Modern Warfare and International Humanitarian Law

Evolving Challenges and Normative Developments

Modern Warfare
and
International Humanitarian Law
Evolving Challenges and Normative Developments

Edited by

Dr Parineet Kaur
Dr Kanika Sharma

Published in association with

The Indian Society of International Law
New Delhi

Vij Books
New Delhi (India)

First Published in India in 2025

Published by

Vij Books
(An imprint of Vij Books India Pvt Ltd)
(Publishers, Distributors & Importers)
4836/24, Ansari Road
Delhi – 110 002
Phones: 91-11-43596460, Mob: 98110 94883
e-mail: contact@vijpublishing.com
web : www.vijbooks.in

ISBN: 978-93-48738-43-1 (PB)

Contents

Foreword

It gives me immense pleasure to write the Foreword to this second book being published by the International Society of International Law this year. This timely work on ***International Humanitarian Law (IHL)*** arrives as global conflicts become increasingly complex, often driven by advanced technologies and rising civilian casualties. Conflicts in regions like Ukraine, Gaza, Iran, Israel and others continue to result in mass casualties and destruction. The link between technology and armed conflict is constantly evolving, where the latest advancements dictate each move and countermove. A short-armed conflict in May 2025, between two nuclear-armed states, India and Pakistan, has demonstrated the use of Artificial Intelligence (AI), missiles and loitering drones and space technology. Advances in AI are likely to bring benefits but they could also create threats to international peace and security. Civilian AI developments also pose a threat to security; a malicious actor may develop and use prohibited biological or chemical weapons. In addition, many states are experiencing extreme levels of violence in non-international armed conflicts (NIAC), which include: Myanmar, Syria, Palestine, Mexico, Nigeria, Brazil, Colombia, Haiti, Yemen, Sudan, and Pakistan, causing enormous destruction and deaths of many innocent civilians. Violations of IHL in NIAC by one side encourage reciprocal misconduct by the other, thereby igniting a cycle of violence and destruction. The deliberate destruction of religious and cultural property in a few NIAC has also been reported in the recent past.

Recent armed conflicts have seen the use of digital technologies of warfare, including the use of artificial intelligence in military decision-making and weaponisation of space; in addition to numerous violations of IHL, including attacks on civilians, killing of journalists, use of prohibited weapons, and targeting of humanitarian workers. The possibility of future weaponisation of outer space cannot be ruled out. Excessive use of explosive weapons and urban fighting across the world continues to cause immense suffering and devastation for civilians. These violations, which may amount to war crimes, undermine the fundamental principles of IHL. These developments have given new urgency to the issue and highlighted the relevance of IHL in addressing it. In the face of ongoing armed conflicts worldwide, study and research in IHL is highly relevant today.

The relevance of IHL remains immense. Its rigorous application is essential to reduce the human cost of crises—including those involving Israel and Iran—and to uphold the rule of law in armed conflict. As warfare evolves, so must our commitment to these legal protections.

This volume, *Modern Warfare and International Humanitarian Law: Evolving Challenges and Normative Developments*, features 15 insightful chapters exploring contemporary legal challenges. I commend the authors and editors of the Indian Society of International Law for their valuable contribution to this critical discourse.

Prof (Dr.) Manoj Kumar Sinha
President,
The Indian Society of International Law, New Delhi.

Preface

On the night of June 12, 2025, Israel launched a massive air offensive targeting Iranian nuclear sites, military bases, several top military officials, the police chief and top nuclear scientists. This operation also destroyed residential buildings in Tehran, including a 14-storey housing complex where 60 people, including 20 children, were reportedly killed.[1] In retaliation, Iran fired around 400 ballistic missiles and drones at Israel in the next few days, causing widespread damage in communities in northern Israel, killing a few civilians and injuring dozens. As the conflict intensified, on June 22, the US dropped Massive Ordnance Penetrators (MOP), the GBU-57, each carrying a 30,000-pound warhead capable of penetrating 200 feet underground. As claimed, it destroyed Iran's fortified nuclear facilities at Fordo, Natanz and Isfahan.[2] The two other ongoing international armed conflicts, Russia-Ukraine and Israel-Gaza wars, have taken the lives of nearly 65,000 individuals, besides causing massive damage to infrastructure and the environment. The number of troops killed or wounded in Russia-Ukraine war has topped one million, apparently a huge price the two countries have paid in this conflict.[3] Little earlier, the

1 Israel launched a series of surprise attacks against Iran in the morning hours of 13 June 2025, targeting the Iranian nuclear programme and dealt a major blow to the country's military chain of command, hitting nuclear sites, missile facilities and air defences and killing a number of top military/ security officials. The Israeli military says more than 200 warplanes carried out the overnight attack, dropping hundreds of bombs across Iran. https://www.nytimes.com/2025/06/13/world/middleeast/israel-attacks-iran.html.

2 What we know about US strikes on three Iranian nuclear sites, BBC, June 23, 2025, available at: https://www.bbc.com/news/articles/cvg9r4q99g4o..

3 Helene Cooper, Troop Casualties in Ukraine War Near 1.4 million, Study Finds, *The New York Times*, June 2, 2025, available at: https://www.nytimes.com/2025/06/03/us/politics/russia-ukraine-troop-casualties.html. Also see: https://www.csis.org/analysis/russias-battlefield-woes-ukraine.

two nuclear-armed adversaries, India and Pakistan were involved in a brief 88-hour intense military conflict.[4]

Technological developments have given rise to new means and methods of warfare, such as hypersonic missiles, cyber-attacks, armed drones and robots, MOPs, raising unique humanitarian and legal challenges. Besides the five nuclear-weapon states involved in recent armed conflicts (India, Israel, Pakistan, Russia and the US), the People's Republic of China is developing military capabilities that could alter the strategic landscape in most regions of the world, including the Asia-Pacific. These international armed conflicts, besides using technologically advanced weaponry in innovative ways, have also generated unprecedented levels of mis- and disinformation.

International Humanitarian Law (IHL) provides an important framework for regulating armed conflict, limiting suffering, and protecting civilians who are not directly involved in armed conflict. IHL also prohibits wanton destruction and requires that any means of violence employed be justified by a real and direct military necessity, be directed to a military objective, and be proportionate to the threat. The study and research of IHL is highly relevant today, particularly due to the increasing number of armed conflicts and the complex challenges they pose to civilian populations and humanitarian actors. Accordingly, this book, comprising three sections and 14 chapters, looks at emerging IHL issues and challenges in modern warfare.

Section I considers emerging domains and methods of warfare. In the contemporary landscape information and computer technologies have become omnipresent and integral to various facets of modern life. Unlike traditional physical actions that necessitate extensive preparation, cyberattacks, in their simplest form, only require a mouse click after a specific plan has been crafted or malware has been deployed. This novel mode of warfare empowers less economically endowed states to engage in cost-effective and swift military strategies. Chapter 1 of the book delves into the existing governing rules that regulate the use of force in the contemporary context, exploring their relevance and applicability to the realm of cyber warfare.

4 Christopher Clary, Four Days in May: The India-Pakistan Crisis of 2025, May 28, 2025, available at: https://www.stimson.org/2025/four-days-in-may-the-india-pakistan-crisis-of-2025/#elementor-toc__heading-anchor-4.

In recent years, the use of 'fake news' during an armed conflict has become a global phenomenon. Fake news refers to the intentional release of fabricated information designed to mislead its audience. In today's digital age, unregulated social media platforms have facilitated the widespread dissemination of fake news and manipulated videos. Chapter 2 of the book covers the use of fake news as a weapon of war in recent armed conflicts. Social bots can automatically generate online communications, such as tweets and comments. They can thus fabricate trends and false news to influence people's opinions about the level of support for particular political candidates or other contentious subjects. The Russia-Ukraine war did not just play out in trenches and towns, it spilled onto X, where both sides turned to bots to churn up the death toll of their enemy. Chapter 3 of the book demonstrates that bots on Twitter, now referred to as X, have significantly influenced public perception of the Russia-Ukraine war. The new phrase "lawfare" is a compound of the words law and warfare. Lawfare is the use of international law and legal procedures with the strict aim of making a claim against another state, especially in spheres connected with national security. It now encompasses all state actions that employ domestic or international law to achieve a state's objectives. Law is no longer used solely to achieve a military objective. In Chapter 4, the concept of Lawfare is covered in detail. This is an updated version of article appeared in the ISIL Yearbook of IHL and Refugee Law Vol. XXIII. In the history of international relations corporations and business entities have been closely associated with conflicts. Well-known corporate entities have played a direct and key role in conflicts by providing the support that fuels the conflicts. Chapter 5 of the book aims to explore the evolving concept of corporate liability under international humanitarian law, focusing on how corporations can be held accountable for complicity in war crimes, genocide, and crimes against humanity.

The term 'weapon' has been broadly defined as: "Any device constructed, adapted, or used to kill, harm, disorient, incapacitate, or affect a person's behaviour against their will, or to damage or destroy buildings or materiel. A weapon acts through the application of kinetic force or of other means, such as the transmission of electricity, the diffusion of chemical substances or biological agents or sound, or the direction of electromagnetic energy. The term 'weapon' includes cyber weapons that damage computer systems and networks or result in physical harm to people or objects."[5] The deployment of multi-satellite constellations, long-range missiles, and

5 Stuart Casey-Maslen (ed.), Weapons Under International Human Rights Law, Cambridge University Press (2015), p. xx.

drones for security and military purposes is a frequent phenomenon of State practices in the present era. Section II of the book examines the evolution of weapons, technologies, and doctrines in recent armed conflicts.

Unmanned systems like drones have revolutionised military operations worldwide, and several countries have effectively incorporated cutting-edge drones into their strategic arsenals. There is a growing trend among developed nations to manufacture drones and counter-drone systems at a speed and scale that meets the requirements of contemporary conflicts. Chapter 6 on Drone Technology analyses how increased speed of new technologies and the integration of innovation will be a force multiplier in winning the conflict in time to come. The Loitering Munitions (Kamikaze Drones or Suicide Drones), are autonomous or remotely piloted aerial weapons that carry a warhead and are intended to self-destruct upon impact with their target. While promising enhanced efficiency and reduced risk to human combatants, Loitering Munitions carry profound strategic, ethical, and legal implications and are discussed in Chapter 7. The ongoing armed conflicts have proved that loitering munitions have the accuracy of missiles with the versatility of drones.[6] In the 2000s, they were developed for additional roles, from long-range strikes and fire support to short-range tactical systems that fit in a backpack. During conflicts in the 2010s and 2020s, a few militaries and even non-state actors modified commercial drones into loitering munitions by attaching a small explosive ordnance such as a grenade or IED and used them against tactical targets.

Since the sole use of atomic bombs in 1945, proliferation has continued despite efforts to prevent it. Nine nations currently possess nuclear weapons. Nuclear weapons have always rested at the intersection of immense destructive power and human frailty. The use of nuclear weapons in Armed Conflict, including their legal and humanitarian dimensions, have been covered under Chapter 8 of the book. In modern times, claims and conflicts of human society are no longer limited to this planet and the airspace above it. With the escalation of armed conflicts to the fourth

6 The US has supplied Ukraine with two forms of Switchblade Loitering Munitions: the smaller 300 model, suited for lighter targets, and the more powerful 600 model, capable of destroying tanks. Both systems are designed to give soldiers precision strike capabilities and can abort and re-engage targets if needed. The sophistication of a loitering munitions device ranges from a drone with explosives attached to purpose-built munitions elaborate in flight and control capabilities, warhead size and design, and onboard sensors for locating targets. Loitering Munitions and the Future of Modern Artillery, IDGA, available at: https://www.idga.org/land/articles/loitering-munitions-and-the-future-of-modern-artillery?ty-ur.

frontier of warfare, outer space is being viewed as the ultimate high ground from which the earth below can be controlled. Space weaponisation and military activities within space environments present an important and sophisticated international security element. Modern technological advancements lead countries to recognise outer space as an essential military territory for national defence operations. The Militarisation and weaponisation of Outer Space has been elaborately covered in Chapter 9 of the book. With the advancements in space technology and the potential use of such technology in military operations and warfare, Chapter 10 explores the nuances of space warfare and its environmental impacts, as they have a direct correlation with the survival of the human species.

Airpower has evolved dramatically over the past century, transforming from a fledgling military experiment into a dominant force in modern warfare. The combat role for aircraft defined missions for air superiority and primitive bombing raids. Larger aircraft allowed for faster transportation of troops, equipment, and munitions, as well as novel airborne operations. Helicopters and Carrier-based aviation altered the role of airpower. Aerial refuelling extended operational ranges and the introduction of precision-guided munitions (PGMs) refined the strike paradigm. During this journey of airpower, IHL too evolved with multiple incarnations. However, to date, there is little clarity on the definitive legal position regarding the use of various aspects of airpower in conflicts. The evolution of airpower over the past 115 years has revolutionised warfare, introducing new capabilities and challenges. Chapter 11, 'Evolving Air Power in Modern Conflicts,' reflects on the evolutionary journey of air power and its various verticals and their impact on legal aspects of conflict dynamics.

Globally, the number of conflicts, whether political, criminal, or military in nature have doubled in the recent past and this is reflected in the increasing number of killings and kidnapping of civilians, who do not participate but remain in conflict zones due to their profession. Section III of the book deals with the protection of such persons during an armed conflict. Chapter 12 deals with the Protection of Journalists in Conflict Zones, while Chapter 13 deals with the challenges and threats faced by Medical Personnel during an armed conflict.

In an armed conflict, where the loss of human lives becomes an important issue, the destruction of a few buildings, books or artefacts may appear insignificant. However, some of these buildings, statues, and books represent the endeavour of generations of the local population in various fields. For instance, Nalanda was a major hub for educational and intellectual exchange and dissemination of knowledge among Asian societies. In its glorious days, from approximately 425 CE onwards, it had the best library in the world. In 1193, on their conquest march, Bakhtiyar Khilji commanded forces to attack the university complex and the library to obliterate local culture and identity. The Nalanda Library was set on fire and millions of books and manuscripts were burnt to ashes. Chapter 14 of the book discusses the Protection of Cultural Property during Armed Conflicts.

The International Criminal Court (ICC), established in 2002, plays a crucial role in punishing individuals for the most serious international crimes, including war crimes and the crime of aggression. Chapter 15 discusses the scope and content of the ICC jurisdiction over the nationals of non–Party States accused of committing crimes on the territories of States Parties.

The editors of the book are grateful to Prof V G Hedge, Executive President and Chairman Research & Publication Committee, the Indian Society of International Law, New Delhi for encouragement. We are also thankful to Vij Books for bringing out this edition.

Dr Parineet Kaur

New Delhi — Dr Kanika Sharma

Contributors

Dr. Benarji Chakka is currently working as Dean and Professor of Law at VIT-AP School of Law (VSL), VIT-AP University, Andhra Pradesh. He graduated from Andhra University, with B.A.L, LL. B (Hons), LL.M from School of Oriental African Studies (SOAS), University of London and obtained M. Phil., and Ph. D., from Centre for International Legal Studies, Jawaharlal Nehru University, New Delhi. He also earned Postgraduate Diploma Course in Learning, Teaching and Research in Higher Education, National University of Ireland (NUI), Galway, Republic of Ireland and he was awarded with the prestigious British Chevening Scholar at SOAS in 2015-16. Dr. Benarji was previously associated as Professor and Dean of Alliance School of Law, Alliance University Bangalore; Associate Professor of Law and Registrar at National Law University and Judicial Academy, Assam (NLUJAA). He was Lecturer at the School of Law, National University of Ireland, Galway (NUIG). He was Regional Legal Adviser to the International Committee of the Red Cross (ICRC), based in Geneva and its Regional Delegation for South Asia, New Delhi. He also worked as Research Associate at the Indian Society of International Law. He has expertise in International Aviation Law, International Space Law, International Humanitarian Law and International Law and Transitional Justice. He published research articles and books in the field of International Aviation and Space law and international humanitarian law.

Dr. Mohammad Bitar was a Research Scholar from the VIT-AP School of Law, VIT-AP University, Andhra Pradesh, India. He is currently working as a Legal Assistant at Internationaler Bund (IB Nord), Norderstedt, Germany.

Dr. Parineet Kaur has worked as an Assistant Professor at the Indian Society of International Law (ISIL), New Delhi, India and was Course Coordinator of the Post Graduate Diploma in Intellectual Property Laws and International Trade Law, which is conducted by the Indian Academy of International Law and Diplomacy, a teaching wing of ISIL. She has been the Head, Centre of Advanced Studies in Intellectual Property and Technology Law. Prior to this, she had experience working for an IP Law firm. Dr Parineet is a graduate in Economics from Sri Guru Gobind Singh College of Commerce, University of Delhi, and has completed her LL.B. from Campus Law Centre, Faculty of Law, University of Delhi, and also LL.M. She has a Ph.D. in the area of Copyright and Competition Law in Entertainment Industry from Dr. Ram Manohar Lohiya National Law University Lucknow, India. She is UGC NET qualified. She also represented India at the prestigious "BRICS Forum of International Rule of Law" in Beijing and has presented papers at various national and international conferences and has many publications to her credit. Her areas of specialization include Intellectual Property Law, Entertainment Law, Competition Law, International Law, and Human Rights Law. She is presently Assistant Professor at Indian Law Institute, New Delhi.

Prof (Dr) Sanghamitra Choudhury teaches Political Science at Bodoland University. She is currently the Dean, Social Sciences and the Head of the Department of Political Science. Dr Sanghamitra was awarded Ph D by Jawaharlal Nehru University and completed her post-doctorate in Asian Studies from the University of Oxford, UK. She holds 20 years of Teaching and Research experience and has worked with organisations like the UNIFEM, Jamia Millia Islamia, etc.

Rhitwique Dutta is a doctoral scholar in the Department of Political Science, Bodoland University. He has completed his masters in Peace and Conflict Studies from Tata Institute of Social Sciences, Guwahati. Further, he holds MA in Political Science from IGNOU. He has also qualified UGC NET in Defence and Strategic Studies.

Dr U C Jha has earned his Ph D from Jawaharlal Nehru University, where he also served as a Visiting Fellow at the Centre for the Study of Law and Governance. His expertise has been shared on various prestigious platforms where he has presented papers and offered insights on international humanitarian law and military law. These venues include the UN High Commissioner for Human Rights in Geneva, the Diplomatic Academy of the Ministry of Foreign Affairs in Russia, and multiple South Asian Teaching Sessions organised by the International Committee of the Red Cross. His contributions also extend to numerous universities in India and the Indian Army Commands. His work includes the authorship of 35 books, contributions to six additional books, and the publication of over 160 papers.

Dr. Indirani K.S. is a Professor of Law and Principal, Bishop Cotton Women's Christian Law College, Bangalore. She holds a PG Diploma in Personnel Management and Industrial Relations, a BA LL B in General Laws, an LL M in Labour Law, a Master in Human Resource Management, and a Ph D degree as well. Furthermore, she has also qualified for the Karnataka State Eligibility Test. She has been at Bishop Cotton Women's Christian Law College since 2009 but has also worked at Al Ameen College of Law in Bangalore and KLE College of Law. Dr. Indirani also has experience working as an Advocate in the industry.

Group Captain Amitabh Mathur (Retd) was commissioned in the IAF in 1987 in the Aeronautical Engineering (Electronics) Branch. The officer has served in the maintenance and operation of surface-to-air missile systems, as well as airborne and ground-based Electronic Warfare systems, and the maintenance of specialist air weapons. He holds a degree in Electrical Engineering and a postgraduate degree in Defence Studies from the University of Madras. In addition to several service courses, he has completed a PG Diploma course in Intellectual Property Rights from NLSIU, Bangalore. He has worked as a Senior Research Fellow at the Centre for Air Power Studies and the Centre for Joint Warfare Studies and has written numerous papers on technology.

Ms Yash Sinha is a final-year student at South Asian University, New Delhi, deeply committed to the evolving field of International Humanitarian Law and International Human Rights Law. Her academic pursuits are centred on understanding and addressing complex global challenges, from the protection of civilians in armed conflict to advocating for fundamental freedoms worldwide. With a keen eye on the future, she aims to contribute to meaningful change in the international legal landscape, whether through policy advocacy, legal practice, or academic research, ensuring that human rights and humanitarian principles remain at the forefront of global discourse.

Gp Capt Kishore Kumar Khera, Vayu Sena Medal, served as a fighter pilot in the Indian Air Force for 33 years including command of a fighter squadron. He was a pioneer member of Composite Battle Response and Analysis (COBRA) Group and headed the Operational Planning and Assessment Group at Air HQ. He served as a Research Fellow at the Institute of Defence Studies and Analyses (IDSA), New Delhi, from 2017-2019. Post retirement, he operates as an independent analyst and has authored nine books and scores of articles on military matters.

Prof (Dr) DK Pandey, a Group Captain, has served the IAF for more than three decades. He has experience of more than 2500 Air combats. In the course of his service, As part of Air Staff Inspections team, at Air HQs, he inspected and audited AD ops at various AF Stations, including AWACS. He has commanded six Air Defence (C&R) Units and was awarded Best Unit Trophies twice. He retired as Director, Joint Control and Analysis Centre. He was Associate Dean & Professor at the School of Business (Aviation Management) at Galgotia University. He co-edited the book 'Road to Atmanirbhar Bharat in Aerospace'. He is currently a Senior Fellow and RCO at CAPS; Adjunct Faculty, Rastriya Raksha University (RRU), a member of the Advisory Council of 'Greater Noida Institute of Technology' (GNOIT) and a member of the Advisory Board (Academic Affairs) at 'Foreign Policy School, New Delhi'.

Mr. Ajay Revansidha Tambulkar is a conscious human-being with professional roles as a research scholar, law academician, and artist at the core of the heart. He has secured Masters in International Law and Human Rights from Department of Law, Savitribai Phule Pune University, India. Presently, he is pursuing Doctoral research in International Space Law from University of Delhi. He is serving as a faculty at Army Law College, Pune, under Savitribai Phule Pune University. Mr. Ajay has read, researched, published and delivered academic services in the domains of Constitutional Law, Jurisprudence, Research Methodology and Competence Development, International Law and its branches, like, International Air, Space and Sea Law, International Economic Law, Humanitarian and Refugee Law, etc. He is associated with various academic and professional institutions in inter-disciplinary manner, like, India Chapter of AI and Space Law Society, Netherlands, Visiting Lecturer of Indian Society of International Law, etc.

Prof. Dr K. Ratnabali is a Professor of Law in the Faculty of Law, University of Delhi, with more than twenty years teaching and research experience. She has majorly published in the areas of International Humanitarian Law as well as in interdisciplinary areas of law with Social & Cultural Anthropology, Environmental studies, developmental issues, etc. In the last four years, she has been critically involved in bringing transformation in the academic landscape of the University of Delhi. These transformative initiatives have also influenced other universities in the country. Prior to joining as teaching faculty in Delhi University, she had worked as in intern in the office of the United National High Commissioner for Refugees, New Delhi and State Human Rights Commission, Manipur.

Dr. Kanika Sharma, is an Assistant Professor and Head-Centre for Advanced Studies in International Humanitarian Law and Military Law at the Indian Society of International Law, New Delhi. Did her Ph.D. in International Refugee Law and LLM from University of Jammu, Jammu & Kashmir. She has qualified UGC NET-JRF and awarded Gold Medal in LLM. She has delivered lectures in the field of refugee law and humanitarian law at national and international universities, National Human Rights Commission, New Delhi. She has published various papers in Journals of repute and also presented papers in National and International Conferences. She is a course coordinator of PG Diploma Course in International Law and Diplomacy and PG Diploma Course in Human Rights, International Humanitarian and Refugee Law conducted by the Indian Academy of International Law and Diplomacy, the teaching wing of the Indian Society of International Law.

Dr. Anna Bashir is a Senior Assistant Professor at the School of Law, University of Kashmir, with over a decade of academic and research experience in international law, human rights, and intellectual property rights. She holds a Ph.D. from the University of Delhi and dual LLM degrees, including one from WIPO. Dr. Bashir has previously served at the Indian Society of International Law (ISIL), New Delhi, where she coordinated numerous national and international academic programs. She has presented papers at prestigious forums, including The Hague Academy, WIPO, and ISIL conferences, and has published extensively in peer-reviewed journals. A recipient of multiple international fellowships, Dr. Bashir is actively involved in institutional development as the Coordinator of the IPR Cell and a member of the Executive Council at ISIL. Her academic contributions reflect a commitment to advancing legal education and research in India and beyond.

Ms. Mehvish Mehraj is an Assistant Professor in the Department of Management at the University of the People, where she teaches business law, ethics, and social responsibility, emphasising critical thinking and ethical decision-making. Also, a researcher focusing on the education rights of refugees in India, her academic interests include humanitarian law, refugee rights, and child protection under international legal frameworks. Committed to raising awareness about the intersection of education and human rights, she strives to empower marginalised communities through knowledge and advocacy.

Prof. Dr. Rashmi Salpekar, Professor of International Law and Dean, Vivekananda School of Law and Legal Studies, Vivekananda Institute of

Professional Studies-TC, Delhi, affiliated to GGSIPU, Delhi. She is a Ph.D. in International Law, a doctoral fellow of the Indian Council of Social Science Research (ICSSR). She is LL.M., Master of Human Rights and Duties (MHRDE) and M.A. in Sociology. She has more than fifteen years of experience in teaching and research, including experience working as a Research Officer in the Maharashtra State Human Rights Commission, Mumbai. She has a specialisation in Public International Law and its various branches. She has written extensively on International Criminal Law, International Humanitarian Law, International Trade, Economic, Investment and Commercial Law and Legal Research Methodology. She has been invited as a speaker all over the country as well as in foreign countries, mainly in international conferences held in Hong Kong, Australia and the Hague.

Dr. Vinai Kumar Singh is an Associate Professor at Centre for International Legal Studies (CILS), School of International Studies (SIS), JNU, New Delhi. He completed his M. Phil and PhD from CILS, SIS, JNU, New Delhi and LLM from Delhi University, Delhi. Earlier he served as Deputy Director and Senior Assistant Professor at the Indian Society of International Law, New Delhi from 2004 to 2024. He is also Associate Editor of Environmental Policy and Law (EPL) published from IOS Press, the Netherlands.

Dr. Meenakshi Harith is the Librarian at the Indian Society of International Law (ISIL), New Delhi, with over 25 years of experience in library and information science. She holds a Ph.D. in Library Science, Master's degree in Library Science and Sociology, LL B, and a Postgraduate Diploma in International Law and Diplomacy. Dr. Harith has contributed extensively to legal bibliography, having compiled numerous subject-specific bibliographies for the Indian Journal of International Law and the ISIL Yearbook of International Humanitarian and Refugee Law since 2001. Her expertise includes bibliometrics, information retrieval, digital resource management, and legal information systems. She has actively participated in national and international conferences, professional training programs, and webinars. Dr. Harith continues to lead efforts to digitise and expand access to international legal literature, aiming to develop ISIL's e-library into a specialised national resource on international law.

Section I

Emerging Domains and Methods of Warfare

Chapter 1

Cyber Warfare and International Law: Charting the Legal Frontiers in the Digital Realm

-Benarji Chakka and Mohammad Bitar

Introduction

In the intricate tapestry of global affairs, the emergence of cyberspace as a dynamic arena for conflict has fundamentally altered the landscape of warfare. Defined by the amalgamation of generated, saved, and shared digital data, cyberspace extends beyond the confines of a virtual realm, interweaving itself with the systems and infrastructures that enable the seamless flow of information. This distinctly man-made space is characterized by its inherent fragment ability, where the mere click of a button can set in motion the activation or deactivation of its various components.

In recent years, the international community has borne witness to a series of remarkable cyber events that transcend the conventional boundaries of conflict. The distributed denial of service (DDoS) attacks on Estonia in 2007,[1] triggered by geopolitical tensions, the cyber onslaught during the South Ossetia War in Georgia in 2008, the deployment of the Stuxnet virus disrupting Iran's uranium enrichment centrifuges in 2010,[2] and

1 Ottis, Rain. "Analysis of the 2007 cyber-attacks against Estonia from the information warfare perspective." In *Proceedings of the 7th European Conference on Information Warfare*, p. 163. Reading, MA: Academic Publishing Limited, 2008.

2 Simonenko, Maksim. "Stuxnet and nuclear enrichment of the cyber security regime." *Security Index: A Russian Journal on International Security* 19, no. 2 (2013): 85-97.

the extensive cyber assaults on Saudi Aramco in 2012 underscore the transformative nature of warfare in the digital realm.[3]

These cyber incidents, akin to traditional conflicts, have brought to light the potential for warfare to extend beyond physical battlefronts, with non-state actors assuming pivotal roles in shaping the dynamics of these cyber confrontations. The absence of explicit international legal frameworks addressing cyber-attacks has created a void, compelling nations to grapple with the application of traditional principles of jus ad bellum to this contemporary form of warfare.

In the ever-evolving realm of cyberspace, the fusion of international law with digital realities prompts a critical revaluation of foundational principles like sovereignty and non-intervention. As cyber operations increasingly challenge traditional notions of state authority by blurring physical and virtual boundaries, questions arise regarding jurisdiction and control over digital infrastructure. In this context, the principle of non-intervention gains renewed significance as cyber activities transcend borders, involving both state and non-state actors and raising complex issues of permissible conduct. In this dynamic landscape, due diligence emerges as a key concept, necessitating proactive measures to mitigate cyber threats originating from various sources. Policymakers and legal experts grapple with these challenges as they seek to adapt traditional legal norms to the complexities of cyberspace.

This research delves into the existing governing rules that regulate the use of force in the contemporary context, exploring their relevance and applicability to the realm of cyber warfare (lex lata). [4] Concurrently, it endeavours to identify the lacunae in these governing rules, presenting a comprehensive analysis of the challenges posed by cyber warfare, and suggesting optimal regulatory measures that could bridge the gap between current legal frameworks and the evolving nature of cyber conflict (lex ferenda).[5]

As the international community navigates through the absence of specific treaties or conventions explicitly addressing cyber-attacks, the urgency

3 Alsaeed, Alaa. "The Cyber Attack on Saudi Aramco in 2012." *Asian Journal of Engineering and Applied Technology* 10, no. 2 (2021): 25-28.

4 Sommario G, 'Applying the Jus in Bello in the Cyber Domain: Navigating between lex lata and lex ferenda' (2016) 3 *Questions of International Law* 13.

5 Hobe S. 'The Legal Framework for a Lunar Base Lex data and Lex Ferenda' In *Outlook on Space Law Over the Next 30 Years* (Brill Nijhoff, 1997) 135.

for a comprehensive legal framework becomes increasingly apparent. This research, therefore, engages in a nuanced examination of international law concerning the use of force and armed attacks, contemplating how traditional principles can be adapted to the novel challenges presented by cyber warfare. Additionally, it scrutinises the limitations of existing approaches and proposes a new analytical framework, offering insights into how nations can navigate the legal intricacies associated with cyber warfare in an evolving global landscape.

Sovereignty in Cyberspace

The utilization of territorial sovereignty concerning states' conduct in cyberspace has sparked considerable debate. Historically, the violation of a state's territorial sovereignty typically pertains to physical encroachment onto its land, sea, or airspace. Nonetheless, cyber operations encompass both physical and virtual aspects, encompassing tangible hardware in conjunction with the transmission of content and data between computers.

Unlike physical territories, cyberspace lacks fixed boundaries and can transcend geographical borders due to diverse network architectures and data storage methods. Moreover, global tech corporations like Google and Meta often wield more regulatory control in cyberspace than individual states.[6] Nonetheless, cyberspace is rooted in the physical world, with its infrastructure located within states' territories and owned by governments and companies.[7]

States retain sovereignty over cyber infrastructure within their borders, along with authority over individuals within their territories and citizens abroad.[8] This sovereignty extends to regulating cyber activities domestically, though it must comply with international human rights laws. Some states, particularly authoritarian ones, enforce stringent controls over internet access and personal data, known as "cyber sovereignty."[9] However, the powers exercised by states in regulating cyber activities, regardless of

6 Efrony D, Shany Y, 'A Rule Book on the Shelf? Tallinn Manual 2.0 on Cyberoperations and Subsequent State Practice' (2018) 112 American Journal of International Law 652.

7 Zeng J, Stevens T and Chen Y, 'China's Solution to Global Cyber Governance: Unpacking the Domestic Discourse of "Internet Sovereignty"' (2017) 45 Politics & Policy 432.

8 Tsagourias N, 'Law, Borders and the Territorialisation of Cyberspace' [2018] SSRN Electronic Journal, p. 16.

9 Buchan R, Cyber Espionage and International Law (Hart Publishing Limited 2018)50.

compatibility with international laws, are distinct from their inherently sovereign functions.[10]

The concept of inherent sovereign functions in international law refers to the fundamental activities of a state, such as foreign affairs, military operations, legislation, police power, and the administration of justice. It is important to note that these functions do not extend to a state's regulation of private or commercial affairs. This understanding is supported by the ICJ ruling in the Nicaragua case, where it acknowledged a state's autonomy in determining its political, economic, social, and cultural systems, as well as crafting foreign policies. Therefore, it is essential to have a clear understanding of what is meant by "inherently sovereign functions" in order to fully grasp their significance in international law.

Violation of Sovereignty

A breach of sovereignty transpires when a state asserts its jurisdiction within the territory of another state without consent, thereby infringing upon the latter's exclusive prerogative to exercise its own state authority autonomously. [11] This principle, upheld in international legal practice, stipulates that unless there exists a specific authorisation to the contrary, a state is prohibited from exercising its authority within the territorial domain of another state. [12]

The ICJ has consistently upheld this principle in several cases, including "Certain Activities Carried Out by Nicaragua in the Border Area (Costa Rica v. Nicaragua)"[13] and "Military and Paramilitary Activities in and against Nicaragua". [14] These instances underscore scenarios wherein the actions of one state encroached upon the sovereignty of another by exerting authority within its territory without consent. [15]

Violations of sovereignty aren't limited to physical intrusions; they can also occur remotely, without direct physical effects in the affected territory.

10 Goldsmith JL, 'Against Cyberanarchy' (1998) 65 The University of Chicago Law Review 1199.

11 Oppenheim L and others, Oppenheim's International Law (Longman 1996) 385.

12 S.S. 'Lotus', 'France v Turkey, Judgment, Judgment' No 9, PCIJ Series A No 10, ICGJ 248 (PCIJ 1927), 18.

13 ICJ GL No 150 [2018] ICJ Rep 15.

14 'Certain Activities carried out by Nicaragua in the Border Area' (Costa Rica v Nicaragua), Judgment, ICJ Reports 2015, paras 221.

15 Ibid., para 93

Similarly, activities conducted from outside a state's territory with physical effects within the target state, such as pollution, can breach sovereignty[16].

Establishing remote violations of sovereignty may be challenging as they lack tangible presence, but the same principles apply whether the exercise of authority is physical or remote. However, coercive remote violations are often scrutinized under the non-intervention principle or specific international laws.[17]

There's debate over whether every non-consensual incursion constitutes a violation of sovereignty or if there's a threshold for such violations. Some argue that any unauthorised state incursion constitutes a violation, while others suggest a more nuanced approach, considering factors like the degree of political independence affected. This ambiguity extends to activities of intelligence agencies operating in other states without disclosure, with differing views on whether they violate sovereignty.[18]

Ultimately, the assessment of sovereignty violations depends on the specifics of each case, particularly in the absence of more specific international laws governing the situation.

Infringements on Sovereignty in the realm of cyberspace

In the context of cyberspace, some scholars contend that there is no identifiable rule of sovereignty that carries legal consequences.[19] They suggest that sovereignty in international law varies across different domains like space, air, and seas, and is more flexible, subject to the practical needs of states. However, despite this debate, case law demonstrates that a state's sovereignty can indeed be violated without reliance on specific international laws pertaining to particular areas.[20] Specter contends that regardless of the terminology used—whether sovereignty, territorial sovereignty, or

16 Handl G, 'Territorial Sovereignty and the Problem of Transnational Pollution' (1975) 69 American Journal of International Law 50.

17 Chatinakrob T, 'Interplay of International Law and Cyberspace: State Sovereignty Violation, Extraterritorial Effects, and the Paradigm of Cyber Sovereignty' [2024] Chinese Journal of International Law.

18 Higgins R, 'Themes and Theories: Selected Essays, Speeches, and Writings in International Law' (Oxford University Press 2009) 275.

19 Michael S N and Liis V, 'Respect for Sovereignty in Cyberspace' (2017) 95 Texas Law Review 1639.

20 Cohen JL, 'Whose Sovereignty? Empire versus International Law' (2004) 18 Ethics & International Affairs 1-24.

territorial integrity—international law unmistakably prohibits one state from taking public actions or exerting authority within another state's territory without consent or contrary to international law.[21]

Rule 4 of the Tallinn Manual 2.0 bolsters this principle by asserting that states should abstain from engaging in cyber operations that infringe upon another state's sovereignty. [22] This prompts inquiries into the conditions under which a cyber operation sponsored by a state constitutes a violation of sovereignty.

More commonly, state cyber intrusions occur remotely from outside the target state's territory. For example, a state may hack into and disrupt another state's national power grid from abroad.[23] Even if the cyber intrusion causes physical effects within the victim state's territory, such as damage to computer systems, or if there is no physical trace left, such as gathering information from a server, it still constitutes unauthorised access to the victim state's infrastructure without consent.[24] Hence, whether executed physically within the territory or remotely, unauthorised cyber activities constitute a breach of the victim state's sovereignty.

This analysis asserts that sovereignty entails a spectrum of interrelated rights. Cyber intrusions not only disrupt the victim state's autonomous exercise of its state powers but also possess a territorial aspect as they occur within the victim state's territory. Consequently, there exists no inherent differentiation between physical infringements perpetrated by state agents within the victim state's territory and remote violations executed from outside. Both scenarios amount to violations of sovereignty.

The scope Application of Sovereignty in Cyberspace

In the context of cyberspace, there is ongoing debate about whether any unauthorised exercise of authority in a state constitutes a violation of sovereignty, or if there is a minimum threshold at play. Taking a maximalist approach to sovereignty as a 'catch-all' would imply that a wide range of

21 Schrijver N, 'The Changing Nature of State Sovereignty' (1999) 70 British Yearbook of International Law 65.

22 Sam S. 'Sovereignty in Cyberspace A study on Customary International Law on the Principle of Sovereignty' (2020).

23 Buchanan, Ben. 'The hacker and the state: Cyber attacks and the new normal of geopolitics' (Harvard University Press, 2020).

24 Buchan R, 'Cyber Attacks: Unlawful Uses of Force or Prohibited Interventions?' (2012) 17 Journal of Conflict and Security Law 212.

activities could be considered violations. This could include actions such as installing access mechanisms on another state's infrastructure without impacting its functionality, engaging in espionage, or examining cyber vulnerabilities. It is important to note that this broad interpretation could lead to a situation where many routine activities are inadvertently classified as violations.

In the cyber realm, there is an ongoing discussion about whether any unauthorised exercise of power within a country constitutes a breach of sovereignty or if there is a minimum threshold for such violations.[25] Adopting a maximalist view of sovereignty as an all-encompassing concept could mean that almost any action could be seen as a breach. For instance, actions such as installing a mechanism to access another country's infrastructure without affecting its operation, engaging in espionage, or probing cyber vulnerabilities could all be considered violations under this broad interpretation.

Indeed, this expansive approach often clashes with the practical realities of state operations in cyberspace. The interconnected nature of the internet frequently results in unintentional encroachments on the jurisdictions of other states.[26] States, including their intelligence agencies, regularly traverse each other's cyber boundaries without explicit permission, particularly in urgent situations like counterterrorism efforts. Adhering strictly to the concept of sovereignty as a 'pure sovereigntist' would mean that states' sovereignty would be constantly breached without consequence.

Moreover, labeling such activities as violations of sovereignty could heighten tensions and risks of escalation.[27] States with expansive views of sovereignty, such as Russia and China, might exploit this concept more frequently to condemn other states' actions. This subjective interpretation of sovereignty poses challenges as international law should be applied objectively, but the lack of specific criteria for sovereignty violations increases the likelihood of subjective interpretations.

---

25 Baldwin CB, 'The Dilution of State Sovereignty: Legal Justifications and Strategic Consequences' [2009] SSRN Electronic Journal.

26 Egan BJ, 'International Law and Stability in Cyberspace' (2019) 35 Berkeley Journal of International Law 169.

27 Kolton M. 'Interpreting China's pursuit of cyber sovereignty and its views on cyber deterrence' (2017) 2 The Cyber Defense Review 119-154.

Interestingly, when states comment on cyber intrusions, they rarely categorise them as violations of sovereignty.[28] It's unclear whether this is to avoid escalating the situation or because they genuinely don't view the activity as breaching sovereignty. The assumption that all unauthorized cyber activities violate sovereignty does not reflect actual state practice. Conversely, completely disregarding sovereignty violations in the cyber realm contradicts international court judgments, which suggest that sovereignty principles apply broadly to unauthorised state actions, whether cyber-related or not.

When contemplating violations of sovereignty in the cyber domain, some commentators advocate for a middle-ground approach wherein certain state cyber activities breach another state's sovereignty only if they exceed a particular threshold. However, the challenge lies in establishing the criteria for this threshold. [29] Should they be rooted in quantitative factors like the severity of harm inflicted in the target state,[30] the number of affected citizens, or the geographical scope of the cyberattack? Alternatively, should they be based on qualitative factors such as the nature of the attack itself?

The experts behind the Tallinn Manual 2.0 explored the concept of delineating breaches of a target state's 'territorial integrity' by suggesting a hierarchy of scenarios characterized by varying degrees of harmful effects.[31] These scenarios encompassed instances of physical damage or injury, exemplified by operations like Stuxnet causing equipment malfunction, as well as the loss of functionality of cyber infrastructure, as seen in the 'Shamoon' cyber operation against Aramco. [32] Additionally, the hierarchy included activities falling below the threshold of loss of functionality, such

28 Harriet Moynihan, "The Application of International Law to State Cyberattacks Sovereignty and Non-intervention", International Law Program Research Paper, December 2019, published by, The Royal Institute of International Affairs, Chatham House, London, P. 8. Available at https://www.chathamhouse.org/2019/12/application-international-law-state-cyberattacks/2-application-sovereignty-cyberspace, visited on 9 May 2025

29 Baldwin CB, 'The Dilution of State Sovereignty: Legal Justifications and Strategic Consequences' [2009] SSRN Electronic Journal.

30 Hüsch P, 'Non-Intervention Thresholds in Cyberspace – in the Shadow of the Sovereignty Debate?' (2023) 92 Nordic Journal of International Law 371.

31 Ahmed Ghappour, Tallinn, 'Hacking, and Customary International Law' (2017) 111 AJIL Unbound 224. Law.

32 Bronk C and Tikk-Ringas E, 'The Cyber Attack on Saudi Aramco' (2013) 55 Survival 81.

as the slowing down of computers or the alteration/deletion of data without resulting in physical consequences.

Indeed, this concept of sovereignty violation pivots on the severity of harmful effects, akin to the 'effects doctrine' deliberated within the framework of regulations governing the use of force. However, determining a de minimis threshold based on effects poses challenges. Experts hold differing views on where to draw this line, whether it's based on loss of functionality or damage below that level.[33]

Some states consider not only the severity but also the societal impact of cyberattacks when assessing violations of sovereignty. For instance, France views any cyber operation producing effects on French territory as a breach of sovereignty.[34] Similarly, the EU's cyber sanctions regime assesses the significant effects of cyberattacks on economic activities, essential services, public order, etc., to determine wrongfulness.[35]

An effects-based approach, considering both quantitative and qualitative effects, offers a pragmatic way to address cyber intrusions that fall below the threshold of intervention but still cause harm. However, defining parameters for sovereignty violations remains challenging, both in the cyber and non-cyber contexts. The lack of consensus on criteria for delineating violations underscores the subjectivity inherent in assessing sovereignty breaches in cyberspace until states reach a mutual understanding on its application.

The Application of Due Diligence in Preventing Harmful Cyber Activities

International law stipulates that a state must refrain from allowing its territory to be utilised for hostile activities targeting another state.[36] There is ongoing debate about whether this obligation extends to requiring a state to take due diligence in preventing harmful cyber activities

33 Schmitt MN, 'Grey Zones in the International Law of Cyberspace' (2017) 42 Yale Journal of International Law 11.

34 Adams J and Albakajai M, 'Cyberspace: A New Threat to the Sovereignty of the State' (2016) 4 Management Studies.

35 Rusinova V and Martynova E, 'Fighting Cyber Attacks with Sanctions: Digital Threats, Economic Responses' (2023) 57 Israel Law Review 135.

36 Corfu Channel Case (United Kingdom v. Albania 22.

emanating from its territory in the context of cyberspace.[37] However, there is a counterargument suggesting that there is no legal obligation in the cyber context, but rather applying due diligence would be a commendable practice. The United Nations Group of Governmental Experts (UN GGE) supports the latter view, indicating that some states do not consider it a legally binding obligation in cyberspace. Nevertheless, some states advocate for its application, suggesting that it is becoming a binding principle in the cyber domain.

However, the distinction between "shall" and "should" holds limited practical significance at present. This is because it remains uncertain what applying the due diligence principle to cyberspace would entail. To be applicable in a specific context, the principle must encompass various smaller duties,[38] which states have yet to clarify in the cyber realm.[39] Indeed, due diligence in the context of cyberspace would encompass various obligations, such as investigating identified activities and responding to them appropriately, Importantly, the principle emphasizes conduct rather than outcomes; it necessitates states to take reasonable measures to try to prevent harmful cyber activities, rather than guaranteeing their complete prevention.

Nevertheless, applying due diligence to cyber activities offers potential benefits, such as fostering a proactive approach rather than a reactive one and easing the challenges associated with attributing cyber activity to a state.[40] Hence, there's a need for further refinement of principles outlining what could reasonably be anticipated from a state in applying the due diligence principle to cyberspace. Additional efforts are required before the principle can be effectively utilized to its fullest extent.

37 UN, 'Group of Governmental Experts on Developments in the Field of Information and Telecommunications in the Context of International Security' 2015 UN A/70/174, para 13(c).

38 Sklerov, MJ, 'Solving the Dilemma of State Responses to Cyberattacks: A Justification for the Use of Active Defenses against States Who Neglect Their Duty to Prevent (2009) 201 Military Law Review 1–85.

39 Liu IY, 'State responsibility and cyberattacks: Defining due diligence obligations' (2017) 4 Indon. J. Int'l & Comp. L. 191.

40 Green, JA, 'Disasters Caused in Cyberspace' in Breau, S. C. and Samuel, K. L. H. (eds) Research Handbook on Disasters and International Law, (Edward Elgar, 2016) 406–427.

The Principle of Non-Intervention

The principle of non-intervention is rooted in the concept of sovereignty and precludes states from employing coercive measures to meddle in the internal affairs of other sovereign states.[41] While some contend that this principle is difficult to apply due to the need for coercive behaviour by the intervening state, others opine that coercion is a relatively rare occurrence that is reserved for exceptional circumstances.[42] However, the Chatham House Report suggests that the principle of non-intervention can be extended to encompass a wider range of situations in practical application.[43]

As per the ICJ's Nicaragua case[44] and the Friendly Relations Declaration, coercive behaviour can be characterized as the use of force to restrict a state's freedom to exercise its sovereign powers. This coercion is aimed at compelling a specific outcome or behaviour concerning matters within the target state's jurisdiction, [45] and it is intended to benefit the perpetrating state, regardless of whether or not it is successful. The pressure exerted is sufficient if it hinders the target state's ability to exercise its free will.

Coercive actions by a state can take on various forms, such as direct and indirect, overt and covert techniques. These actions may aim to limit or obstruct the target state's ability to perform its functions in order to gain an advantage for the perpetrating state. This can range from forcing a policy change to merely causing chaos and instability in the target state. If state-to-state cyber interactions lead to the target state losing control over its sovereign functions, then the principle of non-intervention could apply broadly under this interpretation.

Cyber actions that may be considered as violations of the principle of non-intervention include but are not limited to: intentional cyberattacks on critical infrastructure of another state, such as transportation or power grids, with the aim of weakening the target state's control; tampering with electoral infrastructure to alter election results, as alleged by the United

41 Schmitt MN, Liis V, 'Sovereignty in cyberspace: lex lata vel non?' (2017) 213.

42 Kilovaty I, 'The Elephant in the Room: Coercion' (2019) 113 AJIL Unbound 87.

43 Moynihan H, The Application of International Law to State Cyberattacks: Sovereignty and Non-Intervention (The Royal Institute of International Affairs 2019).

44 'Case Concerning Military and Paramilitary Activities in and Against Nicaragua' (Nicaragua v. United States of America); Merits, ICJ, 27 June 1986,

45 Tsagourias N, 'Electoral cyber interference, self-determination and the principle of non-intervention in cyberspace' (2020) Governing Cyberspace: Behavior, Power, and Diplomacy 45.

States, [46] the United Kingdom[47], and Australia; and conducting covert cyber operations to stealthily manipulate public opinion. For example, a state's extensive use of disinformation and micro-targeting to sway the electorate could jeopardize the target state's ability to hold free and fair elections. Moreover, the principle of non-intervention could be applied to cyber activities that have an impact on the essential operation of parliament or the stability of a state's financial systems, as highlighted by the United Kingdom and Australia.

In brief, the principle of non-intervention is essential for preserving sovereignty and preventing undue interference in a state's internal affairs, and its application in cyber interactions underscores its relevance in contemporary international relations. Those advocating for sovereignty as the guiding principle for state cyber operations and those, particularly the UK, who assert that the non-intervention principle is the appropriate rule for state-to-state cyber activities below the use of force threshold, find themselves closer in practice than one might assume. [48] In fact, the international experts involved in crafting the Tallinn Manual 2.0 acknowledged that a state's sovereignty could be compromised when another state's cyber actions lead to the "usurpation of the target's government functions." [49] They also recognized that real-world scenarios often entail violations of both sovereignty and the non-intervention principle.

While sovereignty and the prohibition of non-intervention are closely intertwined, the latter does not necessitate coercion, unlike the former. The requirement of coercion ensures that only specific state actions are considered transgressions; mere attempts to influence another state's governance processes do not suffice. In practical terms, when one state usurps another's government functions, resulting in detrimental effects on critical national infrastructure, it frequently meets the criteria for coercion.[50]

46 Egan B, 'Remarks on international law and stability in cyberspace' (2016) 10 Berkeley Law School, California 2009.

47 Wright J, 'Cyber and international law in the 21st century' (2018) Chatham House 23.

48 Watts S, 'Low-intensity cyber operations and the principle of non-intervention' (2015) 14 Baltic Yearbook of International Law 137.

49 Jensen, TE, 'The Tallinn Manual 2.0: Highlights and Insights' (2016) 48 Geo. J. Int'l L. 735.

50 Borghard DE, and Shawn LW, 'The logic of coercion in cyberspace' (2017) 26 Security 452-481.

Debates ensue regarding the threshold at which a cyber incident becomes coercive, a determination heavily reliant on the circumstances of each case. However, the criteria for applying the non-intervention principle are relatively well-defined compared to sovereignty. While discussions persist regarding the criteria for sovereignty violations in both cyber and non-cyber contexts, the non-intervention principle rests on discernible parameters – specifically, the utilisation of coercive behaviour by one state to deprive another of its free will concerning the exercise of its sovereign functions.

Cyber Warfare and the Use of Cyber Force

Article 2(4) of the UN Charter, a cornerstone of customary international law, establishes a fundamental principle governing international relations: "All Members shall refrain in their international relations from the threat or use of force against the territorial integrity or political independence of any state, or in any other manner inconsistent with the Purposes of the United Nations." This provision establishes a broad prohibition against the use of force, with two specific exceptions delineated in the Charter. The first exception pertains to force authorised by the Security Council under Article 42. The second exception relates to self-defence, as outlined in Article 51. It is crucial to recognise that Article 2(4) and its customary equivalent exclusively apply to actions carried out by states or those imputable to them based on the principles of state responsibility. These provisions do not encompass the actions of non-state actors, including terrorist organisations.

With the emergence of cyber operations, there has been significant debate among states and scholars regarding the criteria for defining when an act constitutes a "use of force." Indeed, cyber operations that result in physical damage or injury fall within the scope of actions covered by Article 2(4) and its customary equivalent.

However, the challenge lies in determining whether cyber operations that produce severe non-physical consequences, without causing physical harm, should also be considered a use of force.[51] This poses an interpretive dilemma, raising questions about whether such operations, without legal justification, violate the prohibition on the use of force. Rule 10 of the Tallinn Manual broadens the scope of this prohibition by asserting that any cyber operation which poses a threat or employs force against a state's

51 Roscini M, 'Cyber Operations and the Use of Force in International Law' (Oxford University Press 2016) 37.

territorial integrity or political independence, or is inconsistent with the United Nations' objectives, is deemed unlawful. This rule aligns with Article 2(4) of the UN Charter and customary international law. Importantly, it applies specifically to actions carried out by states and does not encompass the actions of non-state actors, including terrorist organisations.[52]

In the Case 'Concerning Military and Paramilitary Activities in and Against Nicaragua', ICJ rejected a rigid, literal interpretation of the concept of "use of force".[53] Notably, the ICJ concluded that certain activities, such as arming and training rebels, could indeed be considered as involving the threat or use of force. However, the mere provision of funds did not meet the criteria for such force. Additionally, the ICJ asserted that assistance to rebels, which includes providing weapons or logistical support, might also fall within the scope of force or threat of force. Importantly, this broad interpretation extends beyond physical actions and encompasses non-destructive cyber acts. For example, supplying malicious software to rebel groups or training them in its use could potentially be categorized as actions falling under the umbrella of the use of force. If, for instance, malware was provided to a rebel group with instructions on deploying it for destructive purposes, such conduct would likely be deemed as a use of force.

While acknowledging that not every aggressive action constitutes the use of force, it is crucial to note that not all acts of force are necessarily hostile. ICJ ruled in the Nicaragua case that financing guerrilla groups, though unlawful, did not amount to a use of force.[54] Furthermore, the drafters of the UN Charter rejected a proposal to include economic coercion within the definition of the term. As a result, cyber operations aimed at economically coercing another state or funding a rebel group's cyber activities would not be considered uses of force. However, despite these examples, the precise location of the threshold remains ambiguous.[55]

The International Group of Experts, comprised of individuals charged with the formidable task of devising a universally applicable, clear-cut criterion, has formulated a comprehensive, non-restrictive array of

52 'Tallinn Manual on the International Law Applicable to Cyber Warfare', 42-43.

53 'Military and Paramilitary Activities in and Against Nicaragua' (Nicar. v. U.S.), 1986 I.C.J. 14.

54 Schabas W, 'The Use of Force in the Nicaraguan Cases' [2017] Nicaragua Before the ICJ 305.

55 Kilovaty I, 'Rethinking the prohibition on the use of force in the light of economic cyber warfare: towards a broader scope of Article 2 (4) of the UN Charter' (2014) 4 JL & Cyber Warfare 210.

elements that determine how states characterise cyber operations as acts of force. Encompassing aspects such as severity, promptness, directness, intrusiveness, quantifiability, martial nature, state participation, and presumed legitimacy, these factors are further supplemented by contextual nuances such as the prevailing political climate, the correlation between an operation and potential military force, the attacker's identity and track record in cyber warfare, and the characteristics of the target. [56]

The Group suggested that the severity of a cyber operation is the only criterion that can classify it as an act of force. As far as the experts are concerned, any cyber activity that causes significant harm or injury would meet this criterion. The Stuxnet virus's impact on Iranian nuclear facilities in 2010, which resulted in more than minor damage, was cited as an instance that surpassed this threshold. However, it is important to note that states evaluate cyber incidents on an ad hoc basis, and this position is not universally accepted. [57]

The way countries respond to cyber operations and define their own cyber activities will have a significant impact on shaping the development of interpretive frameworks. The increasing reliance of countries on cyberspace is likely to result in a decrease in the threshold for determining what constitutes a use of force. [58] While it is difficult to predict whether a definitive test will emerge or if countries will adopt more flexible interpretations of force, several possible paths for clarifying this threshold exist. One approach is to view cyber operations targeting specific types of assets as indicative of force, creating a rebuttable presumption to that effect. For example, non-destructive cyber activities aimed at critical infrastructure could increasingly be viewed by countries as equivalent to a use of force. [59] This perspective could also extend to cyber-attacks on military targets or state systems dedicated to cybersecurity. Another possibility is that countries will start treating data destruction in the same way as physical destruction when it comes to characterizing force, especially when such destruction significantly disrupts societal, economic or governmental

56 Foltz, AC, "Stuxnet," Schmitt Analysis, and the Cyber use of Force Debate' (2012) 4 Joint Force Quarterly 40-48.

57 Holloway M, 'Stuxnet worm attack on Iranian nuclear facilities' (2015) Stanford University.

58 Schmitt MN, 'Taming the lawless void: Tracking the evolution of international law rules for cyberspace' (2020).

59 Delibasis D, 'The right of states to use force in cyberspace: Defining the rules of engagement' (2002) 11 Information & Communications Technology Law 255-268.

functions. Regardless of the approach taken, countries will inevitably be forced to take a stance on whether particular cyber operations breach the prohibition on the use of force. These assessments will significantly contribute to refining the normative framework governing cyber activities, adding intricate details to the understanding of force within the cyber domain.

Self-defence in the context of cyberwarfare

The prohibition of the use of force is the principle that distinguishes between lawful and unlawful cyber operations conducted by states or attributed to them. In contrast, the right of self-defence relates to the conditions under which states may resort to force in response to cyber operations. Article 51 of the United Nations Charter, similar to customary international law as expressed in Article 2(4), defines this right as follows: "Nothing in the present Charter shall impair the inherent right of individual or collective self-defence if an armed attack occurs against a Member of the United Nations, until the Security Council has taken the measures necessary to maintain international peace and security."

The proper interpretation of terms is essential in defining the right of self-defence, much like the use of force. The International Group of Experts made a distinction between "armed attack" and "use of force,"[60] building on the ICJ's ruling in the Nicaragua case, which highlighted the importance of differentiating between severe uses of force that constitute an armed attack and less severe forms. This interpretation acknowledges that all armed attacks are considered uses of force, but not all uses of force can be classified as armed attacks.

The unanimous opinion among experts is that any act of violence resulting in injury, death, or property damage can be considered an armed attack, which may justify a state's use of force in self-defence. Nevertheless, there is some disagreement regarding the level of damage or injury required to reach this threshold. For instance, the ICJ has excluded minor incidents like "mere frontier incidents" from the definition of armed attacks, a decision that has faced criticism. [61] On the other hand, the court has indicated in other cases that a single attack on a military platform or installation can meet the threshold for an armed attack. The exact threshold remains a

60 Schmitt MN., ed. 'Tallinn manual on the international law applicable to cyber warfare' (Cambridge University Press, 2013) 47.

61 'Nicaragua, Military and Paramilitary Activities in and Against Nicaragua' (Nicar. v. U.S.), 1986 I.C.J., 195

subject of debate, but it is clear that significant harm or damage caused by a cyber operation qualifies as an armed attack. In contrast, non-destructive cyber operations, such as espionage, cyber theft, or intermittent disruption of non-essential cyber services, do not reach this threshold. [62]

Two aspects of self-defence law that are uncertain create ample room for interpretation. Initially, there is confusion about whether a cyber operation, which does not produce physical harm, can still be labeled as an armed attack if it results in severe non-destructive consequences. [63] Some experts hold a narrow view, restricting the current law to situations involving physical effects, while others advocate for a more expansive interpretation based on the severity of the consequences rather than their physical nature. This is illustrated by the example of a large-scale cyber operation targeting a state's economic infrastructure. Proponents of this viewpoint argue that it would be illogical to classify such an operation as falling short of the armed attack threshold while considering an operation causing physical damage to a few factories as meeting it. [64]

According to the prevailing perspective, the law of self-defence has not yet reached the point where non-damaging or non-injurious cyber operations are considered armed attacks due to the lack of definitive state practice. [65] However, it is highly probable that states will increasingly view such cyber operations as armed attacks warranting forceful responses when the consequences are severely detrimental. Cyber operations possess the potential to significantly hinder a state's normal functioning and impose non-destructive consequences to an unparalleled degree, much like a military attack. This alteration in the security landscape will undoubtedly prompt the development of self-defence law. [66]

62 Dinstein Y, 'Computer network attacks and self-defence' (2002) 76 International Law Studies 20.

63 Wallace DA. 'Christopher JW, 'Conflict Classification and Cyber Operations: Gaps, Ambiguities and Fault Lines' (2019) 40, Pa. J. Int'l L. 643.

64 Horatiu M, Boşcoianu M, 'Delia Ungureanu, Florin Sandu, and Rzvan Boboc. Network of Unmanned Systems Cyber Attacks over National Economy Infrastructures' (2017) 859 Applied Mechanics and Materials 144.

65 Roscini M, 'World wide warfare–Jus ad bellum and the use of cyber force' (2010) 14 Max Planck Yearbook of United Nations Law 85-130.

66 Couzigou I, 'The Challenges Posed by Cyber Attacks to the Law on Self-Defence' (2014) In 'European Society Of International Law, 10th Anniversary Conference', Vienna 4.

The debate among international legal experts revolves around the distinction between the use of force and armed attack. The United States maintains that any illegal use of force warrants a self-defence response. On the other hand, others argue for a gap between the two thresholds, which could offer states more flexibility in responding to cyber operations without provoking forceful countermeasures.[67]

The understanding of anticipatory self-defence is progressing, especially in the context of cyber threats.[68] Conventional ways of determining imminence may not be applicable in cyberspace, where attacks can happen swiftly and discreetly. The emphasis is moving towards the ability to defend oneself rather than the moment the attack will take place.[69]

The question of whether non-state actors can carry out armed attacks under international law is a topic of ongoing debate. Although the majority of states attribute these actions to states supporting them, the growth of cyber capabilities is causing this distinction to become increasingly unclear. As cyber operations conducted by non-state actors become more common and destructive, states may be tempted to adopt a more forceful approach in response.[70]

The issue of the legality of cyber operations that target groups launching attacks from other countries is a contentious one. The United States justifies such actions by claiming that the territorial state is either unwilling or unable to stop the attacks. This rationale is particularly relevant in cyberspace due to the ease with which attacks can be launched from anywhere with internet connectivity, as well as the speed at which they can occur.[71]

---

67 Schmitt MN, 'Below the threshold cyber operations: The countermeasures response option and international law' (2013) 54 Va. J. Int'l L. 697.

68 Gill T. D., 'Ducheine PA, Anticipatory Self-Defence in the Cyber Context', (2013) 89 INT'L L. STUD, 438.

69 DeWEESE GS, 'Anticipatory and Pre-emptive Self-defense in cyberspace: the challenge of Imminence' In '2015 7th International Conference on Cyber Conflict: Architectures in Cyberspace', IEEE 81-92.

70 Sigholm, Johan. "Non-state actors in cyberspace operations." Journal of Military Studies 4, no. 1 (2013): 1.

71 Thøgersen M, 'Obligations of Non-participating States When Hackers on Their Territory Engage in Armed Conflicts' In 2023 15th International Conference on Cyber Conflict: Meeting Reality (CyCon), IEEE 39.

In summary, the evolving landscape of cyber warfare poses challenges for traditional legal frameworks governing the use of force and self-defence, prompting the need for nuanced interpretations and responses to emerging threats.

Conclusion

In conclusion, the conversations presented provide valuable insights into the intersection of international law and cyberspace. The discussions highlight the ongoing challenges of applying traditional legal principles to the rapidly evolving domain of cyber operations. Key issues addressed include the interpretation of sovereignty and non-intervention in the context of cyber intrusions, the delineation of thresholds for acts constituting the use of force, and the implications for state behaviour and responses in cyberspace. While there is consensus on some aspects, such as the prohibition of certain cyber activities, significant nuances and interpretive dilemmas remain unresolved. Moving forward, continued dialogue, legal scholarship, and international cooperation will be essential to develop clearer frameworks and norms that effectively address the complexities of cyberspace while upholding fundamental principles of international law.

Chapter 2

Fake News as a Weapon of War

-Parineet Kaur

In the wake of Indian military retaliation under *Operation Sindoor*,[1] Pakistan started a digital smear campaign through a number of Pro-Pakistan social media handles to weaponise the news. Fake narratives consisting of shocking videos and unverified claims were widely amplified by the media; shaping public fear and support for war. In one of such narratives, it was reported that Indian Air Force pilot Shivangi Singh, only woman Rafale pilot, had been captured in Pakistan. Her photos and old videos were posted with captions declaring she had been detained in POK. Fakes of Indian Armed Forces personnel were also used. One handle pretended to be an Indian Navy officer posted a fake photo to add weight to his narration. On May 11, 2025, a pro-Pakistan online user posted a satellite image purportedly showing damage caused by Pakistani forces on Jammu airbase in India. This image was supposedly taken after Pakistani strikes. It depicted a series of six craters on the airport's runway and adjacent buildings. However, an image taken by the Sentinel satellite showed that the Jammu airbase was actually intact.[2]

The Pakistani army officially claimed the destruction of an S-400 missile battery in Indian military base in Adampur. The Press Information Bureau (PIB) debunked the fake news claiming that Pakistan destroyed India's air

1 Operation Sindoor was launched by India on May 7, 2025 in response to the April 22, 2025 Pahalgam terrorist attack in which 26 civilians' tourists were killed.

2 Observers, "India-Pakistan conflict: AI-generated or edited fake satellite images flood social media", France 24 Observers, 16 May 2025, available at: https://observers.france24.com/en/asia-pacific/20250516-india-pakistan-conflict-ai-generated-or-edited-fake-satellite-images-flood-social-media (last accessed 09 June 2025).

defence system S-400.[3] Another piece of misinformation stated that the Indian Army raised a white flag and surrendered at Chora Post in Kashmir. According to a news report, "Pakistan fired missiles by night, fake videos by day in coordinated social media war."[4] Fake news has thus emerged as not only the weapon of war, but is viewed as one of the serious threats to democracy and freedom of expression. The aim of fake and misinformation is to flood the information space with a falsehood so quickly that it becomes difficult to separate facts from fiction, thus weakening public trust in the government and the armed forces.

The use of fake news in war is not a new concept. On September 17, 2024, pagers belonging to members of Hezbollah were simultaneously detonated. The next day, walkie-talkies all over Lebanon began exploding. These explosions killed at least 32 people and wounded thousands of others. Hezbollah accused Israel of these blasts.[5] The very next day, a video with the logo of the Cable News Network (CNN) with journalist Jake Tapper hosting a show was shared on social media platforms. The host in this clip spoke about the pager attack in Lebanon and mentioned that another attack took place where the rectum of goats exploded, killing an additional 1,800 people and injuring thousands of others as well as killing countless goats. Lastly, the anchor added, "People for the Ethical Treatment of Animals has just issued a statement denouncing the actions of the Israeli Defence Forces for the senseless killing of all those goats." On fact-checking it revealed that the voice of the anchor in the video has been manipulated using Artificial Intelligence (AI). The reporter's actual name is Danny Polishchuk, a Toronto-based comedian and the video is a satire taken on the situation in Lebanon.

In 2002, US President Bush and a few top government officials made false allegations that the Iraq Government was preparing weapons of mass destruction (WMD)--nuclear, biological or chemical weapons. As a result of this false campaign, a multinational coalition led by the US invaded

3 PIB Fact Check (@PIBFactCheck, X (formerly Twitter)), "S400 Destroyed by Pakistan? Here's the Truth!", 15 May 2025 (online), available at https://x.com/PIBFactCheck/status/1921051899006005308 (last accessed 01 June 2025).

4 Shipra Parashar, "IndiaPakistan conflict: Disinformation — fake socialmedia video of army attack in Sindoor" (*India Today*, 9 May 2025) (online), available at: https://www.indiatoday.in/india/story/india-pakistan-conflict-disinformation-fake-social-media-video-army-attack-sindoor-2721971-2025-05-09 (last accessed 31 May 2025).

5 Matt Murphy & Joe Tidy, "What we know about the Hezbollah device explosions", *BBC News* (20 September 2024) (online), available at: https://www.bbc.com/news/articles/cz04m913m49o (last accessed 2 June 2025).

Iraq on March 19, 2003, without any mandate from the United Nations. Within weeks, the US achieved the primary objective of ousting the regime of Saddam Hussein.[6] In reality, there was no threat of weapons of mass destruction, because they did not exist.

Defining Fake News

In recent years, fake news has become a global phenomenon. However, the term 'fake news' remains undefined under international law. In general, information disorder can be categorised into three major types: disinformation, misinformation, and mal-information.[7] The Council of Europe distinguishes three types of information disorder: dis-information (information that is false and deliberately created to cause harm), mis-information (information that is false, but not created with the intention of causing harm), and mal-information (information that is based on reality, used to inflict harm on a person, organisation or country).[8] According to Kai Sui (2020), disinformation is fake or inaccurate information that is intentionally spread to mislead and/or deceive; misinformation is false content shared by a person who does not realise it is false or misleading; and mal-information is to describe genuine information that is shared with an intent to cause harm.[9] Disinformation consists of operations

6 Carroll Doherty & Jocelyn Kiley, "A Look Back at How Fear and False Beliefs Bolstered U.S. Public Support for War in Iraq", *Pew Research Center* (14 March 2023) (online), available at: https://www.pewresearch.org/politics/2023/03/14/a-look-back-at-how-fear-and-false-beliefs-bolstered-u-s-public-support-for-war-in-iraq/ (last accessed 2 June 2025).

7 Claire Wardle & Hossein Derakhshan, *Information disorder: Toward an interdisciplinary framework for research and policy making*, Council of Europe, Report No 162317 (Sept. 2017) (online), available at: https://edoc.coe.int/en/media/7495-information-disorder-toward-an-interdisciplinary-framework-for-research-and-policy-making.html (last accessed 2 June 2025).

8 Council of Europe, *Information Disorder: Toward an Interdisciplinary Framework for Research and Policy Making* (October 2017), p. 20, available at: https://edoc.coe.int/en/media/7495-information-disorder-toward-an-interdisciplinary-framework-for-research-and-policy-making.html (last accessed 3 June 2025).

9 The spread of false or misleading information often has a dynamic nature, causing the exchanging among different types of information disorder. On the one hand, disinformation can become misinformation. For example, a disinformation creator can intentionally distribute the false information on social media platforms. People who see the information may be unaware that it is false and share it in their communities, using their own framing. On the other hand, misinformation can also be transformed into disinformation. For example, a piece of satire news may be intentionally distributed out of the context to mislead consumers. Kai Sui, Suhang Wang, Dongwon Lee &

(open or secret) designed to favour any of the parties by using informative manipulation that ends up modifying the position of the citizens who remain oblivious while believing they act according to their free will, because the civil population is the main object of the attacks.[10]

Fake news and disinformation content are created and disseminated for a number of reasons. According to Bartlett (2020) disinformation is essentially driven by an agenda, stating that it is "deliberately false information, especially when supplied by a government or its agent to a foreign power or to the media, with the intention of influencing the policies or opinions of those who receive it".[11] Allcott and Gentzkow (2017) have identified two motives for producing fake news that spreads disinformation: (i) The financial incentive because they are sensational and thus draw the clicks of the audience, which in turn brings in advertising revenue; and (ii) Fake news that disseminates disinformation allows its creators to propagate certain ideas and gain backing for the people they support.[12]

According to Wardle and Derakhshan (2017), disinformation is false information that is deliberately created or disseminated with the express purpose to cause harm. Producers of disinformation typically have political, financial, psychological or social motivations. Mal-information is genuine information that is shared to cause harm. This includes private or revealing information that is spread to harm a person or reputation. Misinformation is information that is false, but not intended to cause harm. For example, individuals who do not know a piece of information is false may spread it on social media in an attempt to be helpful.[13]

Huan Liu, *Disinformation, Misinformation, and Fake News in social media: Emerging Research Challenges and Opportunities* (Springer, 2020), p. 4.

10 Chema Suárez Serrano, "From bullets to fake news: Disinformation as a weapon of mass distraction. What solutions does International Law provide?", *The Spanish Yearbook of International Law*, vol. 24 (2020), pp. 129–154.

11 J.C. Bartlett, "Information Literacy and Science Misinformation", in N. Greene (ed.), *Navigating Fake News, Alternative Facts, and Misinformation in a PostTruth World* (IGI Global, Hershey, PA, 2020), pp. 1–17.

12 Hunt Allcott & Matthew Gentzkow, "Social Media and Fake News in the 2016 Election", *Journal of Economic Perspectives*, vol. 31, no. 2 (2017), pp. 211–236.

13 Claire Wardle & Hossein Derakhshan, *Information Disorder: Toward an Interdisciplinary Framework for Research and Policy Making*, Council of Europe (2017), p. 107, available at: https://edoc.coe.int/en/media/7495-information-disorder-toward-an-interdisciplinary-framework-for-research-and-policy-making.html (last accessed 2 June 2025).

The issue of fake news is as old as news. Collins dictionary defines it as "false, often sensational, information disseminated under the guise of news reporting."[14] According to Routledge Handbook of Discourse and Disinformation (2024), the term "fake news" is inadequate to capture the variety of information "pollution" that stifles public discourse. Misleading content can take many forms: satire, clickbait, inaccurate captions, images or statistics, manipulated quotes and images, and made-up stories. Almost none of these details are captured by the term "fake news;" therefore, the term "fake news" should be avoided.[15] The terms, "disinformation" and "misinformation" both refer to false information but are separated by an element of intentionality in the former: disinformation is "deliberately misleading or biased". "Fake news" is often a form of disinformation or misinformation. Other related concepts, such as "propaganda", "psychological operations", "influence operations", "information operations", "information warfare" and "cognitive warfare", may also feature some combination of disinformation, misinformation, misleading information and accurate information.[16] In this chapter the term "fake news" has been used to include all fabricated misleading content which confuses the recipient and originated by a state, its agents and sympathisers during grey-zone or armed conflict against its adversary. Fake news operators may be state-sponsored or may consist of volunteers. In China, for instance, fake news agency is called "information troops" or the "50-cent army," and consists of independent operators including student volunteers at universities, Communist Youth League members, and government bureaucrats.[17]

14 *Collins English Dictionary*, "fake news" defined as "false, often sensational, information disseminated under the guise of news reporting" (*Collins English Dictionary* 2017) (online edn, accessed 12 June 2025).

15 Stefania M. Maci, Massimiliano Demata, Mark McGlashan & Philip Seargeant (eds.), *Routledge Handbook of Discourse and Disinformation* (Routledge, London, 2024), pp. 1–15.

16 Elan Katz, "Liar's War: Protecting Civilians from Disinformation During Armed Conflict", *International Review of the Red Cross*, vol. 102, no. 914 (2020), pp. 659–682.

17 *The Washington Post*, "The Chinese Government Fakes Nearly 450 million Social Media Comments a Year. This Is Why" (19 May 2016) (online), available at: https://www.washingtonpost.com/news/monkey-cage/wp/2016/05/19/the-chinese-government-fakes-nearly-450-million-social-media-comments-a-year-this-is-why/ (last accessed 12 June 2025), as cited in Norman Vasu *et al.*, *Fake News: National Security in the Post-Truth Era*, S. Rajaratnam School of International Studies (January 2018), p. 36, available at: https://www.rsis.edu.sg/wp-content/uploads/2018/01/CO18018.pdf (last accessed 3 June 2025).

Fake News During Armed Conflict

New revolutions in technologies have amplified the power of states to wage war in ways that were previously inconceivable: the use of unmanned autonomous weapons, loitering munitions, and sophisticated GPS-guided missiles. However, the most crucial weapon in modern warfare is the ability of states to outsource the role of propaganda and information warfare to the public itself. [18] The use of fake news as a military tactic is not a modern concept. Fake news or rumours of tallow and lard-greased cartridges played an important role in the Sepoy Mutiny of 1857 in India. Many sepoys believed that the cartridges that were issued with the new 'Enfield' rifle were greased with pork and cow fat. The soldiers were required not only to handle the cartridges, but also to bite off the ends before loading the rifles. Hindus believed cows were sacred, and Muslims considered pigs unclean and therefore forbidden from consumption. This was against the Hindu and Muslim sentiments and was believed to be the immediate factor for the revolt of 1857. [19]

The Mahabharata, an ancient Indian epic also contains the story of Ashwatthama's death resulting from the use of disinformation.[20] During the war, *Dronacharya* was destroying the *Pandava's* army with his relentless attacks and was required to be stopped. But he was a great warrior and his only weakness was his affection for his son, *Ashwatthama*. Thus, *Krishna* advises *Yudhisthir* that there is but one thing that will make him desist from fighting. If he hears that *Ashwatthama*, his son, is dead, *Dronacharya* will lose all interest in life and throw down his weapons. Someone must therefore tell *Dronacharya* that *Ashwatthama* has been killed. As *Yudhisthira* ponders this, *Bhima* lifted his iron mace and killed a huge elephant called *Ashwatthama*. After killing the elephant, Bhim went near *Dronacharya* and roared so that all might hear. "I have killed *Aswatthama*." *Dronacharya* comes to *Yudhisthir* and asks him: "Is *Ashwatthama* dead?" *Yudhisthira* replies, "Yes *Ashwatthama* is dead," he pauses and adds, "I don't know if it is man or elephant (*Ashwatthama hathaha iti narova kunjarova*)." His last part, deliberately ambiguous, was lost in the noise of war. *Dronacharya*,

18 Grayson S. Walker, "From Instagram to Infowar: The Weaponisation of Social Media and Its Consequences", *Emory International Law Review*, vol. 38 (2024), pp. 673–710.

19 C. Claire Summers, "The Indian Rebellion of 1857", *Tenor of Our Times*, vol. 4, article 6 (Spring 2015) (online), available at: https://scholarworks.harding.edu/tenor/vol4/iss1/6 (last accessed 4 June 2025).

20 C. Rajagopalachari, *Mahabharata* (Retold), (online edn), available at: https://www.hariomgroup.org/hariombooks_shastra/mahabharata.pdf (last accessed 5 June 2025).

who knows that *Yudhisthir* can never lie, believes that his son is dead. He surrenders his weapons, sits down, and begins to meditate. Taking advantage of the situation, *Dhristadyumna* killed *Dronacharya*, changing the tide of the war.

Social media platforms have become the main battlefield for competing discourses in every armed conflict. Reportedly, the Digital Ministry of Ukraine has pressured social media companies like Facebook and Twitter to engage in information war on their behalf, which has been effectively implemented.[21] Since the beginning of Israeli-Hamas war, false and misleading information has been spreading on social platforms by many media outlets. Hamas used information warfare to damage Israeli morale and confidence.[22] On October 17, 2023, a blast stroked Al-Ahli Hospital in Gaza, killing more than 500 civilians. Immediately, Palestinian authorities blamed Israel for the attack. The public opinion in the Arab world appeared to take the side of Palestinians, condemning Israel for committing war crimes. However, the Israeli government firmly denied any involvement with the bombing, claiming that Hamas struck its hospital. According to the Israeli Defence Force (IDF) analysis of footage, the crater created by the blast would be too small to be caused by Israeli weapons. Moreover, the IDF released a conversation presumably between two Hamas militants in which they acknowledged to have stricken Al-Ahli hospital.[23]

Although the phenomena of mis/ disinformation are not new, they have gained significance recently with the widespread availability of sophisticated digital media. Today, the Internet is the primary vehicle for disseminating messages to the masses. The sharing of text, images, videos, or links online, for example, allows information to go viral within hours. Once 'such' information is believed by the receiver, it is difficult to undo it for two reasons: first, people persuaded by the false information very rarely

---

21 Liqiang Wang & Ruonan Wang, "Cyber Warfare: A Study of Zelenskyy's Social Media Political Performance Strategies and Effects", *Frontiers in Psychology* (10 December 2024) (online), available at: https://www.frontiersin.org/journals/psychology/articles/10.3389/fpsyg.2024.1478639/full (last accessed 1 June 2025).

22 Jacob Olidort, *The Other Front of Israel's War: Disinformation Operations by Hamas and Its Supporters*, The Jewish Institute for National Security of America (19 October 2023) (online), available at: https://jinsa.org/the-other-front-of-israels-war-disinformation-operations-by-hamas-and-its-supporters/ (last accessed 3 June 2025).

23 P. Brown *et al.*, "Gaza Hospital: What Video, Pictures and Other Evidence Tell Us About the AlAhli Hospital Blast", *BBC News* (2023) (online), available at: https://www.bbc.com/news/world-middle-east-67144061 (last accessed 4 June 2025).

encounter the truth themselves; secondly, even if they later encounter the truth, they are reluctant to adjust their beliefs.[24]

Impact during Armed Conflict

According to Claudia (2012), dissemination of false and misleading information has been made possible by two main factors: assessing the truthfulness of facts is highly complex in war, and media outlets are often inclined to lower the bar of the fact-checking process to provide information as fast as possible to people.[25] During 'grey-zone conflict' or 'armed conflict', fake news can lead to death, injury, imprisonment, discrimination or displacement. Unreliable information can prevent people from accessing safe places, causing them to withdraw from certain areas through dangerous passages, or prevent access to essential services or humanitarian assistance. The International Committee of the Red Cross (ICRC) is of the view that the spread of fake news containing misleading/ hateful narratives may undermine the protection and safety of people affected by armed conflict. According to ICRC, a few consequences of fake information during armed conflict could be as follows.[26]

- Fake news can harm people's physical, economic and social well-being. They may be misdirected away from life-saving information or led into making decisions which may cause physical harm. They may become targets of violence, harassment or intimidation.
- Fake news can fuel hatred, unrest and encourage violence. During armed conflict, it may undermine people's protection and any opportunities for conflict resolution.
- Fake/ harmful information may influence the actions of combatants or arms bearers leading to avoidable violence against adversaries thus violating IHL.

24 Chema SuárezSerrano, "The Limits of Fake News as Methods of Warfare", in Pablo Antonio FernándezSánchez (ed.), *The Limitations of the Law of Armed Conflicts: New Means and Methods of Warfare* (Brill, The Netherlands, 2022), pp. 231–253.

25 Claudia Padovani *et al.*, "Italy: A Highly Regulated System in Search of Equality", in Josef Trappel *et al.* (eds.), *The Media for Democracy Monitor 2021* (Nordicom, 2021), pp. 315–386.

26 It is not only bullets and rockets that harm people in war. Information – its absence or its manipulation – is part and parcel of the theatre of war and can lead to serious consequences on people affected. Jolle Rizk, Why the ICRC in concerned by 'harmful information' in war? ICRC, September 20, 2024.

- Fake news about humanitarian organisations could erode people's trust in their activities, including their neutrality and independence and may incite violence against their staff.

The use of fake news or disinformation is one of the prominent methods of hybrid warfare. Disinformation campaigns are used to create mistrust and chaos to influence public opinion. Pakistan and China have made extensive use of fake news and disinformation against India as a tool in the recent past. Fake news has been spread through two social networks – Facebook and Twitter. India has banned a large number of YouTube channels for dispensing fake news and promoting anti-India propaganda. The channels and websites belong to a coordinated disinformation network operating from Pakistan and spreading fake news about various sensitive subjects in a coordinated manner on topics like Kashmir, Indian Army, minority communities in India, and Ram Mandir, etc.[27] India and China are not engaged in direct military conflict, but China has launched a misinformation warfare against India and has been flooding the internet with fake news and views to discredit India on the world stage.[28] China has been using disinformation to influence its standing in the world on various issues of strategic importance.

Fake News and Hybrid Warfare

The use of fake news or disinformation is one of the prominent methods of hybrid warfare. Disinformation campaigns are used to create mistrust and chaos to influence public opinion. Pakistan and China have made extensive use of fake news and disinformation against India as a tool in the recent past. Fake news has been spread through two social networks

27 The Ministry of Information and Broadcasting has acted to secure the information space in India, and utilized emergency powers under the Rule 16 of the Information Technology (Intermediary Guidelines and Digital Media Ethics Code) Rules, 2021. The Ministry observed that Most of the content pertains to subjects sensitive from the perspective of national security and are factually incorrect, and are being mainly posted from Pakistan as a coordinated disinformation network (as in the case of Naya Pakistan Group) against India and thus deemed it fit for action under the provisions to block content in case of emergency. Press Information Bureau, "India dismantles Pakistani coordinated disinformation operation", *PIB: Press Release* (21 DEC 2021) (online), available at: https://pib.gov.in/PressReleasePage.aspx?PRID=1783804 (last accessed 2 June 2025).

28 Pradip R. Sagar, "How China has unleashed a misinformation war on India", *India Today Insight* (18 October 2023) (online), available at: https://www.indiatoday.in/india-today-insight/story/how-china-has-unleashed-a-misinformation-war-on-india-2450656-2023-10-18 (last accessed 1 June 2025).

– Facebook and Twitter. India has banned a large number of YouTube channels for dispensing fake news and promoting anti-India propaganda. The channels and websites belong to a coordinated disinformation network operating from Pakistan and spreading fake news about various sensitive subjects in a coordinated manner on topics like Kashmir, Indian Army, minority communities in India, and Ram Mandir, etc.[29] India and China are not engaged in direct military conflict, but China has launched a misinformation warfare against India and has been flooding the internet with fake news and views to discredit India on the world stage.[30] China has been using disinformation to influence its standing in the world on various issues of strategic importance.

International Law and Fake Information

International law does not prohibit states from spreading misinformation or disinformation. International humanitarian law (IHL) permits acts to confuse or mislead an enemy as a "ruse of war," as far as these actions comply with other applicable rules of international law.[31] Belligerents have long exploited the military value of disinformation as 'ruses of war' for deceiving their enemies. Ruses of war are methods, resources, and techniques that can be used to convey false information or deny information to opposing forces. They can include (i) Electronic war-fare measures; (ii) False intelligence information; (iii) Utilisation of enemy codes and signs; and (iv) Transmission of misleading messages. Clandestine or treacherous attempts to injure the enemy are prohibited under IHL. It is prohibited to kill, injure, or capture an adversary by resorting to perfidy.[32]

Circulating misleading messages, according to the International Committee of the Red Cross (ICRC), is a form of ruse.[33] Several national military manuals endorse the use of misinformation, disinformation, false

29 PIB, *note 27.*

30 Pradip, *note 28.*

31 Article 37(2) of the 1977 Additional Protocol I explicitly permits "ruses of war" – "acts which are intended to mislead an adversary or induce him to act recklessly but which infringe no rule of international law applicable in armed conflict and which are not perfidious."

32 JeanMarie Henckaerts & Louise DoswaldBeck (eds.), *Customary International Humanitarian Law*, vol. 1: Rules (Cambridge University Press/International Committee of the Red Cross, 2005), Rule 57.

33 *Ibid.*

information, or psychological operations.[34] Under the Tallinn Manual 2.0 on the International Law Applicable to Cyber Operations, 'ruses of war'[35] which are intended to mislead the enemy or to induce enemy forces to act recklessly, but that do not violate the law of armed conflict are permitted in warfare. For instance, a party to the conflict may issue a warning as a ruse, that is, in order to mislead the enemy (Rule 123). For instance, a false announcement of a cyber-attack affecting dual-use systems might prove militarily useful in causing the enemy to take its military assets off-line. However, even though ruses of war are not prohibited in this regard, they are unlawful if they have the effect of influencing the population to disregard future valid warnings of attack. The following are examples of permissible ruses:[36]

- Transmission of false information causing an opponent to erroneously believe operations are about to occur or are underway
- The use of false computer identifiers, computer networks (e.g., honeynets or honeypots), or computer transmissions
- Bogus orders purporting to have been issued by the enemy commander
- Psychological warfare activities
- Transmitting false intelligence information intended for interception
- Use of enemy codes, signals, and passwords

34 For instance, The US Law of War Manual provides: Ruses of war are considered permissible. Ruses of war are methods, resources, and techniques that can be used either to convey false information or deny information to opposing forces. In general, a belligerent may resort to those measures for mystifying or misleading the enemy against which the enemy ought to take measures to protect itself. The US Department of Defence, *Law of War Manual*, Office of the General Counsel (June 2015, updated July 2023), pp. 334–335, available at: https://dod.defense.gov/Portals/1/Documents/pubs/Law-of-War-Manual-July-2023.pdf (last accessed 2 June 2025).

35 'Ruses of war' are acts intended to mislead the enemy or to induce enemy forces to act recklessly, but that do not violate the law of armed conflict. They are not perfidious because they do not invite the confidence of the enemy with respect to protected status.

36 Michael N. Schmitt (gen. ed.), *Tallinn Manual 2.0 on the International Law Applicable to Cyber Operations* (Cambridge University Press, Cambridge, 2017), Rule 123, para. [X].

According to Katz (2021), disinformation in armed conflict may cause serious harm to civilians including severe mental suffering. Modern disinformation operations disproportionately target civilian populations and circulate at unprecedented speeds and scales and cannot be considered as a ruse of war. The concept of 'ruse' is the practice of an era when deception was supposed to yield tactical gains without harming the civilians. [37]

Fake News and Human Rights

Article 19 of the Universal Declaration of Human Rights (UDHR) and Article 19 of the International Covenant on Civil and Political Rights (ICCPR) protect the right to freedom of expression. Article 19 of the ICCPR states: "2. Everyone shall have the right to freedom of expression; this right shall include freedom to seek, receive and impart information and ideas of all kinds, regardless of frontiers, either orally, in writing or in print, in the form of art, or through any other media of his choice. 3. The exercise of the rights provided for in paragraph 2 of this article carries with it special duties and responsibilities. It may be subject to certain restrictions, but these shall only be such as are provided by law and are necessary: a. For respect of the rights or reputations of others; b. For the protection of national security or of public order or of public health or morals." Article 20(2) of the ICCPR subsequently provides that propaganda for war and "any advocacy of national, racial or religious hatred that constitutes incitement to discrimination, hostility or violence shall be prohibited by law." Under international legal standards, limitations of the right to freedom of expression are permissible but should meet certain conditions. They must be: (i) "provided by law" which is sufficiently clear and precise; (ii) pursue a legitimate aim set out in Article 19 para 3 of the ICCPR (the "rights or reputations of others" or "the protection of national security or of public order or of public health or morals"); and (iii) conform to the "strict tests of necessity and proportionality".[38]

Fake News and UN General Assembly

In 2017, in the context of growing unrest about the potential impact of false information campaigns in electoral processes, the theme was chosen by the

37 The gravity of these harms, along with the modern nature of wartime disinformation, is out of keeping with the traditional classification of disinformation in IHL as a permissible ruse of war. Elan Katz, Liar's war: Protecting civilians from disinformation during armed conflict, *International Review of the Red Cross*, vol. 102, no. 914 (2020).

38 Human Rights Committee, *General Comment No. 34: Article 19 – Freedoms of Opinion and Expression*, CCPR/C/GC/34 (12 September 2011), para. 22.

UN Special Rapporteur on the promotion and protection of the right to freedom of opinion and expression. The free speech rapporteurs took note of the growing prevalence of disinformation and propaganda in legacy and social media, fuelled by both States and non-State actors alike, and the various harms to which they may be a contributing factor or primary cause. The rapporteurs expressed their concern that disinformation and propaganda are often designed and implemented so as to mislead a population. Further, some forms of disinformation and propaganda may harm individual reputations and privacy, or incite to violence, discrimination or hostility against identifiable groups in society. The rapporteurs agreed that the states may impose restrictions on the right to freedom of expression only in accordance with the test for such restrictions under international law, namely that they be provided for by law, serve one of the legitimate interests recognised under international law, and be necessary and proportionate to protect that interest. Such restrictions may also be imposed, as long as they are consistent with the requirements noted in paragraph (a), to prohibit advocacy of hatred that constitutes incitement to violence, discrimination or hostility in accordance with Article 20(2) of the ICCPR.[39]

The UN General Assembly Resolution 36/103, provides that states must abstain from any defamatory campaign, vilification or hostile propaganda to intervene or interfere in the internal affairs of others. It prohibits states from exploiting and distorting human rights issues as a means of interference in the internal affairs of states or creating distrust and disorder within and among states or groups of states.[40] The General Assembly report on "Countering disinformation for the promotion and protection of human rights and fundamental freedoms" describes the challenges posed by disinformation and the responses to it, sets out the relevant international legal framework and discusses measures that States and technology enterprises reported to have taken to counter disinformation. The spread of disinformation can have a devastating impact on our societies, undermining a broad range of human rights. Countering the different manifestations of disinformation requires addressing underlying

39 Andrey Rikhter, *International Law and Policy on Disinformation in the Context of Freedom of the Media*, Brief Paper for the Expert Meeting organized by the Office of the OSCE Representative on Freedom of the Media (14 May 2021) (online), available at: https://www.osce.org/files/f/documents/8/a/485606.pdf (last accessed 2 June 2025).

40 UN General Assembly, *Declaration on the Inadmissibility of Intervention and Interference in the Internal Affairs of States*, GA Res 36/103, UN Doc. A/RES/36/103 (9 December 1981).

societal tensions, fostering respect for human rights, online and offline, and supporting a plural civic space and media landscape.[41]

Report by the Secretary General states, "There is no clear definition of, or shared common understanding and approach to, the term "disinformation". The term has been used by the International Telecommunication Union and the United Nations Educational, Scientific and Cultural Organisation (UNESCO) to describe false or misleading content that can cause specific harm, irrespective of motivations, awareness or behaviours. The Special Rapporteur on the promotion and protection of the right to freedom of opinion and expression similarly defines disinformation as "false information that is disseminated intentionally to cause serious social harm". Disinformation can have a variety of motives, including political, ideological or commercial, or a combination thereof. When used by those with power and influence, it can undermine trust in public institutions and contribute to polarising societies and exacerbating social divisions, thus creating fertile ground for populism and authoritarianism to flourish. When disinformation threatens human rights, States have a duty to take appropriate steps to address these harmful impacts. Further, States have a crucial role to play in combating the impacts of disinformation, both with regard to their own actions and relating to their duty to protect against human rights abuses by third parties. Some temporary or extended Internet shutdowns, including restricting access to the Internet and blocking certain websites or platforms, have been explained as measures to tackle disinformation. [42]

Action by the States

Fake news can affect a broad range of human rights and increasing tensions in times of armed conflict or public emergencies. In place of imposing restrictions, states must promote and protect free and independent media and access to information. It will develop trust in public institutions and governance. States should also undertake digital and media literacy programmes to enable more resilient and meaningful participation online. In Europe, Stopfake.org was launched in 2014 to combat fake news spreading across the internet during Ukraine's crisis in Crimea. This site checks facts, verifies information, and refutes inaccurate reports and propaganda about events in Crimea. In

41 UN Secretary-General, *Report of the Secretary-General*, UN Doc. A/77/287 (12 August 2022).

42 Report of the Secretary-General, UN General Assembly doc A/77/287, August 12, 2022.

Qatar, "Lift the Blockade" is a government website set up in September 2017 to counter what Qatar regards as fake news distributed by geopolitical rivals to justify the imposition of economic sanctions amid the Gulf crisis. Several states have taken regulatory measures to combat misinformation and disinformation on the grounds of the protection of national security of public order or public health or morals. Several states have also established government fact-checking departments.[43]

In India, Facebook, YouTube, and WhatsApp are most vulnerable to fake news. There is no specific law against fake news in India.[44] Free publication of news flows from Article 19 of the Constitution, guaranteeing freedom of speech.[45] The Indian police, over the last few years, have opened investigations against a large number of people for allegedly spreading misinformation and fake news. Fake news and spreading mis/ disinformation is a crime under the Bharat Nyaya Sanhita, 2023, the Disaster Management Act 2005, and the Information Technology Act, 2000. The Press Information Bureau (PIB) Fact Check Unit in India takes up queries related to the Government of India, its Ministries, Departments, Public Sector entities etc. Any matter that does not pertain to the Union Government is not taken up for evaluation/fact-checking by the PIB Unit. After Operation Sindoor, the PIB has countered a number of instances of misinformation, including altered images, recycled footage, and false attributions. Fact-checking agencies and independent researchers observed that disinformation exploited emotionally charged content in order to drive engagement, escalate nationalist sentiment and manufacture support for an all-out war.[46]

---

43 Ali Strongwater, "Combating Disinformation Through International Law", *New York University Journal of International Law and Politics*, vol. 55 (2023), pp. 33–41.

44 In India, the government recently passed a policy that bans members of the military from using social networking platforms like Facebook, Instagram, Twitter etc. Further, the government ordered the military members to delete their social media accounts. Delhi High Court in the case of *Lt Col Pk Choudhary v. Union of India* (decided on August 5, 2020) held, ".... if the government, after complete assessment, has concluded that permitting the use of certain social networking websites by personnel of its defence forces is enabling the enemy countries to gain an edge, the Courts would be loath to interfere."

45 On April 2, 2018, the Indian Government amended the 'Guidelines for Accreditation of Journalists', to tackle fake news across media by providing for cancellation of accreditation of journalists even before the completion of the proposed 15-day inquiry. It was withdrawn in 15 hours after protests by the media.

46 Mainstream Indian news channels played a significant role in amplifying misinformation throughout the conflict. Their position as established brands lent undue credibility to fabricated stories, which were packaged with "Breaking News" banners, militaristic

Conclusion

The term "fake news" is a highly contested term as it has a number of distinct meanings and uses. Fake news refers to intentionally releasing fabricated information that is designed to mislead its audience. In today's digital age, unregulated social media platforms have facilitated the widespread dissemination of fake news and manipulated videos. In India, prominent social media platforms are Facebook, Instagram, Twitter, YouTube, and WhatsApp. Our adversaries use these platforms to spread false news and misleading reports against the country. It is generally created with malicious intent to cause harm by both the state and non-state actors. It can be used to harm the reputations and integrity of individuals and organisations and is often employed as a means of swaying public opinion. International law does not prohibit a state from disseminating misinformation in another State unless it amounts to an intervention due to the coercive nature of interference with the domestic affairs of the latter state. In such scenario, states reserve the sovereign right to employ any effective means of combating fake news within their own jurisdiction which is justifiable under the applicable rules of international or domestic human rights law. The best strategy for the against fake news will be to create a "digital defence force" to combat mis/ disinformation on social media networks. counter-narratives that challenge fake news must be taken expeditiously as fake news can spread at great speed due to technology.

graphics, and loud siren effects. In numerous instances, these outlets aired unverified claims or repackaged unrelated footage to portray Pakistani aggression or Indian military successes and then further propagated those false narratives through their social media accounts. Inside *the Misinformation and Disinformation War Between India and Pakistan*, The Centre for the Study of Organized Hate (2025), p. 48.

Chapter 3

Fake News and Propaganda on the Ukraine War by Social Media 'bots' and Their Effects

---

-Rhitwique Dutta and Sanghamitra Choudhury

Introduction

Social bots can automatically generate online communications like tweets and comments. They can thus fabricate trends and false news to influence people's opinions about the level of support for particular political candidates or other contentious subjects (Li, Liu, & Zhang, 2023) . The war between Russia and Ukraine, which began in February 2022, is not just about soldiers and tanks, it is also about what happened online, where bot accounts turned into major players. These bot profiles churned out messages fast, and became extremely important, especially when neither side could win on the actual battlefield in the early phase of the war, there was no strategic victory for either side. On platforms like Twitter, now called X, bots shaped how people perceived the fight and psychologically manipulated them, making the social media war almost as key as the real one. Russia initiated its attack, expecting to conclude it quickly, and according to the information space, the predicted timeline was three days. Yet, Ukraine fought back hard, way tougher than Moscow anticipated. That resistance did not remain silent, it hit Twitter with videos of destroyed Russian gear, and dead soldiers, spreading fast and wide on X.

Disinformation campaigns are a crucial component of Putin's regime's military operations, and their use against Ukraine represents a dramatic shift in their approach to combat. This fundamental change in Russian military policy is reflected in the creation of the "Gerasimov Doctrine," which highlights the importance of misinformation campaigns, cyber operations, and psychological warfare. In order to accomplish strategic military goals (Marigliano, Ng, & Carley, 2024). A Twitter spokesperson stated during the early phase of the war "Since the war in Ukraine began, we have removed more than 75,000 accounts for violations of our platform manipulation and spam policy" (Purtill, 2022). When Russia rolled in on Ukraine, it did not count on Ukraine holding out so strongly. Soon enough, videos depicting blown-up T-90 M tanks by Javelin missiles, burned-out trucks, and all the mess of dead Russian soldiers who were blasted into smithereens, popped up online, mostly on X. People saw it, and the number of interactions increased (it can be identified from the interaction bar on X). Bot accounts made sure it went even further, hitting Russia's tough-guy image hard. Ukrainians and the users rooting for them, capitalized on this, poking fun at Russia for not winning quickly like they initially planned. The trolling was nonstop and extremely brutal, turning X into a place where Russia got laughed at, and their military was deemed incompetent by the X community. As Ukraine kept standing up to Russia's army, that online buzz grew, pulling in support from all over the world.

The longer Ukraine was able to hold off Russia, the more the world noticed. X posts were full of shaky videos showing Ukrainian soldiers taking on tanks, or drones dropping bombs on Russian lines, which got lots of interactions. The defence of Hostomel airport was of particular interest to many X users. Ukrainian forces were seen in a new video using precision attacks to destroy Russian vehicles. Their concerted actions thwarted the enemy's objectives. Two Russian infantry fighting vehicles were destroyed by the Ukrainian defences, and at least one more was damaged (Nazarenko, 2025). People in the West, watching these events take place, started to increase their support for Ukraine, and their leaders also found an opportunity in this and, promised more guns and aid to Ukraine. Helping Ukraine could have a significant impact on the elections as so many people in the West were united on this issue, it was a vote bank in the making. Regular folks were moved by stories of brave Ukrainians, examples like one guy facing down a convoy, and stories like that, spread like wildfire on X. The Ukraine-aligned bots helped push it, making sure everyone saw the bravery of Ukrainians, and it worked, raising awareness, and getting more eyes on their fight.

In addition to the fact that Russian information operations have been actively targeting Ukraine since at least 2014, there is evidence that domestic Ukrainian political players use social media manipulation tactics (Urman

& Makhortykh, 2025). The Ukrainians used bots to sow disinformation, pumping out fake stories sometimes, stretching the truth about Russian losses and cowardice. Videos of ruined Russian weapons backed it up and made it look real, even if the numbers were far from reality. Then there was the sad side, civilian deaths, and bombed-out homes, which were carefully caught on drone-based cameras, and shared everywhere on X. Bots kept pushing these posts, hitting Westerners' hearts and minds, turning them against Russia fast. That anger became apparent in the X posts, which were directed towards Russia, and it got Ukraine real war-fighting equipment, like weapons from NATO, and cash from regular people too, all due to the online push. Russia could not ignore this. Ukraine's social media game was strong, bringing in aid, and boosting morale, and this even had the possibility of messing with Russia's weapon sales. Countries thinking about buying T-90s or Ka-52 choppers saw them getting destroyed online, which is not a good look for business prospects. Plus, all that support Ukraine raked in, from missiles to crowdfunding for weapon platforms, made their new units war-ready, which were raised in urgency. Moscow had to fight back, so they utilised their own bots on X, spreading lies, denying the negative information about itself, and terming Ukrainians as Nazis. It also raised significant interactions on X, confused some people, and gave Russia a bit of breathing room in the narrative war.

Social media, especially X, turned into a wild zone for this conflict. Ukraine showed off every Russian loss, sometimes Russia also shared its own losses and termed those as Ukrainian losses. Ukraine made sure that its posts garnered a lot of interaction on X and kept spirits up. Russia was caught off guard and scrambled to catch up, throwing bots into the mix to flip the narrative. Winning online meant more than just looking strong, it brought actual help, like guns, tanks, ammunition, and financial aid, or hurt real plans, like tank deals. Both sides knew it, fought hard for it, and turned X into a battleground where likes and retweets hit as hard as missiles. This chapter looks into that online battle, looking at how bots on X shaped the Ukraine war story. It utilizes special content analysis techniques to identify bot behavior. Repetition patterns, followers, posts made by the followers, activity range, and replies to posts are coded to identify the probability of being a bot account or bot-supported account. However, identifying bot accounts is no easy feat as Xs' algorithms have already hidden many bot posts from public view in an attempt to curb bot activities. However, upon closer inspection, bot activities can still be identified with proper coding techniques. More than 100 probable bot and bot-supported accounts are taken for this study. This study relies on a high degree of confidence;

however, 100 percent accuracy is difficult to claim. This study aims to open the chapter on bot war, how it changed what people think, and how it pushed the real war along too.

Why does this matter? The Ukraine fight, still going strong in July 2025, keeps shifting, and social media is right in the middle. Bots do not just echo what is happening, they make new tales and steer the crowd. Ukraine used it to stay alive, grabbing help from the West. Russia used it to dodge blame and muddy the water. It is not just talk, it is raw power, affecting deals, wars, and maybe how fights go down from now on. This chapter shows who did what, how it landed, and what it all means. Moreover, this chapter will examine the moves made by bots, Ukraine's big wins online, and Russia's pushback with fake tales. It will check how they played X's rules, hooked real people, and played with human emotions. Western aid, sparked by all this, gets a look, plus Russia's tricks to break it up. By analysis of Twitter posts and some deep thinking, this study paints the full picture, of how bots and lies on X messed with the Ukraine war, and changed how the world saw it. This start sets it all up, a war where tweets pack a punch, where winning might come down to who scrolls the most.

Narrative of Losses

Researchers from the University of Adelaide in Australia discovered that between 60 and 80 percent of Twitter accounts that tweet on the conflict between Russia and Ukraine may be bot accounts (Mihindukulasuriya, 2022). The Russia-Ukraine war did not just play out in trenches and towns, it spilled onto X, where both sides turned to bots to churn up the death toll of their enemy, a messy scramble to look righteous in a fight where how things seemed mattered almost as much as what happened. Russia set its automated voices loose, spreading misinformation about Ukrainian soldiers cut down and Western gear torn apart, trying to cast itself as a juggernaut smashing through Kyiv's hopes and its foreign friends. Ukraine fired back, its own bots piling up Russian losses, painting a picture of grit and guts even as the ground shifted under its feet. This chapter digs into that digital fight, the way it shook up the weapons trade, the hints of Western hands stirring the pot, a story where losses were not just numbers, they were bargaining chips. By utilizing bots Russia's game was to make Ukraine look like it was falling apart, its bots flooding X with news of whole units wiped out, fancy NATO equipment like HIMARS blasted to bits, a story meant to rattle Kyiv's backers into second thoughts. Every post about dead Ukrainians or wrecked aid was a one-two punch, lifting spirits at home while whispering to the West that their help was pointless. But it was not that clean-cut, things got messy fast, take the T-90 tank, a Russian export worth millions, each one lost was a bruise on Moscow's reputation, and countries like India or Egypt could start eyeing other sellers, a hit to Russia's wallet that bots could not allow to happen.

On the day when the UN General Assembly passed Resolution ES-11/2, denouncing the invasion of Ukraine, the number of pro-Russian communications reached its highest point. The bots' location analyses showed that they were most active in nations that did not cast ballots on UN Resolution ES-11/1 on March 2, 2022. These included countries like Pakistan, South Africa, and India. On this day, pro-Russian Twitter activity was particularly dense in these nations. Although pro-Russian propaganda on Twitter continued to reach its highest levels on this day, this remarkable regional dispersion had vanished by the next day (LMU, 2023). However, Ukraine made a powerful comeback, its bots targeted Russian body counts, every soldier gone, every tank trashed, a chance to wave a flag of defiance. The T-90s, Su-34 jets, warships, and BTRs, were not just battlefield casualties, they were cracks in Russia's arms business, the Su-34, a pricey $36 million bird (Airplane Update , 2019). The Moskva warship sank back in 2022 and Ukraine claimed it struck the vessel with its Neptune missiles (Sands, 2022). This ship was supposed to be a power-projecting weapon which ended up as a cautionary tale. Ukraine kept the spotlight on them, turning losses into a warning for buyers in places like India and China, a way to say Russia's weapons were of poor quality.

Then there were the big-ticket weapons, the ones that really moved the scales. When Ukraine took out an S-400, Russia's top-shelf air defense missile, it was not just a tactical win, it was a punch to Moscow's sales pitch, the S-400, a hundreds of million-dollar system meant to rival the West's best, lost its shine, nations like Turkey or India could think twice before ordering more such systems, a single blow rippling far beyond the front lines. Already, the Indian Ministry of Defence signed a $5.5 billion agreement in October 2018 to purchase four regiments of Russian S-400 surface-to-air missiles (SAM) (Wilson & Parachini, 2020). Flip that coin, and you have got the Patriot missile system. The American-made air-defense missile, which knocked out a Kinzhal hypersonic missile according to the Ukrainians (Neuman, 2023). Russia's so-called unbeatable wonder, suddenly the Patriot started looking like a good buy and raised the number of prospective buyers for the Patriot air-defence missile system. Ukraine's bots latched onto those wins, showing to the world how great Western gear was, a habit that makes you wonder who was really steering the ship. They were not just cheering for Kyiv, they were practically selling Patriot systems, S-400's destruction doubling as advertisements for NATO's edge, it is hard not to peek behind the curtain and see Washington or London in the background, nudging things along, though pinning it down is not an easy possibility, the whole thing is too murky, too slippery to nail shut, still, the feeling is there, Ukraine's digital hustle lining up a bit too neatly with Western dreams.

The money side of this was huge, every loss could hit the arms market like a stone in a pond. Russia's T-90, a steady earner, took a beating on its reputation with each wreck. High-resolution footage of a drone attack against a Russian T-90M traveling at high speed on a dirt road was posted on official information platforms run by the Security Service of Ukraine (SBU), the nation's law enforcement and intelligence organisation. Later impact photos taken by a different drone reveal the tank completely destroyed by a huge explosion (Korshak, 2024). The Su-34, marketed to far-off buyers, looked less convincing when it crashed, warships, and BMPs, all fed Russia's billions of dollars' worth of arms haul, bots pushing this news made the damage bigger, and Ukraine twisted that social media knife, showing the world Russian gear was not worth the price tag, and pointing towards Western sellers who would happily step in. However, the actual amount of damage in monetary terms to Russia and win for Western arms suppliers remains outside the scope of this chapter.

Ukraine's bots were not just about economics; they kept Kyiv looking strong even when losing ground against the Russians. Bakhmut and Soledar were nightmares for Ukraine, Ukraine lost ground and lost lives of significant numbers of soldiers and civilians, yet online it was all Russian corpses, numbers thrown out in thousands, no proof needed, what made it stick was the videos, Ukraine had cracked the code for filming Russian equipment blowing up, T-90s in flames, Su-34s being blown from the sky, BMPs shredded, those clips ran loops around the truth, kept spirits up, kept the world watching, a lifeline when the war map was not kind to Ukraine.

It was a tug-of-war over who looked worse, Russia's bots pushing Ukrainian graves to scare off the West, every HIMARS, Leopard or Abrams wreck a plea to pull the plug on supplies to Ukraine, Ukraine hitting back, making Russian losses a sales disaster, every tank kill made a mark against Moscow's name. The S-400 going down would hurt Russia's bottom line, and the Patriot's Kinzhal kill had possibly pumped-up America's, bots were not counting bodies, they were counting contracts, shaping who would buy what from Delhi to Riyadh.

Figuring out who ran these bots is a headache, and the West's role, is a guess wrapped in the fog of war, Ukraine's cheerleading for NATO gear feels too perfect, but there is no smoking gun, just shadows, Russia's claims, Ukraine's counters, they built a story where losses sold more than weapons, the T-90's troubles, the Patriot's rise, those were the prizes, not just morale boosts. Ukraine had the upper hand with cameras, and Russia stuck to numbers, cold and plain, Ukraine paired its tallies with footage, a Javelin ripping a T-90 apart, replayed until it stuck, that beat Russia's advantage in troop numbers and weapons, kept Kyiv's head high even as Bakhmut crumbled, bots made sure the world saw Russian wrecks, not Ukrainian tears, a trick that worked because people believe their eyes.

It completely destroyed the authenticity of information, even news channels could not keep track of what was real. Russia's bots, Ukraine's bots, spinning out continuous lies and fake narratives, each one with a different objective, a sale, a lifeline. The S-400's failure, the Kinzhal's fall, these were market moves, not just war stories, the T-90's fate, the Su-34's destruction, they hit wallets, Ukraine's videos, Russia's counts, they fought for more than pride. In Ukraine's lens, they wrote a tale where every Russian loss was leveraged, garnering more financial and military aid to Ukraine as it seemed that it was possible to defeat the once enormous and widely feared Russian army. This fight over losses, played out on X, was a fight in the dark, Russia and Ukraine, duking it out with bots, piling up the dead to claim the high ground, the arms game hung on every word, T-90s and Patriots, Su-34s and Kinzhals, their worth tied to the noise, they turned carnage into capital, a war where winning meant selling and losing meant more than dying.

Aftermath of Kursk

In a surprise move, the Ukrainian army advanced rapidly up to 30 kilometers inside Russia (Murphy, 2024). The Ukrainian push into Russian territory was a move that took everyone by surprise and was unlike anything seen before. Finally, Ukraine, a country that had spent years holding its ground, crossed the border and took over Sudzha, a small but important town close to the edge of Russia. This attack, which was carefully planned and carried out quickly, caught Russia off guard, showing significant problems in its border security and causing damage to its pride, as nobody could imagine a nuclear power being invaded by a non-nuclear power in the 21st century. Sudzha, though not a big place, meant a lot because of its location, and losing it was a slap in the face to the Kremlin, which had warned that crossing certain red lines would bring serious trouble. Those warnings, often talked about by Russia's leaders and military bloggers as limits no one should test, seemed empty when nothing huge happened afterward, making people wonder if Russia's threats, especially about nuclear weapons, were just propaganda.

This event raised one of the highest interaction phases on X since the beginning of the war, it was Kursk, a place already known from a giant tank battle in World War II, in which Tiger tanks and T-34s dueled it out, now back in the news for a different reason. Notably, there was no fight between Leopard 2s and T-90s, which many users on X hoped. However, the Ukrainians used German symbols in their vehicles which crossed over to Kursk, meant to remind the Russians of the historical trauma. People everywhere, from experts to regular folks, were stunned at Ukraine's gutsy move, a big shift from the slow, tough fighting that had been the story of the war so far. Ukrainian troops, using weapons from Western countries and confident from earlier wins, moved quickly, taking advantage of a border area Russia had not guarded well, may be comfortable with the thought that Ukraine would not dare try something like this. Russia's first response was far from satisfactory, with leaders rushing to send help to civilians rather than having a clear plan to deal with the Ukrainian forces, which made it look like they were not ready for this at all.

The world reacted quickly, with all kinds of opinions flying around. News reports from different places showed pictures of Ukrainian soldiers putting their flag up in Sudzha, a sign of their success. On social media, especially on X, the word "Kursk" with a hashtag in front of it started popping up everywhere, a way for people to follow what was happening. The button of X that shows the latest posts for a particular hashtag was filled up with real, rough clips of the fighting. Videos spread showing entire Russian units surrendering, giving up to Ukrainians, while others showed wrecked convoys hit hard by HIMARS rockets, weapons Ukraine got from the United States. Video of a severely damaged convoy in the Kursk area of Russia has been analyzed by BBC and verified. It depicts several wrecked Russian military vehicles abandoned on the road, some of which are loaded with wounded or deceased soldiers, as a few uniformed individuals stand by the side of the road (BBC, 2024). These moments, filmed by Ukrainian fighters or which at times come from the Russian side were used by Ukraine to show off their win, they did not need fake accounts to push them, they stood out on their own in those early days.

For Russia, it was a brutal reality check on their military capabilities, a low point that needed more than just fighting back. Losing Sudzha, even if it was not a huge city, hurt because it is near a big gas pipeline that matters to the country. Russia's government tried to brush it off, saying extra troops were coming, and that Ukraine's push was stopped. But stories from the area did not match that, with Ukrainian soldiers still holding their ground, digging in trenches, despite Russia's efforts. President Vladimir Putin spoke to the country, calling it a big problem and blaming Ukraine for attacking regular people, though there was not much proof of that. Russian President Vladimir Putin said that Kyiv is attempting to halt Moscow's operation in the Donbas region of eastern Ukraine by allowing the Ukrainian army to invade the Kursk region, which has forced over 100,000 residents to escape (NBC News, 2024). The emphasis on civilians having to bear the brunt of the troubles was to show that Ukraine fights unethically. Putin's words, full of anger, could not hide what was clear, Russia had been outsmarted, and its big talk about using nuclear weapons did not scare Ukraine off. Around the world, this made people question if Russia's warnings were serious, something leaders and thinkers kept talking about.

After the first shock wore off, the fight moved online, where X turned into a messy battle of its own. The #Kursk hashtag, at first a clear way to see Ukraine's success, got tangled up in a mess of lies being promoted by Russian bots. Russia which was stuck in a bad spot with everyone watching, leaned on a trick from the Ukrainian playbook of spreading fake stories by utilizing fake users. This time the Russians were not concerned about giving a real user-like image to the bots, they made it apparent and easy to identify, as their sole objective was to hide the news. Soon, a bunch of new accounts started posting on X, all saying the same thing, that Ukraine lost a large number of soldiers, some putting the figure in thousands, and that Russia has already managed to throw out the Ukrainians. These posts, claiming Ukraine was crushed and the Kursk region was back in Russian hands, flooded the hashtag, repeating it over and over until it was hard to find any real updates. The accounts were easy to spot as fakes, with no past posts, no one following them, clearly made just to mess with the story. Looking through the newest posts turned into a slog, just the same lies again and again, hiding what was happening.

This surge of fake posts, even if it was not real-like, did its job for a while. For a few days, it buried the real news coming from the battlefield, making it tough for anyone to figure out what was true about Kursk. People could tell these accounts were not legitimate, with nothing to them but the same copied messages, but there were so many that it clogged everything up. One could not scroll down as the Kursk hashtag had an endless amount of the same posts, which were posted in a gap of a few seconds. Users started complaining, pointing out the problem to X, yet it took time for anything to change. Eventually, after enough people spoke up, X stepped in, probably shutting down lots of those fake accounts and fixing things so real posts could show up again. By then, though, Russia had gotten what it wanted, the clear story of Ukraine's win was rigged, replaced with a made-up version of Russia bouncing back.

That online push from Russia, although it was short-lived, it gave them some breathing room. It mixed up what people thought, slowed down Ukraine's big moment online, and gave Russia time to get itself together. It was vital for Russia to get back control of the information space. Back in Kursk, Russian troops, helped by tougher units and even some soldiers from another country, started pushing back, taking some ground again. Sudzha stayed with Ukraine, though, a spot they would not let go of, no matter how hard Russia tried. What this whole move meant, whether it pulled Russia's attention away from other fights or gave Ukraine something to use in talks later, kept people arguing, but it hit Russia hard in the head. It showed Russia was not as strong as it acted, not in fighting or in keeping its story straight. So, Kursk was a mix of big wins and big problems, Ukraine's daring attack getting overshadowed by Russia's fight back in social media, a short time of clear news on X swallowed up by a pile of fake information. The #Kursk hashtag, once a straight look at what was happening, turned into a picture of the war itself, truth and lies all jumbled together. For everyone watching, it showed something new, Ukraine, always seen as the weaker side, could hit Russia where it hurt, while Russia, knocked down but not out, used fake stories and used bots to try to stand back up. As the war kept going, what happened in Kursk stuck around, proof that fights can change fast, on the ground and online, and that lines Russia said no one could cross were not as solid as they seemed.

Credibility and Fundraising

One of the big pieces in the information war between Russia and Ukraine came down to credibility. It was not just about who could look the most legitimate online, it was about who people actually believed. Even when real accounts posted about Russian or Ukrainian losses, those accounts had to seem trustworthy. A simple way to look legitimate was grabbing that blue tick on X, you know, the one you could pay for. But there was more to it than that, having a huge follower count mattered too. The more followers an account had, the more people assumed they knew what it was talking about when it came to the Russia-Ukraine war. Numbers gave weight, even if they did not always mean being truthful. Created in February 2022, the social bot @UAWeapons, also known as Ukraine Weapons Tracker, gained 410,000 followers in just one month and more than 480,000 by the end of April 2022. In a parallel study, Shen et al. (2023) gathered 3,816 randomly selected bot accounts on the Russian-Ukrainian war between February 17 and March 17, 2022. They found that the average number of bot account followers was 988, while the median was 174. Another research found that over the period of 42 days, 96 bots were placed on a social media site and amassed a total of 5,546 followers (Li, Liu, & Zhang, 2023).

Russia started picking up an edge in this game once Ukraine got its hands on Leopard 2 tanks from Germany and M1A1 Abrams tanks from the U.S. These were supposed to be game-changers, big symbols of Western support. But then came Russia's Lancet drones, little kamikaze weapons that could swoop in and blow them up. And they did, a lot. In part, because Russian drone warfare had made it too difficult for the Abrams to operate, the Ukrainians were forced to sideline the tank as a result of the ongoing Abrams losses (Kass, 2024). Videos of these tanks getting wrecked spread quickly on X, posted by Russian bots and real users alike. The footage was real, no one could deny that, burning hulks of metal in Ukrainian fields. Destroying them was not the end of it though, Russia went further. Some of these tanks got captured, not totally trashed, just damaged enough to be towed away. They hauled them back to Russia, took them apart, and filmed the whole thing. Those clips hit X too, shared over and over, all part of a plan to make American and European weapons look weak. It was not just about battlefield wins, it was about hurting the export market for those tanks. If Russia could show the world these "superior" weapons failing, then countries thinking about buying them might hesitate. That was a smart move from the Russians.

But here is the thing, bot accounts were a double-edged sword. They could push those videos out, and flood the platform with them, but they did not always get tons of views on every single post. Their strength was in repetition, posting the same information again and again until it stuck in people's heads. The problem is, bots are kind of obvious sometimes. You see the same wording, and the same clips, it is not hard to spot. So both sides, Russia and Ukraine, started leaning harder on real accounts. People with actual faces, actual names, not just faceless programs. The problem was, that those real accounts still needed some credibility. The blue tick helped, sure, anyone with a few dollars could buy it after X changed the rules. But followers, that was the real prize. More followers meant more trust, and both sides knew it.

This is where bots became important again. They were not just meant for spreading videos and tweets anymore, they were used to increase follower counts. Russia and Ukraine both did it, creating thousands of fake profiles to follow their war-blogger accounts. An account with 30,000 followers will always look more legitimate than one with 300, even if a large number of those followers are bots. The same reason why Instagram users buy bot followers. For Russia, this was perfect for sending their message about Western weapons to prospective buyers. When an Abrams got taken out by a Lancet drone, or a Leopard 2 got captured, they would have these war-blogger accounts boosted by bots post about it. The bigger the account, the more people interacted with the story. They zeroed in on American weapons especially, like the Abrams, because it is considered a formidable weapon platform and epitome of American technology. A video of one burning, posted by an account with a blue tick and a ton of followers, puts a strong message across. It is not just propaganda at that point, it is a pitch to make the U.S. weapons look bad.

Ukraine, interestingly, took a different route with this credibility game. They were not just trying to win the online battles; they were raising cash. Real accounts, sometimes even soldiers on the front lines, started to put up with payment links. PayPal or Venmo whatever worked, they would share it and ask for donations to fund their units or requests to get them a particular weapon system. These were not bots pretending to be people, these were actual Ukrainians, guys in uniform, posting from muddy trenches, their faces covered with dust from the battle or military news reporters. That made it feel real, raw even. But if you looked closer, something stood out. A lot of these accounts had crazy high follower numbers, way more than you would expect for some random sergeant or a reporter. Dig into it, and you will see the same trick, tons of those followers were bots. They would build up these accounts to look huge, credible, and trustworthy. It worked too, Western users, especially in the U.S. and Europe, saw these posts and wanted to help. They would send money, thinking it was going straight to the fight against Russia.

This whole credibility battle with bots was not just about winning likes or retweets. It opened the door to bigger problems, like fraud. Think about it, some random account says it is raising funds for a Ukrainian battalion, shows a few gritty photos, has a blue tick, and has 100,000 followers. Looks real enough, right? Westerners, eager to support the underdog, start sending cash. But there is no guarantee that money is going where it is supposed to. Could be a scam, could be someone pocketing it, and the bots propping up the account make it harder to tell. Ukraine's side probably had some legitimate fundraisers, no doubt, soldiers do need gear and supplies. But the setup was ripe for abuse. Russia did not seem to lean into fundraising the same way, their focus stayed on tearing down the West's image. Two different strategies, the same reliance on fake followers to sell the story.

Let us back up a bit, the tank thing is worth digging into more. The Leopard 2 and Abrams were not just random targets. They were icons, right? Germany and the U.S. staked a lot of pride on those machines. When Russia started knocking them out, it was not just a military win, it was a propaganda goldmine. The Lancet drones were cheap compared to a tank, like a few thousand dollars versus millions. That is the kind of math Russia loved to show off. They would post a clip, "See, our little drone took out your invincible tank," and let it spread. Real accounts with big followings, boosted by bots, made sure it hit every corner of X. Ukraine tried to counter this, posting their wins, like taking out Russian T-90s. But the Western tanks getting wrecked, that stuck more, because they were supposed to be untouchable.

Credibility was not static either, it shifted with the war. Early on, Ukraine had the edge, the world rallied behind them, and their accounts got natural followers fast. Russia was playing catch-up, leaning on bots to close the gap. But as the fighting dragged on, and those Western tanks started blowing up, Russia clawed back some ground. Their real accounts, the ones with the huge follower lists, got better at pushing the narrative. Ukraine, meanwhile, had to keep the cash flowing. Their fundraising posts would mix with sad stories, photos of kids in bomb shelters, anything to tug at heartstrings. Bots helped amplify it, but the real power was in the human touch, a soldier saying, "We need this to survive."

The weird part? Both sides were gaming the same system. X became this battlefield where followers and blue ticks were weapons, bots were soldiers, and credibility was the prize. Russia wanted to embarrass the West, and Ukraine wanted money to keep fighting. Neither could do it without looking legitimate. Fraud was a risk, sure, especially on Ukraine's end, but the bigger issue was how this warped the truth. People scrolling X, would see a post from a "credible" account, assume it was real, and move on. Did not matter if half the followers were fake, or if the tank video was staged. Perception won out. So there was also an online fight for credibility, it showed how contagious the war got online. Real events, like tanks blowing up, were mixed with fake hype from bots. Real soldiers asking for help, pushed up by fake fans. Russia and Ukraine both used all means available. Followers did not just mean popularity, they meant power, trust, and cash. And bots, they were the engine making it all work, even if everyone knew they were there.

Conclusion

In conclusion, this chapter demonstrates that bots on Twitter, now referred to as X, have significantly influenced public perception of the Russia-Ukraine war and the positions individuals have adopted. Both factions have employed these automated accounts in a covert conflict, promoting their narratives while attempting to suppress the opposing side's. Consider the Ukrainian advance into Kursk; Russian bots inundated the #Kursk hashtag with irrelevant tweets and deceptive assertions to obscure the actual events, complicating the ability of users on X to discern the truth. Both Russia and Ukraine have manipulated the figures regarding each other's casualties. Russian bots were actively disseminating figures of Ukrainian casualties and territorial losses, attempting to persuade the West that further financial and military support for Ukraine is futile and resource-draining. Conversely, Ukraine's bots exaggerated Russian casualties, specifically targeting Russia's known weapon platforms to diminish their export potential. It was a chaotic contest to determine who would appear victorious or defeated. Additionally, both parties have employed bots to enhance the follower counts of authentic accounts, thereby augmenting the perceived legitimacy of their posts. Russia has undertaken this action to amplify support for the Kremlin, whilst Ukraine's augmented users present their perspective. However, it is not solely a matter of perception; certain Ukrainian fundraising accounts with numerous bot followers raise concerns. It is difficult to ascertain whether the requested funding stems from urgent military need, which creates opportunities for fraudulent schemes where individuals may contribute to dubious causes unknowingly. Considering this, bots are not merely disseminating falsehoods; they are integral to a broader strategy aimed at distorting public perception of the conflict and influencing financial allocations. Whether by inundating X with misinformation regarding Kursk or distorting casualty figures, these examples illustrate the ease with which a platform may be compromised when the stakes are elevated. And augmenting follower counts to fabricate credibility? This strategy has proven effective for both parties, although it has raised some uncertainties regarding aspects such as funding. As the conflict persists, X will remain a theatre for such maneuvers, necessitating vigilant observation to discern the implications for truth, trustworthiness, and global responses.

References:

Airplane Update . (2019). *Sukhoi Su-34 Fighter Bomber Specs, Engine, Cockpit and Price.* Retrieved from Airplane Update : https://www.airplaneupdate.com/2019/04/sukhoi-su-34.html.

BBC. (2024). *Footage posted online shows destroyed Russian convoy.* Retrieved from BBC: https://www.bbc.com/news/videos/c24p5l64dg2o.

Kass, H. (2024). *Ukraine Has A Problem: 20 out of 31 M1 Abrams Tanks Have Been Destroyed.* Retrieved from The National Interest : https://nationalinterest.org/blog/buzz/ukraine-has-problem-20-out-31-m1-abrams-tanks-have-been-destroyed-212760.

Korshak, S. (2024). *Russia's Mighty T-90 Tank: Not Exactly as World-Beating as Putin Wants.* Retrieved from Kyiv Post : https://www.kyivpost.com/post/42946.

Li, Q., Liu, Q., & Zhang, H. (2023). Influence of social bots in information warfare: A case study on @UAWeapons Twitter account in the context of Russia–Ukraine conflict. *Communication and the Public.* doi:https://doi.org/10.1177/20570473231166157.

LMU. (2023). *Russia's war against Ukraine: the bot offensive flanking the invasion.* Retrieved from LMU: https://www.lmu.de/en//newsroom/news-overview/news/russias-war-against-ukraine-the-bot-offensive-flanking-the-invasion.html.

Marigliano, R., Ng, L. H., & Carley, K. M. (2024, August). Analyzing digital propaganda and conflict rhetoric: a study on Russia's bot-driven campaigns and counter-narratives during the Ukraine crisis. *Social Network Analysis and Mining.*

Mihindukulasuriya, R. (2022). *60-80% of Twitter accounts posting on Russia-Ukraine war bots, 90% 'pro Ukraine', finds new study.* Retrieved from ThePrint : https://theprint.in/tech/60-80-of-twitter-accounts-posting-on-russia-ukraine-war-bots-90-pro-ukraine-finds-new-study/1114878/.

Murphy, M. (2024). *Ukrainian troops now up to 30km inside Russia, Moscow says.* Retrieved from BBC: https://www.bbc.com/news/articles/crkm08rv5m0o.

Nazarenko, V. (2025). *Defense forces halt Russian convoy heading toward Ukrainian border.* Retrieved from RBC-Ukraine: https://newsukraine.rbc.ua/news/defense-forces-halt-russian-convoy-heading-1737027778.html.

NBC News. (2024). *Russian President Putin Comments on Ukraine's Kursk Offensive* . Retrieved from NBC News: https://www.nbcnews.com/video/russian-president-putin-comments-on-ukraine-s-kursk-offensive-217048133745.

Neuman, S. (2023). *Ukraine says its newly fielded U.S. Patriot system downed a Russian hypersonic missile.* Retrieved from NPR: https://www.npr.org/2023/05/06/1174505616/ukraine-patriot-defense-russian-hypersonic-missile-kinzhal.

Purtill, J. (2022). *Twitter bot network amplifying Russian disinformation about Ukraine war, researcher says.* Retrieved from ABC Science: https://www.abc.net.au/news/science/2022-03-30/ukraine-war-twitter-bot-network-amplifies-russian-disinformation/100944970.

Sands, L. (2022). *Sunken Russian warship Moskva: What do we Know,* BBC, available at: https://www.bbc.com/news/world-europe-61103927.

Chapter 4

Lawfare: The Strategic Use of Law as a Weapon

-U C Jha

After the April 22, 2025, Pahalgam terror attack, India has used international law as a tool to achieve its objective of diminishing Pakistan's support to cross-border terrorism. By putting the 1960 Indus Waters Treaty (IWT) in abeyance, India has used lawfare to gain its political objectives to end Pakistan's support for terrorism. Indian action is grounded in the customary international law of *clausula rebus sic stantibus* and countermeasures.[1] The customary nature of this doctrine, enshrined under Article 62 of the Vienna Convention on the Law of Treaties, 1969 (VCLT),[2] makes it

1 *Clausula rebus sic stantibus* is a clause in international agreements or treaties that provides for the unenforceability of a treaty due to fundamentally changed circumstances. The doctrine is one of the oldest norms of customary international law. https://www.law.cornell.edu/wex/rebus_sic_stantibus.

2 Article 62, the Vienna Convention on the Law of Treaties, 1969: Fundamental change of circumstances: 1. A fundamental change of circumstances which has occurred with regard to those existing at the time of the conclusion of a treaty, and which was not foreseen by the parties, may not be invoked as a ground for terminating or withdrawing from the treaty unless: (a) the existence of those circumstances constituted an essential basis of the consent of the parties to be bound by the treaty; and (b) the effect of the change is radically to transform the extent of obligations still to be performed under the treaty. 2. A fundamental change of circumstances may not be invoked as a ground for terminating or withdrawing from a treaty: (a) if the treaty establishes a boundary; or (b) if the fundamental change is the result of a breach by the party invoking it either of an obligation under the treaty or of any other international obligation owed to any other party to the treaty. 3. If, under the foregoing paragraphs, a party may invoke a fundamental change of circumstances as a ground for terminating or withdrawing from a treaty it may also invoke the change as a ground for suspending the operation of the treaty.

applicable to the IWT. The doctrine permits states to suspend, withdraw, or terminate treaty obligations in the light of fundamental changes in the circumstances surrounding the agreement.[3] The Indian government has issued a notification to its Pakistani counterpart explaining the reasons for suspending the IWT and also highlighted the significantly altered population demographics, the urgent need to expedite the development of clean energy, and shifts in the assumptions related to water sharing under the IWT as fundamental changes that have led to its decision to suspend its treaty obligations.

The wording of the Cabinet Committee on Security clarifies that India is temporarily suspending its treaty obligations. As stated, the IWT will be in abeyance as long as Pakistan supports cross-border terrorism. The Indian response to the killing of 26 innocent civilians is not excessive since the Pakistan government and military regime have been openly supporting terrorism on Indian soil. The dispute resolution mechanism under the IWT has no reference to settling any differences before the ICJ.[4] Instead, the IWT has set up a graded system, which includes submission of disputes to the Indus Water Commission, consequently to a neutral expert and later to a court of arbitration if the issue remains unresolved. Lawfare is a viable instrument to further political interests, and India has reaffirmed its stand that blood and water cannot flow together. The use of lawfare is becoming a new weapon of war in modern times.

Defining Lawfare

The new phrase "lawfare" is a compound of the words law and warfare. One of the first records of it can be traced back to an article published in 1975, in which it was claimed that "lawfare replaces warfare, and the duel is with words rather than swords".[5] The modern usage was coined by Charles J.

3 Certain conditions must be met to invoke the doctrine of fundamental change in circumstances: (i) the change must be objective and not merely a subjective change in the attitude of the party invoking it; (ii) as noted by the International Court of Justice (ICJ) noted in the Fisheries Jurisdiction Case, the fundamental change should be radical; (iii) the clausula doctrine should be invoked within a reasonable timeframe; and (iv) the change must be unforeseen when parties conclude the treaty.

4 Article IX of the 1960 Indus Waters Treaty dealing with Settlement of Differences and Disputes, states, "(1) Any question which arises between the Parties concerning the interpretation **or** application of this Treaty or the existence of any fact which, if established, might constitute a breach of this Treaty shall first be examined by the Commission, which will endeavour to resolve the question by agreement.

5 Carlson John and Yeomans Neville, "Whither goeth the law: Humanity or barbarity," in Smith M. and Crossley, D., (ed.), 1975, *The Way Out - Radical Alternatives in Australia*,

Dunlap Jr., defining it as "a method of warfare where law is used as a means of realizing a military objective." According to Dunlap, there are many dimensions to lawfare, but the one frequently used (by the US opponent) is a cynical manipulation of the rule of law and the humanitarian values it represents.[6] Dunlop later refined the definition of lawfare as "the strategy of using-or misusing-law as a substitute for traditional military means to achieve an operational objective."[7]

According to Scharf and Anderson (2010) lawfare is the use of international law and legal procedures with the strict aim of making a claim against another state, especially in spheres connected with national security.[8] Tropin (2021) provides a comprehensive definition, suggesting lawfare is the "use of law aimed at delegitimising the actions of an opponent (or legitimising one's own) and to tie up the time and resources of the opponent and achieve advantages in military activity or in any sphere of social relations."[9] However, Beck (2014) considers that lawfare is a misuse of the law to achieve a military objective and to undermine the legal framework.[10] This definition try to represent lawfare in a narrow sense the use of legal means in the context of military activity alone. Trachtman defined lawfare (2016) as "legal activity that supports, undermines, or substitutes for other types of warfare."[11] This definition is too broad to be useful.

Jill (2021) has defined lawfare as the purposeful use of law taken toward a particular adversary with the goal of achieving a particular strategic, operational, or tactical objective. In other words, the purposeful use of law to bolster the legitimacy of one's own strategic, operational, or tactical

Melbourne: Lansdowne Press, pp. 155-163.

6 Charles J. Dunlap Jr., "Law and Military Interventions: Preserving Humanitarian Values in 21st Century Conflicts," presented at "Humanitarian Challenges in Military Interventions Conference," Washington, DC, 29 November 2001, available at https://people.duke.edu/~pfeaver/dunlap.pdf, accessed 26 May 2025.

7 Charles J. Dunlap, "Lawfare Today: A Perspective", *Yale Journal of International Law*, Vol. 3, p. 146.

8 Scharf M. and Andersen E., "Is Lawfare worth defining?" Report of the Cleveland Experts Meeting, September 11, 2010, *Case Western Reserve Journal of International Law*, 43(1), 2010, pp. 11–27.

9 Zakhar Tropin, Lawfare as part of hybrid wars: The experience of Ukraine in conflict with Russian Federation, *Security and Defence Quarterly*, Vol. 33(1), 2021, pp. 15-29.

10 Beck A., 'China's strategy in the Arctic: a case of lawfare?', *The Polar Journal*, Vol. 4(2), 2014, pp. 306–318.

11 Joel P. Trachtman, "Integrating Lawfare and Warfare", Vol. 39, *B.C. INT'L & COMP. L. REV*, 2016, pp. 267-268.

objectives toward a particular adversary, or to weaken the legitimacy of a particular adversary's particular strategic, operational, or tactical objectives.[12] Any side of a conflict can exercise lawfare. It can be used by civilian agencies and the military alike and could be employed by the military at the strategic, operational, and tactical levels. This definition of lawfare is neutral and is being followed by most academicians. According to Dunlop, there are two constitutive elements of lawfare: (i) Its effects must be the same as or similar to those traditionally sought from conventional military action, and (ii) It must intend to weaken or destroy an adversary.[13] According to Kittrie (2016), lawfare is "the strategy of using or misusing law as a substitute for traditional military means to achieve a war-fighting objective." Further, an action qualifies as lawfare if it satisfies two basic conditions: (i) The actor uses law to create the same or similar effects as those traditionally sought from conventional kinetic military action; and (ii) One of the actor's motivations is to weaken or destroy an adversary against which the lawfare is being deployed.[14]

In the last twenty-five years since introduction of the term, the concept of lawfare has expanded into all domains of state power beyond just military operations. It now encompasses all state actions that employ domestic or international law to achieve a state's objectives. Law is no longer used solely to achieve a military objective. It is used to file claims against opponents in international courts, using legislation to disadvantage an opponent, and to influence public opinion to win support.[15]

Lawfare and International Law

The mechanics of international law functions differently from a state's domestic legal system. In the absence of any supranational legislature to pass statutes that bind all states to a common code, international law is based on the consensus of sovereign states. The main reason for international law to be respected is that it serves the national interest by a set of rules, norms and principles based on equality and reciprocity. This is

12 Jill I. Goldenziel, "Law as a Battlefield: The U.S., China, and the Global Escalation of Lawfare", *Cornell Law Review, Vol.* 106, no. 5, 2021, pp. 1085-1071.

13 Dunlap Charles J. Dunlap Jr., "Lawfare Today...and Tomorrow", *International Law Studies*, Vol. 87, 2011, p. 315.

14 Orde F. Kittrie, 2016, *Lawfare: Law as Weapon of War*, Oxford: Oxford University Press, p. 8.

15 Zoey Kotzambasis, "Lawfare: A New Tool for Fighting Terrorism?" *Arizona Journal of International & Comparative Law*, Vol. 35, No. 1, 2018, pp. 165-194.

referred to as the Lotus principle, after a case before the Permanent Court of International Justice between France and Turkey (1927). In its ruling, the court held: "*International law governs relations between independent States. The rules of law binding upon States therefore emanate from their own free will as expressed in conventions or by usages generally accepted as expressing principles of law and established in order to regulate the relations between these co-existing independent communities or with a view to the achievement of common aims. Restrictions upon the independence of States cannot therefore be presumed.*" In essence, the Lotus principle means that international law is only binding on states that consent to being bound by it. [16] There is no official hierarchy for sources of international law. The most recognized precedence follows the order in which the ICJ statute lists them. Treaties create binding obligations on the states that join them. Therefore, a violation of the terms of a treaty by a party state is a clear violation of international law. However, the interpretation of the rules of a treaty are left to each state. Originalism is not a hard rule for treaties, and states may change their interpretation of a treaty over time. If there is no treaty governing a certain international legal question, then customary international law becomes the primary focus.[17]

A rule based international order highlights the importance of international law in resolving conflicts. The effects of lawfare impacts diplomatic relations, and the very foundations of international law. For instance, in the Russian-Ukraine War, international law has played a crucial role in framing narratives around sovereignty and territorial integrity. The ongoing Israeli-Hamas conflict demonstrates the role of international law, as both sides utilise legal arguments to justify their actions. The Chinese claim in

16 In late 1926, France and Turkey agreed to bring a case before the Permanent Court of International Justice PCIJ asking the Court whether Turkey acted in accordance with the principles of international law when it brought criminal proceedings under Turkish law against a French national, Lieutenant Demons, for the involuntary manslaughter of Turkish nationals aboard the Turkish steamship *Boz-Kourt*, which had collided on the high seas with the French steamship *Lotus* for which Demons was responsible.

17 Most of the contemporary lawfare activity is centred on making changes to customary law, which is based on the practice and opinions of states. When a broad coalition of states share the same opinion and practice, a legal element can become a norm. However, neither practice nor opinion are static. Certain states today seek to modify customary norms by initiating new practices or publishing new interpretations of both treaty and customary rules. States can also use their representation on international boards and tribunals to assert these new interpretations of the rules. If enough states accept and practice under the new interpretations, these can become the new norms. Justin Malzac, "A Special Operations Approach to Lawfare", *The US Naval War College Review*, Vol. 77, No. 2, Spring 2024, p. 86.

the South China Sea,[18] an economically critical region that handles half of the world's daily merchant shipping, a third of global oil shipping, and 12 percent of the world's total fish catch' is another example of the use of lawfare.[19] These are a few examples of the use of lawfare as a weapon against the adversaries.

Lawfare involves the strategic deployment of legal mechanisms to gain an advantage and may entail leveraging legal norms, treaties, and courts to influence or disrupt an adversary's actions. Lawfare represents a critical intersection of law and conflict in the modern era. The convergence of legal and military strategies alters both the conduct and perception of conflicts. Today, lawfare is the strategy of using or misusing law as a substitute for traditional military means. Legal arguments are being frequently used to shape international public opinion and justify actions taken in conflict zones.[20]

Several recent conflicts highlight the important role of lawfare. For instance, after the Russian invasion of Ukraine, lawfare has been utilised through ICC investigations into war crimes, the imposition of international sanctions based on legal grounds, and cases brought against Russia before the International Court of Justice for alleged violations of

18 The 2023 edition of China's "standard map," published on August 28, 2023 on China's Ministry of Natural Resources website, claimed the Indian state of Arunachal Pradesh and the Aksai Chin plateau as Chinese territory. It also included part of Malaysia's maritime area off Borneo, as well as Taiwan and swaths of the South China Sea. The Chinese Foreign Ministry responded on August 30, calling on relevant parties to remain objective. Chinese spokesperson Wang Wenbin said, "It is a routine practice in China's exercise of sovereignty in accordance with the law; We hope relevant sides can stay objective and calm, and refrain from over-interpreting the issue." Available at: https://asia.nikkei.com/Politics/International-relations/Malaysia-India-and-Taiwan-reject-China-s-new-territorial-map.

19 In 2012, the Philippines referred the issue of China's vast (and unlawful) territorial claims to the Permanent Court of Arbitration (PCA), as allowed by the UN Convention on the Law of the Sea (UNCLOS). The court largely sided with the Philippines in a ruling that declared China's sweeping claims over the areas that overlapped with the territorial claims of other states to be invalid. China maintains to this day that the decision "seriously violates international law" and that it is "illegal, null, and void." Daniza Fernandez, "China Claims Arbitral Ruling on South China Sea 'Seriously Violates International Law,'" *Asia News Network*, July 15, 2022.

20 Dan Kuwali, *Local Conflict, Global Impact: Lawfare in Warfare*, Raoul Wallenberg Institute, September 24, 2024, available at: https://rwi.lu.se/blog/local-conflict-global-impact-lawfare-in-warfare/.

international law, including genocide.[21] Legal frameworks are used to document abuses, advocate for accountability, and influence the conflict's dynamics. The states have used "legal warfare" as a major component of their strategic doctrine. Lawfare is a good substitute for kinetic warfare; the States need to exploit it for strategic advantages. It is becoming a powerful 'force multiplier', reminding one of Sun Tzu, who once said that supreme excellence consists in breaking the enemy's resistance without fighting. In a legally-sophisticated era, international law has been deployed as a weapon of war by the states and non-state actors to weaken legitimacy of their adversaries.[22] Lawfare is a means to compel specified behaviour with fewer costs than the use of weapons, bringing peace, stability and development.

Types of Lawfare

Five types of lawfare have been employed by the states in recent times. These are: (i) Battlefield exploitation lawfare in which law is used for the exploitation of an adversary's law-abidingness, usually, its compliance with international humanitarian law (IHL). For example, embedding civilians within legitimate military targets or hiding armed fighters in a large crowd of civilians.[23] (ii) Instrumental lawfare, wherein law is used as legal tools to achieve the same or similar effects as those traditionally sought from conventional kinetic military action. For instance, US sanctions against Iran. The US could have launched a military strike against Iranian nuclear facilities to cause Iran to abandon its nuclear programme. Instead, the US

21 Ukraine has launched a legal counter-attack against Russia in various international tribunals like International Criminal Court, International court of Justice and the European Court of Human Rights. The issue of arrest warrant against Russian President Putin by the International Criminal Court for war crimes is a strategic lawfare action and should not be undervalued. Kelly Michael, The Role of International Law in the Russia-Ukraine War, *Case Western Reserve Journal of International Law*, Vol. 55, Issue 1-2, Spring 2023, pp. 61-92

22 Waseem Ahmad Qureshi, "Lawfare: The Weaponization of International Law", *Houston Journal of International Law*, Vol. 42, 2019-2020, p. 39.

23 For instance, the Taliban placed military assets within or around schools, religious sites, and hospitals, with the aim of either deterring attacks or being able to accuse the United States and its allies of harming innocent civilians and sites protected under international law. This exploitation of international humanitarian law obliged the United States to adopt targeting standards more stringent than those required by international law. Thus, for the Taliban, lawfare served as a substitute for conventional air defences. Eric Chang, Lawfare in Ukraine: Weaponizing International Investment Law and the Law of Armed Conflict Against Russia's Invasion, Strategic Perspectives 39, Centre for Strategic Research, Institute for National Strategic Studies, National Defence University, Washington DC, August 2022, p. 6.

launched sanctions to achieve the same effect. (iii) Proxy lawfare, which involves taking legal actions using adversary proxies. Lawfare between the US and the Chinese company Huawei. (iv) Information lawfare is the use of law to control the narrative of the conflict. One party to a conflict may gain an advantage by portraying its actions as legal, or the other side's as illegal. This type of lawfare is especially important in the battle for hearts and minds. Information lawfare could be used in conjunction with other types of lawfare.[24] (v) Institutional lawfare, which creates the purposeful new domestic and international laws and institutions to achieve one's military or strategic efforts. The US has practiced this type of lawfare for years by serving as the primary funder of the United Nations and China is now beginning to build international institutions of its own to counter US efforts. These forms of lawfare are not new and could be employed before, during, and after armed conflict at the strategic, operational, and tactical levels of war. It can also set the terms for conflict or for negotiation.

According to Tiefenbraun (2010), there are three types of lawfare:

(i) Filing malicious defamation, harassment or hate speech actions before international and national courts to silence the enemy;

(ii) The abuse of legal terminology to manipulate international institutions and create negative opinions about the enemy;

(iii) The process of foreign nations in domestic courts for civil and military actions.[25]

However, this categorization appears insufficient to cover the possible forms of lawfare when compared to the other proposals.

Strategic Uses of Lawfare

Strategic use of the law can take four forms: (i) Re-interpreting existing norms; (ii) Establishing new norms; (iii) mobilizing legal effects to constrain a party; and (iv) making accusations of unlawful acts to cause

24 The US and the Soviet Union frequently used information lawfare during the Cold War, criticizing each other's commitments to international human rights law, which resulted in two separate core human rights conventions: the International Covenant on Civil and Political Rights (ICCPR) backed by the US, and the International Covenant on Economic and Social Rights (ICESCR), backed by the USSR.

25 Tiefenbrum Susan W., "Semiotic Definition of Lawfare", *Case Western Reserve Journal of International Law*, Vol. 43, Issue 3, 2020, pp. 29-60.

reputational damage.[26] Lawfare can take the form of reinterpreting a principle of law in favour of one or more actors in strategic competition. This could be a principle codified in a treaty or included in national laws, or a standard of behaviour. The law of armed conflict has multiple sources like treaties, customs, and doctrines. Their interpretation may give rise to divergent, even contradictory opinions. As the objective of International Humanitarian Law (IHL) is to determine the behaviour of actors in an armed conflict, tension arises between that law and military objectives. Therefore, there is a strong temptation for states and their armed forces to propose adjustments to the law that allow greater freedom of action.[27]

Another category of lawfare consists of establishing new norms through legal lobbying to gain the upper hand. This strategic use of the law is favoured by the many civil and military applications of contemporary technological advances, particularly in the cyber and outer-space domains. A third category of lawfare actions involves mobilizing legal effects to constrain an adversary, sometimes called strategic litigation. Both national and international courts can be used to limit a party's freedom of action. This type of litigation allows citizens to contest the policies of the state in the courts, for example questioning the criminal responsibility of members of the armed forces, the state's responsibilities toward soldiers and their families, or decisions to export armaments.[28] The fourth category of lawfare concerns mobilizing legal arguments to adversely affect the reputation of a practice and the parties involved in it. The law's power to confer and destroy legitimacy makes it an outstanding tool of influence. Legal arguments are therefore also communication tools. Accusing a state of not respecting international legality, even in the absence of evidence, may for example damage the legitimacy of a military operation in progress or cast doubt on a foreign policy stance.

26 Ferey Amelie, "Towards a War of Norms: From Lawfare to Legal Operations", Security Studies Centre, *Focus Strategique*, April 2022, p. 36.

27 For example, post-9/11, on October 26, 2001, the US Congress adopted the Patriot Act, which allowed restrictions on detentions to be relaxed by ad hoc application of the status of "illegal combatant" to members of Al Qaeda and their associates who did not fit the category of lawful combatant as defined by the 1977 Additional Protocol (I) to the Geneva Conventions.

28 For example, the Palestinian Authority has used various legal mechanisms and courts at its disposal to oblige Israel to respect international law in an armed conflict. In March 2021, the ICC prosecutor, Fatou Bensouda, officially opened an investigation into the crimes committed on Palestinian territory.

Lawfare in Action

A word of caution, lawfare is not a perfect substitute for armed conflict. The purpose of lawfare is to use the law to achieve a military advantage for a political purpose, considering war as a political instrument. The states are weaponizing the law in different ways to achieve political goals while limiting adversarial military responses. Strategic use of the law in Russia, the US, and Israel has demonstrated how states exploit legal norms to serve their foreign policies and strengthen their position on the international stage.

A. China

Chinese lawfare development is consistent with Sun Tzu's maxim "to fight and conquer in all your battles is not supreme excellence; supreme excellence consists in breaking the enemy's resistance without fighting."[29] Developing on this conception, in 1999, Colonels Qiao Liang and Wang Xiangsui, articulated 'Unrestricted Warfare' stating that "all boundaries lying between the two worlds of war and non-war, of military and non-military, should be removed." These assessments collectively fed into the development of China's official conception or strategy of political warfare, which the Central Military Commission officially introduced in 2003 that had lawfare as an important vertical.

Today, China has the most developed lawfare strategy.[30] China institutionalized its use of lawfare at the beginning of the 21st century. This policy grew out of China's observations of the superb speed at which information in all forms became key to societies and integral to national infrastructure and power.[31] The Chinese Communist Party (CCP) followed

29 Tzu Sun, *The Art of War*, (Attack by Stratagem), New York: Fall River Press, 2014, pp. 92

30 'Three Warfares' is consistent with guidelines issued to the PLA's Political Work Department since at least 1963, which directed 'Give full play to the combat function of political work: organize public opinion warfare, psychological warfare, and legal warfare; do a good job of disintegrating the enemy's activity; and prevent the enemy's efforts to incite discord.'

31 Chinese political analysts defined what they called *xinxihua* as: "A comprehensive system of systems, where the broad use of information technology is the guide, where information resources are the core, where information networks are the foundation, where information industry is the support, where information talent is a key factor, where laws, policies, and standards are the safeguard. Cheng Dean, 2016, *Cyber Dragon: Inside China's Information Warfare and Cyber Operations*, Praeger Publishers Inc., p. 304.

President Jiang Zemin's guidance to a group of international law experts in 1996, where he said, "We must be adept at using international law as a weapon." The outcome was the conception of lawfare (*falu zhan*), as one of the 'three warfares (*san zhan*).'[32]

In 2003, the PLA incorporated the three warfare concepts into its training and education. China views the 'three warfares' as a force multiplier in military or political conflict. The Chinese government entities have also published several texts emphasizing that lawfare is critical to advancing Chinese interests in peacetime and wartime.[33] From the Chinese perspective, political warfare, including legal warfare, is seen as a form of combat.

In 2015, China created an international law committee under its foreign affairs ministry to advance its interests through treaties and legal provisions. According to Chinese writings, lawfare or legal warfare (*falu zhan*) is the use of domestic law, the laws of armed conflict, and international law in arguing that one's own side is obeying the law, the other side is violating the law, and making arguments for one's own side in cases where there are also violations of the law. The essence of legal warfare, like psychological and public opinion warfare, is to help one side secure the initiative in wartime and also to gain greater support, both at home and abroad.[34]

32 The three warfare are: (i) Psychological Warfare: the use of propaganda, deception, threats, and coercion to affect the enemy's ability to understand and make decisions; (ii) Media Warfare: the dissemination of information to influence public opinion and gain support from domestic and international audiences for China's military actions; and (iii) Legal Warfare (*falu zhan*): the use of international and domestic law to gain international support and manage possible political repercussions of China's military actions. The Chinese term, "falu zhan," has been translated as lawfare. Lawfare involves shaping the legal context for Chinese actions using both domestic and international law. Kittrie Orde F., 2016, *Lawfare: Law as Weapon of War*, Oxford: Oxford University Press, pp. 161-162.

33 The People's Liberation Army publication, *Analysis of 100 Cases of Legal Warfare* (2004) demonstrates legal warfare in strong terms as a tool to control the enemy with the law or constrain the enemy. In 2005, the PLA published another book titled *Legal Warfare in Modern War*, written by Xun Hengdong, an attorney who was a high-ranking military officer. According to Xun Hengdong, no country involved in armed conflict complies fully with the law of armed conflict, since the pressures of war do not allow such restraint. He concludes that the law of armed conflict should therefore be seen not as an inviolable set of boundaries but rather as a weapon to achieve such objectives as manipulating the perceptions of the international community.

34 The Chinese have taken concrete steps towards implementing legal warfare. The Anti-Secession Law, passed by China on March 14, 2005, serves as a form of military deterrent/coercion (*junshi weishe*), through the use of legal warfare. As the law's

China's aggression on the Doklam plateau and its reliance on an 1890 treaty between itself and Britain to claim sovereignty over the 89 square mile territory perfectly demonstrates its strategy of using 'lawfare' to achieve military objectives. Apart from land reclamation, China also passed a series of legislations aimed at legitimising its so-called 9-dash line which encompasses vast swathes of the South China Sea (SCS).[35] As long as China is on the rise, it will plan to change the norms of international law through its doctrinal legal warfare strategy and the domains that will see it first and most dramatic are in outer space, cyberspace, and other areas of advanced technological innovation.[36] In April 2020, the Chinese Ministry of Civil Affairs' website published the names of 25 islands and reefs and 55 seafloor geographical entities. As a part of the lawfare strategy, the PRC asserts that it has historic rights in the SCS.

China has also used lawfare domestically to delegitimize an independent Taiwan and its proponents. In 2005, the Chinese Communist Party (CCP) passed the Anti-Secession Law, giving it the authority to use non-peaceful means against secessionists, thus changing its Taiwan policy from a mere political statement to a legal basis for invasion of Taiwan. China has updated this law in 2024 to criminalize secessionist acts by issuing interpretive guidelines by the Supreme People's Court and several other state bodies.[37] The guidelines authorize the trials in absentia and even the death penalty for anyone asserting Taiwan's independence. China is using these new guidelines as a scare tactic to dissuade individuals from supporting Taiwan's independence. Any may lead to life imprisonment or even death sentence.[38]

---

preamble sets forth, the goal is to prevent secessionist behaviour and maintain national sovereignty and territorial integrity. It is simply the means and the battlefields that have shifted. Cheng Dean, The Heritage Foundation, Testimony before the US-China Economic and Security review Commission, January 27, 2011. Available at: https://www.uscc.gov/sites/default/files/1.27.11Cheng.pdf.

35 Deo Akhil, Standoff on the Doklam plateau: Another instance of Chinese lawfare, July -7, 2017. Available at: https://www.orfonline.org/expert-speak/standoff-doklam-plateau-another-instance-chinese-lawfare/.

36 White Bret Austin, "Reordering the Law for a China World Order: China's Legal Warfare Strategy in Outer Space and Cyberspace", *Journal of National Security Law and Policy*, Vol. 11, 2021, pp. 435-487.

37 Donald C Clark, *China's Anti-Secession Law: Background, Legal Significance, and Recent Developments*, GW Law Faculty Publications, 2024, available at: https://scholarship.law.gwu.edu/cgi/viewcontent.cgi?article=3001&context=faculty_publications.

38 Jody Chen, Chinese Government Expands Criminalisation of Taiwanese Identity, Human Rights Watch, July 04, 2024, available at: https://www.hrw.org/

China has published several texts emphasizing that lawfare is critical to advancing Chinese interests in peacetime and wartime. China's lawfare tactics have been followed by Russia and other state and non-state actors across the globe. The Office of the Legal Advisor at NATO's Supreme Headquarters Allied Powers Europe (SHAPE), one of NATO's strategic commands, also has personnel working on lawfare. Israel has personnel dedicated to lawfare within its Ministry of Justice.[39]

B. The USA

The US Department of Defence has been of view that "lawfare is what others do" by suggesting that recourse to international law, much like terrorism, is for the weak and generally in defiance of US interests: "Our strength as a nation will be continued to be challenged by those who employ a strategy of the weak, using international fora, judicial processes and terrorism."[40] The US has now developed complex legal strategies capable of serving its interests on the international scene. These strategies are well-served by certain particularities of the American system: a legal culture that encourages soft law; justice based on negotiation and compromise; and the extraterritoriality of American law, with the Department of Justice leading the charge. These characteristics enable the US to act in all categories of lawfare discussed above.[41] Though the US does not explicitly claim to have a lawfare policy and uses this term to make critical remarks about international law, analysis of its legal practice shows how it exploits legal instruments to serve its geopolitical interests. [42]

news/2024/07/04/chinese-government-expands-criminalization-taiwanese-identity.

39 Jill I. Goldenziel, "Law as a Battlefield: The U.S., China, and the Global Escalation of Lawfare", *Cornell Law Review, Vol.* 106, no. 5, 2021, pp. 1085-1071.

40 Dill Janina, "Abuse of Law on the Twenty-First-Century Battlefield," in pp. Gross Michael L. and Tamar Meisels (ed.), 2017, *Soft War: The Ethics of Unarmed Conflict, Cambridge*: Cambridge University Press, pp. 119-133.

41 In October 2001, the US Government executed an exclusive legal contract, with SPACE IMAGING INC to obtain exclusive rights to imaging of its then-expected operational areas in Afghanistan. This action both allowed the US military to obtain unimpeded, exclusive use of the finest imaging technology available, and also prevented other individuals or states from taking satellite pictures in a war zone. The advantages of this type of Lawfare is that it gets neutral private businesses involved and tends to mask the strategic intentions with a veneer of businesslike detachment. Moore John, *The Three Swords Magazine*, Vo. 31, 2017, pp. 39-43.

42 Ferey Amelie, "Towards a War of Norms: From Lawfare to Legal Operations", Security Studies Centre, *Focus Strategique*, April 2022, p. 36.

According to China, the Western states, particularly the US have been proficient in using lawfare as weapons of war.[43] According to the PLA analyses, in the recent conflicts, including the two Gulf Wars and the US actions in Kosovo under the aegis of NATO, the US has successfully exploited lawfare as cover for its military actions. In the field of cyber law, Chinese academics are of the view that the US is engaging in a legal warfare strategy for the development and international adoption of "Tallinn Manual 2.0: On the International Law Applicable to Cyber Operations." The US is attempting to draw rules for cyberwarfare to put a cloak of legality on its 'pre-emptive strike' strategy in cyberwarfare." [44] Apparently, there is no systematic, coordinated US lawfare effort against competitors that are trying to dominate the strategic legal terrain. Key global competitors, such as Russia and China, appear to be advancing faster than the US. For the US, lawfare at the strategic level must include national-level involvement in the evolution and employment of the law in offence as well as defence.[45]

C. Ukraine

Following Russia's 2014 invasion of the Crimean Peninsula, Ukraine did not use its military forces to confront Russian forces. Instead, Ukraine opted for the use of lawfare, focusing on international investment law as a legal means to "wage war" against Russia.[46]Ukraine has launched a legal counter-attack against Russia in various international tribunals. There

43 Dean Cheng, *Winning Without Fighting: Chinese Legal Warfare*, The Heritage Foundation, May 21, 2021.

44 The Tallinn Manual is an ambitious effort by legal experts to study and propose ways that international law would apply to transnational cyber activity and cyberwarfare. Convened by a North Atlantic Treaty Organization cyber institute, the experts published the "Tallinn Manual on the International Law Applicable to Cyber Warfare" in 2013. Although many of the experts, including chief editor Michael Schmitt, have affiliations with the United States or other NATO country armed forces, the Tallinn Manual represents the independent views of the expert authors rather than the views of their employers or home governments. A second publication by the same group, dubbed "Tallinn 2.0," examined how international law treats cyber operations that do not rise to the level of "armed attack" under the law of jus ad bellum. Chinese commentators specifically state that Tallinn Manual 2.0 would serve only to legitimize the US abuses in cyberwarfare. Ku Julian, How China's Views on the Law of Jus ad Bellum Will Shape Its Legal Approach to Cyberwarfare, Aegis Series Paper No. 1707, Hoover Institution, 2017, pp. 28, at pp. 16-17.

45 Justin Malzac, "A Special Operations Approach to Lawfare", *Naval War College Review*, Vol. 77, No. 2, 2024, pp. 83-103.

46 Eric Chang, "Lawfare in Ukraine: Weaponising International Investment Law and the Law of Armed Conflict Against Russia's Invasion", *Strategic Perspectives* 39, Centre

are at least five international law forums that Ukraine has successfully activated against Russia.[47] Ukraine is not a signatory to the Rome Statute that created the International Criminal Court (ICC); however, it has accepted the court's jurisdiction through a declaration under Article 12(3) for war crimes taking place on Ukrainian territory from February 20, 2014, without any temporal limitation. Consequently, the ongoing conflict with Russia is also covered. On March 17, 2023, the ICC, issued an international arrest warrant for President Vladimir Putin and Ms Maria, Commissioner for Children's Rights in the Russian Federation. The arrest warrant alleges that they were responsible for war crimes, namely the 'deportation of population (children) and that of unlawful transfer of population (children) from occupied areas of Ukraine to the Russian Federation.' Such acts qualify as war crimes under 'articles 8 (2) (a) (vii) and 8 (2) (b) (viii) of the ICC's Statute, the Rome Statute of the International Criminal Court.'[48]

After Russia annexed Crimea, Ukraine brought a claim against Russia before the International Court of Justice (ICJ) in 2017. Immediately after Russia invaded Ukraine in February 2022, Ukraine approached the ICJ again this time accusing Russia of breaching the Genocide Convention. Ukraine managed to obtain an order from the ICJ that Russia should immediately halt its military actions against Ukraine till the time the court decides on the issue of the breach of the Genocide Convention. However, Russia has not complied with this order and has continued its military offensive. Ukraine has also moved the Strasbourg-based European Court of Human Rights (ECtHR) against Russia filing multiple petitions since 2014.

In February 2022, Ukraine alleged massive human rights violations committed by Russian troops in Ukraine. The European Court of

---

for Strategic Research, Institute for National Strategic Studies, National Defence University, Washington DC, August 2022, pp. 54.

47 Ranjan Prabhash, Ukraine's lawfare against Russia, Raisina Debate, November 11, 2022, Observer Research Foundation, available at: https://www.orfonline.org/expert-speak/ukraines-lawfare-against-russia/.

48 Based on the Prosecution's applications of 22 February 2023, the Pre-Trial Chamber II considered that there are reasonable grounds to believe that each suspect bears responsibility for the war crime of unlawful deportation of population and that of unlawful transfer of population from occupied areas of Ukraine to the Russian Federation, in prejudice of Ukrainian children. Situation in Ukraine: ICC judges issue arrest warrants against Vladimir Vladimirovich Putin and Maria Alekseyevna Lvova-Belova, Press release March 17, 2023, available at: https://www.icc-cpi.int/news/situation-ukraine-icc-judges-issue-arrest-warrants-against-vladimir-vladimirovich-putin-and.

Human Rights (ECtHR) instructed Russia in March 2022 to refrain from military attacks against civilians and civilian objects. The Hamburg-based International Tribunal of the Law of the Sea is dealing with a case brought by Ukraine against Russia. This case is based on Russia detaining three Ukrainian naval vessels. Ukraine alleges that Russia has breached its obligations under the United Nations Convention on the Law of the Sea. Ukraine has been backing its companies to make use of the Investor-State Dispute Settlement (ISDS) mechanism under the 1998 Ukraine-Russia bilateral investment treaty (BIT) to challenge Russia's seizures of Ukrainian companies in Crimea. Ukraine's strategic lawfare salvos should not be undervalued.[49]

D. Russia

Russia is quite seasoned at exploiting international law to expand its power. The concept of lawfare was in use by the Soviet Union long before the term became known. As early as 1933, the Soviet Union devised to insert the state crime of aggression into a treaty with Afghanistan, Estonia, Latvia, Persia, Poland, Romania, and Turkey to obtain a measure of predictability regarding the conduct of those nations. Through both domestic and international communication, Russia attempted to portray the US as an aggressor in Korea, Vietnam, and Syria. In the Syrian conflict, Russia has simultaneously argued that its military action is authorized under the UN Charter because the government of Syria requested Russia's assistance, while also condemning US and coalition activity as violating international law. The Russian "peacekeepers" were able to accomplish the Kremlin's strategic objectives in West Asia and confound coalition forces without openly engaging them.[50] The Russian Federation deploys legalistic discourse informed by a sound understanding of international law and refers to international norms to criticize the actions of its competitors and justify its foreign policy. Russian lawfare in the Arctic has culminated in the August 2015 Russian appeal to the UN for the recognition of a large expanse of approximately 460,000 square miles of the Arctic Sea, including

49 Kelly Michael, "The Role of International Law in the Russia-Ukraine War", *Case Western Reserve Journal of International Law*, Vol. 55, Issue 1-2, Spring 2023, pp. 61-92.

50 Schiffman Stephen R., Great Power Use of Lawfare: Is the Joint Force Prepared? Joint Force Quarterly, No. 107, National Defence University Press, October 24, 2022, pp. 15-20.

the North Pole, as forming part of Russia's EEZ, which directly conflicts with claims from other countries.[51]

The Russian legal narratives are well-informed, falling within the domain of information weaponry. Russia has developed a legal rationale for its policy of territorial expansion into Georgia, Crimea, and the Donbas, as well as concerning the current operation in Ukraine. As part of this strategy, Russia took action—both before military action and then in parallel with it—to establish legal grounds for the use of force.[52]

E. NATO

Within NATO, the use of lawfare is emerging as a major trend in international relations and is set to increase in the short and medium term. The Office of Legal Affairs has identified three lines of work: (i) Preparation for legal operations: raising the defence community's awareness, integrating legal operations into training exercises, strengthening interdepartmental synergies. (ii) Legal intelligence: monitoring to anticipate threats and identify opportunities, building a network of intermediaries. (iii) Toolbox development: identifying legal attacks, producing counternarratives, disseminating France's legal positions more widely at the NATO Strategic Communication Centre of Excellence (StratCom) level, working on establishing common legal positions with France's allies.[53]

---

51 Bachmann Sascha-Dov and Andres B Munoz Mosquera, "Current Developments: Battleground Arctica and Lawfare Opportunities", *Amicus Curiae*, Issue 108, Winter 2016, pp. 19-22.

52 Russia recognized the independence of the Luhansk People's Republic and the Donetsk People's Republic and used this development to justify its "special military operation". Russia's letter to the United Nations Security Council on February 24, 2022 announced a Russian military intervention in the region under Article 51 of the UN Charter, on the grounds of legitimate self-defence, which constitutes an exception to the prohibition on the use of force contained in Article 2(4). Russia's legal interpretation therefore relies on a principle of selective self-determination. Ferey Amelie, "Towards a War of Norms: From Lawfare to Legal Operations", Security Studies Centre, *Focus Strategique*, April 2022, p. 36.

53 Amelie Ferey, "Towards a War Norms? From Lawfare to Legal Operation", *Focus stratégique*, French Institute of International Relations (IFRI), April 2022, pp. 40. Available at: https://www.ifri.org/sites/default/files/migrated_files/documents/atoms/files/ferey_lawfare_2022_us.pdf, accessed 25 May 2025.

F. Israel

Israel's use of lawfare centres on military matters. The state makes a unique contribution to the emergence of global thinking about the integration of law into state military strategies. The Israeli Defence Forces (IDF) have increasingly viewed international law not as an external constraint but as an element of the Israeli national interest. Interpreting the law of armed conflict and promoting alternative norms, where necessary, has come to be seen as a way of advancing Israel's interests in wartime as in peacetime. The Military Advocate General (MAG) Corps is responsible for exploiting the grey areas of international law to allow the IDF freedom of action.[54] The Israeli military continues to grapple with the challenges posed by Hamas battlefield lawfare.[55] The Supreme Court also plays an important key role, though indirectly, in Israeli lawfare strategy concerning the Palestinians. This role of the Court is particularly important for Israel, which has no constitution. Its judges are simultaneously the guarantors of democracy and entrusted with a leading political role of interpreting and updating the state's basic laws.[56]

Integration of Lawfare and Kinetic Warfare

There have been numerous ways in which law could be used to peacefully substitute for other military methodologies. Lawfare can be used to win or to hamper enemies. Areas in which an integrated legal component may improve tactical or strategic outcomes are:[57]

54 The Military Advocate General (MAG) Corps provides legal assistance to members of the Israeli defence Forces. By making military command responsible for ensuring that international legality is respected, soldiers are supposed to be protected against criminal prosecution because orders are checked for legality before being issued, thus reducing the moral solipsism of soldiers who may be placed in a difficult position if asked to assess for themselves the legality of the orders received. While the armed forces want their decisions to be approved as much as possible, they also have to protect their credibility with the public and with organizations that defend human rights. Ferey Amelie, Towards a War of Norms: From Lawfare to Legal Operations, Security Studies Centre, *Focus Strategique*, April 2022, p. 36.

55 Orde F. Kittrie, 2016, *Lawfare: Law as Weapon of War*, Oxford: Oxford University Press, p. 292.

56 Amelie Ferey, "Towards a War Norms? From Lawfare to Legal Operation", *Focus stratégique*, French Institute of International Relations (IFRI), April 2022, pp. 40. Available at: https://www.ifri.org/sites/default/files/migrated_files/documents/atoms/files/ferey_lawfare_2022_us.pdf, accessed 25 May 2025.

57 Trachtman Joel P., "Integrating Lawfare and Warfare", *Boston College Int'l & Comp. L. Rev.*, 2016, pp. 267-282

- Training of select military lawyers (judge advocates) in offensive lawfare and actively promoting ancient Indian interpretations of international law.
- Negotiating treaties to India's advantage and representing international courts along with the law officers of Law and Treaty Division of the Ministry of External Affairs.
- Ensuring the presence of military lawyers in or alongside the chain of command, and legal review of military practices.
- Identification of disputes in which legal resolution is unlikely to accurately predict the context for kinetic disputes.
- Developing new weapons or methodologies to maximise effectiveness given legal restraints.
- Anticipating challenges to rules of engagement and target policies and identifying methods to maximise effectiveness despite potential challenges.
- Identification of circumstances where opponents are creating legal facts on the ground that may give them an advantage in future conflicts, such as the Chinese claims of territories in India.
- Identifying circumstances in which opponents are seeking to create international legal rules or modify existing international legal rules that will restrict the use of weapons in which your forces have an advantage.
- Making proposals for modifying existing international legal rules that will restrict the use of weapons in which your forces are at a disadvantage.

Lawfare and Internal Security in India

Today, lawfare is being used to manipulate legal standards to confine traditional military means and operations and to limit both state responses to insurgency and the use of force. Several national and international NGOs have used lawfare to engage the government to create a perception that the security forces are waging internal conflicts in violation of international law. In India, between 2012 and 2016, nearly 200 complaints of human rights violations by defence personnel were filed in the states where the AFSPA has been in force.[58] Reacting to a petition filed by an NGO, the Supreme Court of India in its order in July 2017 issued directions for the lodging of an FIR in every case of encounter death against members of the forces involved in counter-insurgency operations in Manipur.[59] In almost every encounter death in areas infested with non-state actors, activists move the human rights commissions and the courts, claiming the encounter to be fake. Pellet guns have been portrayed as inhuman weapons, compelling the government to limit their use in India.

The Supreme Court has recently pointed out that over the period, it has become a norm, that false petitions are filed by individuals and organizations who are either supporters of Left-Wing Extremism or benefit, financially and politically, from Left-Wing Extremist activities and protective orders are obtained from the courts by playing fraud. [60] The Supreme Court held,

> In addition ... the purpose and motive of the present petition was also to derail the ongoing efforts of security forces in neutralizing the Left-Wing Extremism movement and the armed Left-Wing Extremists; to take away the dignity and credibility of security forces and the attempts made by them to neutralize the armed rebellion by Left-Wing Extremists; to lower the moral of the security agencies by portraying them as demons and national villains, i.e. slayers of innocent tribal people; and to foist false cases on them so that in future the said false cases acts as a deterrent and chilling factor for the rest of the members of the armed forces in planning or participating in similar operations. It is submitted that all this was done before the highest court of the country and at the altar of national security. This was a fraud played

58 For more details see: Chadha Vivek, 2016, *Indian Army's Approach to Counter Insurgency Operations: A Perspective on Human Rights*, New Delhi: Institute for Defence Studies and Analyses, pp. 42.

59 *Extra Judicial Execution Victims Families Association v. Union of India*, WP (Criminal) 129 of 2012, judgement dated July 14, 2017.

60 The Supreme Court of India pointed out, "False allegations have been levelled on the police and the paramilitary forces with a *mala fide* intention to change the narrative of the incidents, i.e., to portray the dreaded Left-Wing Extremists (Naxals), who were waging an armed rebellion against the security forces of the country and threatening the sovereignty and integrity of the country, as innocent tribal victims being massacred by the security forces court." This was done with a deceitful design to instigate an instantaneous response of outrage by this Hon'ble Court and mislead it to pass adverse orders against security forces under an erroneous assumption of facts causing an adverse and deterrent effect on the operations and morale of the security forces. The Court imposed a penalty of Rs 500,000 on the petitioner. *Himanshu Kumar v. State of Chhattisgarh*, WP (Criminal) No. 103 of 2009, decided on July 14, 2022.

> on the constitutional remedies and an abuse thereof of the highest order. Scurrilous allegations made against the security personnel of the country have nevertheless brought about a chilling effect of demoralising the esprit de corps and self-esteem of the members of the forces, which has since then acted against national interests. [61]

Conclusion

Law is a contested domain like battlefield and states are evolving lawfare strategies. It involves the use of national and international law to constrain and restrict an opponent's ability to wage war. It does not involve any soldiers, weapons, or battlefields. The reasons behind the rise of lawfare are the increasing reach of human rights organisations, a revolution in information technology, unaccounted sources of finance and the ease with which the legal system can be exploited. Today, domestic law, international law and judicial institutions are being exploited to influence the military policies of the armed forces. Lawfare poses a serious threat to the effective functioning of the security forces. There is a need for a realistic assessment of this threat and the responses to it by the military commanders. The law needs to be incorporated into their thinking and planning. Lawfare can be integrated into military command structures to bring about the desired outcomes and must be exploited to downsize insurgency and subdue non-state actors. The government must identify circumstances in which opponents may create legal facts that could give them an advantage in the future. While inducting new weapon systems for use in internal security situations, it must advance international legal rules that would not restrict the use of weapons. The government must identify insurgents' needs for material and resources, and attempt to block access within applicable law. Law is a good substitute for kinetic warfare; the government needs to exploit it for strategic advantages. It must develop a lawfare doctrine to incorporate defensive measures into its strategic, operational, and tactical policies. Based on current trends to conserve resources and prevent destruction of property and loss of life, the use of lawfare is likely to increase in the future.

61 *Himanshu Kumar v. State of Chhattisgarh*, WP (Criminal) No. 103 of 2009, decided on July 14, 2022, para 11, 12 and 14.

Chapter 5

Corporations in Conflict Zones: Regulations of Corporate Behaviour in Armed Conflict under International Humanitarian Law

-Benarji Chakka, Indirani K.S. and Mohammad Bitar

Introduction

The international community in today's competitive world is always under the threat of violence and conflict, is under constant consideration to resolve the disputes and safeguard the interest of the innocent civilian population from atrocities. Most of the conflicts in the international scenario are related to the economic interest, and corporations play a very important and dominant role in the international relations. These types of conflicts may be called socio–economic conflicts, which are usually under represented, the reasons being the perpetrators are the corporations. There is a general trend in this regard is lack of political will that is also coupled with absence of effective legal mechanisms to make the corporations accountable for the atrocities and crimes that it conducts in course of its operations in various international scenarios. Some of the atrocities conducted by the corporation are – they are involved in armed conflicts where they facilitate rather fuel armed conflicts either by supplying arms as vendors, or supply required economic assistance to groups to sustain the conflict. Further they also involve in perpetrate and support the acts of torture, persecution, extermination, disappearance of people, employ forced labour, and also maintain relations with the conflict groups and even with the State entities.

Here the term corporations or corporation[1] refers to a legal entity with limited liability and is recognised by the State as a juridical or legal person. Corporations are legal entities where a group of individuals join together and make decisions on behalf of the entity[2]. If these corporations are legal entities, now the question that arises is when these corporations can be held liable for the human rights violations and gross violation of people's rights during the conflict situations. The terminology - human rights violation and gross violation of people's rights, in the first instance was understood as violations or crimes committed under the specific branch of international law ie., international humanitarian law. However, is there a mechanism where corporations can be held responsible for their actions in the conflict situation as violations under International Humanitarian Law and prosecute them for their gross violations under international criminal law International Criminal Court- Rome Statute or any other mechanism which permits to do so. The attribution of liability or responsibility upon the Corporation has always been a challenge and it requires addressing several pertinent questions in this regard before attribution.

The Challenges to impose Liability on the Corporations

There had always been a dire need to impose accountability on corporations for the various human rights violations they carried out in the course of their interactions with various States. It is found that as early as 1789; the Judiciary Act[3] allowed the suing of the foreign nationals committing torts

1 The term has been used in Curran, Vivian Grosswald, and David Sloss. "Reviving Human Rights Litigation After Kiobel." American Journal of International Law 107, no. 4, p. 858-863, 2013, 85 and also see Garner, Bryan A. Blacks Law Dictionary 8th Edition, St. Paul, MN: West Group. 2004.

2 De Schutter, Olivier. "The challenge of imposing human rights norms on corporate actors" in Olivier De Schutter (ed), Transnational Corporations and Human Rights, Hart Publications, 2006.

3 Savanovic, Armina Tanja. Transnational Corporations and Human Rights Corporate Criminal Liability in International Criminal Law, unpublished thesis at Centre for Human Rights, Faculty of Law, Lund University, 2017. In this judicial act the word "foreign cubed" has been adopted to describe in which the foreign defendants are sued by foreign plaintiffs for torts committed on foreign soil. The term has been used in Curran, Vivian Grosswald, and David Sloss. "Reviving Human Rights Litigation After Kiobel." American Journal of International Law 107, no. 4, p. 858-863, 2013, p.858.

on foreign soil being capable to be sued in US.[4] The human rights lawyers found this provision of the Act and quickly anchored themselves in Human Rights cases. Therefore, the formation of the Alien Tort Statute mandated the US Federal Courts to have jurisdiction over "civil action by an Alien for a tort only, committed in violation of the Law of Nations or a Treaty of United Nations"[5]. However, there had been a broader applicability of this provision as it adopted the universal jurisdiction that enabled the US courts to open their doors, to hold Corporations liable for human rights violation conducted beyond the borders of US jurisdiction[6].

The provision that was adopted for the civil remedies also found its applicability in criminal law after 1990. The three major bodies who worked upon the accountability are the UN, OECD, and the ILO. While this was the improvement happening under the civil law, the position of many countries who are fragile due to the armed conflicts or war like environment, were exploited economically by the corporations who commit serious international crimes, and they go unpunished or they are under punished.

The accountability for the offence of human rights violation was the responsibility of the State, however after the Second World War, the situation changed where other actors other than the State could be held liable for the violation of the rights of human beings. There was a pressing need to set up separate courts to deal with the crimes conducted by the corporation especially for criminal liability, because during the World War II and thereafter came a consensus in the world that wars caused various human rights violations and also have affected the lives of many people adversely, paving way to the approach of protection of human rights and human rights law regime[7]. It was found during the World War II, some German Industrialists were found to be involved as accomplice in war crimes[8]. The question arose as to whether individuals can be held liable

4 Bellia Jr, Anthony J., and Bradford R. Clark. The Alien Tort statute and the law of Nations. *U. Chi. l. rev.* 78, 2011, p. 445.

5 Lee, Thomas H. "The Safe-Conduct Theory of the Alien Tort Statute." Colum. L. Rev. 106, 2006., p.830.

6 Grear, Anna, and Burns H. Weston. "The betrayal of human rights and the urgency of universal corporate accountability: Reflections on a post-Kiobel lawscape." Human Rights Law Review 15, no. 1, p.21-44, 2015.

7 Bullard, Alice, ed. Human rights in crisis. Ashgate Publishing, Ltd., 2008 p.51.

8 Danner, Allision Marston. "The Nuremberg industrialist prosecutions and aggressive war." Va. J. Int'l L. 46, p.651, 2005.

for war crimes individually when they supported Germany to wage war, to secure economic support through military investments[9], and indulging in acts such as slave labour, property crimes or for aggressive war, or any act that furthered the object of war crime[10]. These questions led to the setting up of the Nuremburg Trials, the Genocide Convention, and ad hoc International Criminal Tribunal for Yugoslavia, Rwanda, and Tokyo[11]. The accountability under the International Humanitarian Law is one such area, where IHL helps in identifying the violators of human rights when the war is in progress, and the perpetrators have violated the norms laid down in the Geneva Convention in regards aiding and abetting war crimes, and crime against humanity.

Corporation as subject of International Law

The Traditional view is that States alone can be the subjects of international law,[12] as it regulates the relationship between the nation- states. Philip C. Jessup[13], was of the view that pawns (individuals, NGO's, corporations etc.,) are objects and subjects are players in the game of chess. But the with the broadening of the international law, players, who were one's considered as objects are now being questioned to be included as subjects. First the United Nations through its Preamble in addressing "People of United Nationals" has included individuals as also subjects of international law. Though the individuals pose the rights, the procedural capacity is through state, and has been highlighted by ICJ in many cases[14]. This position again changed when the Nuremberg trial stated that international law imposes

9 Ibid.

10 United States v. Flick (The Flick Case), in 6 Trials of War Criminals Before The Nuremberg Military Tribunals Under Control Council Law 10, at 1192 (1952).

11 Skinner, Gwynne. "Nuremburg's Legacy Continues: The Nuremburg Trials' Influence on Human Rights Litigation in U.S. Courts Under the Alien Tort Statute", 71 Alb. L. Rev. 321, p. 340–41, 2008.

12 Macdonald, Ronald St John, and Douglas M. Johnston, eds. *The Structure and Process of International Law: Essays in Legal Philosophy, Doctrine and Theory*. Vol. 6. Martinus Nijhoff Publishers, 2024.

13 Jessup, Philip C. "The Subjects of a Modern Law of Nations." Michigan Law Review 45, no. 4, p. 383-408, 1947.

14 "It is elementary principle of international law that a State is entitled to protect its subjects when injured by acts contrary to international law committed by another State, from whom they have been unable to obtain satisfaction through the ordinary channels. By taking up the case of one of its subjects and by resorting to diplomatic action or international judicial proceedings on his behalf, a State is in reality asserting its own rights-its right to ensure, in the person of its subjects respect for the rule of

duties and liabilities upon individuals and states. The International Criminal Tribunal held that crimes against international law are committed by men, not by abstract entities and only by punishing individuals who commit such crimes can the provisions of international law be enforced[15].

The non-state actors' reception and perception has becoming glaring in the international stage, especially in regards the Human Rights and Humanitarian law. In the age of Globalisation and liberalisation trade and investment gained importance and corporations became significant players in the global market and they participated with great vigor. They gained recognition and participated in many international treaties, thus were assigned certain duties directly like in case of environmental law. However to hold them liable for the atrocities they committed in the area of environment and human rights law, many felt only domestic law can be made applicable, some others debated that responsibility need be imposed by framing policies and locate a proper place to make them directly liable and the also prescribe the extent of responsibility. Thus, the transformation is to bring the non-state actors under the direct purview of international law. The notion of corporate criminal liability was first looked into by the Nuremberg Trail, where the question individuals were also raised, after the World War II in the trails of German War Criminals[16]. The United Nations Organization, in the 1949 Reparation Case[17], where it was held that subject is capable of being developed. This left a see-saw effect on including the corporation and individuals as subject among scholars under international law[18]. This paved way to look into the broader aspects of crediting Corporations with duties and rights as they donned various roles under international law in their day to day business. The Corporations financial regulations are governed through the international economic

---

international law", Hudson, Manely O. "The Mavrommatis Palestine Concessions Case 1924, World Court Repots 934", Vol.1, p.297.

15 Article 7 of the Nuremberg Charter, 8th August,1945.

16 The Charter of the International Military Tribunal - Annex to the Agreement for the prosecution and punishment of the major war criminals of the European Axis ("London Agreement"), 8 August 1945, available at https://www.un.org/en/genocideprevention/documents/atrocity-crimes/Doc.2_Charter%20 of%20IMT%201945.pdf visited on 12 September 2021.

17 ICJ 'Advisory Opinion on Reparation for Injuries suffered in Service of United Nations' (11 April 1949) 174.

18 Aust, Anthony. Handbook of International Law 180. 2nd edn, Cambridge, 2010.

law[19] for its trading, States enter into individual treaties with corporations considering them as subjects of international law[20], UDHR and European Union governments[21] have been applying their provisions to corporations also in regards human rights violations. The Article 4 of the Genocide Convention[22] in regards the term 'person' does not distinguish between natural and judicial persons, and therefore in its interpretations it can be stated that corporations are included, the lack of clarification prevailed even in the ad hoc Tribunals. The Rome Statue specifically wanted to avoid the corporations therefore did not leave uncertainty and explicitly referred to persons in Article 25 as only natural persons, thus removing corporations from the ICC jurisdiction. The Nuremberg trail showed that the corporations can be held liable for war crimes against humanity and are bound by the international criminal law,[23] thus leaving room for challenge, as to why the extension cannot be provided at the International Criminal Court the Rome conference. However the extension of the role of corporation especially Corporations who contribute to a substantial creation and also formulating solution to problems that confront humanity are still debatable.

The Secretary General's Representative (SRSG) of United Nations in 2005, under the UN Human Rights Commission was given the task of identifying and clarifying on the obligations of Corporations under International law, to John Ruggie of Harvard University, the then UN Secretary General Kofi Annan. SRSG came to a concluded that the position of corporation has

19 Joyner, Christopher C. International law in the 21st century: rules for global governance. Rowman & Littlefield, 2005.

20 Ratner, Steven R. "Corporations and human rights: a theory of legal responsibility." Yale Law Journal 111, no. 3, p. 443-546, 2001.

21 Clapham, Andrew. "Human rights obligations of non-state actors in conflict situations." International review of the Red Cross 88, no. 863. p. 491-523, 2006. Also see: Clapham, Andrew, Human Rights Obligations of Non-state Actors. Oxford University Press, Oxford, 2006. p. 61.

22 UN General Assembly, *Convention on the Prevention and Punishment of the Crime of Genocide*, 9 December 1948, United Nations, Treaty Series, vol. 78, p. 277. Also see Kelly, Michael J. "The status of corporations in the travaux Preparatories of the Genocide convention: The search for personhood." Case W. Res. J. Int'l L. 43, p.583, 2010.

23 Zakir, Muhammad Hamza, Mehnaz Begum, Ataur Rahman, Muhammad Bilal, Arsalan Tayyab, and Sudais Khan. "The Role Of International Criminal Law In Addressing War Crimes and Crimes Against Humanity." *Kurdish Studies* 12, no. 4, 2024, p. 535-543.

changed tremendously over the period of time under international law[24]. The transcend shift is that, corporations are now considered as duty bearers under international criminal law[25].

Corporations and business entities- closely associated with conflicts

1. Associated to acts of Genocide
2. Under Humanitarian Law
3. Conflict zones
4. Vicarious criminal liability
5. Financial contributions
6. Provide war outsourcing
7. Conduct militarised commerce

Associated to the acts of Genocide

The Vienna Convention did not specifically exclude corporation from the term 'person', at its treaty making conference, Soviet Union was of the view all who committed Genocide need be punished[26], however some Civil Law nations especially Sweden who did not have provisions under criminal laws/code to penalise corporations did not want to include corporation. The term 'person'[27] in general usage means human being (natural person), though by Statute the term may include labour organisations, partnerships, associations, corporations, legal representatives, trustees, bankruptcy or receivers, therefore including both natural and artificial persons. The Genocide Convention Article 3 and 4 specifies that persons conducting

24 The UN Protect, Respect, Remedy Frame Work and Guiding Principles: Driving Change? (CIDSE Briefing March 2013).

25 Andrew Clapham, as he expressed his views in 'The Question of Jurisdiction under International Criminal Law over legal Persons: Lessons from the Rome Conference on an International Criminal Court' in Kamminga, Menno T., and Saman Zia-Zarifi, eds. Liability of multinational corporations under international law. Vol. 7. Brill, 2021. in Emeka Duruigbo, 'Duruigbo, Emeka. "Corporate accountability and liability for international human rights abuses: recent changes and recurring challenges." Nw. UJ Int'l Hum. Rts. 6, 222, 2007.

26 Abtahi, Hirad, and Philippa Webb. The Genocide Convention: The Travaux Préparatoires (2 vols). Vol. 2. Brill, 2009.

27 Gifis, Steven H. Law dictionary. Simon and Schuster, 2010.

the act of genocide shall be punished[28]. In the case of genocide, the State cannot be held liable[29], therefore it becomes important for the prosecutors to find the initiator or instigator who is equally liable—might fund or back the atrocities of the state. Corporation can be held liable because of its position includes Command Responsibility, Respondent Superior and a Notion of Agency

The US Alien Tort Statute, the question of respondent responsibility and knowledge was recognised, where a foreign national could be sued in the Federal Court for violation of international law.[30] The same came to be applied upon the multinational corporations the Canadian energy concern Arakis Energy in 1998, who were defendants in the Presbyterian Church of Sudan case (genocide)[31], as they acquired the Sudanese Oil Company. Ratner adopts the view that, the corporate liability is one that originates from State responsibility, when both State and Companies are perpetrators and abusers of human rights[32]. When corporate is the Principal and the State the agent, then corporate liability is superior to the state, then it can be understood that corporation is the subject of the international law. The concept of respondent superior may be used on the multinational corporations because of their economic enterprise, and they do not involve directly and liability is vested upon the corporation. In Zyklon B Case[33] the defendant argued that the prosecution had to prove that the gas was for extermination and the court felt it was enough for the prosecution to prove that the allied nation was gassed and the defendants were aware that Zyklon

28 Convention on the Prevention and Punishment of the Crime of Genocide (entered into force 12 January 1951) 78 U.N.T.S 277 (Genocide Convention), Article III of the states the following acts shall be punishable: a) Genocide, b) Conspiracy to commit Genocide, c) Direct and public incitement to commit genocide, d) Attempt to commit genocide, e) complicity in genocide. Article IV states Persons committing genocide or any other acts enumerated in Article III shall be punished, whether they are constitutionally responsible rulers, public officials or private individuals.

29 Bosnia and Herzegovina v Serbia and Montenegro, [2007] ICJ 2.

30 Ewell, Christopher, Oona A. Hathaway, and Ellen Nohle. "Has the Alien Tort Statute Made a Difference?: A Historical, Empirical, and Normative Assessment." *Cornell L. Rev.* 107, 2021, p. 1205.

31 Business & Human Rights Resource Centre, Talisman lawsuit (re Sudan). 2014. available at https://www.businesshumanrights.org/en/latest-news/talisman-lawsuit-re-sudan-2/ visited on 9 August 2021

32 Ratner, Steven R. "Corporations and human rights: a theory of legal responsibility." Yale Law Journal 111, no. 3, p. 443-546, 2001.

33 In re Tesch (The Zyklon B Case) (1946) 13 Ann. Dig. 250, British Military Ct.

B was used to gas and kill humans. In *United States v Krupp*[34], forced labour was used in Nazi industrial machines, knowledge was what was established in these cases, and the International Criminal Tribunals held the director was liable. In Tadic case[35], instances of hiding weapons in coffee companies that were used for act of genocide for the use by companies' police to disperse the striking workmen, ICTY described as acts that maybe direct or substantial and there indeed was a prior interest to commit the crime.

Corporations operating in conflict zones, whether through direct involvement or by supporting state or non-state actors, can become complicit in serious violations of international law, including Crimes Against Humanity, War Crimes, and Genocide.[36] These violations, which constitute grave breaches of international law, are not limited to physical perpetrators alone but can also extend to entities that provide financial, logistical, or technological support to those engaged in such actions.[37] By supplying resources such as arms, technology, or fuel, corporations may contribute to the commission of these atrocities, making them liable under international law. Their involvement, even if indirect, can be viewed as aiding and abetting the acts, thereby invoking principles of vicarious criminal liability and corporate complicity in international crimes.

Legal frameworks, including the Geneva Conventions and the Genocide Convention, highlight those entities involved in such crimes must be held accountable. Historical precedents, such as the Zyklon B Case[38] and United States v Krupp[39], demonstrate that corporate actors can be prosecuted for their role in enabling grave breaches of international law. Additionally,

34 Heller, Kevin Jon. The Nuremberg military tribunals and the origins of international criminal law. Oxford University Press, 2011.

35 Heller, Kevin Jon. The Nuremberg military tribunals and the origins of international criminal law. Oxford University Press, 2011, also see Howen, Nicholas, and M. Shinn. "Responsibility and complicity from the perspective of international human rights law." In The 2005 Business & Human Rights Seminar Report. Exploring Responsibility and Complicity (Business & Human Rights Seminar Ltd, London), pp. 12-15. 2005.

36 Olson, Danielle. "Corporate complicity in human rights violations under international criminal law." *DePaul Int'l Hum. Rts. J.* 1, 2015.

37 Kaleck, Wolfgang, and Miriam Saage-Maaß. "Corporate accountability for human rights violations amounting to international crimes: The status quo and its challenges." *Journal of International Criminal Justice* 8, no. 3 , 2010, p. 699-724.

38 The Zyklon b, case trial of Bruno Tesch and two others British military court, Hamburg, 1st-8th March, 1946.

39 United States Military Tribunal at Nuremberg - United States v. Alfried Krupp et al., Judgment of 31 July 1948

modern international legal principles, such as the UN Guiding Principles on Business and Human Rights (UNGPs), emphasise the responsibility of corporations to ensure that their operations do not contribute to violations of humanitarian law. The potential for corporate liability in conflict zones underscores the need for rigorous due diligence and adherence to international legal standards to prevent corporate complicity in atrocities that breach jus cogens norms, which safeguard fundamental human rights.

Corporations in Conflict zones

The notion of corporate criminal liability is still evolving, reason being after the Second World War the International Criminal Tribunal were set up for assigning liability for gross violation of Human Rights.[40] The charter authorised the Tribunal to criminalise legal entities under Article 9[41], however this was hardly used and the International Military Tribunal held that 'Crimes against international law are committed by men, not by abstract entities'[42], giving edge to punish individuals rather than the corporations

In *United States v Krupp*[43], in this case the Krupp firm acquired materials, machines and properties, in collaboration with the government, and they took part in activities like plundering, slave trade and used prisoners as laborers, they also misappropriated the factories, in Netherland and France, but the Tribunal held the individuals liable did not hold the firm liable as criminal organisation. In another case United States v Krauch[44], in this again the officials of the firm Farben were held liable, for the acts of plunder, and taking away the factories instead of the firm. In United States

40 De Tommaso, Alessandra. *Corporate liability and international criminal law*. Taylor & Francis, 2023.

41 'At the trial of any individual member of any group or organization the Tribunal may declare that the group or organization, of which the individual was a member, was a criminal organization'. Charter of the International Military Tribunal - Annex to the Agreement for the prosecution and punishment of the major war criminals of the European Axis (8 August 1945) 1544 82 UNTS 279 (London Agreement) art 9,

42 Presbyterian Church of Sudan v Talisman Energy Inc (2009) 582 F.3d 244 2d Cri.

43 9 Trials of War Criminals before the Nuremberg Military Tribunals under Control Council Law No.10, at 1372(1952), also see http://www.mazal.org/archive/nmt/09/NMTO9-COO1.htm.

44 United States v. Krauch, 8 Trials of War Criminals before the Nuremberg Military Tribunals under Control Council Law No.10, at 1081(1953), at available at <http://www.mazal.org/archieve/nmt/08/NMTO8-COO1.htm>.

v Bruno[45], Tesch the owner of the company was held liable in his personal capacity for supplying Zyklon B gas, to concentration camps. Here also though the agreement was with the corporation the individual was held liable in his individual capacity.

In the cases before the two ad hoc Tribunals for Former Yugoslavia and Rwanda, the Security Council upheld individual criminal liability; even corporate liability was proved the prosecution avoided the liability. In *Nahimana Case*[46], though the act of genocide was committed in the course of the corporate activity of the Radio station (RLM Radio Station), the International Tribunal for Rwanda held the directors liable in their personal capacity as a de jure head of the radio station, for the acts of Genocide. Corporations have been found in various other areas of abuses, in their ancillary roles, which may include as financial contributions[47], provide war outsourcing[48] and conduct militarised commerce.[49]

The corporation's control of mining operations during war and during internal conflicts through the use of military and security forces, also the presence of police, mercenaries and causing gross violence to take control of a territory[50], are acknowledged by the World Bank Extractive Industries Group. Therefore the acts committed by the Corporations are both direct and indirect, in direct acts they are forced labour, deploy child soldiers, enslavement, and other war crimes. And in indirect acts it is by way of aiding, abetting, complicit with the governments or paramilitary groups[51].

45 The Zyclon B case, 1 Law repots of Trials of War Criminals 93, 1947.

46 *Prosecutor v. Nahimana*, Case No. ICTR-99-52-T, judgment and sentence 99-101 (Dec.3, 2003).

47 Int'l Peace Acad. & FAFO, "Business and International Crimes: Assessing the Liability of Business Entities for Grave Violations of International Law" (FAFO and International Peace Institute 2004).

48 UN Security Council, 1999. Report of the Secretary-General to the Security Council on the Protection of Civilians in armed Conflict. UN Doc. S/2001/331. available at < https://undocs.org/ Home/Mobile?FinalSymbol= S%2F2001%2F331& Language=E&DeviceType= Desktop& LangRequested= False>, also see UNGA Report of the Secretary General to the Security Council on the Protection of Civilians in Armed Conflict (26 November 2002) UN Doc S/2002/1300

49 Forcese, Craig. "Deterring militarised commerce: The prospect of liability for privatised human rights abuses." Ottawa L. Rev. 31. 171, 1999.

50 Jose Luis Gomez del Prado, President of the Working Group on *the Use of Mercenaries as Means of Violating Human rights and Impeding the Rights of Peoples to Self-Determination, Oral Statement at the Human Rights Council,* (10 March 2008).

51 *Prosecutor v Tadic* (Judgment) IT-94-1-T (7 May 1997).

Under the International law, the international conventions and treaties (bilateral or multilateral) are legally binding the state parties or the parties to the convention or treaty, but in case of International Humanitarian Law, the Geneva Convention is not just to the state parties but non-state actors also.[52] The Humanitarian Law is made applicable under two circumstances the international armed conflict (to parties in conflict) and the non-international armed conflict (even when they are no more involved like the wounded, sick the shipwrecked, medical persons, prisoners of war, civilians). Every state party therefore takes upon itself a duty to punish persons who violate the humanitarian law under the domestic courts, and their state have jurisdiction shall hand over the violators to state that has jurisdiction. War crimes need be prosecuted and punished at all times by all courts, as it has universal jurisdiction. The Security Council of the UN has set up the International Military Tribunal Nuremberg, and International Criminal Tribunal for Former Yugoslavia[53](where mass killing, organised and systematic violations, rape of women, detentions, and continued practice of ethnic cleansing, that threatened the international peace and security) and Rwanda, and it has explicitly given three counts of crimes-crimes against peace, crimes against humanity and war crimes.

Liabilities of the Corporations

Wars and its events have been asymmetrical; there had been an ever-increasing influence of corporations on the events of war, to this the collateral application of Humanitarian Law led to the development of modern approach of corporate liability[54]. The influence of corporations especially in the war conflict zones have contributed to the gross violations of human rights directly and indirectly and also violations of International Humanitarian Law. The nature of Criminal law is that it always imposes punishments for crimes conducted by individuals and not for collective actions as such by corporations' collective punishments[55]. But the positive

52 Dunoff, Jeffrey, Monica Hakimi, Steven R. Ratner, and David Wippman. International Law: Norms, Actors, Process. Aspen Publishing, 2023.

53 ICTY at a Glance-General Information', ICTY website, available at <http://www.icty.org/en/content/welcome-new-icty-website>, visited on 7 September 2021.

54 Batesmith, Alex. The Business and Human Rights Movement, Corporate Criminal Responsibility for War Crimes and other Violations of International Humanitarian law: The Impact of the Business and Human Rights Movement. Cambridge University Press, 2014, p.285.

55 Hasnas, John. "The centenary of a mistake: One hundred years of corporate criminal liability." Am. Crim. L. Rev. 46, 2009 in Batesmith, Alex. The Business and Human

aspect of it was that, it found its first mention –Corporate Liability, at the International Military Tribunal, where there was enough evidence to prove that corporations played a major role in the Nazi war[56]. There was a tremendous involvement of the corporation big or small, helping the Nazi's in all activities like, transferring prisoners, enslaving them, produced deadly weapons, supplying poisonous gas, that were later used on the civilians at the concentration camps. The evidences were strong during the trial, prosecutors Allies, Robert Jackson[57] wanted to indicate them, but the judge did not allow the indictment of the corporations.

This had been the foundation laid, where discussions on corporate criminal liability started rolling. The Control Council Law Number 10- cases such as I. G. Farben, Roechling, Krupp and Flick, and other who supplied poisonous gas, to kill civilians and prisoners, were decided keeping in mind the views laid down by Robert Jackson. In all these cases though Corporations were not held liable, it became a common knowledge that it is not the legal aspect that could not hold the corporation liable rather the lacuna was in the political will. Thus evidence showed that, it was corporations that are equally liable along with the employees (individuals) in violation of International Humanitarian Law. The International Tribunal for Former Yugoslavia also tried to hold the corporations liable but again did not materialise. The Then Secretary General of the United Nations Boutros Gali made a reference to hold certain organisations liable, but they ultimately focused on the individual liability.

Rights Movement, Corporate Criminal Responsibility for War Crimes and other Violations of International Humanitarian law: The Impact of the Business and Human Rights Movement. Cambridge University Press, 2014, p. 285.

56 Balouziyeh, John MB, and Stephen J. Rapp. "The Role of Civil Society in Promoting Corporate Accountability for International Crimes." *Journal of International Criminal Justice*, 2024.

57 This was answer given by the United States Prosecutor to the motion on behalf of the Defendant Gustav Krupp von Bohlen, International Tribunal Document, 12th November 1945. Document available at http://avalon.law.yale.edu/imt/v1-11.asp, in Batesmith, Alex. "Corporate criminal responsibility for war crimes and other violations of international humanitarian law: The impact of the business and human rights movement." Contemporary Challenges to the Laws of War: Essays in Honour of Professor Peter Rowe. Cambridge: CUP (2014): 285-312.

Application of Corporate Liability on Israel's Actions in Gaza

Since October 2023, Israel has conducted extensive air and ground offensives against Gaza[58] in response to Hamas-led attacks on Israeli territory. These operations have resulted in the deaths of thousands of Palestinians, predominantly unarmed civilians, and have forced most of Gaza's population to flee their homes.[59] The scale and nature of these actions have raised serious concerns, with a preliminary verdict from the International Court of Justice (ICJ),[60] along with various U.S. courts[61] and the UN experts,[62] suggesting they may constitute genocide. Simultaneously, there has been a surge in Israeli violence in the occupied West Bank,[63] as well as confrontations with militant groups in Lebanon and air strikes in Syria.[64]

The ICJ has delivered an interim ruling on 26 January 2024, responding to South Africa's case against Israel[65], which alleged breaches of the Genocide Convention due to Israel's actions in Gaza starting from 7 October 2023.

---

58 Qiblaw, Tamara et al., "Not seen since Vietnam': Israel dropped hundreds of 2,000-pound bombs on Gaza, analysis shows" 2023 https://edition.cnn.com/gaza-israel-big-bombs/index.html

59 Leatherby, Lauren, "Gaza Civilians, Under Israeli Barrage, Are Being Killed at Historic Pace" 2023, available at https://www.nytimes.com/2023/11/25/world/middleeast/israel-gaza-death-toll.html

60 Casciani, Dominic,"What did ICJ ruling mean in South Africa's genocide case against Israel?" 2024 available at https://www.bbc.com/news/articles/c3g9g63jl17o

61 Center for Constitutional Rights, "U.S. Court Concludes Israel's Assault on Gaza Is Plausible Case of Genocide", 2024 https://ccrjustice.org/home/press-center/press-releases/us-court-concludes-israel-s-assault-gaza-plausible-case-genocide.

62 OHCHR, "Gaza: UN experts call on international community to prevent genocide against the Palestinian people", 2023 available at https://www.ohchr.org/en/press-releases/2023/11/gaza-un-experts-call-international-community-prevent-genocide-against

63 Amnesty, "Israel/OPT: Palestinians face drastic escalation in unlawful killings, displacement as Israel launches West Bank military operation",2024 available at https://www.amnesty.org/en/latest/news/2024/08/israel-opt-palestinians-face-drastic-escalation-in-unlawful-killings-displacement-as-israel-launches-west-bank-military-operation/

64 Dhaybi, Jana and Hussein, Mohammed, "Mapping Israel-Lebanon cross-border", 2024 available at https://www.aljazeera.com/news/longform/2024/4/15/mapping-israel-lebanon-cross-border-attacks

65 Application of the Convention on the Prevention and Punishment of the Crime of Genocide in the Gaza Strip (South Africa v. Israel) available at https://www.icj-cij.org/case/192

The ICJ acknowledged that "at least some of the rights" asserted by South Africa, particularly those concerning the protection of Palestinians in Gaza from genocide, are credible. Furthermore, the Court recognised a "real and imminent risk" of irreversible harm to these protected rights under the Convention. This ruling has significant implications for corporations operating in or engaging with Israel, as it highlights the critical importance of adhering to international humanitarian law and the potential for corporate liability in such conflict zones.[66]

Corporate Complicity and Liability Under International Humanitarian Law

The ICJ's ruling underscores the importance of the jus cogens norm prohibiting genocide, which is a fundamental principle of international law that no entity, including corporations, can violate.[67] This principle has particular relevance for businesses operating in conflict zones, where their actions, directly or indirectly, may contribute to violations of international humanitarian law. The notion of corporate complicity in such crimes, as explored earlier, becomes crucial when considering the activities of companies in Israel, especially those involved in providing military support or other resources to the Israeli government.[68]

The ICJ's findings reinforce the principle that corporations and their executives could be held liable for acts of genocide.[69] Article VI of the Genocide Convention clearly states that individuals, including business leaders as natural persons, and potentially corporations as legal entities, may be accountable for genocidal acts.[70] While the International Criminal Court (ICC) does not have jurisdiction over legal entities, it does have the authority to prosecute individuals, including corporate personnel from

66 Ibid

67 Kelly, Michael J. "Prosecuting corporations for genocide under international law." Harv. L. & Pol'y Rev. 6, 2012, p.339.

68 Pietropaoli, Irene, Obligations of Third States and Corporations to Prevent and Punish Genocide in Gaza, "Obligations of Third States and Corporations to Prevent and Punish Genocide in Gaza", 2024 available at https://www.somo.nl/wp-content/uploads/2024/06/Obligations-of-Third-States-and-Corporations-to-Prevent-and-Punish-Genocide-in-Gaza-3.pdf

69 Dąbrowski, Łukasz Dawid. "Transnational corporations' liability for genocide under international law." In The Concept of Genocide in International Criminal Law, pp. 117-138. Routledge, 2020.

70 Kelly, Michael J. "Prosecuting corporations for genocide under international law." Harv. L. & Pol'y Rev. 6, 2012, p.339.

States Parties to the Rome Statute, who contribute to the commission of such crimes.[71] This creates a substantial risk for companies and their executives who might be implicated in aiding or abetting genocidal actions through their business activities.

Implications for Corporations Engaged with Israel

The decision by the ICJ places additional scrutiny on companies that invest in or collaborate with Israeli governmental bodies or state-controlled entities.[72] The involvement of businesses in providing arms, munitions, vehicles, technology, fuel, or other military resources to Israel's armed forces is particularly concerning. These activities are essential for the operations of Israel's military, which the ICJ has indicated may pose a "real and imminent risk" of contributing to genocidal acts in Gaza.[73] Thus, firms that continue to supply these critical resources could be seen as complicit in the violations of international humanitarian law, including genocide.

Historical precedents, such as the cases discussed in this article, illustrate how companies have been implicated in war crimes and crimes against humanity through their financial contributions, militarised commerce, and other forms of support to states engaged in such actions. The Krupp and Zyklon B cases from the Nuremberg Trials, as well as more recent cases before the International Criminal Tribunals for the Former Yugoslavia (ICTY) and Rwanda (ICTR), demonstrate that corporations can be held responsible, particularly when their actions significantly impact the commission of international crimes, which provided under the IHL treaty mechanisms.

Risk of Corporate Liability and the Need for Responsible Disengagement

Given the ICJ's ruling, companies operating in or with Israel must reassess their roles and responsibilities under international law. The UN Guiding Principles on Business and Human Rights (UNGPs) and OECD Guidelines urge companies to respect IHL, particularly in conflict zones.[74] This means conducting thorough human rights due diligence to assess

71 Scheffer, David. "Corporate liability under the Rome Statute." Harvard International Law Journal 57, no. 2016, p. 35-38.

72 ICJ, Summary of the Advisory Opinion of 19 July 2024 available at <https://www.icj-cij.org/node/204176>

73 Ibid para 4.

74 OHCHR, guiding principles on business and human rights, 2011, p. 3.

and mitigate the risks of contributing to serious violations, including genocide. If a company finds that its operations are contributing to the risk of genocide or other severe human rights abuses, it has an obligation under international law to reconsider its involvement.[75] This may involve disengagement from partnerships or contracts that directly or indirectly support the Israeli government's military operations in Gaza. The earlier discussion on corporate liability makes it clear that mere compliance with domestic laws is insufficient; companies must adhere to international standards, even if this requires taking difficult steps, such as terminating profitable business relationships.

In conclusion, the ICJ's interim ruling against Israel serves as a crucial reminder of the evolving nature of corporate liability in international law, particularly concerning genocide and other serious human rights violations. Corporations must recognise the potential for legal accountability and take proactive steps to ensure that their operations do not contribute to such atrocities. The responsibility to prevent complicity in genocide extends beyond legal obligations to encompass ethical considerations, demanding that companies act with the highest regard for human rights and international humanitarian law.

The direct or indirect involvement of corporations in supporting Israel during its operations in Gaza, whether through providing financial aid, supplying weapons, or maintaining operations in the conflict environment, constitutes a serious violation of international law. These corporations, by contributing resources essential to military actions, become complicit in the resulting humanitarian violations, including potential war crimes or genocide, as indicated by the ICJ's findings. The grave breaches of international humanitarian law committed with corporate assistance demand accountability. Accordingly, international courts must exercise their jurisdiction to attribute responsibility to these corporate entities, ensuring that they are held accountable under established legal frameworks for their role in facilitating such acts.

Conclusion

The corporations play a major role in making the wars violent, as they played the role of perpetrators either by helping the state in war by supplying money or funded them supplied materials like gas, arms ammunitions, or personnel / military, or technology and thus took active

75 Kinley, David, and Junko Tadaki. "From talk to walk: The emergence of human rights responsibilities for corporations at international law." Va. J. Int'l L. 44, 2003, p. 931.

part in the gross human rights violations. The International Committee of the Red Cross (ICRC) has been assisting the states to understand the intensity of the weapons used and the pain and sufferings it causes in the war front. The Geneva Convention has given right to the state parties to prosecute those involved in war, especially conducting war crimes, crimes against humanity, and genocide as an international customary law. With the adoption of the Rome Statue and formulating and working of the permanent International Criminal court (ICC) is another major step towards locking on the criminal liability of the corporations, but lack out political will again excluded the corporations from the ambit of the ICC. With the passage of time now again the non-governmental organisations are on the campaign of inclusion of corporation into the ambit of ICC, thus making it the Global Ombudsman as envisaged by John Ruggie. As this move is still taking time the responsibility rests on the state parties to adopt corporate criminal liability within its domestic legal system/ jurisdiction. Some of the states that have become successful in adopting are Australia, UK and Canada. Though political will becomes the major concern of the domestic law of the states, curbing the atrocities of the corporations and prosecuting the corporations for their criminal liability is the need of the hour for a peaceful society.

References

Abtahi, Hirad, and Philippa Webb. The Genocide Convention: The Travaux Prépáratoires (2 vols). Vol. 2. Brill, 2009.

Amnesty, "Israel/OPT: Palestinians face drastic escalation in unlawful killings, displacement as Israel launches West Bank military operation",2024 available at https://www.amnesty.org/en/latest/news/2024/08/israel-opt-palestinians-face-drastic-escalation-in-unlawful-killings-displacement-as-israel-launches-west-bank-military-operation/

Application of the Convention on the Prevention and Punishment of the Crime of Genocide in the Gaza Strip (South Africa v. Israel) available at https://www.icj-cij.org/case/192

Aust, Anthony. *Handbook of International Law*. 2nd edn, Cambridge, 2010.

Balouziyeh, John MB, and Stephen J. Rapp. "The Role of Civil Society in Promoting Corporate Accountability for International Crimes." Journal of International Criminal Justice, 2024.

Batesmith, Alex. "Corporate criminal responsibility for war crimes and other violations of international humanitarian law: The impact of the business and human rights movement." Contemporary Challenges to the Laws of War: Essays in Honour of Professor Peter Rowe. Cambridge: CUP (2014): 285-312.

Batesmith, Alex. The Business and Human Rights Movement, Corporate Criminal Responsibility for War Crimes and other Violations of International Humanitarian law: The Impact of the Business and Human Rights Movement. Cambridge University Press, 2014.

Bosnia and Herzegovina v Serbia and Montenegro, [2007] ICJ 2.

Bullard, Alice, ed. Human rights in crisis. Ashgate Publishing, Ltd., 2008.

Business & Human Rights Resource Centre, Talisman lawsuit (re Sudan). 2014. available at https://www.businesshumanrights.org/en/latest-news/talisman-lawsuit-re-sudan-2/ visited on 9 August 2021

Casciani, Dominic,"What did ICJ ruling mean in South Africa's genocide case against Israel?" 2024 available at https://www.bbc.com/news/articles/c3g9g63jl17o

Center for Constitutional Rights, "U.S. Court Concludes Israel's Assault on Gaza Is Plausible Case of Genocide", 2024 https://ccrjustice.org/home/press-center/press-releases/us-court-concludes-israel-s-assault-gaza-plausible-case-genocide.

Charter of the International Military Tribunal - Annex to the Agreement for the prosecution and punishment of the major war criminals of the European Axis (8 August 1945) 1544 82 UNTS 279 (London Agreement) art 9.

Clapham, Andrew, *Human Rights Obligations of Non-state Actors*. Oxford University Press, Oxford, 2006.

Clapham, Andrew. "Human rights obligations of non-state actors in conflict situations." International review of the Red Cross 88, no. 863 (2006): 491-523.

Convention on the Prevention and Punishment of the Crime of Genocide (entered into force 12 January 1951) 78 U.N.T.S 277 (Genocide Convention).

Curran, Vivian Grosswald, and David Sloss. "Reviving Human Rights Litigation After Kiobel." American Journal of International Law 107, no. 4, p. 858-863, 2013.

Dąbrowski, Łukasz Dawid. "Transnational corporations' liability for genocide under international law." In The Concept of Genocide in International Criminal Law, pp. 117-138. Routledge, 2020.

Danner, Allision Marston. "The Nuremberg industrialist prosecutions and aggressive war." Va. J. Int'l L. 46, p.651, 2005.

De Schutter, Olivier. "The challenge of imposing human rights norms on corporate actors" in Olivier De Schutter (ed), Transnational Corporations and Human Rights, Hart Publications, 2006.

De Tommaso, Alessandra. Corporate liability and international criminal law. Taylor & Francis, 2023.

Dhaybi, Jana and Hussein, Mohammed, "Mapping Israel-Lebanon cross-border", 2024 available at https://www.aljazeera.com/news/longform/2024/4/15/mapping-israel-lebanon-cross-border-attacks

Dunoff, Jeffrey, Monica Hakimi, Steven R. Ratner, and David Wippman. International Law: Norms, Actors, Process. Aspen Publishing, 2023.

Forcese, Craig. "Deterring militarised commerce: The prospect of liability for privatised human rights abuses." Ottawa L. Rev. 31. 171, 1999.

Garner, Bryan A. Blacks Law Dictionary 8th Edition, *St. Paul, MN: West Group*. 2004.

Gifis, Steven H. Law dictionary. Simon and Schuster, 2010.

Grear, Anna, and Burns H. Weston. "The betrayal of human rights and the urgency of universal corporate accountability: Reflections on a post-Kiobel lawscape." Human Rights Law Review 15, no. 1, p.21-44, 2015.

Hasnas, John. "The centenary of a mistake: One hundred years of corporate criminal liability." Am. Crim. L. Rev. 46, 2009 in Batesmith, Alex. The Business and Human Rights Movement, Corporate Criminal Responsibility for War Crimes and other Violations of International Humanitarian law: The Impact of the Business and Human Rights Movement. Cambridge University Press, 2014.

Heller, Kevin Jon. The Nuremberg military tribunals and the origins of international criminal law. Oxford University Press, 2011.

Howen, Nicholas, and M. Shinn. "Responsibility and complicity from the perspective of international human rights law." In The 2005 Business & Human Rights Seminar Report. Exploring Responsibility and

Complicity (Business & Human Rights Seminar Ltd, London), pp. 12-15. 2005.

ICJ 'Advisory Opinion on Reparation for Injuries suffered in Service of United Nations' (11 April 1949) 174, available at https://www.icj-cij.org/node/100032

ICJ, Summary of the Advisory Opinion of 19 July 2024 available at <https://www.icj-cij.org/node/204176>

ICTY at a Glance-General Information', available at <http://www.icty.org/en/content/welcome-new-icty-website>.

In re Tesch (The Zyklon B Case) (1946) 13 Ann. Dig. 250, British Military Ct.

Int'l Peace Acad. & FAFO, "Business and International Crimes: Assessing the Liability of Business Entities for Grave Violations of International Law" (FAFO and International Peace Institute 2004).

Jessup, Philip C. "The Subjects of a Modern Law of Nations." Michigan Law Review 45, no. 4, p. 383-408, 1947.

Jose Luis Gomez del Prado, President of the Working Group on *the Use of Mercenaries as Means of Violating Human rights and Impeding the Rights of Peoples to Self-Determination, Oral Statement at the Human Rights Council,* (10 March 2008).

Joyner, Christopher C. International law in the 21st century: rules for global governance. Rowman & Littlefield, 2005.

Kaleck, Wolfgang, and Miriam Saage-Maaß. "Corporate accountability for human rights violations amounting to international crimes: The status quo and its challenges." Journal of International Criminal Justice 8, no. 3, 2010, p. 699-724.

Kamminga, Menno T., and Saman Zia-Zarifi, eds. *Liability of multinational corporations under international law.* Vol. 7. Brill, 2021. in Emeka Duruigbo, 'Duruigbo, Emeka. "Corporate accountability and liability for international human rights abuses: recent changes and recurring challenges." Nw. UJ Int'l Hum. Rts. 6, 222, 2007.

Kelly, Michael J. "Prosecuting corporations for genocide under international law." Harv. L. & Pol'y Rev. 6, 2012, p.339.

Kelly, Michael J. "Prosecuting corporations for genocide under international law." Harv. L. & Pol'y Rev. 6, 2012, p.339.

Kelly, Michael J. "The status of corporations in the travaux preparatoires of the Genocide convention: The search for personhood." Case W. Res. J. Int'l L. 43, p.583, 2010.

Kinley, David, and Junko Tadaki. "From talk to walk: The emergence of human rights responsibilities for corporations at international law." Va. J. Int'l L. 44, 2003, p. 931.

Leatherby, Lauren, "Gaza Civilians, Under Israeli Barrage, Are Being Killed at Historic Pace" 2023, available at https://www.nytimes.com/2023/11/25/world/middleeast/israel-gaza-death-toll.html

Lee, Thomas H. "The Safe-Conduct Theory of the Alien Tort Statute." Colum. L. Rev. 106, 2006.

OHCHR, "Gaza: UN experts call on international community to prevent genocide against the Palestinian people", 2023 available at https://www.ohchr.org/en/press-releases/2023/11/gaza-un-experts-call-international-community-prevent-genocide-against

OHCHR, guiding principles on business and human rights, 2011, p. 3

Olson, Danielle. "Corporate complicity in human rights violations under international criminal law." DePaul Int'l Hum. Rts. J. 1, 2015.

Pietropaoli, Irene, Obligations of Third States and Corporations to Prevent and Punish Genocide in Gaza, "Obligations of Third States and Corporations to Prevent and Punish Genocide in Gaza", 2024 available at https://www.somo.nl/wp-content/uploads/2024/06/Obligations-of-Third-States-and-Corporations-to-Prevent-and-Punish-Genocide-in-Gaza-3.pdf

Presbyterian Church of Sudan v Talisman Energy Inc (2009) 582 F.3d 244 2d Cri.

Prosecutor v Tadic (Judgment) IT-94-1-T (7 May 1997).

Prosecutor v. Nahimana, Case No.ICTR-99-52-T, judgment and sentence 99-101 (Dec.3, 2003).

Qiblaw, Tamara et al., "Not seen since Vietnam': Israel dropped hundreds of 2,000-pound bombs on Gaza, analysis shows" 2023 https://edition.cnn.com/gaza-israel-big-bombs/index.html.

Ratner, Steven R. "Corporations and human rights: a theory of legal responsibility." Yale Law Journal 111, no. 3, p. 443-546, 2001.

Savanovic, Armina Tanja. Transnational Corporations and Human Rights Corporate Criminal Liability in International Criminal Law, unpublished thesis at Centre for Human Rights, Faculty of Law, Lund University, 2017.

Scheffer, David. "Corporate liability under the Rome Statute." Harvard International Law Journal 57, no, 2016, p. 35-38.

Skinner, Gwynne. "Nuremburg's Legacy Continues: The Nuremburg Trials' Influence on Human Rights Litigation in U.S. Courts Under the Alien Tort Statute", *71 Alb. L. Rev.* 321, p. 340–41, 2008.

The Charter of the International Military Tribunal - Annex to the Agreement for the prosecution and punishment of the major war criminals of the European Axis ("London Agreement"), 8 August 1945, available at <https://www.un.org/en/genocideprevention/documents/atrocity-crimes/Doc.2_Charter%20 of%20IMT%201945.pdf> visited on 12 September 2021.

The UN Protect, Respect, Remedy Frame Work and Guiding Principles: Driving Change? CIDSE Briefing March 2013.

The Zyclon B case, 1Law repots of Trials of War Criminals 93, 1947.

The Zyklon b, case trial of Bruno Tesch and two others British military court, Hamburg, 1st-8th March, 1946.

Trials of War Criminals before the Nuremberg Military Tribunals under Control Council Law No.10, at 1372(1952).

UN General Assembly, *Convention on the Prevention and Punishment of the Crime of Genocide*, 9 December 1948, United Nations, Treaty Series, vol. 78, p. 277.

UN Security Council, 1999. Report of the Secretary-General to the Security Council on the Protection of Civilians in armed Conflict. UN Doc. S/2001/331. available at < https://undocs.org/Home/ Mobile?FinalSymbol=S% 2F2001%2F331& Language=E&DeviceType= Desktop&LangRequested=False>

UNGA Report of the Secretary General to the Security Council on the Protection of Civilians in Armed Conflict (26 November 2002) UN Doc S/2002/1300.

United States Military Tribunal at Nuremberg - United States v. Alfried Krupp et al., Judgment of 31 July 1948

United States v. Flick (The Flick Case), Trials Of War Criminals Before The Nuremberg Military Tribunals Under Control Council Law 10, at 1192, 1952.

United States v. Krauch, 8 Trials of War Criminals before the Nuremberg Military Tribunals under Control Council Law No.10, at 1081(1953), available at <http://www.mazal.org/archieve/nmt/08/NMTO8-COO1.htm>.

Woodhouse, Charles Douglas. "The Mavrommatis Palestine concessions case." Ph D diss., University of California. May, 1925.

Section II

Evolving Weapons, Technologies, and Doctrines

Chapter 6

Dawn of Drones in War Fighting

-Amitabh Mathur

Introduction

The Russia-Ukraine conflict, referred to as a 'Special Operation' by Moscow, has been ongoing for nearly three years since the full-scale invasion in February 2022. Similarly, the unexpected attack on Israel by the Harakat al-Muqawama al-Islamiyya (Hamas) on October 07 2023, has resulted in the loss of thousands of civilians. These conflicts involving state and non-state actors have transformed the nature of air warfare, where the role of traditional crewed aircraft in the application of force is expanding to include missiles and unmanned aerial vehicles (UAVs), also known as drones. Low-cost, precision strike capabilities, operational flexibility, and extended missions with minimal risk to the aircrew are significant attributes that have contributed to the growth of drones as force multipliers in all three domains. Due to the opportunities for rapid innovation, their role in these conflicts has made combat faster and more intense. Tools like space, precision weapons, cyber, electronic warfare (EW) and drones have been employed for escalation control in the Ukraine conflict. There is a growing trend among developed nations to manufacture drones and counter-drone systems at a speed and scale that meets the requirements of contemporary conflicts. With the arrival of modern reconnaissance and surveillance assets available to the adversary, the Air Power offers advantages such as flexibility, accuracy, rapid reaction times, the ability to reposition forces, and the capacity to operate from various directions simultaneously at a high pace.

Current Trends

The battlefield has served as a testbed for new technologies. Unmanned systems have revolutionised military operations worldwide, and several countries have effectively incorporated cutting-edge drones into their strategic arsenals. As per the United Nations (UN), at least 139 civilians were killed and 738 wounded in January 2025, with 27% of the deaths and 30% of the injuries being caused by short-range drones, even though the drones were fitted with onboard cameras which could identify military targets and civilians.[1] Russia and Ukraine were expected to produce well over one million drones in 2024. Ukraine's defence ministry says drone strikes are now responsible for up to 80 per cent of Russian battlefield casualties. In May 2025 alone, Ukrainian drones destroyed over 89,000 Russian targets.[2]

"Operation Spider Web" operation launched by Ukraine on June 01,2025. It was aimed at degrading Russia's long-range strike capabilities by smuggling FPV drones to attack airfields in the Murmansk, Irkutsk, Ivanovo, Ryazan, and Amur regions, where several aircrafts were hit. It was a combined operation involving remote human control with elements of autonomy and potentially AI-assisted functionality has led to new dimension of hybrid warfare.

"Op Sindoor" has highlighted that a seismic shift is underway into the age of autonomous warfare. The highlight of the operation was the role of combined Air Defence in successfully countering drone threats. The Indian Air Force's Integrated Air Command and Control System (IACCS) and the Indian Army's "Akashteer" provided a digitised command layer for Air Force and Army Air Defence units, enabling seamless coordination between sensor units and weapon platforms. The IACCS creates a centralised yet dispersed command-and-control network by combining surveillance inputs from satellites, aircraft, early warning and control platforms, ground-based radars, and other sensors. It allows for the quick identification, tracking, and interception of low-altitude threats,

1 "Drones Become Most Common Cause of Death", Reuters February 11, 2025, https://www.reuters.com/world/europe/drones-become-most-common- cause-death- civilians-ukraine- war-un-says-2025-02-11/?utm_source =Sailthru& utm_ medium=Newsletter& utm_campaign=Daily-Briefing &utm_term=021125 &lctg=62ccd2e4936 1eaef0b0a0fc5, Accessed on February 12, 2025.

2 Newsweek, June 25, 2025, Ukraine's New Drone Boss is Getting Results On and Off the Battlefields", https://www.newsweek.com/robert-brovdi-ukraine-russia-war-drones-2090785,Accessed on June 29, 2025

such as drones, by integrating with fighter aircraft and SAM systems. The "Akashteer" is an Indian Army's air defence shield built around a layered architecture that combines retrofitted legacy Low-Level Air Defence (LLAD) systems with advanced missile platforms.

Evolution in Warfighting Role

The drones employed in earlier conflicts could fly higher and had carbon wing coatings, making them more challenging to shoot down. The most widely used technology on either side is drones for intelligence, surveillance, and reconnaissance (ISR) purposes, as well as targeting. In the future, the role of logistics supply will also gain prominence. Technological advancements in Artificial Intelligence (AI), sensor miniaturisation, and autonomous navigation have expanded their capabilities. Through the use of platforms like the MQ-9 Reaper and RQ-4 Global Hawk for long-range surveillance and targeted strikes, the United States played a vital role in the wars in Afghanistan, Iraq, and Syria. These drones are instrumental in terrorist operations because of their precision strike skills, which have drastically decreased collateral damage. China's military maintains a diverse fleet that includes aircraft such as the CH-4, CH-5, CH-7, Wing Loong series, and the stealthy GJ-11 Sharp Sword, all designed to strengthen its aviation capabilities.

The Russia-Ukraine conflict has seen the use of not only purpose-built drones, such as the Russian Orion and Orlan-10, the Iranian Mohajer-6, and the Turkish Bayraktar TB2, but also loitering munitions like the American Switchblade, the Iranian Shahed-136, and the Russian Lancet, as well as many others, which are cheap commercial drones modified with high-resolution cameras. The armies today have to fight on what is called the transparent battlefield. Surveillance today is layered with satellites scanning the Earth above 200 km, and surveillance drones with First Person Views (FPVs) are used to spot and destroy soldiers on the ground. Using thermal imaging cameras lets the drone operator identify the target in open fields and the woods at night. The transparent battlefield gives the defenders an advantage over the adversary.

While the US, Israel, and China have made significant strides in developing kamikaze and long-range reconnaissance drones, even smaller nations have joined the march. The US Centre for a New American Security (CNAS) recently released a report that states that Turkey has overtaken world leaders like America, China and Israel in terms of drone technology and supply[3]. The Turkish TB2 drone, manufactured by the Turkish firm Baykar, demonstrated combat in the Nagorno-Karabakh conflict in September 2020, in African countries and the current Ukraine conflict. The Akinci, which was inducted into the Turkish armed forces in 2021, is a high-altitude, long-endurance drone armed with various air-to-air and air-to-ground missiles. The TB3, developed recently, has foldable wings and can take off from a small runway. In addition, Baykar is also developing an unmanned fighter jet, the 'Kizilelma', that is expected to carry out a wide range of military operations, including Close Air Support (CAS), missile offensives, Suppression of Enemy Air Defences (SEAD), and Destruction Of Enemy Air Defences (DEAD)[4].

The Iranian Army has inducted the Ababil-4 and Ababil-5 drones, which can be used for reconnaissance, patrol missions, EW, data collection, and aerial combat. The Shahed-3 are kamikaze drones with short ranges compared to the Arash drones, capable of carrying out "long-range suicide" missions[5]. The Iranian Revolutionary Guard Corps (IRGC) Naval Forces have released footage of their new drone carrier ship, the IRGC "Shahid Mahdavi"[6], that can launch and retrieve unmanned combat aircraft and operate various attack reconnaissance drones. It has a runway of about 180 meters and an impressive operational range of 22,000 nautical miles[7]. Israel's Heron TP and Harop drones are celebrated for their endurance and precision "kamikaze" strike capabilities, with the Harop designed explicitly as a loitering munition capable of autonomously targeting enemy radars.

Pakistan has increased its drone fleets, escalating the competition in the region. These aircraft have sophisticated observation and combat capabilities. An estimated 150–200 drones are operated by Pakistan,

3 Tahir Qureshi, "Turkey Has a Secret Weapon That worries Superpower's", India.com, November 03,2025 https://www.india.com/news/world/turkey-has-secret-weapon-that-worries-superpowers-like-us-china-russia-and-israel-the-deadly-weapon-is-drones-ukraine-iraq-iran-7368983/,Accessed on February 06, 2025.

4 Sakshi Tiwari. "From Car Spare Parts to World Leader in UAV", **Eurasian Times**, February 3, 2025 https://www.eurasiantimes.com/from-auto-spare-parts-to-world-leader/,Accessed on February 04, 2025.

5 "Iran Gets Major Drone Boost Amid Growing Tensions With Israel", **Newsweek**, January 13, 2025, https://www.newsweek.com/iran-gets-major-drone-boost-amid-growing-tensions-israel-2013837,Accessed on February 5, 2025.

6 Twitter OSINT Defender, February 06, 2025, https://x.com/sentdefender/status/1887395971753255376?t=kFhg2_z41n5ADMGQnjOoTQ&s=08.

7 Sakshi Tewari, **Eurasian Times**, February 06, 2025, https://www.eurasiantimes.com/iran-adds-serious-firepower-to-deter-u-s-after/,Accessed on February 08, 2025.

including the Turkish Bayraktar TB2, and Akinci variants, as well as the CH-3-based Burraq and CH-4B. While the introduction of the Bayraktar TB2 drones has improved Pakistan's ISR and striking capabilities along the Line of Control (LoC), the Burraq has been extensively utilised in counter-terrorism operations inside its borders[8]. Pakistan has, in the recent Op Sindoor, used quadcopters, Turkish Songar, and eYatri drones to test gaps in the Indian Air Defence.

In addition to Defence Research and Development Organisation (DRDO) products, such as the Rustom-II and Archer-NG, India's drone startups have made remarkable strides in recent years, with the country achieving a second ranking in the manufacture of commercial drones, following the US, according to the 2024 Global Drone Survey Industry insights. The next major challenge lies in expanding globally[9].

Current Trends in various roles

The current trends in the application of drones in the current conflicts are given below:

(a) Reconnaissance Drones. In addition to the High-Altitude Long Endurance (HALE) and Medium-Altitude Long Endurance (MALE) drones, which can loiter for extended durations, tethered drones have an advantage in that they can remain in a fixed position for an extended period above defence establishments, providing 360-degree surveillance capability. The tethered drone can hover over its target to collect updated information by processing data from various cameras and sensors, offering multiple visual feedback options at roughly real-time speeds via a cable connected to the control panel. Since the drones fly for long hours, the data they collect is extensive. The battlefield information combines live camera feeds and sensor data from multiple sensors, including infrared, night-vision, electromagnetic spectrum, gamma-ray, biological, and chemical sensors.

One of the most popular drone sensors onboard is the LiDAR (Light Detection and Ranging), which enables real-time object detection and

8 Rishabh Manvendra Pratap, Times Now, February 7, 2025, https://www.timesnownews.com/india/strengthening-the-indian-armys-unmanned-aerial-fleet-for-future-challenges-article-118030197,Accessed on February 08, 2025.

9 Ritu Sharma," From Armenia To America, Demand For Indian Drone, AntiDrone System Increases; Billions In Revenue Expected", Eurasian Times, February 22, 2025, https://www.eurasiantimes.com/from-armenia-to-america-demand-for-indian/ Accessed on February 23, 2025.

safe navigation in dynamic driving environments. It is an advanced remote sensing technology that uses electromagnetic energy in the optical range for detection and classification based on phenomena such as scattering, absorption, reflection and fluorescence. LiDAR sensors are equipped with high-speed optical transceivers, including laser emitters and photodetectors, which enable them to transmit and receive information through light pulses. LiDAR can produce incredibly accurate spatial data by measuring the time it takes for these pulses to return to a sensor, vastly outperforming more traditional techniques like radar and sonar. The reflected laser pulses create highly detailed, three-dimensional maps of the surrounding environments[10]. A few military applications of LiDAR are listed below:

- **Battlefield Mapping.** Enables precise terrain analysis, including in urban environments
- **Enemy Detection** helps locate enemy positions and infrastructure.
- **Navigation**: Enhances movement by providing detailed spatial awareness.
- **Sea Mine Detection**: Identifies the depth of underwater threats.
- **Laser Weapon Support**: Predicts performance by analysing atmospheric conditions.
- **High-Altitude Surveillance**: Systems rapidly map large areas from the air, offering advanced data collection capabilities above 100,000 feet.
- **Infra-Red (IR) and Hyperspectral.** Infrared and hyperspectral imaging can potentially determine the chemical and material composition of the surface being monitored. The sensor's ability to detect various camouflage materials is used to identify concealed weapon systems.
- **Synthetic Aperture Radar (SAR).** These sensors can capture images of the Earth under various atmospheric conditions, both during the day and at night. India's first drone-based SAR

10 Fernandez Diaz J.C., Carter W.E., Shrestha R.L., Glennie C.L. (2013) "Lidar Remote Sensing". in: Pelton J.N., Madry S., Camacho-Lara S. (eds) **Handbook of Satellite Applications**, New York, Springer, 2013, accessed on February 04, 2025

system for fog penetration and tactical ISR, displayed at Aero India 2025, was developed by Idea Forge and Galax Eye.

- **SIGINT (Signal Intelligence) Sensors**. These communication and electronic intelligence-gathering sensors can identify, detect and pinpoint the location of radio frequency signals for military use.

The fusion of data from various types of sensors can yield accurate results. Some examples are:

- **Hyperspectral + SAR**. Hyperspectral imagery collects and processes information across the electromagnetic spectrum to obtain the spectrum of each pixel, which helps identify camouflage materials. By seeing through clouds and some foliage, SAR confirms the locations of these potential targets.
- **Optical + Infrared + Radar**. Optical imagery provides high-resolution visual detail, while infrared sensors detect heat signatures from vehicles and activity. Radar can see through adverse weather conditions and even offer ground-penetrating capabilities. Fusing these delivers a clearer picture, by day or night, in rain or sunshine.
- **Signals Intelligence (SIGINT) + Geospatial Data**. Geotagged SIGINT data (like intercepted communications and radar emissions) fused with satellite or drone imagery can reveal the disposition of enemy forces or the location of hostile transmissions.

In addition to the Heron and Searcher MALE (Medium Altitude Long Endurance) drones for ISR, the Indian armed forces are inducting the MQ-9B Sea Guardian drones, which offer enhanced ISR and precision strike abilities, with the capability to carry Hellfire missiles and precision-guided munitions. The Indian Archer-NG drone is scheduled to make its first flight in March 2025 and is expected to be weaponised within the next three years. Many seafaring countries are integrating carrier-based drones into their naval fleets. On January 28, 2024, Airbus Defence, along with Spanish shipbuilder "Navantia", are exploring the potential integration of the SIRTAP drone into the Spanish Navy's Landing Helicopter Dock (LHD) flagship, the "Juan Carlos I"[11]. China has launched a 40,000-ton

11 Ashish Dangwal," After Bayraktar TB#, SIRTAP Could Become Next Drone To Operate From Short Runway Carrier", January 29, 2025, https://www.eurasiantimes.

076 amphibious assault ship, *Sichuan*, where test trials of the WZ-9 "Divine Eagle" drones were reported.

(b) First-Person View (FPV) Drones. In 2023 came the drone revolution. Ukraine pioneered the use of FPV drones to search, track, and destroy enemy targets with pinpoint accuracy. FPV drones bring a real-time, first-person perspective to tactical reconnaissance, enabling precise intelligence gathering while keeping personnel out of harm's way. FPV drones are based on racing quadcopters. The operator wears goggles that display a video feed from the drone during flight, with a flight time of between 20 and 40 minutes. The munitions dropped are mortar shells, grenades, canisters containing shrapnel or darts, or bottles of petrol that ignite. In December 2024, for the first time, Ukrainian forces successfully attacked Russian positions using the FPV drones. These drones are particularly suited for urban warfare, search-and-rescue missions, and counter-infiltration efforts. Ukraine has used these FPV drones extensively, and the largest share of the destruction of Russian key infrastructure and military assets, some 49%, has been attributed to them[12]. To increase the operational range of FPV kamikaze drones, the Russian troops have increased their usage of drone motherships. By acting as transporters and data-link nodes, these motherships enable FPV drones to be deployed over far greater distances than they could independently. The mothership enables the FPVs to operate beyond their 10km operating range by acting as a relay for control signals and video communication, while neutralising the impact of EW jammers in the vicinity.[13] Ukraine has deployed a mobile radar system to provide early warning for incoming FPV drones several kilometres away. Once they detect the threat, the unit then launches its drones to intercept the Russian ones before they can reach their targets.

Increased use of fibre optic guided FPV drones, where an extremely thin but strong wire, with the help of a large spool, links the drone with its controller. The Russians were the first to deploy fibre-optic drones in this war and, as of early 2025, are widely using this solution across various

com/after-bayraktar-tb3-u-s-mojave-sirtap-could/#google_vignette, Accessed on February 3, 2025.

12 Ashish Dangwal, Eurasian Times, 7 February 2025 https://www.eurasiantimes.com/drones-responsible-for-66-of-russian-equipment-losses/,Accessed on February 8, 2025.

13 Vijainder K Thakur, "Russian Drone Motherships Carrying FPV Drones", January 31, 2025, https://www.eurasiantimes.com/ukraines-next-big-headache-russian-drone-motherships/, Accessed on February 2, 2025.

sections of the front line. The cables can stretch varying distances and often go up to around 10 kilometres. This capability enables the drones to operate in a communication-degraded environment, while flying very low to the ground, a technique used by the Russians. Russia developed the Vandal FPV Kamikaze Fibre Optic Cable-Controlled Drone. This drone utilises a wired connection via a fibre optic control cable, rendering its communication link virtually immune to electronic jamming and interference. The drone's digital flight control electronics are also jam-resistant. Other significant advantages that drone provide from the use of fibre optic cable include high bandwidth, low latency communication, stealthy operation, and the ability to fly at extremely low altitudes. This has led to Ukrainians using techniques such as short-wavelength radar to spot slow-moving drones. The short-wavelength radars have a limitation of short ranges, thereby providing early warning for short detection ranges and reaction times for counter-drone systems. Once detected, the Ukrainians launch their drone to intercept the Russian drones before they can reach the target.

(c) Loitering Munitions. The role of loitering munitions, which were initially developed as anti-radiation drones, has proved to be more lethal than that of armed drones. These drones comprise a diverse group of aircraft in various sizes and weights, ranging from small, gun- and hand-launched drones to those weighing up to 200 kg (440 pounds) with electric propulsion, controlled by a tablet that displays images from an onboard optical camera and an infrared thermal imager. Originally designed to counter radar, loitering weapons are now used to attack a range of other combat targets, including hostile soldiers, armoured vehicles, ships, and even adversary drones. Loitering munitions that operate at lower altitudes, in the gaps between the ground and air forces, can be challenging to identify, target, and engage before becoming a threat. Russia has used the Shahed Unmanned Aerial Vehicles (UAVs), or so-called "kamikaze" drones, to strike at Ukrainian infrastructure, such as energy sites. The drones had been fitted with thermobaric warheads, which caused more destructive explosions[14]. Piston engines mainly powered the drones. Ukraine has used jet-powered UJ-22 Kamikaze drones to strike deep into Russian territory.

14 "Russia Deploys Deadly New Weapon in Drone Race", Newsweek November 2, 2024 https://www.newsweek.com/russia-ukraine-drones-shahed-race-deadly-new-weapon-1979040,Accessed on February 4, 2025.

Russia is also developing the Geran-3 jet-powered drones[15]. Dynatron Systems has designed India's first jet-powered loitering munition[16].

(d) Unmanned Underwater Vehicles (UUVs). The drone's capacity to operate over large distances has also proven crucial for maritime domain awareness, particularly in the Indian Ocean Region (IOR), where persistent surveillance is vital to counter potential threats, including piracy, trafficking, and maritime terrorism. The widespread application of Unmanned Underwater Vehicles (UUVs) in the Ukrainian conflict has given rise to asymmetric warfare, as operating in the undersea domain is more complex than in other domains. The USVs cost a fraction of the price of traditional warships, thereby offering a playbook that war planners can use around maritime chokepoints.[17] UUVs are of two variants: Remotely Operated Underwater Vehicles (ROVs) or Autonomous Underwater Vehicles (AUVs), depending on their mode of operation. AUVs differ from ROVs in that they are self-propelled and retain some human control autonomy. Recent advances in sensors, communication, and processing tools, such as big data and machine learning, are poised to impact underwater warfare, potentially shifting from defensive to offensive roles. The new emerging threats are drone swarms and submersible kamikaze USVs, which approach targets stealthily before surfacing for high-speed attacks. They are fast becoming a pressing issue for modern navies to deal with.

Kyiv has successfully targeted the Crimean Peninsula, which has served as a central hub for the Russian Black Sea Fleet. The UUVs have forced the Russian Navy to move its fleet further east in the Black Sea. On February 14, 2024, Ukraine used the "MAGURA V5" USVs to sink the Caesar Kunik, a Pr. 775 landing ship[18]. Ukrainian forces were able to shoot down

15 Vijender K Thakur, "Russia Set To Unleash Geran-3 Jet Powered Kamikaze Drones", Eurasian Times, February 19, 2025, https://www.eurasiantimes.com/russia-set-to-unleash-new-gen-geran-3-jet/,Accessed on February 20, 2025.

16 Raghav Patel, "Kaatil India's New Jet Powered Drone" DEFENCE.IN, February 11,2025, https://defence.in/threads/kaatil-indias-new-jet-powered-loitering-munition-turns-heads-with-f-5-fighter-jet-resemblance.12838/,Accessed on February12, 2025,

17 Geoff Ziezulewicz, "What The Navy's Massive Orca Submarine Drone is Actually Capable of", January 14, 2025,https://www.twz.com/news-features/what-the-navys-massive-orca-submarine-drone-is-actually-capable-of, Accessed on January 16, 2025.

18 Jon Hemler and Derek Bisaccio 'Ukraine's USVs Write New Rules For Asymmetric Naval Warfare', June 13, 2024, https://dsm.forecastinternational.com/2024/06/13/ukraines-usvs-write-new-rules-for-asymmetric-naval-warfare/ Accessed on January13, 2025.

Russian helicopters flying over the Black Sea with missiles launched from Magura V5 naval strike drones.[19]Both tactics and technology continue to evolve. Moscow reportedly destroyed one uncrewed boat on February 01, 2025, using an airborne Orion missile-capable drone[20]. The US Navy, too, is developing UUVs of all sizes, which will revolutionise undersea warfare. Non-state actors like the Houthis, in the group's first successful USV attack, have attacked commercial shipping off the coast of Yemen, severely damaging the carrier *Tutor*[21].

Future Trends in Drone Warfare: New Applications

There are four main versions of drones: single-rotor, multi-rotor, fixed-wing, and hybrid Vertical Take-off and Landing (VTOL). In December 2024, Ukraine carried out all drone assaults on Russian positions, where dozens of FPV drones, reconnaissance drones, turret-mounted, and kamikaze drones all worked in tandem on the ground and the air. The Russians and the Ukrainians are also engaged in the war of waves, the Electronic Warfare (EW) race, which is a key component of the conflict. Continuous changes are driven by fierce competition between jammers and munitions. Both sides try to locate, track, occupy, and attack using rare gaps in the spectrum where signals can pass through. As jammers become more numerous and more sophisticated, the quest for jam-proof drones becomes inevitable. Current drones can switch between Global Positioning System (GPS)- assisted navigation and inertial navigation systems, which utilise gyroscopes and accelerometers. The new solutions are incorporating technological advancements such as artificial intelligence, communication via beacons on the ground, and fibre cable-assisted navigation. The use of Optical navigation, combined with inertial data from accelerometers and gyroscopes, and Eagle Eye AI-assisted software, enables the comparison of live video of the terrain below with an onboard map stitched together from photographs and videos stored by reconnaissance sensors. This is the new solution to counter EW, which has become the new norm.

19 Newsweek, "Russian Black Sea Fleet Debuts New Method To Offset Ukrainian Droines", February 02, 2025, https://www.newsweek.com/russia-black-sea-fleet-new-method-ukrainian-naval-drones-crimea-2024791,Accessed on June 29, 2025

20 Ellie Cook, "New Method" to Offset Ukrainian Drones, 2 February 2025, https://www.newsweek.com/russia-black-sea-fleet-new-method-ukrainian-naval-drones-crimea-2024791, Accesed on February 03, 2025.

21 Howard Altman, Houthi Drone Boat Strikes Ship For Fits Time Since Red Sea Crisis Erupted, June 12, 2024, https://www.twz.com/news-features/houthi-drone-boat-strikes-ship-for-first-time-since-red-sea-crisis-erupted,Accessed on February 2025.

The future trends in the growth of various types of drones and their roles are discussed as follows:-

(i) **Logistics: Vertical Take-off and Landing** (VTOL) systems are tailored for operations in extreme environments, offering unparalleled flexibility by enabling vertical take-off and landing in areas where runways are unavailable, such as mountainous regions and urban conflict zones. Indian startups are manufacturing drones powered by fuel and hybrids that use hydrogen-electric propulsion. These systems are finding applications in the civil world, and the Government of India is developing a regulatory framework for Unmanned Aircraft Traffic Management (UTM) systems to enable eVTOL aircraft to operate alongside existing Air Traffic Management (ATM) systems.[22]

(ii) **Hybrid Manned-Unmanned Operations**: Manned-Unmanned Teaming (MUMT) involves a human pilot and an unmanned robotic platform working together on land, sea, and air, with the air domain experiencing the most growth compared to the land and sea domains. These semi-autonomous UAVs are designed to serve as "loyal wingmen" to crewed fighter jets, offering enhanced capabilities and adaptability in complex combat situations. These drones' advanced AI allows them to work in unison with piloted aircraft, increasing their efficacy and reach in dangerous situations [23], enabling the pilot to direct the drones in flight and freeing them to focus on higher-priority combat objectives. Operational flexibility is enhanced by this AI-driven coordination, allowing a more dynamic response to rapidly changing battlefield scenarios.

Lockheed Martin released a significant update in 2024, which will enable the F-35 fighter jets to control drones as part of the development of the Collaborative Combat Aircraft (CCA) fleet, a key element of the strategy for achieving air dominance in the coming decade. In addition to performing various tasks, such as air-to-air and air-to-ground combat, EW, and ISR, the CCAs can

22 *The Economic Times*, February 03, 2025, available at: https://economictimes.indiatimes.com/industry/transportation/airlines-/-aviation/dgca-developing-regulatory-framework-for-evtols-ops-to-be-managed-strategically-tactically-govt/articleshow/117891080.cms?from=mdr,Accessed on February 5, 2025.

23 Defence News Aerospace 2025,24 January 2025, https://armyrecognition.com/news/aerospace-news/2025/exclusive-us-lockheed-martin-f-35-fighter-jet-controls-drone-in-flight-using-ai-technologies,Accessed, Accessed on 2 February 2025.

work alone or in coordinated groups under the guidance of human pilots. Russia has utilised drones integrated with manned aircraft, such as the Su-34, to enhance engagement efficiency, primarily in terms of overall awareness and target acquisition. The Indian MUMT project is the Hindustan Aeronautics Limited (HAL) Combat Air Teaming System (CATS)[24]. The CATS Warrior can perform multiple tasks, such as scouting, absorbing enemy fire, and attacking targets. It can be controlled by a mothership aircraft and can return to base after missions. In high-risk scenarios, it can be directed to sacrifice itself by crashing into critical targets, thereby preserving manned assets. The drone features stealth capabilities, internal weapon bays, and advanced avionics. An Indian startup, New Space Research and Technologies, has unveiled the design of its collaborative aircraft, the Abhimanyu, which utilises a MUMT aircraft to execute missions for ISR, decoys, kinetic attacks, and EW roles, leveraging AI.[25] Based on the "Abhimanyu", the Indian Navy has chosen the startup to develop its Naval Collaborative Combat Air Vehicle (N-CCAV).

(iii) **High Altitude Pseudo-Satellite (HAPS):** Significant capabilities have already been established, enabling the armed forces to operate through the Low Earth Orbit (LEO) region. Near-space, between 20 and 100 km, is called the 'near-space' region. It can augment and support military applications, such as surveillance, reconnaissance, and communication. Lighter-than-air vehicles operating in near space could use high-altitude drones to provide communications, network relays, and ISR capabilities. The High-Altitude Pseudo Satellite (HAPS) drones, flying in the stratosphere, powered by solar radiation, which can stay aloft for 60 to 90 days, have provided low-cost solutions and technological advantages compared to LEO satellites. These HAPS can provide persistent coverage over the chosen area and can be utilised to fill gaps, particularly in countering threats from ballistic missiles and hypersonic weapons. The key advantages lie in these platforms'

24 Gp Capt (Dr) DK Pandey," Manned-Unmanned Teaming" January 09, 2025, https://cenjows.in/manned-unmanned-teaming-enhancing-lethality/ Accessed on January 25, 2025.

25 "New Space Unveils Abhimanyu: Redefining Air Warfare", IDRW, February 7, 2025, https://idrw.org/newspace-unveils-abhimanyu-redefining-air-warfare/,February, 08, 2025.

persistent loitering ability and survivability while escaping detection in covert missions.

(iv) **Hypersonic Drones**. These compact drones can reach speeds above Mach 5 and operate autonomously at near-space altitudes. They feature an advanced aerodynamic architecture, including a wedge-shaped fuselage optimised to reduce drag, delta wings for enhanced lift at high speeds, and canted vertical tails for improved stability. They can be launched from high-altitude balloons and aircraft, operate at extreme altitudes and fly at hypersonic speeds, which gives them a crucial advantage in flying at unpredictable flight paths against modern air defence systems for reconnaissance and kamikaze strike roles. While surveillance satellites follow predictable trajectories, making them vulnerable to open conflict between the major powers, hypersonic reconnaissance aircraft offer significant strategic flexibility. These drones, capable of unexpected flight paths and hidden in underground hangars, provide a valuable alternative to satellites.

China had taken the lead in operationalising the WS-8, the world's first hypersonic military surveillance drone. Now, China has developed the MD-22 "Mingdi", MD-19, MD-21, and MD-2 versions, designed to be launched from the H-6 M aircraft and showcased at the 2022 Zhuhai Air Show. Measuring between 8 and 11 meters in length, this compact drone can reach speeds above Mach 5 and operate at near-space altitudes. Q-Alpha Aerospace is developing a state-of-the-art turbojet engine designed for use by hypersonic platforms.[26] China has also developed a long-range early warning radar, reportedly capable of detecting threats, including hypersonic ones, thousands of miles away.[27] Beyond surface-based defences, China claims to have created the world's first 'seabed radar,' allegedly capable of detecting high-altitude aircraft from a depth of 1,000 metres.

26 Raghav Patel, "Bangalore's Q-Alpha Aerospace Developing QAL-J10 Turbojet Engine",Defence .In, January 22,2025, https://defence.in/threads/bangalores-q-alpha-aerospace-developing-ai-powered-qal-j10-turbojet-engine-for-next-gen-drones-and-hypersonic-ucavs.12464/ Accessed on 05 February 2025.

27 Shubhangi Palve, "China Flashes "Anti-Hypersonic" Gigantic Radar That It Claims Can Detect & Track Every Kind Of Missiles", Eurasian Times, February 05, 2025, available at: https://www.eurasiantimes.com/china-flashes-anti-hypersonic-gigantic-radar/, Accessed on February 06, 2025.

(v) **Micro Drones and Stealth.** Due to the miniaturisation of electronics and the combination of stealth with reduced payload size, micro drones will increasingly find applications in expendable roles, such as surveillance by military combat units and law enforcement agencies, by carrying out vertical delivery of munitions. Though performance-wise, they may not be as good as the other drones, their application in warfare is significant. Such micro drones are AI-enabled and very small, roughly around three centimetres. They have voice recognition software and can hold a few grams of RDX, which explodes on contact. India has developed a flame-throwing drone, a low-cost, high-impact device designed for close-quarters dominance.

(vi) **AI-Powered drones:** The current ongoing conflicts in Gaza and Ukraine have demonstrated the role of AI in warfare, where killer robots and autonomous drones are being used for targeting. AI-driven autonomy will revolutionise decision-making, enabling drones to analyse the data and execute missions independently. This reduces human intervention, enhances speed and improves operational efficiency. It is used to analyse surveillance data and cross-reference it with SIGINT and open-source information. Russia and Ukraine have been developing drones which are assisted by AI that can deploy automatically to engage a threat once a surveillance system flags an enemy drone. A programme known as "The Gospel" generates suggestions for the buildings and bunkers to be hit, whereas "Lavender" and the facial recognition software system Clearview AI are used to identify the foot soldiers by tracking and identifying them. Ukraine also utilised an AI-powered acoustic monitoring system, the Zvook, developed by a Ukrainian startup, which can detect the direction and speed of incoming aircraft and missiles using a network of sensors. The acoustic counter drones detect drones and aim the acoustic beam at them. The system records sound waves from approaching drones. It uses a computer to concentrate energy into a narrow acoustic "laser" that disrupts, among other things, the gyroscopes these drones require for stable flight. Germany is supplying an HX-2 attack drone that uses AI to resist electronic warfare. IIT Kanpur has developed the SABAL-50 drone, which utilises AI to fly in rugged terrain at high altitudes, equipped with stealth features for both surveillance and combat, including aerial attacks.[28] The impacts of AI on warfare are given below:

- **Shift in Human Role**. Experts on the laws of war, already alarmed by the emergence of AI in military applications, express concerns about "automation bias" on the part of the operator. It is not that the robots will take control over the operator, but that AI will supplant them without realising that they are already controlling the operator's mind. Hence, policymakers should ensure that AI enhances the ability to constrain the operator more effectively in managing unfolding events.
- AI will make war more lethal and uncontrollable. AI-powered cyberattacks degrade adversary networks, and advanced algorithms accelerate decision-making. Experts warn that automated decision-making could lead to rapid escalation.
- The Large Language Model (LLM) can empower the weak by enabling non-state actors to utilise AI to coordinate drone swarms, thereby narrowing the gap between developed and underdeveloped nations.
- The Future of Manned Aircraft in a Drone-Dominated Battlefield: The role of traditional aircraft in the AI-drone-dominated battlefield will be reduced considerably.
- Swarm Tactics: Swarm tactics, involving the deployment of many drones that operate autonomously to overwhelm the adversary, will be utilised for both offensive and defensive roles to counter such threats using AI tools.

Evolution of Counter-Drones

Earlier conflicts witnessed the role of manned aircraft. Current conflicts have transformed into more cruise missiles and drones, with aircraft being used extensively at the start of the conflict. Therefore, only heterogeneous counters can effectively match the threats posed by heterogeneous air power. However, this is inherently complicated and costly as these counters must match multiple dissimilar air power components. Unlike

28 Indian Defence News, June 27,2025,"IIT -Kanpur is Rolling Out SABAl-50 Drones in India", https://www.indiandefensenews.in/2025/06/iit-kanpur-is-preparing-to-roll-out.html,Accessed on June 29,2025

air defence operations used for manned platforms, like the Close Air Support (CAS), missile offensives, SEAD, and DEAD operations, the same methodology cannot be applied to counter drone operations. Counter drone systems include warning sensors, backpack- and vehicle-mounted electronic jammers, gun systems, hard-kill interceptors, and laser-blinding devices deployed at the front lines as well as in depth. Many deception techniques are used to render the Counter-Unmanned Aerial Systems (C-UAS) systems inoperable. Soldiers wear multi-spectral camouflage nets to block heat signatures and evade detection by thermal cameras. Using stroboscopes to lash lights to dazzle the drone's camera is also being tested[29]. The armoured tanks will require radars covering 360 degrees, along with electro-optical sensors, for situational awareness and threat identification. Passive and active countermeasures are required against different types of threats. Soft and hard kill measures, such as smoke grenade launchers or jamming, are used when a threat is detected. For the hard kill, explosively formed projectiles (EFPs) are used to destroy the incoming projectile in mid-air. Despite all the countermeasures, new technological solutions are being developed to outsmart these techniques. Layered AD systems with AI-driven networks capable of countering manned and unmanned threats must be relied upon. The methodology can be described as follows:

(a) **Readiness.** It includes activities related to threats and preventive measures to understand offenders and protect high-value assets.

(b) **Detection and Decision-Making.** Measures include detection, tracking, identification, threat evaluation, and decision-making.

(c) **Influence.** Active countermeasures encompass both destructive and non-kinetic impacts on drones.

(d) **Evaluation.** For improvements in the counter-drone counter-action system.

Non-Kinetic. According to EW theorists, the competition for dominance in EW command and control systems, while degrading the adversary's EW systems and units, is the foundation for the competition for information superiority during a campaign. This is the only course of action that gives the actor with fewer resources a chance to win a war. Additionally, cyberattacks against the adversary's EW command and control systems play

29 "Fighting The War In Ukraine On The Electromagnetic Spectrum, Science and Technology", The Economist 5Fenruary 2025, https://www.economist.com/science-and-technology/2025/02/05/fighting-the-war-in-ukraine-on-the-electromagnetic-spectrum,Accessed on February 14, 2025.

a crucial role. The Russians have carried out the offensive with cyberattacks involving Distributed Denial of Service (DDoS) to disrupt internet connectivity in Ukraine. This has incapacitated the latter's command and control centres, advanced artillery and missile systems, and EW systems and disrupted radar and communication systems. According to reports, the Russians regularly sent numerous text messages using devices (Leer-3 systems) mounted on the Orlan-10 long-range surveillance drone to imitate cellular base stations to which phones automatically connect, thereby affecting Ukrainian communication systems.

EW systems act as a force multiplier by creating a protective dome around their base location and sending out powerful radio frequency signals that disrupt communication between drones and their pilots, causing them to lose control of the craft and miss their target.[30] The operation of electronic warfare systems requires state-of-the-art sensors to detect drones. Phased-array radar technology offers significantly faster scanning speeds and greater accuracy than traditional radars. Unlike conventional systems that physically rotate, phased-array radars utilise electronically controlled arrays to rapidly shift focus in multiple directions, thereby enhancing tracking efficiency. Small drones pose challenges for radars to differentiate between birds and drones. China's Chengdu Aircraft Design Institute has developed a Large Language Model (LLM) for drones, enabling them to rapidly disrupt the enemy's radar and radio communications[31]. Ukraine has acquired its first lightweight two-seater SHARK aircraft from a Czech-Slovak firm, equipped with an electronic warfare system specifically designed to counter threats such as the Shahed and Orlan drones. It is equipped with an antenna for detecting and tracking drone threats and can neutralise them using jammers mounted on the aircraft. It has two components: one targets the GNSS positioning systems, and the other jams the video and control links of drones, while flying at an altitude of 1,800 metres and having a coverage of 4.5 km radius.

Kinetic. Artillery reconnaissance can detect drones and destroy them, as well as their ground control systems. A MANPAD essentially forms a lower layer of a country's air defence network. The MANPADS deployed by

30 "Ukraine Rolls Out Dozens of AI Systems To Help Its Drones Hit Targets", Reuters, October31 2024, https://www.deccanherald.com/world/ukraine-rolls-out-dozens-of-ai-systems-to-help-its-drones-hit-targets-2-3257443, Accessed on January 10, 2025.

31 "China Unveils"ChatGPT" That Can Attack Enemy Radars and Communications", November 5,2025, https://www.eurasiantimes.com/chinas-j-20-mighty-dragons-designer/Accessed on February 6, 2025.

Ukraine were instrumental in denying Russia air superiority. To defend a given geographical area, the prerequisite is to shift layers and have mobility, along with the capability to engage at different ranges. The Ukrainian military has used various MANPADS in the ongoing conflict, including Soviet-era Igla, Swedish RBS-70 NG, French Mistrals, US Stingers, and British Starstreak. The Indian Army is modernising its ageing ZSU-23-2 anti-aircraft systems, focusing on converting them into self-propelled units to counter modern aerial threats such as drones and low-flying aircraft[32]. The Defence Research and Development Organisation (DRDO) has successfully conducted flight trials of the Very Short-Range Air Defence System (VSHORADS) against high-speed targets flying at very low altitudes, with reduced thermal signatures that mimic those of low-flying drones under various flight conditions. The missile is 2 meters long and weighs about 21 kilograms. It has an effective operational range of up to 6 kilometres. Designed to neutralise low-altitude aerial threats at short ranges, the missile features an Imaging Infra-Red (IIR) seeker. Additionally, it has a miniaturised Reaction Control System (RCS) to increase mid-air manoeuvrability and integrated avionics. Economic Explosives Ltd has developed the 'Bhargavastra' counter-drone system, which can neutralise the growing threats of small incoming drones, including swarms[33].

During the ongoing operations "Op Sindoor", kinetic actions were taken by using Pechora and OSA-AK, Israeli SPYDER, Akash and Akash-NG (New Generation) long-range Barak-8 SAM systems and ZSU-23-4 Shilka, ZU-23-2 twin barrel 23mm anti-aircraft (AA) guns from Soviet times, and the L/70 Bofors 40mm AA platform defended high-value assets and strategic nodes from aircraft, drones, and ballistic/cruise missiles. These were all backed by Russia's Almaz-Antey S-400 'Triumf' self-propelled surface-to-air missile system. In an era of extended operations, there will be a limit on the number of own missiles being expended. Hence, there will be a need to have directed energy weapons to neutralise drones using laser or microwaves. The IACCS also demonstrated its Directed Energy Weapons (DEWs) capability, which involves high-powered lasers or microwaves, via

32 Raghav Patel, " Indian Army Explores Modernising Ageing ZSU-23-2 into Self Propelled Anti-Aircraft Weapons", February 02,2025, https://defence.in/threads/indian-army-explores-modernizing-aging-zsu-23-2-into-self-propelled-anti-aircraft-system-aiming-for-improved-counter-drone-capabilities.12660/,Accessed on February 3, 2025.

33 Defence.IN. January 22,2025, https://defence.in/threads/newly-tested-bhargavastra-detects-drones-at-6km-targets-at-2-5km-capable-of-firing-64-micro-missiles-to-counter-swarms.12465/Accessed on February 11, 2025.

a real-time network, detecting, tracking, and neutralising airborne threats like drones speedily. The indigenous DEW system, equipped with a 30-kW power weapon, could neutralise a swarm of drones.

Challenges

Growth in drone technologies and tactics has been at high-speed, and therefore, the challenges for the armed forces are:

(i) **Need for Integrated Air Defence System:** Ukrainian drones hit an oil pumping station and a missile arsenal in Russia's Tver region on January 28, 2025, located approximately 750 km inside the Russian territory from the Ukrainian border[34]. This highlighted the vulnerabilities in the Russian military air defences. The drones had highly automated capabilities and were partly piloted by an operator and partly by artificial intelligence, which enabled them to fly along a pre-planned route. Nations must develop an integrated air defence system to tackle threats from manned platforms, cruise missiles, and drones, even at depth.

(ii) **Integration in the Armed Forces**: In June 2024, Kyiv established a new branch of its military dedicated exclusively to drone warfare, and the Russian armed forces have also formed separate branches. This move reflects a pivot to maximise the use of unmanned systems on the front lines [35] by combined arms.

(iii) **Cyber Threats**: As LiDAR's signal processing capabilities advance, the sensor's supporting hardware utilises embedded processors that rely on embedded operating systems, such as Linux, and use Ethernet standards for data transmission. These are vulnerable to firmware backdoors or malicious code, which are difficult to detect. As a result, these sensor systems typically connect to the broader internet, significantly increasing their vulnerability to cyberattacks[36].

34 "Russian Missile Arsenal Hit By Ukrainian Drones", January 29, 2025, https://www.newsweek.com/russian-missile-arsenal-oil-facility-hit-ukrainian-drones-reports-2023200,Accessed on February 3, 2025.

35 ibid,https://www.eurasiantimes.com/drones-responsible-for-66-f-russian-equipment-losses/

36 Craig Singleton and RAdm Mark Montgomery, "Laser Focus: Countering China's LiDAR Threat", FDD, December 02,2024 ,https://www.fdd.org/analysis/2024/12/02/laser-focus-countering-chinas-lidar-threat-to-u-s-critical-infrastructure-and-military-systems/Accesed on February 04, 2025.

(iv) **Development of Indigenous AI Tools.** The use of AI in drones and counter-drone systems has raised a crucial issue of the reliability and fairness of algorithms. Human intentional or subconscious biases can infiltrate algorithms, shaping their results. Modern AI systems, built by OpenAI or Meta AI, rely on data-driven architecture. The nation should harness the local talent, resources and vision to establish a fair technological order by investing in distributed computing and grassroots innovation.

(v) **Indigenous Components.** Keeping in mind the supply chain disruptions, there is a need for the development of an indigenous industry that can manufacture components for all types of drones. Use of 3D printing facilitates manufacturing new drones on-site and on scale allows faster production of drones, faster technological upgrades and improvements in tactics.

Drones and International Humanitarian Law (IHL)

Drones are used to perform different functions in an armed conflict, including reconnaissance, surveillance and attacks. They are increasingly used in armed conflicts and counter-terrorism operations to undertake targeted killings. Drones as autonomous weapon systems[37] are not explicitly regulated by IHL treaties. IHL consists of several fundamental principles which states must consider before undertaking a strike in armed conflicts. These principles include military necessity, humanity, honour, distinction, precaution and proportionality. IHL requires all parties to an armed conflict to distinguish between civilians who are not participating in hostilities and combatants who are, and to always protect the property of civilians. The International Committee of the Red Cross (ICRC) thinks that neither civilians nor individual property may be attacked during times of armed conflict. IHL mandates that combatants follow the rules that protect civilians and their property. That is, any military attacks should not be directed at civilians, but rather at combatants. IHL maintains that any combatant who has ceased fighting and no longer participates in

37 An autonomous weapon system is defined as follows: Any weapon system with autonomy in its critical functions—that is, a weapon system that can select (search for, detect, identify, track or select) and attack (use force against, neutralize, damage or destroy) targets without human intervention. Neil Davison, A legal perspective: Autonomous weapon systems under international humanitarian law, Scientific and Policy Adviser Arms Unit, Legal Division, International Committee of the Red Cross, available at: https://www.icrc.org/sites/default/files/ document/file_list/autonomous_weapon_systems_ under_international_humanitarian_law.pdf.

armed conflicts must be spared and protected. Further, those people who are not participating in the armed conflict must be protected and treated with humanity without any discrimination. IHL also prohibits the use of weapons and any other means that are likely to result in excessive suffering to a combatant. Armed drones are generally considered to be a legitimate means of warfare, and they must be used following IHL.[38]

Conclusion

The rise of combat drones will challenge the role of combat aircraft for air superiority. The Ukraine war has shown that missiles and drones, in addition to fighter jets, are now pivotal to adequate air power. The role of manned platforms in contested airspace will be augmented, with AI-driven autonomous drones operated by manned aerial platforms as command-and-control centres. The role of legacy combat platforms, such as tanks, ships, and aircraft, will not cease; however, drones will augment their capabilities. The increased speed of new technologies and the integration of innovation will be a force multiplier in winning the conflict. Ukraine's defence ecosystem evolved in wartime conditions by turning commercial start-up innovation, which was faster than the conventional military-industrial complex.

The "Operation Spiderweb" has highlighted the vulnerability of the Air Defence system, where the threats to homeland security were demonstrated by smuggling FPV drones inside wooden containers and eventually being driven by trucks close to the bases. Op Sindoor has shown that a combined air defence system can effectively mitigate drone threats at an economical cost.

State and non-state actors will have access to this technology, which will call for revisiting military doctrines, investment priorities, and force structures. The current conflicts have been ongoing for prolonged durations across differing timelines. In building a nation's air power, the possibility of needing to engage in air operations across extended periods, possibly in a non-linear manner, needs to be included in the force structure. In

38 For more details see: Rebecca Mignot-Mahdavi, *Drones and International Law: A Techno-Legal Machinery*, Cambridge University Press, 2023; Stuart Casey-Maslen, et.al., *Drones and Other Unmanned Weapons Systems under International Law*, Leiden: Brill, 2018, pp. 267; Oren Gross, The New Way of War: Is There is Duty to Use Drones? *Florida Law Review*, Vol. 67, 2015, pp. 1-72; John Kaag and Sarah Kreps, *Drone Warfare*, Cambridge: Polity Press, 2014, pp. 152; Vivek Sehrawat, *Legal Status of Drones Under LOAC and International Law*, *Penn. St. J.L. & Int'l Aff*, Vol. 5(1), p. 164.

addition to the induction of UUVs, many seafaring countries are engaged in integrating carrier-based drones into their naval fleets. The complexity of technologies in lethal drones challenges traditional understandings of IHL. Commanders must minimise civilian harm due to the use of deadly drones in military operations.

'Counter drones' systems technology has advanced significantly, with various methods to detect, track, and neutralise hostile drones by using two methods: drone detection and, thereafter, their mitigation or interception. The growth of counter-drone techniques is challenging the rise of drones on the battlefield.

Chapter 7

Loitering Munitions and Its Implications Under IHL

-Yash Sinha

Introduction

The dawn of the 21st century has ushered in an unprecedented era of technological innovation, profoundly reshaping nearly every facet of human existence, including the grim realities of armed conflict. This has led to a radical transformation in the means and methods of warfare, driven by emerging capabilities and requirements. Central to this paradigm shift is the burgeoning field of autonomous warfare, with capabilities now being developed not only by traditional armed forces but also by agile private companies.

With the advent of Artificial Intelligence (AI) and machine learning, the development of Autonomous Weapons Systems (AWS) has significantly accelerated. The evolution has moved the development from traditional and rudimentary automated defence systems to highly sophisticated platforms capable of complex decision-making. They are not only capable in analysing a vast amount of data but also learning from their environment and experiences to make real-time decisions. The modern AWS encompass a wide range of systems, including unmanned aerial vehicles (UAVs), ground robots, naval drones, and the latest of all are the loitering munitions, each equipped with advanced sensors, AI algorithms, and communication networks that allow them to operate independently or collaboratively in various combat scenarios. Further, the operation of these modern systems vary in degrees of independence from human intervention. They have the potential to enhance operational efficiency, reduce human casualties, and revolutionise combat tactics.

Historically, war and warfare have been defined by human agency, decision-making, and direct participation. From the earliest conflict to the most complex modern operations, the human element—the soldier, the commander, the political leader—has been indispensable. The first properly modern loitering munition was introduced in 1988 by Israel Aerospace Industries (IAI) and was designed to attack hostile radar systems or mobile missile launchers, under the name "HARPY".[1]

Since then, the rise of autonomous systems has threatened to disrupt the long-standing paradigm. The ability of autonomous warfare capabilities refers to the ability of machines to perform tasks, from surveillance to targeting and engagement, with varying degrees of independence from human oversight. They are usually launched from the ground, after which they fly autonomously or can be steered manually as well. The drones use electro-optical systems to locate their targets and carry small warheads used to destroy radars, vehicles and more. Some countries have developed their variants of this technology, such as the Switchblade in the United States, Shahed in Iran and Harop in Israel, including India, which has developed its own loitering munitions, namely Nagastra-1[2] and FWD-LM01[3]; which offer a unique set of new capabilities compared to traditional alternatives such as missiles, rockets, mortars, etc. The development of these capabilities is spurred by several factors. Militaries seek to reduce risk to personnel, enhance precision, increase speed of response in contested environments, and overcome human limitations such as fatigue or emotional bias. Also, private companies, driven by innovation and profit, are increasingly entering the defence sector, leveraging their expertise in artificial intelligence, robotics, and data processing to develop sophisticated

1 Disarmament and International Security Committee, 'Measures to Regulate the Production, Stockpiling, and Usage of Loitering Munition' (Report, Model United Nations of Bucharest) <https://www.munob.ro/importantd/rr/RR_DISEC_Topic%202_MUNOB%202024.pdf> accessed 12 June 2025

2 'Indian Army receives supply of 480 indigenous loitering munitions' *Business Standard* (3 December 2024) https://www.business-standard.com/india-news/indian-army-receives-supply-of-480-indigenous-loitering-munitions-124120300091_1.html accessed 10 June 2025

3 'Meet FWD-LM01, the Indian drone that flies 100km, finds targets, and hits on its own' *The Economic Times* (20 June 2025) https://m.economictimes.com/news/defence/meet-fwd-lm01-the-indian-drone-that-flies-100km-finds-targets-and-hits-on-its-own/articleshow/121978030.cms accessed 10 June 2025

autonomous platforms. This dual-track development, by both state actors and commercial entities, accelerates the pace of innovation and complicates regulatory efforts.

The Operational Concept

The Kamikaze drones, or suicide drones, are autonomous or remotely piloted aerial weapons that carry a warhead and are intended to self-destruct upon impact with their target.[4] In the World War I-era Kettering Bug, was regarded to be one of the first drones which was designed to deliver an explosive charge by crashing into its targets, more like a rocket than the reconnaissance and strike aircraft that are associated with the word "*drone*" today.[5] Later, the United States military began using laser-guided bombs and cruise missiles during the 1970s, which exhibited autonomous aspects in their deployment, as their targets would be marked by an operator beforehand, and the bombs would independently follow the marked target until destruction.[6]

Though the first significant instance of developing and producing LMs lies with Israeli weapons manufacturers, who successfully launched and employed them in the 1980s.[7] The operation Mole Cricket 19 carried out by the Israeli Air Force (IAF) in Lebanon on the 9th of June 1982, led to the first time in history that a Soviet-made Surface-to-Air Missiles (SAM) network was defeated by an air force equipped with western technology.[8] The airstrike was successful, without taking any losses, due to the Israelian innovation of engaging unmanned drones to provide real-time targeting links to warplanes, giving the IAF an advantage against the Syrian Integrated Defence System.[9] However, the term "*Kamikaze*" came into existence from the World War II-era Japanese tactic of suicide missions,

4 Victor Growth, 'Kamikaze Drones: The Rise of Loitering Munitions in Modern Warfare' *Victor Growth* (12 May 2023) https://victorgrowth.com/kamikaze-drones-the-rise-of-loitering-munitions-in-modern-warfare/ accessed 10 June 2025.

5 Dan Gettinger and Arthur Michel, 'Countries with Loitering Munitions' (Drone Center, February 2022) https://dronecenter.bard.edu/files/2017/02/CSD-Loitering-Munitions.pdf accessed 29 June 2025

6 Disarmament and International Security Committee (n 1)

7 ibid

8 ibid

9 ibid

which is now repurposed for modern precision-guided systems that offer strategic advantages without sacrificing human pilots.[10]

Currently, the LMs are considered as a new generation of unmanned aerial vehicles that are designed to provide unprecedented levels of flexibility and precision in modern warfare. Unlike traditional UAVs, which were used for reconnaissance or surveillance. These UAVs are specifically designed to attack targets directly, making them a game-changer in modern warfare. With their ability to loiter in the air for extended periods and conduct autonomous missions, LMs are rapidly becoming a critical tool in the arsenal of modern militaries around the world. They are equipped with a range of advanced sensors, guidance systems, and explosive warheads that enable them to locate, track, and engage high-value targets with pinpoint accuracy. These systems are launched from a hidden safe position, with very low signature, fly to the target area, loiter above a target, locate and verify targets and strike precisely when the opportunity arises, even if the target appears for only an instant.

Further, these LMs are controlled by an operator who sees a real-time image of the target and its surrounding area, allowing the capacity to control the exact time, direction and angle of the attack on a static or moving target. This capability provides a significant contribution to the formal target identification and confirmation process. Also, if the operational situation changes at the last minute, the operator can abort the mission in mid-air, go back to loitering mode, assign a different target or re-engage the same target when conditions are more favourable, or even stop the mission completely. Hence, LMs provide small tactical units with independent fire support, with a "one-shot, one-target" accuracy. The spectrum of these advanced LMs ranges from "human-in-the-loop" systems, where a human operator maintains final control over critical decisions, to "human-on-the-loop" systems, which allow for greater autonomy but still permit human intervention, and ultimately to "human-out-of-the-loop" systems, which can execute missions independently once activated.

In addition, due to their characteristics, this emerging field of unmanned aircraft has blurred the line between drones and missiles.[11] As LMs fall somewhere between drones and missiles, they cannot be purely defined as

10 Growth (n 4)

11 Gettinger and Michel (n 5)

a missile or a drone separately.[12] When compared to traditional missiles, mortars, and rockets, LMs have the advantage of being fired from either land, sea, or air.[13] Furthermore, these weapons can be launched from man-portable systems, combat vehicles, and even rotary and fixed-wing aircraft, which are cost-efficient compared to anti-tank guided missiles (ATGMs).[14] Also, with the advanced technology of artificial intelligence (AI), some of these munitions are capable of returning to the launch positions if the target is not found, thus saving significant amounts of money.

Current Capabilities

Undoubtedly, the ongoing advancements in artificial intelligence (AI) and machine learning have significantly enhanced the capabilities of autonomous weapons systems (AWS). These advancements have allowed AWS to perform more complex tasks and operate effectively in dynamic environments. It has not only shifted the dynamics of warfare tactics, but also the strategy of how wars can be or should be waged. However, the potential implications of fully autonomous warfare capabilities are vast and complex. Strategically, these systems do promise to redefine the concept of deterrence, potentially enabling swift, decisive strikes without direct human risk, thereby lowering the political threshold for engaging in conflict. This introduces a new form of warfare, leading to a highly automated battlefield, where conflicts are fought at machine speeds, potentially reducing reaction times for human decision-makers and the risk of unintended escalations.

In terms of the integration of LMs with national defence systems, there has been a rapid proliferation over the past decades. Today, more than 20 States are producing and employing such systems, and the trend is expected to increase in the coming years.[15] It is due to the super abilities of these unmanned munitions that are particularly designed to identify, track, and engage beyond-visual range with an explosive warhead of varying weight. They are structured to be portable, easy to launch, and single-use, making them a cost-effective, safer, and more flexible alternative to

12 Centre for Air Power Studies, 'ALS-50: A Boon for the Indian Defence System' (CAPS In Focus, 27 June 2023) https://capsindia.org/als-50-a-boon-for-the-indian-defence-system/ accessed 5 June 2025

13 ibid

14 ibid

15 Gettinger and Michel (n 5)

expensive artillery and complex missile systems.[16] These advanced systems are also capable of conducting multiple types of missions (intelligence, surveillance, reconnaissance, precision strike, counter-battery, etc.) while loitering above a certain area for an extended period, allowing for greater decision-making options.[17] For instance, LMs such as the Israeli Harpy and Harop drones, the Russian Lancet-3, the Turkish Kargu-2, as well as the American Switchblades (300 and 600 series) are all equipped with GPS guidance, electro-optical and infrared sensors with image processing, allowing them (with varying degree) to autonomously identify and track objects.[18]

In addition, the use of LMs provides opportunities to enable an increased capacity to discriminate between combatants and non-combatants in armed conflict as compared to equivalent weapons such as mortars, rockets, and small missiles etc.[19] With the loiter capability of these systems, the operator can detect and track potential targets for extended periods of time before a strike. It enables improved precision compared to any other equivalent weapon. For example, the AeroVironment Switchblade creates a forward-facing blast that makes the detonation more targeted than a grenade, which creates a 360-degree blast.[20] Also, these LMs are steerable and much cheaper than guided missiles that provide a similar level of precision.[21] Further, various munition models also feature a "wave off" feature that allows operators to cancel an attack in mid-flight and ditch the aircraft harmlessly, which was not possible through traditional weapons systems.

16 Francesco Ancona, 'AI in Warfare: Loitering Munitions – Current Applications and Legal Challenges' *Mondo Internazionale* (26 February 2024) https://mondointernazionale.org/focus-allegati/ai-in-warfare-loitering-munitions-current-applications-and-legal-challenges accessed 15 June 2025

17 UVision Smart Loitering Systems, 'About Loitering Munitions' (2023) https://uvisionuav.com/loitering-munitions/ accessed 15 June 2025.

18 Ancona (n 16)

19 'Loitering Munition Review' *IMR - Indian Military Review* (19 May 2020) https://imrmedia.in/loitering-munition-review/ accessed 15 June 2025

20 ibid

21 ibid

India's Use of Loitering Munitions

For India, the integration of LMs into India's military arsenal marks a significant shift in its counter-terrorism strategy.[22] It is with the view that the use of precision LMs aligns with India's stated objective of conducting 'focused, measured, and non-escalatory' operations.[23] India as a state has been actively adaptive to this evolving technological landscape in its defence strategies, impelled by escalating geopolitical tension and persisting border challenges, particularly with its nuclear-armed neighbours. This strategic evolution signifies its departure from the conventional military approaches, shifting from the traditional air strike conducted by manned aircraft towards an era increasingly defined by unmanned systems, precision-guided munitions, loitering drones and hypersonic missiles.

India's strategic imperatives, driven by a complex regional security environment and a strong push for indigenous defence capabilities, have positioned LMs as critical force multipliers. India, in its recent operation Sindoor, showcased the operational utility of various LM types, highlighting their precision strike capabilities against high-value targets. The integration of AI into LMs fundamentally altered the operational dynamics, enabling greater autonomy in target acquisition and engagement, offering speed and efficiency.

In early May 2025, India launched its 'Operation Sindoor' and crossed a significant threshold in its military modernization, marking its first operational deployment of loitering munitions.[24] It occurred through a retaliatory strike against terror targets in Pakistan and Pakistan-Occupied Kashmir (PoK)—underscoring a shifting landscape in contemporary warfare. The operation was reportedly executed in response to the brutal terrorist attack in Pahalgam, which claimed the lives of 26 civilians, including 25 Indians and one Nepali national.[25] The Indian forces utilised a range of precision strike weapon systems, including loitering munitions.

22 Purtika Dua, 'What is Loitering Munition that India used against Pakistan in Operation Sindoor?' *The Hindu* (10 March 2025) https://www.thehindu.com/news/national/what-is-loitering-munition-that-india-used-against-pakistan-in-operation-sindoor/article67936166.ece accessed 21 June 2025

23 ibid

24 ibid

25 ibid

A series of strikes targeting nine terror camps linked to Jaish-e-Mohammed (JeM) and Lashkar-e-Taiba (LeT) were conducted by the Indian army.[26] These sites were located in Muridke, Muzaffarabad, Kotli, Bhimber, Narowal, Sialkot and Bahawalpur, which were selected based on credible intelligence inputs suggesting the presence of terrorist infrastructure.[27] These striking required certain time-sensitive targets without triggering full-scale retaliation, making the operation extremely complex.[28] The hits by India were done using precision strikes to avoid damage to the civilian population and infrastructure, aiming to hold the perpetrators accountable while avoiding direct attacks on Pakistani military facilities.[29] The strikes were conducted from Indian soil, with the stated aim of neutralizing key terrorist leadership and infrastructure, dismantling terror network operating across the line of control and inside Pakistani territory. Hence, the possible LMs speculated to be used in the operation were the HARPY & HAROP, Skystriker, Warmate (micro loitering munition), etc.

Interestingly, India's foray into loitering munitions was not merely through acquisition but with a testament to its burgeoning indigenous defence capabilities. As these LMs used in the operation were developed by a Bengaluru-based private company, which has a joint venture with an Israel-based military technology company.[30] The Israeli firm provided transfer of technology under the joint venture named 'AVision', which later led the Indian army to procure more than 100 of these drones under the brand PALM (Precision Attack Loitering Munition) Hero Systems.[31] These munitions are of fully autonomous Unmanned Aerial Vehicle Systems (UAVs) that can locate, acquire, and strike operator-designated targets

26 ibid

27 Meghna Pradhan, 'SILENT WINGS OVER VERMILION SKIES: Contextualising SEAD and Loitering Munitions in the 2025 India-Pakistan Conflict' (Issue Brief, Society for the Study of Peace and Conflict, 29 March 2024) https://www.sspconline.org/issue-brief/silent-wings-over-vermilion-skies-contextualising-sead-and-loitering-munitions-2025 accessed 25 June 2025

28 ibid

29 ibid

30 Hemanth C S, 'Operation Sindoor: Loitering munition used against terror bases developed in Bengaluru' *The Hindu* (1 June 2025) https://www.thehindu.com/news/national/operation-sindoor-loitering-munition-used-against-terror-bases-developed-in-bengaluru/article69550708.ece accessed 25 June 2025

31 ibid

with a warhead installed inside the fuselage, enabling high-precision performance.[32]

Other than that, the 'Nagastra-1' developed by Solar Industries' Economic Explosives Limited (EEL) stands as a prime example of self-reliance; the first indigenous advanced loitering munition.[33] This man-portable, fixed-wing electric UAV has been designed for precision strikes, boasting GPS-enabled accuracy within two meters and capable of carrying a 1 kg high-explosive warhead. Notably, it features a unique parachute recovery mechanism that allows operators to abort the mission mid-flight and potentially reuse the munition. In addition, it features both remote control and autonomous functionality, with ranges of 15 km and 30 km, respectively.[34] It signals towards varying degrees of human intervention.

Hence, these advanced systems of warfare offer a significant strategic advantage, including reduced risk to human personnel, enhanced precision, extended surveillance capabilities, greater operational flexibility in dynamic environments and cost efficiency. This integration of advanced drone technology as a part of India's broader defence modernisation drive aims to leverage technological superiority in asymmetric warfare and counter-insurgency operations.

Application of International Humanitarian Law

International Humanitarian Law (IHL) is a branch of international law which limits the use of violence in armed conflicts.[35] The basic principle of IHL is that in any armed conflict, the right of the parties to conflict to choose methods and means of warfare is not unlimited.[36] Although certain international instruments specifically ban or regulate several inherently problematic weapons, such as expanding bullets, poisonous gases, antipersonnel landmines, biological and chemical weapons. However, currently, there is no foundational regime for the use of these advanced AI-driven Munitions.

32 ibid

33 Pradhan (n 27)

34 ibid

35 U.C. Jha, Killer Robots: Lethal Autonomous Weapon Systems Legal, Ethical and Moral Challenges (VIJ Books India Pty Ltd 2016) 69

36 ibid

These munitions represent a sophisticated class of precision-guided weapons. Categorically, they are autonomous missiles that can stay airborne for some time, identify a target, and then attack with pinpoint accuracy.[37] Their unique characteristics, which blend aspects of unmanned aerial vehicles (UAVs) and traditional missiles, offer distinct tactical advantages. However, the profound implications of LMs used under International Humanitarian Law (IHL), particularly concerning with their evolving autonomy of the weapon, represent a pressing issue which requires future regulation.

Ethically, the delegation of lethal decision-making to machines raises profound concerns. According to Paul Scharre, LMs are a type of fully autonomous weapon that can search for, decide to engage, and engage targets on their own in such a way that no human can intervene.[38] This is directly contrasted with semi-autonomous homing missiles, which are human-directed and then have a short flight time in which to find a target.[39] Subsequently, LMs are akin to airborne mines, like landmines or naval mines; they share their explosive nature and sensor-based detection capabilities. However, unlike traditional mines that can persist for long durations indefinitely, these advanced munitions are constrained by flight time, though some models can be refuelled and redeployed.[40] Therefore, it raises questions regarding the ability of an algorithm to truly grasp the nuances of proportionality and distinction in the chaotic fog of war or can these models weigh the value of human life against military necessity. Though the critics argue that removing human judgment from the loop dehumanizes warfare, erodes moral responsibility, and causes devastating consequences.

Consequently, these ethical dilemmas and risks arise from moral concerns in situations of LMs capable of making attack decisions without human intervention ("man out of the loop"), particularly concerning the decision to attack and potentially kill human beings. Also, attributing responsibility for war crimes becomes problematic with AI systems due to their distributed development, limited predictability, and the absence of human

37 Kelsey Atherton, 'Loitering Munitions Preview the Autonomous Future of Warfare' (Brookings, 4 August 2021) https://www.brookings.edu/articles/loitering-munitions-preview-the-autonomous-future-of-warfare/ accessed 1 July 2025.

38 Paul Scharre, Army of None: Autonomous Weapons and the Future of War (WW Norton & Co 2018)

39 Atherton (n 37)

40 ibid

intentionality in their autonomous actions. Experts note that a machine lacks the concepts of justice or mercy, and an algorithm cannot be put on trial for war crimes. In addition, these AI-driven systems operate at machine speeds and have the potential to accelerate the use of force beyond human control. It could lead to conflicts spiralling into unpredictable "flash war" scenarios that are particularly dangerous for nuclear-armed states.

Hence, a fundamental tension exists between the pursuit of efficiency and speed in warfare and the imperative for human control and accountability. As these advanced AI-integrated LMs promise increased speed, efficiency, and the ability to minimize soldier casualties. Concern related to reduced human control, diluted responsibility, and the inability to fully understand or predict system behaviour, creates a fundamental trade-off, potentially leading to unintended consequences that violate IHL provisions. Though in the absence of specific regulations directly addressing such advanced weaponry, the Martens Clause emerges as a crucial interpretive tool, ensuring that the spirit of humanity and the dictates of public conscience continue to guide armed conflict. The clause states:

> Until a more complete code of laws of war has been issued, the High Contracting Parties deem it expedient to declare that, in cases not covered by them, the inhabitants and the belligerents remain under the protection and the rule of the principles of the law of nations, as they result from the usages established among civilized peoples, from the laws of humanity, and from the dictates of the public conscience.[41]

Hence, the Clause serves a powerful reminder that even in the absence of an explicit treaty provision, conduct in armed conflict is not unregulated. It emphasizes on the interconnectedness of the sources of law, i.e., the usages established among civilized peoples (customary international law), the laws of humanity, and the dictates of the public conscience.[42] The provision strictly protects civilians and combatants by the principle of humanity and the dictates of public conscience.[43] Therefore, in application to LMs, the Clause becomes particularly relevant.

41 Preamble to Hague Convention (II) Respecting the Laws and Customs of War on Land, 29 July 1899

42 Jeffrey Kahn, Protection and Empire: The Martens Clause, State Sovereignty, and Individual Rights, 56 Va. J. Int'l L. 1 (2016)

43 Protocol Additional to the Geneva Conventions of 12 August 1949, and Relating to the Protection of Victims of International Armed Conflicts (AP I), 8 June 1977, Preamble.

However, still the IHL has served as the legal framework governing the conduct of armed conflict, aiming to minimize human suffering by balancing military necessity with humanitarian protection. Its core principles are fundamental in ensuring humane conduct in hostilities. All weapons, regardless of their technological sophistication, must be used in strict adherence to these IHL principles.

Distinction

It is a cornerstone principle requiring parties to a conflict to always distinguish between civilians and combatants, and between civilian objects and military objectives.[44] The humanitarian law mandates that parties to a conflict shall prohibit indiscriminate attacks, which strike military objectives and civilians or civilian objects without distinction. The principle of distinction also necessitates that defenders must distinguish themselves from civilians and refrain from placing military personnel or material near civilian objects.[45]

However, the challenge with LMs, especially those with advanced autonomous targeting, lies in their ability to reliably make these complex distinctions in fluid combat environments. Discriminating between combatants and non-combatants or other persons, including civilian workers, aircrew members, war correspondents, military doctors, religious personnel, civilian drivers, porters, as well as combatants who are unwilling to fight or are wounded or sick, will likely be present at the place of conflict. While precision targeting can reduce collateral damage, the concern remains whether algorithms can possess the nuanced judgment required to differentiate legitimate military targets from protected persons or objects, particularly when dealing with complex behaviours or in ambiguous situations. At present, there is no evidence suggesting that a computer has the independent capability to operate on the principle of distinction similar to that of a human soldier.[46]

44 Protocol Additional to the Geneva Conventions of 12 August 1949, and Relating to the Protection of Victims of International Armed Conflicts (AP I), 8 June 1977, art 48; art 51(2); Customary IHL Rule 1, 7) International Committee of the Red Cross (ICRC), Customary International Humanitarian Law, Volume I: Rules (Cambridge University Press 2005) Rule 1; Rule 7.

45 Jha (n35) 71

46 ibid

Proportionality

The principle of proportionality is related to the principle of distinction.[47] This principle prohibits attacks that may be expected to cause incidental loss of civilian life, injury to civilians, or damage to civilian objects, which would be excessive in relation to the concrete and direct military advantage anticipated.[48] It is considered part of customary international law, which binds all states.[49] To make the principle of proportionality more effective, Article 57 of AP I obliges belligerents to take all feasible precautions and constant care to implement proportionality and distinction.[50] For instance, if damage to civilian objects or civilian death or injury is anticipated before targeting a military object, then an assessment must be undertaken in which the anticipated military advantage to be gained is weighed against the anticipated "collateral" damage to protected civilians or civilian objects.[51]

Although LMs, due to their precision, theoretically offer the potential to minimize collateral damages. However, if these systems operate with significant autonomy in densely populated areas, or if their sensors and algorithms are not rigorously tested and validated, there is a risk of disproportionate civilian harm.

Precautions in Attack

IHL, through its provisions, requires that all feasible precautions should be taken by the parties to the conflict to avoid or minimize incidental civilian harm.[52] This includes verifying targets, choosing methods of attack that

---

47 Ibid, 73

48 Protocol Additional to the Geneva Conventions of 12 August 1949, and Relating to the Protection of Victims of International Armed Conflicts (AP I), 8 June 1977, art 51(5)(b); International Committee of the Red Cross (ICRC), Customary International Humanitarian Law, Volume I: Rules (Cambridge University Press 2005) Rule 14.

49 Rule 14 of the ICRC study on customary law provides: "Launching an attack which may be expected to cause incidental loss of civilian life, injury to civilians, damage to civilian objects, or a combination thereof, which would be excessive in relation to the concrete and direct military advantage anticipated, is prohibited." Jean-Marie Henckaerts and Louise Doswald-Beck, 2005, Customary International Humanitarian Law, Cambridge University Press, p. 46.

50 Jha (n35) 73

51 ibid

52 Protocol Additional to the Geneva Conventions of 12 August 1949, and Relating to the Protection of Victims of International Armed Conflicts (AP I), 8 June 1977, art 57; International Committee of the Red Cross (ICRC), Customary International

minimize civilian damage to life and property. The parties to the conflict are under an obligation to spare the civilian population and civilian objects from the effects of armed conflict.[53] Further, it is expected by parties to the conflict to cancel or suspend any attack if it becomes unlawful as per IHL norms. As those who plan or decide upon an attack must do everything feasible to verify that the objectives to be attacked are military objectives and are not under any form of protection.[54] Furthermore, what is 'feasible' shall depend upon the resources and technology available to a commander who is planning an attack.[55]

In case of LMs, since the "loitering" capability of these munitions allows for extended surveillance, potentially enabling better target verification, the degree of "meaningful human control" becomes paramount. If human operators cannot intervene or abort a mission effectively, particularly in autonomous modes, the ability to take all feasible precautions can be severely compromised. Also, this obligation of taking 'feasible precautions' can be justly expected from a military commander in conventional warfare.[56] However, in an armed conflict where all these advanced weapons are deployed, it would be nearly impossible for such systems to take all 'feasible precautions'.[57] While it may be possible for a commander to consider updated information available from the battlefield, a machine cannot be programmed with every futuristic scenario of an armed conflict[58].

In addition, due to the large-scale generalized utilization of LMs, the accountability and responsibility have become a profound IHL concern. The provisions of IHL typically place responsibility for violations on human commanders and operators. However, the questions are raised in the case of a fully autonomous loitering munition making a targeting error, resulting in grave consequences. Time and again, the international community has emphasized the need for "meaningful human control" to ensure human agency and judgment remain central to life-and-death

Humanitarian Law, Volume I: Rules (Cambridge University Press 2005) Rule 15; Rule 16.

53 Jha (n35) 75

54 ibid

55 ibid

56 ibid

57 ibid

58 ibid

decisions, thereby preserving a clear chain of accountability even when no explicit regulation regarding LMs has been developed.

Conclusion

It is proven that technology continues to advance, and the future of AWS holds both promise and uncertainty. India's first use of LMs has established a significant technological advancement and a strategic shift to its military capabilities. The 2025 Indo-Pakistan conflict has marked a historical moment for modern warfare, as it saw possibly the first 'drone' war between two nuclear-armed nations.[59] Beyond India's use of drones for Operation Sindoor, Pakistan also unleashed 'Bunyaan al-Marsoos', wherein over 500 low-cost drones (primarily Chinese commercial-grade drones and Turkish YIHA and Asisguard Songar systems) were launched at 36 military and strategic Indian sites.[60] Clearly, these exchanges indicate that unmanned, AI-enabled platforms are increasingly dominating asymmetrical engagements, offering persistent loitering and rapid target acquisition while minimising risk to human pilots.[61]

However, while offering undeniable tactical benefits, these developments have also underscored the urgent need to balance technological innovation with unwavering adherence to International Humanitarian Law (IHL). Undoubtedly, these nascent capabilities of transformed warfare of the 21st century possess the potential to fundamentally alter the nature and course of conflicts, marking a pivotal moment in human history. While promising enhanced efficiency and reduced risk to human combatants, these advancements carry profound strategic, ethical, and legal implications. The core principles of distinction, proportionality, and precautions in attack, alongside the overarching imperative of meaningful human control and accountability, remain at the forefront of the design, development, and deployment of these systems. The imperative is not to halt technological progress, but to guide its trajectory responsibly.

Hence, the current era necessitates urgent national and international dialogues, development of robust legal frameworks, a commitment to ensure meaningful human control remains central to any lethal decision-

59 Pradhan (n 27)

60 Rajat Pandit, 'Operation Sindoor: Turkish drones to Chinese missiles, India beat them all' (Times of India, 13 May 2025) https://timesofindia.indiatimes.com/india/turkish-drones-to-chinese-missiles-india-beat-them-all-pakistan/articleshow/121121289.cms accessed 1 July 2025.

61 Pradhan (n 27)

making in armed conflict, preserving humanity's core values in an increasingly automated world. These profound ethical reflections shall be indispensable to ensure that these powerful tools serve legitimate security needs without undermining the fundamental principles of humanity and the rule of law in armed conflict. Therefore, establishing a notion of balancing innovation with responsibility.

Chapter 8

Use of Nuclear Weapons in Armed Conflict: Legal and Humanitarian Dimensions

-U C Jha and Kishore Kumar Khera

Introduction

Why now? Nuclear weapons have been in existence for eight decades and have not been used since 1945. Why should these be discussed now?

Since the sole use of atomic bombs in 1945, proliferation has continued despite efforts to prevent it. Nine nations currently possess nuclear weapons—the United States, Russia, France, China, the United Kingdom, India, Pakistan, Israel, and North Korea—while Iran pursues its nuclear capability[1]. 2025 marks a pivotal moment in the history of nuclear weapons. In the first half of this year, five of these nuclear-armed states committed acts of war - Russia, India, Pakistan, Israel and the United States. This has never happened before. Israel launched "Operation Rising Lion" on June 13, targeting over 100 Iranian military and nuclear sites and reportedly killing multiple nuclear scientists and senior security officials[2]. On June 22, the United States joined the campaign, deploying B2 bombers and submarine-launched missiles against the Fordow, Natanz, and Isfahan

1 Strike Set Back Iran's Nuclear Program by Only a Few Months, U.S. Report Says, The New york Times, Jun 24, 2025 available at https://www.nytimes.com/2025/06/24/us/politics/iran-nuclear-sites.html

2 Operation Rising Lion, The Times of India, Jun 14, 2025 available at https://timesofindia.indiatimes.com/world/middle-east/operation-rising-lion-200-jets-hit-100-targets-how-israel-carried-out-covert-strikes-deep-inside-iran/articleshow/121826390.cms

nuclear facilities[3]. While U.S. authorities initially claimed destruction of the sites, international assessments later determined that Iran's nuclear capabilities were only delayed by one to two months. At the same time, North Korean forces[4] reportedly engaged alongside Russian troops in the Ukraine conflict, extending nuclear-armed states involvement into another theatre of war.

These developments shatter decades of nuclear restraint. Nuclear weapons have always rested at the intersection of immense destructive power and human frailty—ego, national prestige, and psychological pressures. With more than half of nuclear-armed states now militarily engaged, the risk of miscalculation driven by wounded pride, domestic pressure, or a leader's reputation has become dangerously real—potentially triggering catastrophic escalation on a global scale.

The events of early 2025 demand urgent legal, strategic, and humanitarian scrutiny. They challenge core international frameworks, from the UN Charter to the Nuclear Non-Proliferation Treaty and International Humanitarian Law. They also undermine the nuclear taboo that has helped prevent nuclear conflict for nearly eighty years. These fissures in our safeguards must now be addressed to avert a broader descent into atomic confrontation.

History of Nuclear Weapons: Mushrooms Over Japan

In August 1945, the United States dropped two atomic bombs—"Little Boy" on Hiroshima and "Fat Man" on Nagasaki—ushering in a profoundly disturbing era in warfare. The detonations obliterated entire urban areas—roughly 13 km^2 in Hiroshima and similarly devastating in Nagasaki—and killed approximately 140,000 and 70,000 people respectively by year's end, with total fatalities likely exceeding 210,000 when accounting for radiation-related illnesses[5]. Beyond immediate destruction, these bombings inflicted enduring humanitarian, legal, and environmental wounds, reshaping national trauma and driving developments in international law.

---

3 Early US intel assessment suggests strikes on Iran did not destroy nuclear sites, sources say, CNN, Jun 25, 2025 available at https://edition.cnn.com/2025/06/24/politics/intel-assessment-us-strikes-iran-nuclear-sites

4 N Korea confirms it sent troops to fight for Russia in Ukraine war, BBC, 28 April 2025 available on https://www.bbc.com/news/articles/ckg25wxvpy2o

5 Michael J Yavenditti, The American People and the Use of Atomic Bombs On Japan: The 1940s, The Historian, Taylor and Francis, 1974, Volume 34 pp. 224-247.

Survivors suffered instantaneous injuries—thermal burns, fractures, blast trauma—compounded by acute and chronic radiation sickness manifesting as haemorrhage, weakened immunity, and deep psychological distress. The scarcity of medical care exacerbated suffering: in Hiroshima, 90 per cent of doctors had been killed or incapacitated, leaving many without even basic treatment.

The ecological impact was catastrophic. Within a radius of 1 to 1.5 kilometres, nearly all trees were incinerated, wildlife decimated, and soil and water contaminated with radioactive isotopes like caesium and plutonium. Fallout produced "black rain" that carried radioactive particles into surrounding regions. Local ecosystems—fish stocks, forests—suffered long-term decline; contamination persisted, affecting agriculture and drinking water.

Infrastructure collapse was near total: approximately 92 per cent of buildings in Hiroshima and about 63 per cent in Nagasaki were destroyed. Across Japan, 2.2 million homes were lost and nine million people were displaced. National wealth plummeted by around 40 per cent, with industrial output reduced to about 6.6 per cent of pre-war levels. The resulting loss of housing, shelter, services, and employment triggered widespread poverty, homelessness, food shortages, and resource scarcity.

Survivors—the *hibakusha*—endured persistent discrimination and psychological trauma. Many faced prejudice in marriage and employment due to fears of radiation effects. Epidemiological studies conducted over decades revealed significantly elevated rates of leukaemia, various cancers, cataracts, and reproductive harm among *hibakusha*, confirming the profound long-term health consequences of the bombings—even as misconceptions around genetic inheritance fuelled discrimination.

The legacy of the atomic bombings is both a stark reminder of nuclear devastation and a testament to resilience. The enduring suffering of *hibakusha*, the environmental scars, and policy responses remain central to ongoing debates about nuclear weapons, humanitarian impact, and international justice.

Outcomes and Humanitarian Impacts of Nuclear Weapons

Immediate Humanitarian Catastrophe

The detonation of a nuclear weapon instantaneously produces a devastating blast wave and fireball, obliterating buildings and generating lethal thermal radiation. Tens to hundreds of thousands of civilians would be killed on the spot, while countless others would suffer fatal burn and blast injuries, acute radiation sickness, and internal trauma—far beyond the capacity of any healthcare system to manage.

Insufficient Humanitarian Capacity

The International Committee of the Red Cross (ICRC) and Red Crescent emphasise that no national or international humanitarian response could cope with the scale of casualties, infrastructure collapse, or radiation harm following even a single city-sized nuclear strike. Indeed, they caution that the catastrophic humanitarian consequences would be "beyond the capacity of any humanitarian organisation to address effectively".

Long-Term Health Effects

Survivors of nuclear detonations (*hibakusha*) endure persistent health challenges, including Radiation-induced cancers (e.g., leukaemia, thyroid), other illnesses such as cataracts and chronic organ damage, elevated risk of congenital defects and inter-generational genetic damage in descendants. Statistical evidence from Hiroshima and Nagasaki shows a significant rise in cancer rates and lifelong health complications among exposed populations.

Psychological and Social Trauma

Nuclear devastation leaves deep psychological scars—post-traumatic stress, depression, anxiety, and survivor stigma persist for years. Social cohesion frays as survivors face ostracism and long-term mental health burdens.

Environmental Destruction & Biodiversity Loss

Radioactive fallout contaminates land, air, and water, poisoning ecosystems and human food sources. Plants and animals perish in the blast zone, while residual radiation disrupts habitats, genetic integrity, and biodiversity. The ICRC notes that such environmental collapse may last generations—imperilling the very basis of agriculture and human survival.

Climatic Catastrophe: Nuclear Winter & Famine

Smoke and soot from widespread firestorms could enter the stratosphere, blocking sunlight. Even a limited nuclear exchange could trigger a "nuclear winter," causing drastic temperature drops, reduced sunlight, and global crop failure—placing billions at risk of starvation. Studies project that millions could die from hunger and disease in the aftermath of such climatic disruption.

Economic Collapse & Infrastructure Breakdown

Economic systems would crumble due to infrastructure loss, market collapse, and post-strike disorder. Reconstruction would require unprecedented resources—far exceeding current capabilities. Essential services (energy, water, healthcare) would become unavailable, further compounding mortality and societal breakdown.

Transboundary and Global Impacts

Radiation, climate effects, and contamination transcend borders, affecting non-combatant nations and triggering global insecurity. No community, even those far from the blast, would remain insulated from cascading effects on the environment and food security.

Ongoing Legal, Ethical, and Security Debates

Are nuclear weapons ever lawful? Can they adhere to proportionality and discrimination? Japanese precedents and experience provide critical reference points for evolving international humanitarian law. Meanwhile, environmental justice, intergenerational harm, and survivor rights animate calls for reparations, compensation, and legal accountability—evident in domestic rulings like the "Overseas *Hibakusha*" case confirming loss-of-benefit claims.

Nuclear Doctrines as They Seem

The doctrines of nuclear-armed states diverge sharply—from strictly defensive NFU (No First Use) stances to assertive first-use postures and doctrinal ambiguity. These variations significantly influence nuclear stability, escalation dynamics, and crisis management. Knowledge of these doctrines is crucial for understanding strategic behaviour and shaping arms-control initiatives in today's fraught geopolitical climate.

United States[6]

The US follows a "flexible response" doctrine, integrating nuclear weapons as part of a range of strategic options—from conventional force to strategic retaliation—and extending deterrence to its allies. The 2022 Nuclear Posture Review highlights that nuclear weapons would only be used in "extreme circumstances" to defend vital national interests while continuing arms-control efforts.

Russia[7]

Russia's 2024 Nuclear Doctrine notably lowers the threshold for nuclear use. It permits nuclear retaliation not only against nuclear attacks but also against large-scale conventional attacks—especially those involving allied support or threats to critical infrastructure. This is often described as escalation dominance, enabling early nuclear use to offset conventional inferiority.

China[8]

China maintains a No First Use (NFU) policy and a minimalist deterrent posture. It pledges never to initiate nuclear attacks and vows to use nuclear weapons only defensively and in retaliation. Its arsenal is kept at a size deemed sufficient to ensure second-strike viability.

France [9]

France employs a strategy of "deliberate ambiguity" signalling that its nuclear forces serve to protect vital national interests (including EU security) while maintaining strategic autonomy. It keeps a relatively small stockpile and is modernising its submarine-launched and air-launched systems.

---

6 2022 Nuclear Posture Review Fact Sheet, U.S. NUCLEAR DETERRENCE STRATEGY AND POLICY available on https://www.defense.gov/Portals/1/Spotlight/2022/NDS/NUCLEAR%20STRATEGY%20AND%20POLICY%20-%20NPR%20Factsheet.pdf

7 Fundamentals of State Policy of the Russian Federation on Nuclear Deterrence, Dec 3, 2024 available on https://www.mid.ru/en/foreign_policy/international_safety/1434131

8 Xia Liping , Impacts of China's Nuclear Doctrine on International Nuclear Disarmament, The Nuclear threat Initiative, 2021/09, available at https://www.nti.org/wp-content/uploads/2021/09/Xia_Liping.pdf

9 French Nuclear Policy, International Centre for Defence and Security, Jan 19, 2023 available at https://icds.ee/en/french-nuclear-policy/

United Kingdom [10]

Like France, the UK adopts strategic ambiguity, retaining ambiguity about whether it would use nuclear weapons first. Its Continuous At-Sea Deterrent (CASD) guarantees at least one submarine at sea at all times. The UK is currently upgrading its deterrent capability with Dreadnought-class submarines while retaining credibility within NATO's extended deterrence framework.

India [11]

India's official doctrine, outlined in 2003, emphasises No First Use, Credible Minimum Deterrence, and Massive Retaliation, including in response to nuclear, chemical, or biological attacks. Its nuclear command authority is civilian-led via the Prime Minister.

Pakistan [12]

Pakistan eschews NFU entirely, instead adopting a posture of strategic ambiguity and full-spectrum deterrence—from tactical to strategic weapons—designed to compensate for conventional imbalance with India. It signals possible first use in response to existential or large-scale conventional attacks.

Israel [13]

Israel maintains a long-standing policy of nuclear ambiguity, neither confirming nor denying its arsenal. Inferred doctrine emphasises deterrence against existential threats, flexibility (including "Samson Option" retaliation), and conditional first use if its existence is imperilled.

10 The UK's Nuclear Deterrent, HM Governement available at https://assets.publishing.service.gov.uk/media/61eea6848fa8f505893f1e03/UK_Nuclear_Deterrence_Policy_Booklet.pdf

11 Cabinet Committee on Securty Reviews Progress in Operationalising India's Nuclear doctrine, PIB, available at https://archive.pib.gov.in/release02/lyr2003/rjan2003/04012003/r040120033.html

12 Sitara Noor, Pakistan's Evolving Nuclear Doctrine, Arms Control Association, 2023/10 available at https://www.armscontrol.org/act/2023-10/features/pakistans-evolving-nuclear-doctrine

13 Arvind Dilawar, The Samson Option: Israel's Plan to Nuke Its Opponents, The Progressive Magazine, Jun 24, 2024, available at https://progressive.org/latest/the-samson-option-israels-plan-to-nuke-its-opponents-dilawar-20240624/

North Korea [14]

North Korea's 2022 law allows nuclear first use pre-emptively or in response to perceived external aggression. Its threats signal readiness to use nuclear weapons to protect the regime and deter adversaries, reflecting an overtly aggressive nuclear posture

Is Nuclear War a Possibility?

Nuclear weapon use is conditioned by a complex interplay of strategic logic and political psychology. The most immediate triggers include existential crises, critical conventional defeats, or defensive moves against perceived nuclear threats. However, accidental launches, miscommunications, or norm erosion pose equally grave risks. The international community continues to rely on doctrines of deterrence, strategic stability, and arms control, but these safeguards must account for emergent risks—such as brinkmanship, AI-driven decision systems, and alliance entanglements—to prevent catastrophic nuclear use. The use of nuclear weapons can be triggered by a range of factors—strategic, political, technological, or accidental.

Escalation from Conventional to Nuclear Warfare[15]

When a conventional conflict reaches a critical juncture, nuclear-armed states may use nuclear weapons to regain the upper hand or to signal resolve. Escalatory dynamics—as described in the *stability-instability paradox*—may lead to limited nuclear use to prevent defeat in conventional war, a concept known as "escalation dominance". Thereby halting conventional combat and compelling adversaries to back down. This doctrine has been explicitly incorporated into Russia's revised nuclear strategy, which permits nuclear retaliation even in response to non-nuclear attacks threatening its sovereignty or key infrastructure. Notably, Moscow's latest doctrine states that:

"Such nuclear deterrence is aimed at safeguarding the sovereignty and territorial integrity… in case of a military conflict, preventing an escalation

14 Understanding the North Korean Nuclear Issue, Ministry of Foreign Affair, Republic of Korea available at https://www.mofa.go.kr/eng/wpge/m_5474/contents.do

15 Jamie Kwong, Anna Bartoux, and James M. Acton, Forecasting Nuclear Escalation Risks: Cloudy With a Chance of Fallout, Carnegie Endowment for International Peace, 2025, pp 26-30.

of hostilities and stopping them on conditions acceptable for the Russian Federation."

This strategy—sometimes referred to as "escalate to de-escalate"—is seen as a high-risk gambit, since it rests on the assumption that nuclear coercion can successfully temper hostile intent without triggering broader conflict.

Pre-emptive or Preventive Strikes [16]

Leaders may resort to strikes first if they believe adversaries are on the verge of launching a nuclear attack or are rapidly developing a nuclear capability. Preventive strikes aim to preclude emerging threats, especially from nascent nuclear programs. Pre-emptive nuclear strikes may occur amid credible intelligence of an imminent attack—though this is a highly risky and rare calculus. Such actions, though rare, are particularly dangerous in a crisis driven by missile accuracy or intelligence suggesting an impending attack.

Regime Survival ("Existential" Threat Perceptions) [17]

Nuclear weapons are sometimes retained for their ultimate defensive value. Several doctrines, including the U.S., Russia, Pakistan and North Korea, reference use in "extreme circumstances of self-defence," particularly to protect the state's existence. In Russia's case, even a significant conventional attack, backed by nuclear powers, may be construed as existential, justifying nuclear use.

Threat Display and "Nuclear Blackmail" [18]

The mere threat of nuclear use can serve coercive objectives- historically termed nuclear blackmail, this involves threats intended to deter adversaries or compel political action. Such threats include North Korea and, at times, Pakistan in its rhetorical escalation toward India. States may drive conflicts toward the nuclear threshold to gain bargaining leverage—a

16 Karl P Mueller et al, Striking First: Pre-emptive and Preventive Attacks, Rand Corporation, 2006, pp 1-18.

17 Laing, Jessica, The use of nuclear weapons under the doctrine of self-defence, 2019, open UCT available at https://open.uct.ac.za/items/ce86db97-1a4c-43b5-9d35-0c69e60d504a

18 Todd S. Sechser and Matthew Fuhrmann, Crisis Bargaining and Nuclear Blackmail, International Organization , Volume 67 , Issue 1 , Cambridge University Press January 2013 , pp. 173 - 195

practice known as brinkmanship. Thomas Schelling famously described nuclear brinkmanship as "manipulating the shared risk of war," where risk itself is a communicative tool. However, this tactic is fraught with peril: miscalculation or misinterpretation can rapidly spiral out of control.

Accidents, Unauthorised Launches, or Miscalculation [19]

Technological failures and human error pose serious risks. The possibility of accidental nuclear war stems from system malfunctions, false alarms, or technical glitches. Unauthorised or misinformed launches, due to rogue actors or poor intelligence, present a credible risk. Perhaps the most unpredictable triggers are accidents, false alarms, or erroneous interpretations of opposing actions such as The 1995 Black Brant rocket launch that triggered a Russian nuclear alert. In 1983, Soviet officer Stanislav Petrov correctly identified a false alarm and prevented retaliatory nuclear launch. High-alert nuclear postures and ambiguous weapon systems (e.g., dual-capable missiles or AI in command-and-control) elevate the risk of miscalculation or unintended escalation.

Breakdowns in Political Restraints and Norms

Even robust deterrents can falter under domestic political pressures. Nuclear use scenarios often assume purely technical logic, but real-world decisions involve psychological, reputational, and political dimensions; once the "nuclear taboo" is eroded, nuclear use becomes more conceivable. Leaders facing grave domestic crises or perceived humiliation—especially under time pressure—may cross rational thresholds.

The triggers for nuclear weapon deployment range from deliberate strategic calculations to unforeseeable technological and cognitive errors. Human misjudgment—amplified by AI or rapid-launch systems—alongside crisis instability and aggressive doctrines, creates a perilous environment. Preventing nuclear use demands not only treaties and deterrence but robust safeguards, transparency, and control mechanisms in nuclear command-and-control architectures.

Legacy and Contemporary Legal Discourse

The Hiroshima and Nagasaki bombings left indelible marks on international discourse:

19 Seth D. Baum et al, A Model For The Probability Of Nuclear War ,Global Catastrophic Risk Institute Working Paper 18-1 8 March 2018 pp 27-32.

- Norm-building: The bombings prompted the emergence of a strong moral and legal taboo against nuclear weapon use.
- Treaty developments: The 2017 Treaty on the Prohibition of Nuclear Weapons explicitly references the humanitarian suffering of *hibakusha* and categorically prohibits nuclear weapons on moral, legal, and humanitarian grounds
- Policy frameworks: Red Cross leadership and humanitarian advocacy (e.g., the ICRC's 2011 resolution) have supported disarmament efforts grounded in human rights and dignity.

Illegality Under International Law?

Japanese courts examined the bombings soon after WWII. In Ryuichi Shimoda v. The State (1963),[20] plaintiffs contended that atomic bombings violated international law's principles of proportionality and distinction. A watershed moment arrived with the decision by the Tokyo District Court on December 7, 1963. The Court concluded *obiter dicta* that the atomic bombings contravened existing international law—specifically, the Hague Conventions of 1907 and the non-binding 1922–23 Hague Rules on Air Warfare—because they constituted indiscriminate attacks on undefended urban populations. The Court held:

- The bombings violated customary law prohibiting "blind aerial bombardment" of civilian areas;
- They breached the prohibition of inflicting "unnecessary suffering";
- However, plaintiffs (individual survivors) could not obtain redress due to Japan's treaty waiver of claims under the 1951 San Francisco Treaty.

This ruling marked a rare judicial determination acknowledging the illegality of nuclear weapons under extant legal principles at the time. The Supreme Court acknowledged these bombs were illicit under 1945 law—they were indiscriminate, targeting undefended cities. This landmark ruling challenged state assumptions and opened discourses on blurring military-hard targets versus civilian spaces, making a compelling case under IHL that the bombings breached key conventions.

20 Ryuichi Shimoda et al. v. The State. Japan. 07 December 1963.Published online by Cambridge University Press: 01 January 2021 available at https://www.cambridge.org/core/journals/international-law-reports/article/abs/ryuichi-shimoda-et-al-v-the-state/8D549534563C89456CD485059DE5511D

Evolution of International Humanitarian Law

The catastrophic consequences of Hiroshima and Nagasaki catalysed normative developments. Subsequent codifications of international humanitarian law reflected an acute awareness of indiscriminate weapons:

- The 1949 Geneva Conventions and the Additional Protocol I (1977) strengthened protections for civilians and clarified principles of distinction, proportionality, and unnecessary suffering;
- The bombings as central to the international legal debate on indiscriminate weapons—whether nuclear arms can ever meet the "principle of discrimination" (attack only military objectives) or "proportionality" (not causing excessive civilian harm). Critics argue the bombings fail both tests, setting an illicit precedent under current international law.

The nuclear weapon outcomes illustrate the incompatible nature of nuclear weapons with the fundamental IHL principles of distinction, proportionality, and necessity. According to ICRC's authoritative interpretation, nuclear weapons are inherently incompatible with IHL's core principles. Although IHL treaties, such as the Geneva Conventions and their Protocols, do not explicitly reference nuclear weapons, the ICJ confirmed that IHL norms imperatively extend to their use. The core principles include:

- Distinction: Requiring combatants to differentiate between military targets and civilians.
- Proportionality: Prohibiting attacks that cause excessive civilian harm.
- Precaution: Mandating necessary steps to minimise unintended destruction.

The ICJ noted that, given their unprecedented destructive capacity and uncontrollable effects, nuclear weapons are "hardly reconcilable" with these humanitarian norms. The Martens Clause affirming consideration of "the principles of humanity" also applies. The scale and indeterminacy of nuclear harm violate core principles of international humanitarian law—distinction, proportionality, and unnecessary suffering—and raise existential concerns. The ICRC has affirmed that nuclear detonations are legally and morally incompatible with humanitarian norms and human dignity. The ICJ reaffirmed that any use or threat must comply with these rigorously, thereby making use in densely populated areas nearly impossible to justify.

International Legal Regime Governing Nuclear Weapons

The global legal framework addressing the development, possession, and use of nuclear weapons is multilayered, evolving through treaties, customary international law, judicial findings, and normative practice.

The Treaty on the Non-Proliferation of Nuclear Weapons (NPT, 1968) [21]

The NPT rests on three foundational pillars: non-proliferation, peaceful use of nuclear energy, and disarmament. Under Article II, non-nuclear weapon states (NNWS) commit to abstaining from acquiring nuclear weapons or facilitating their development. In return, Article IV safeguards the right to develop peaceful nuclear technology under IAEA oversight. Crucially, Article VI obliges all parties—especially nuclear-weapon states (NWS)—to pursue "good faith" negotiations toward nuclear disarmament and the cessation of the nuclear arms race. Moreover, the NPT incorporates a withdrawal clause (Article X), permitting withdrawal upon a three-month notice if a state determines its "supreme interests" are threatened—a provision recently echoed in the context of U.S.–Israeli strikes on Iran and Iran's explicit threats to exit the Treaty. Although the NPT legitimized the possession of nuclear weapons by the five recognized NWS, it also created a legal commitment to disarmament. Nonetheless, critics argue that Article VI's language is aspirational rather than legally binding, specifying no concrete disarmament timelines.

The Comprehensive Nuclear-Test-Ban Treaty (CTBT, 1996) [22]

The CTBT prohibits all nuclear explosions, whether for military or civilian purposes. While widely ratified, it remains legally inoperative due to the absence of ratifications from eight key Annex II states, including the United States, China, India, Pakistan, and North Korea. Entry into force would institutionalise the international norm against nuclear testing through verification mechanisms overseen by the CTBTO.

21 Based on documents of the UN Office of Disarmament Affairs

22 Based on documents of the UN Office of Disarmament Affairs

The Treaty on the Prohibition of Nuclear Weapons (TPNW, 2017) [23]

The TPNW marks the first legally binding, comprehensive ban on nuclear weapons. It prohibits the development, testing, production, acquisition, stockpiling, stationing, deployment, use, or threat of use of nuclear weapons, as well as assistance and encouragement for such actions. For states possessing nuclear weapons, the TPNW mandates a time-bound disarmament trajectory involving verified destruction of nuclear arsenals. Beyond military restrictions, the treaty affirms obligations for victim assistance and environmental remediation. It reflects a humanitarian priorities shift, emphasising human dignity and fundamental rights. With the entry into force in January 2021, its normative power exerts moral and legal pressure—though none of the recognised NWS have yet joined.

Nuclear-Weapon-Free Zone (NWFZ) Treaties [24]

Region-specific treaties—such as Tlatelolco, Rarotonga, and Bangkok—prohibit nuclear weapons within their territories and require NWS to provide negative security assurances, pledging not to use or threaten them against zone members. These protocols bolster broader disarmament and non-proliferation efforts.

Emerging Norms & the Path to Nuclear Disarmament

Beyond formal treaties, there is a gradually strengthening opinio juris—state recognition that nuclear weapons contravene legal and humanitarian norms. The ICJ explicitly recognised a legal obligation to pursue nuclear disarmament in good faith (stemming from Article VI). Additionally, the TPNW embodies a sharp normative break, formally outlawing nuclear arsenals altogether.

Nevertheless, major NWS has not joined the TPNW, often citing deterrence. This highlights the normative tension between legal commitment and strategic calculation. Observers argue that NWFZs, TPNW momentum, and ICJ pronouncements are collectively emerging into a robust regime of customary law and soft norms.

Ultimately, nuclear weapons occupy an uneasy legal and moral space: formally lawful within highly constrained parameters, yet generally incompatible with humanitarian norms and potentially evolving into

23 Based on documents of the UN Office of Disarmament Affairs

24 Based on documents of the UN Office of Disarmament Affairs

a comprehensive illegal status through growing normative consensus. Should current geopolitical tensions—such as crises involving Iran or renewed nuclear rivalries—continue unchecked, they risk undermining the fragile architecture of disarmament and non-proliferation.

International Court of Justice Advisory Opinion (1996)[25]

In response to UN requests, the ICJ delivered a landmark advisory opinion in 1996. Its key conclusions include:

- No existing legal authorisation (customary or treaty) explicitly permits the use or threat of nuclear weapons.
- No comprehensive legal ban on nuclear weapons exists, meaning they remain technically lawful under extremely limited circumstances.
- The use or threat is generally unlawful under international humanitarian law (IHL), particularly when assessed against principles of distinction, proportionality, necessity, and precaution.

The Court could not definitively determine whether extreme cases—such as a last-resort nuclear strike for state survival—might be lawfully justified. Nonetheless, it emphasised the legal obligation of all states to negotiate nuclear disarmament in good faith (NPT Article VI).

Customary International Law and Opinio Juris

Customary international law arises when state practices align with a sense of legal obligation (*opinio juris*). The TPNW and expansive treaty frameworks suggest a growing normative consensus against nuclear weapons. However, the ICJ noted the absence of a universally binding customary prohibition—largely because the worldview and doctrines of NWS do not yet perceive nuclear weapons as illegal per se.

Summation

The architecture governing nuclear weapons is simultaneously robust and fragmented. The NPT defines the status quo, while the CTBT and TPNW represent progressive legal advances. The ICJ opinion and IHL principles affirm that nuclear weapons are largely incompatible with humanitarian constraints.

25 Legality of the Threat or Use of Nuclear Weapons, International Court of Justice available at https://www.icj-cij.org/case/95

However, substantial legal loopholes persist—particularly regarding customary law and the willingness of nuclear-armed states to comply with disarmament norms. Bridging these gaps requires reinforced verification mechanisms, binding NFU agreements, treaty-based criminal accountability, and enhanced normative pressure.

Strengthening Legal Mechanisms to Minimise the Risk of Nuclear Weapon Use

The intersection of law, strategy, and technology demands a multifaceted reform to minimize or eliminate nuclear weapon use to erect effective safeguards in one of humanity's most existential domains.

Reduce Launch Posture: *De-alerting*

De-alerting involves reversible technical changes to nuclear forces, introducing deliberate delays to prevent hair-trigger launches. Proposals suggest instituting a minimum 24-hour delay on launch-authorised systems to eliminate "launch on warning" protocols. This measure has the potential to significantly reduce the risk of accidental or hasty launches.

Constrain Delegation: Authorisation Protocols

Reforms in chain-of-command processes can limit the conditions under which nuclear use can be authorised. Historical practices, such as explicit pre-delegation rules, allowed operational commanders to use nuclear weapons only in specified extreme conditions. Modern legal reforms could codify explicit multi-party authorisation requirements—for example, mandating concurrence from both civilian and military leadership—thereby decreasing the likelihood of unilateral or hasty decisions.

Enhance Verification: Robust Arms Control Regimes

The effectiveness of non-proliferation and disarmament regimes depends on robust verification and transparency:

- Strengthening IAEA safeguards and universal adoption of the Additional Protocol would greatly improve the detection of clandestine weaponisation activities.
- Bilateral or multilateral treaties should incorporate transparent and regular on-site inspections (e.g., for mobile launchers), as outlined in new arms control proposals.

Promote Accountability: UNSC Oversight and Enforcement

Incorporating verification failures into enforceable UN mandates (e.g., under Chapter VII resolutions) could create effective consequences for non-compliance. For instance, requiring UN Security Council review before any NPT withdrawal would serve as an accountability check against states exploiting withdrawal clauses for strategic gain.

Shift Treaty Design: Move Beyond Consensus

Treaty mechanisms that rely on consensus often stagnate. The development of the TPNW—adopted through majority voting—demonstrated that alternative, flexible models can yield stronger disarmament-based results. Similar voting-based procedures could accelerate arms-control development and adoption.

Regulate Emerging Technologies: AI & Autonomy

Given the increasing integration of autonomous systems and AI in military command and control, novel legal standards are needed:

- Protocols for AI use in nuclear decision-making.
- Mandatory fail-safe (lock-out) mechanisms for autonomous delivery platforms.
- Binding agreements to prohibit autonomous nuclear launch systems.

Reinforce the "Nuclear Taboo" through Normative Law

Solidifying the moral and legal stigma against nuclear use—also known as the nuclear taboo—can be supported by legal reinforcement. Explicit normative statements within treaties and UN resolutions, elevated by the ICJ's Advisory Opinion, strengthen the sense that nuclear weapon use is not only strategically irrational but legally and morally unacceptable.

Empower Non-State Oversight: Civil & Parliamentary Involvement

Involving independent oversight bodies—such as parliamentary committees, judiciary review, or empowered civil society institutions—provides transparency and legitimacy. This could complement traditional executive control, ensuring that decisions to use nuclear weapons undergo rigorous democratic and legal scrutiny.

Toward a Nuclear-Weapon-Free World

The elimination of nuclear arsenals, while a monumental challenge, remains both legally conceivable and ethically imperative. Achieving a nuclear-weapon-free world requires a coherent sequence of legal, political, and institutional initiatives—grounded in existing frameworks and bolstered by normative innovation.

Universalising and Enforcing Core Treaties

- Comprehensive Nuclear-Test-Ban Treaty (CTBT)

  The CTBT establishes a global prohibition on nuclear explosions. Its entry into force would codify the norm against weapons development and prevent the refinement of existing arsenals States encompassed by NuclearWeaponFree Zones (NWFZs) are among the strongest supporters; full CTBT ratification would significantly erode the legitimacy of nuclear testing.

- Treaty on the Prohibition of Nuclear Weapons (TPNW)

  The TPNW embodies a comprehensive ban on nuclear weapons, encompassing development, possession, use, and threats—including mandates for victim assistance and environmental remediation encouraging broader participation, including from nuclear-armed or allied states, would deepen its normative weight.

Expanding and Strengthening Nuclear-Weapon-Free Zones (NWFZs)

NWFZs serve as crucial building blocks for non-proliferation efforts. Existing zones (Latin America, Africa, Central Asia, Southeast Asia, and South Pacific) legally prohibit all nuclear weapons within their territories and require legally binding negative security assurances from nuclear-armed states. Regional extensions—to the Middle East, Arctic, or Korean Peninsula—should be prioritised. As noted by the Carnegie Council, NWFZs provide robust verification regimes and reinforce global peace through federal cooperation mechanisms.

Instituting a Global Nuclear Weapons Convention (NWC)

A Nuclear Weapons Convention would create a phased elimination plan—a legally binding framework codifying disarmament. Based on the 1997/2007 model, it includes shifting arsenals off alert, removing warheads, disabling fissile cores, and placing materials under international control.

This regime would include robust verification—akin to chemical weapons frameworks—and enforcement mechanisms, translating Article VI of the NPT into tangible, time-bound action.

Strengthening IAEA Safeguards and Verification Regimes

Restricting nuclear weapons requires universal implementation of the IAEA Additional Protocol, enhancing transparency through more frequent inspections and environmental sampling Embedding such safeguards in all NPT signatories—including nuclear-armed nations—strengthens the institutional architecture that underpins disarmament. Nuclear-weapon-free zones and the CTBT complement these efforts by reinforcing states' compliance and confidence in mutual verification.

Normative Reinforcement and Legal Accountability

- Embedding a Legally Binding "No First Use" Commitment-Negotiated either as a protocol to the NPT or separately, a legally binding NFU treaty would normalise the principle that nuclear arsenals exist solely for deterrence, not for initiation
- Criminalisation of Nuclear Threats and Use -Updating the Rome Statute to encompass nuclear weapons as explicit war crimes would establish individual liability and reinforce deterrence through accountability.
- Codifying the Nuclear Taboo - Legal instruments—such as treaties, UN resolutions, or national criminal provisions—that explicitly outlaw threats or use of nuclear weapons would help transform the global norm against nuclear violence into enforceable law.

Establishing Security Assurances and Conflict Prevention Systems

Binding negative security assurances (NSAs) from nuclear-armed states—formalized in treaties or UNSC resolution—would reinforce NWFZs and reduce incentive to seek deterrence capability in contested regions This should be complemented by robust conflict-prevention architecture, including diplomatic crisis resolution mechanisms and "Pacts for the Future" to manage geopolitical tensions.

Achieving a nuclear-weapon-free world is ambitious, but underpinned by existing treaties and normative frameworks. CTBT ratification, NWFZ expansion, a phased convention, enhanced transparency, and legal accountability together form a coherent architecture. The successful negotiation of a model NWC—as repeatedly encouraged by UNGA and supported by 127 states, including nuclear-armed China and India—demonstrates global endorsement. Civil society momentum and the demand for a "Pact for the Future" among global security actors show that this vision is both legally grounded and politically viable. Success—however—depends on sustained international cooperation, nuclear-armed state buy-in, and civil society engagement to guide humanity away from existential peril.

Conclusion

The use of nuclear weapons presents a profound threat to humanity, the environment, and the foundations of international law. From the devastating impacts witnessed in Hiroshima and Nagasaki to the patchy global legal frameworks and shifting national doctrines, the overwhelming and irreversible consequences of nuclear detonations render any claim of strategic utility meaningless. The growing support for disarmament treaties and humanitarian campaigns reinforces an urgent ethical and legal mandate: nuclear weapons must never be used again and should be systematically removed from global arsenals.

Recent events underscore this urgency. The 2025 attacks on nuclear facilities in Iran—carried out by states outside the Non-Proliferation Treaty—highlight deepening fractures in the global non-proliferation regime. Simultaneously, the potential lapse of the New START agreement risks destabilising the strategic balance between the United States and Russia, paving the way for a renewed arms race. In this context, the Nobel Peace Prize awarded to Japan's hibakusha organisation, Nihon Hidankyo, serves as a stark reminder of the pressing need for decisive arms control measures. Collectively, these developments point to a sobering truth: existing treaties and doctrines fall short of ensuring global security.

The International Committee of the Red Cross has stated unequivocally that nuclear weapons are fundamentally incompatible with humanity, and their use would contravene the principles of international humanitarian law. The 1996 Advisory Opinion of the International Court of Justice supported this position, affirming the general illegality of nuclear use and reinforcing the obligation to pursue disarmament. Though lacking the participation of nuclear-armed states, the Treaty on the Prohibition of Nuclear Weapons establishes a binding framework for disarmament, victim support, and environmental recovery.

This essay outlines a viable path forward: universal ratification of the Comprehensive Nuclear-Test-Ban Treaty; expansion of Nuclear-Weapon-Free Zones backed by enforceable security guarantees; formal adoption of no-first-use policies; a phased elimination process guided by a comprehensive Nuclear Weapons Convention; criminal accountability for nuclear threats or use; and rigorous societal verification mechanisms.

Achieving these goals demands political resolve, legal ingenuity, and collective will. As a prominent editorial once observed, a nuclear war cannot be won and must never be fought. Effective arms control depends on leaders prioritising moral responsibility over strategic calculation. Robert Oppenheimer's warnings about the ethical lag behind technological progress remain deeply relevant—his call for disarmament must not be ignored. In 2025, the world finds itself at a critical juncture. Without meaningful steps toward disarmament, the erosion of trust among nuclear-armed states, the emergence of aggressive nuclear doctrines, and geopolitical instability—exemplified by Iran's potential withdrawal from the NPT—could unravel the fragile barriers that have thus far prevented nuclear conflict. Yet, global humanitarian efforts and civil society activism continue to offer hope for meaningful progress.

The vision of a nuclear-weapon-free world is not mere idealism—it is a moral, legal, and existential necessity. Failure to act risks consequences beyond calculation, threatening not only present generations but the future of life itself. Through cohesive legal reform, enforceable treaties, and widespread public engagement, humanity has the means—and the obligation—to bring the nuclear age to a close before it brings about our undoing.

In today's unstable geopolitical climate, the legacy of Hiroshima and Nagasaki serves as a compelling case study—an enduring testament to the catastrophic human cost of nuclear warfare and the critical need for legal, moral, and humanitarian safeguards. These events reinforce the argument that nuclear weapons, having already been proven historically devastating and legally indefensible, must remain tightly constrained under the strictest international prohibitions.

Chapter 9

Militarisation and Weaponisation of Space

-DK Pandey

Militarisation of Space

Deploying offensive capabilities, such as anti-satellite and laser weaponry, in space is known as the militarisation of space. No nation-state with an active space program has publicly said that it intends to put such a plan into action just yet. Conversely, the military utilisation of space for non-aggressive and passive reasons has been established for an extended period and is essential for air defence, among other applications. Military satellites function as early warning systems, communication devices, and sensors. In certain instances, commercial satellites are also utilised.

The militarisation of space pertains to the enhancement of terrestrial warfare systems through the utilisation of space-based resources.[1] The weaponisation of space is typically characterised by the deployment of weapons or weapon systems, whether terrestrial, maritime, aerial, or extraterrestrial, that target space-based assets or rely on the physical utilisation of space for operation.[2] Space weapons can be deployed in earth-to-space, space-to-earth, and space-to-space configurations, provided that space is a critical component of the trajectory or system. Some definitions suggest that earth-to-earth directed weapons, such as intercontinental ballistic missiles (ICBMs), constitute the weaponisation of space. This

1 "Militarization of space", Rau's IAS Study Circle, August 31, 2023, https://compass.rauias.com/current-affairs/militarization-of-space/. Accessed on April 6, 2025.

2 David C. DeFrieze, "Defining and Regulating the Weaponization of Space", The Weaponization of Space, 3rd Quarter 2014, https://ndupress.ndu.edu/Portals/68/Documents/jfq/jfq-74/jfq-74_110-115_DeFrieze.pdf. Accessed on April 5, 2025.

Future Issue asserts that space has not been militarised, as no earth-to-space, space-to-earth, or space-to-space weaponry has yet been deployed in space.[3]

Historical Context

During the Cold War, space was militarised for primarily two reasons: the space race between the United States and the Soviet Union. Indeed, both superpowers had invested huge amounts in developing military technologies, like ballistic missiles and reconnaissance satellites. The military motivation behind the early exploration of space played a very huge role as both nations were probing to show who is technically advanced and how both countries can use this space to improve their strategic capability.

The most rudimentary grade of space militarisation was their development of reconnaissance satellites. Gathering intelligence on military installations was a critical information for strategic planning, and these satellites were used to do so. The United States, for example, when they launched the Corona program in the 60s, was launching the first successful series of spy satellites. These satellites provided high resolution images of Soviet military bases to the US to monitor the Soviet Union's military activities.

One of the other important developments was research on anti-satellite weapons. The United States and the Soviet Union looked at different ways to try to render or destroy each other's satellites. Almaz space station developed by the Soviet Union deployed a 23mm cannon for the defence against the enemy satellites. Like Project A119, United States also performed the feasibility studies of deploying nuclear weapons in space, for instance, to detonate a nuclear bomb on the Moon as a demonstration of power.

Militarisation v/s Weaponisation

Current global security dynamics crucially involve militarisation and weaponisation of space. Militarisation refers to the use of space for the military purposes of satellite surveillance, communication, navigation and reconnaissance. This is not new, as countries have been deploying satellites to gain strategic intelligence gathering and military operations advantages since the Cold War.

3 Ibid.

Weaponisation includes deployment of weapons in space or creation of space-based systems that can target terrestrial objects or other satellites. Even though the Outer Space Treaty of 1967 prohibits the placement of nuclear weapons or weapons of mass destruction in space, there are no comprehensive accords strictly barring conventional weapons, and the arms race in space technology has ensued.

Technological Advancements: This rapid advancement in technology has made anti-satellite (ASAT) weapons too realistic for active consideration as a kinetic kill vehicle, directed energy weapon, and cyber capabilities to disrupt or destroy satellites.

Strategic Implications: Strategic ascendency in space may bring with it important results, as it increases the command, control, communications, computers, intelligence, surveillance, and reconnaissance (C4ISR) over ranged force, thus effecting conventional combat results.

Current international law and ethical discussions on the militarisation of a domain that has long been perceived as a common heritage of humanity is what makes the weaponisation of space a huge legal issue.

Global Security: The space has become an increasingly recognised domain of national security and thus has become a joint and competitive zone between countries. It includes the creation of space forces or commands within national armed forces.

Due to an arms race in space, there may exist the possibility of inadvertent conflicts due to debris in the form of obliterated satellites in space, which could damage both military and civilian space systems.

International Cooperation: Despite the competition, there are efforts of international cooperation, for instance, the UN Committee on the Peaceful Uses of Outer Space (COPUOS) to prevent a weapons race in outer space.

The militarisation and possibly weaponisation of space have opportunities and challenges. In fact, they underscore the need for diplomacy, reform of the international law and maybe new treaties to minimise the risks of space turning into another theatre of struggle. It is a crucial issue of the 21st century to maintain equilibrium between national security priorities and global tranquillity in space.

Westernisation of Space

The militarisation and westernisation of space represent significant developments in the modern era, driven by technological advancements and geopolitical interests. The militarisation of space involves the deployment of military technology and weaponry in outer space, while westernisation refers to the adoption of Western cultural, economic, and political practices by other nations.[4]

The westernisation of space is a more recent phenomenon, driven by the increasing influence of Western nations and their cultural, economic, and political practices. Westernisation in space can be seen in the way Western countries have dominated space exploration and the establishment of international norms and regulations.

One of the key examples of westernisation in space is the dominance of the United States in space exploration. The United States has invested heavily in space programs, such as NASA, which has been instrumental in advancing space technology and exploration. The United States has also been a leader in establishing international norms and regulations for space activities, such as the Outer Space Treaty of 1967, which prohibits the placement of weapons of mass destruction in space.[5]

Another example of westernisation in space is the influence of Western cultural practices on space exploration. For instance, the naming of celestial bodies often reflects Western cultural and historical references. The International Astronomical Union, which is based in Paris, France, is responsible for the naming of celestial bodies, and many of these names are derived from Western mythology and history.

Current Trends of Militarization of Space

In recent years, there has been the development of new technology and methods as the militarisation of space has progressed. Another trend in point of existence is the rise of anti-satellite weapons, that is to say weapons

4 Thomas D. Bell, "Weaponization of Space: Understanding Strategic and Technological Inevitabilities", Center for Strategy and Technology, Air War College, January 1999, https://www.airuniversity.af.edu/ Portals/10/CSAT/documents/OP/csat6.pdf. Accessed on April 4, 2025.

5 "Treaty on Principles Governing the Activities of States in the Exploration and Use of Outer Space, including the Moon and Other Celestial Bodies", UNOOSA, October 1967, https://www.unoosa.org/oosa/en/ourwork/ spacelaw/treaties/introouterspacetreaty.html. Accessed on April 3, 2025.

having the capabilities of disabling or destroying satellites. For instance, in 2007 China's test launch of an anti-satellite missile blew one of their meteorological satellites into smithereens, leaving behind more than 3,000 pieces of debris in orbit.

Space based missile defence systems also witness a further trend in their advancement. They are engineered to detect and neutralise ballistic missiles in space and that provides an additional layer of ballistic missile attack defence. The Ground Based Midcourse Defence (GMD) is such a system that the United States has excelled in developing, and it uses space-based sensors to detect and intercept incoming missiles.[6]

Militarisation of space refers to the use of space-based capabilities for military purposes, i.e. reconnaissance, communications, navigation, and missile defence. In recent years, many countries have been investing substantial amounts in the development of their military space capabilities.

Types of Military Space Assets

There are several types of military space assets, including:

(a) Reconnaissance Satellites: They use Reconnaissance Satellites that collect intelligence of adversaries' military movements and the deployment of equipment used in their military operations.

(b) Communication Satellites: These satellites allow for secure communication connexions between military units and command centres.

(c) Navigation Satellites: These platforms used to provide locational data and temporal signals for military navigation systems such as GPS.

(d) Missile Defense Satellites: Missile Defence Satellites are satellites employed for their missile detection and tracking capabilities, among other things—providing an early warning and target data for missile defence systems.

Military Assets in Space

Number of military space resources, from various countries, are deployed in space. The military resources of Super powers are appended below.

6 "Ground-based Midcourse Defense (GMD) System", Missile Threat, July 26, 2021, https://missilethreat. csis. org/system/gmd/. Accessed on April 3, 2025.

The US Air Force's Space-Based Infrared System (SBIRS). This network has satellites that locate and track incoming ballistic missiles so as to provide timely warning and targeting data to missile defence systems.[7]

The Russian Federation's Oko-1 Early Warning System is a network of satellites that constitute a precursory observing system and also a target monitor regime aimed at detecting and followed incoming ballistic missiles and providing for early alerts and for targeting data for Russian missile defence systems.[8]

The Beidou Navigation Satellite System of the Chinese People's Liberation Army (PLA) offers locational data and temporal signals for both military navigation systems and civilian users.

Key Players in Space Militarisation

Militarisation of space technology refers to a number of actors participating in the development and deployment of military capabilities in outer space. These players encompass national governments, military organisations, and private corporations, each with distinct roles and motivations.

The leaders are national governments particularly those of the top powers such as the United States, Russia and China. Both their space agencies, such as NASA and Roscosmos, are dedicated to both scientific exploration and improving the military readiness through the developments of advanced space technologies.

Space is used by these nations' military organisations for intelligence gathering, communication and surveillance. Strategic advantages are implemented by these technologies — satellite systems and missile detection — which constitute their technologies.

More and more powerful entities are militarising space technology, and these entities are increasingly private corporations. SpaceX and Lockheed Martin offer cutting edge solutions that advocate for government initiatives to support the furtherance of military satellite systems and launch capabilities.

7 "Space Based Infrared System (SBIRS)", US Space Fprce Fact Sheet, October 2021, https://media.defense. gov/2022/Apr/08/2002973444/-1/-1/1/SBIRS%20 FACTSHEET.PDF. Accessed on April 3, 2025.

8 "US-K and US-KMO constellations", Russian Space Web, November 14, 2024, https:// russianspaceweb. com/ oko.html. Accessed on April 3, 2025.

Technologies Driving Militarisation

Various advanced systems that enable space technology for surveillance, reconnaissance and combat capabilities drives the militarisation of space technology. Satellite systems, nevertheless, are of vital importance in monitoring global activities, thus allowing nations to gather intelligence and remain in a state of operational readiness.

Missile defence systems are another very important technology that uses space-based sensors to detect and neutralise possible threats. These systems are intended to give nations strategic advantage to enable preemptive measures against terrestrial threats emanating from space assets.

In addition, artificial intelligence and machine learning are used more and more on the data collected by different space missions. These technologies help in military operations making decisions in a rapid way while responding to the threat and using resources efficiently.

Robots and drones also help militarise space through the autonomous capabilities of reconnaissance and data collection. Nations keep on investing in these technologies and the very picture of warfare might change, and it would be entangled somewhat more with space operations.

Implications of the Militarisation of Space

Consequently, the militarisation of space has a number of ramifications, including:[9]

(a) Military space assets are used to increase conflict risk in space as nations may be compelled by the threat or assault on their space-based resources to respond in kind.

(b) Arms Race Escalation: The militarisation of space could be an escalator of arms race; the nations will try to develop and deplete advanced military space capabilities.

(c) Military of Space: This may lead to the militarisation of space, and thus poses a threat to civilian space assets such as commercial satellites and space stations who may become collateral damage in a space conflict.

9 https://www.cram.com/essay/Pros-And-Cons-Of-The-Militarization-Of/FCCJJFWZXV. Accessed on March 29, 2025.

Militarisation of Space

The idea of weaponisation of space refers to the making and use of armaments in outer space, which expands the battlefield to space. In other words, it is about the development and deployment of armaments in the vast reaches of outer space and thus extending the parameters of war beyond Earth. It is an exhaustive procedure examination of the motives behind, how it works, what are the potential risks, and a few fixes to the problem.

In the present moment, space is militarised, but it is not weaponised. Directed Energy Weapons (DEW), which are similar to laser systems that have been utilised as terrestrial-to-space targeting systems, are classified as anti-satellite systems (ASAT). However, the categorisation of directed energy weapons as space weapons is up for debate. The military uses of space assets that are most routinely used, such as communications, photography, and navigation, all played a part in the augmentation of military capabilities. However, these applications have now evolved from being enhancements to being enablers of military might.[10]

Recently, there have been operations in space that indicate the beginning of a new era in which space is becoming the medium itself for warfighting. Additionally, offensive space force projection and space denial are both possibilities that could occur in the not-too-distant future. It would appear that some factors, including technological advancements in space, political policy about space exploration, socioeconomic dependence on space, and commercial interests, have pushed the limits of military superiority on Earth. As a result of the fact that space trade and industry have now driven the pursuit of military superiority into space, the development of space weaponry will now be a consequence of the desire to safeguard a space economy that is quickly expanding. Space weapons will find their way into national space policies and doctrines as space technologies continue to advance in order to sustain the thirst for space exploitation and the growing space commerce. This is especially true in the absence of laws that explicitly define the prohibition of space weapons.

10 Betty Wehtje, "Increased Militarisation of Space – A New Realm of Security". Jun 6, 2023, https://behorizon.org/increased-militarisation-of-space-a-new-realm-of-security/. Accessed on March 29, 2025.

The Strategy

Developing space weapons requires a range of technologies, including some still in the theoretical stage. For instance, one such technology could be a laser-based system that can disable enemy satellites from a distance or a particle beam that can disrupt the functioning of space infrastructure.

(a) **Advanced Anti-Satellite Weapons (ASATs)**: These cutting-edge weapons can be kinetic projectiles or advanced directed-energy systems, such as lasers or particle beams. Their purpose is to neutralise or incapacitate adversary satellites.[11]

(b) **Space-based Weapons:** Platforms in orbit equipped with lasers or missiles have the capability to engage targets in space or on Earth.

(c) **Cyber Weapons:** They can disrupt the control systems of satellites or space infrastructure.

Why Weaponisation?

Strategic Importance: Disabling adversary satellites would severely impair their ability to communicate, navigate, and gather intelligence.

Regarding national security, certain countries view space weapons as a means of deterring potential space-based threats.

Status and Power: Spacefaring nations could see having space weapons as evidence of their technological superiority.

Concerns about the Potential for Weaponisation

Space Debris: The destruction of satellites could lead to the creation of a dangerous debris field in orbit, posing a significant risk to upcoming spacecraft and missions. This concern should not be taken lightly. Additional complications arise during the testing and deployment processes. Space debris produced as a result of such actions might cause cascading collisions, which pose a threat to satellites operating for everyone. One of the most compelling arguments against the use of space for military purposes is the presence of orbital debris, as well as the absence of any realistic procedures for debris abatement. The purposeful explosion of satellites by means of anti-satellite weapons (ASATs) and unintentional accidents in orbit have been the single most significant sources of debris.

11 Mark Smith, "Anti-satellite weapons: History, types and purpose", Space.com, August 10, 2022, https://www.space.com/anti-satellite-weapons-asats. Accessed on April 6, 2025.

Escalation of Conflict: The potential for a space war to ignite a broader conflict on Earth is a matter of concern. For example, if a country's satellite communication system is disabled, it could lead to miscommunication or even military miscalculations, escalating tensions and potentially leading to a full-scale war.

Space as a Zone of Conflict: The potential impact on peaceful activities in space, such as scientific research and communication, is a cause for concern.

Westernisation of Space

The westernisation of space continues to be influenced by the dominance of Western nations in space exploration and the establishment of international norms and regulations. One of the key trends is the increasing commercialisation of space, which is largely driven by Western companies. For example, SpaceX, a private company founded by Elon Musk, has been at the forefront of developing reusable rockets and launching satellites into orbit.[12]

Another trend is the influence of Western cultural practices on space exploration. For instance, the naming of celestial bodies often reflects Western cultural and historical references. The International Astronomical Union, which is based in Paris, France, is responsible for the naming of celestial bodies, and many of these names are derived from Western mythology and history.

The westernisation of space refers to the adoption of Western cultural, economic, and political practices in space exploration and development. This has been a growing trend in recent years, with many countries seeking to develop their space capabilities and participate in international space activities.

Types of Westernization of Space

There are several types of westernisation of space, including:

1. **Cultural Westernisation**: This refers to the adoption of Western cultural practices and values in space exploration and development, such as the use of English as the primary language of space communication.

12 IvyPanda. 2020. "Westernization of the World." May 20, 2020. https://ivypanda.com/essays/westernization-of-the-world/. Accessed on Mar 30, 2025.

2. **Economic Westernisation**: This refers to the adoption of Western economic practices and systems in space exploration and development, such as the use of market-based economies and private sector investment.

3. **Political Westernisation**: This refers to the adoption of Western political practices and systems in space exploration and development, such as the use of democratic governance and international cooperation.

Examples of Westernization of Space: Some examples of westernisation of space include:

(a) International Space Station (ISS) Program: This program is a cooperative effort between space agencies around the world, including NASA, Roscosmos, JAXA, and ESA, to develop and operate a habitable artificial satellite in low Earth orbit.[13]

(b) European Space Agency's (ESA) Galileo Navigation Satellite System: This system provides location information and timing signals for European military and civilian users, as well as users around the world.[14]

(c) SpaceX's Reusable Rocket Technology: This technology has been developed by the private sector company SpaceX, which has pioneered the use of reusable rockets for launch and space transportation.[15]

Implications of Westernization of Space

The westernisation of space has several implications, including:

(a) Increased Cooperation and Collaboration: The westernisation of space may lead to increased cooperation and collaboration between countries, as they seek to develop and participate in international space activities.

13 "International Space Station", NASA, May 23, 2023, https://www.nasa.gov/reference/international-space-station/. Accessed on April 5, 2025.

14 Andrew Wilson, "Galileo: The European Programme for Global Navigation Services", ESA International, January 2005, https://www.esa.int/esapub/br/br186/br186e.pdf. Accessed on April 5, 2025.

15 Henry Adrian, "Reusable Launch System: The Gateway to the Future of Space Travel", Pittsburgh Swanson School of Engineering, 2018, https://sites.pitt.edu/~budny/papers/8226.pdf. Accessed on April 5, 2025.

(b) Spread of Democratic Values: The westernisation of space may also lead to the spread of democratic values and practices, such as transparency, accountability, and the rule of law.

(c) Threat to Non-Western Cultures and Practices: The westernisation of space may also pose a threat to non-Western cultures and practices, as Western cultural and economic practices become more dominant in space exploration and development.

Interplay Between Militarisation and Westernisation

The interplay between militarisation and westernisation in space is complex and multifaceted. On one hand, the militarisation of space can be seen as a reflection of Western dominance, as Western nations have been the primary actors in developing military technologies and strategies for space. On the other hand, the westernisation of space can be seen as a result of the influence of Western cultural, economic, and political practices on space exploration and the establishment of international norms and regulations.

One example of the interplay between militarisation and westernisation is the development of international norms and regulations for space activities. The Outer Space Treaty of 1967, which was primarily negotiated by Western nations, prohibits the placement of weapons of mass destruction in space and establishes the principle of non-appropriation of celestial bodies. This treaty reflects the Western emphasis on international cooperation and the establishment of rules and regulations for space activities.

Another example is the influence of Western cultural practices on space exploration. The naming of celestial bodies often reflects Western cultural and historical references, which can be seen as a form of cultural imperialism. For instance, the naming of craters on the Moon and Mars often reflects Western historical figures and events, which can be seen as a form of cultural dominance.

The interplay between militarisation and westernisation of space is complex and multifaceted, reflecting the changing geopolitical landscape and the increasing influence of Western nations in space exploration and development.

Examples of Interplay

Some examples of the interplay between militarisation and westernisation of space include:[16]

US Military's Use of Commercial Satellites: The US military has been increasingly relying on commercial satellites, such as those provided by companies like Intelsat and SES, to support its military operations. This trend reflects the westernisation of space, as commercial companies are playing a larger role in providing space-based services to the military.

European Space Agency's (ESA) Participation in NATO's Space Activities: The ESA has been participating in NATO's space activities, such as the Alliance's space-based surveillance and reconnaissance programs. This reflects the westernisation of space, as European countries are working together to develop and operate space-based systems for military and civilian purposes.

China's Development of Military Space Capabilities: China has been rapidly developing its military space capabilities, including the launch of satellites for reconnaissance, communication, and navigation. This trend reflects the militarisation of space, as China seeks to expand its military presence in space.

Implications of Interplay

The interplay between militarisation and westernisation of space has several implications, including:

(a) Increased Tensions between Nations: The militarisation of space, combined with the westernisation of space, may lead to increased tensions between nations, as countries with differing interests and values compete for influence in space.

(b) Growing Importance of Space in International Relations: The interplay between militarisation and westernisation of space highlights the growing importance of space in international relations, as countries seek to expand their presence in space and protect their interests.

---

16 "Outer Space Becoming Contested Domain for Supremacy with Space-Based Communications, Intelligence Assets, Anti-Satellite Weapons, First Committee Hears", UNO, 19 October 2023, https://press.un.org/en/ 2023/gadis3722.doc.htm. Accessed on April 4, 2025.

(c) Need for International Cooperation and Regulation: The interplay between militarisation and westernisation of space also highlights the need for international cooperation and regulation, as countries seek to prevent conflicts in space and ensure the long-term sustainability of space activities.

The future of space activities will be shaped by the interplay between militarisation and westernisation of space. Some potential future directions include:

(a) Increased Focus on Space Security: As the militarisation of space continues, there may be an increased focus on space security, including the development of systems for detecting and tracking objects in space, as well as the creation of international norms and regulations for space activities.

(b) Growing Role of Commercial Companies: The westernisation of space is likely to continue, with commercial companies playing a larger role in providing space-based services, such as launch and satellite operations.

(c) Expansion of Space Activities to New Regions: As space activities continue to expand, new regions of space, such as the Moon and Mars, may become increasingly important, with countries and companies competing for influence and resources in these areas.

Measures to Check Westernisation of Space

Various countries, across the Globe, can work together to promote the peaceful use of space, prevent conflicts, and ensure the long-term sustainability of space activities. Based on the analysis of the militarisation and westernisation of space, several recommendations can be made:[17]

(a) International Cooperation and Regulation: There is a need for international cooperation and regulation to prevent conflicts in space and ensure the long-term sustainability of space activities.

(b) Transparency and Confidence-Building Measures: Countries should prioritise transparency and confidence-building measures, such as the sharing of information on space activities and the creation of international norms and regulations.

17 Chris Deziel, "What Types Of Measurements Are Used for Measuring in Outer Space?", August 30, 2022, https://www.sciencing.com/types-measurements-used-measuring-outer-space-14340/. Accessed on April 3, 2025.

(c) Investment in Space Security: Countries should invest in space security, including the development of systems for detecting and tracking objects in space, as well as the creation of international norms and regulations for space activities.

(d) Support for Commercial Space Activities: Governments should support commercial space activities, including the development of launch and satellite operations, to promote the growth of the space industry and increase access to space.

Future Projections

The future of the militarisation of space is likely to be shaped by the development of new technologies and the changing geopolitical landscape. One of the key trends is the development of space-based weapons, which can be used to disable or destroy satellites and other space assets. For example, the development of directed-energy weapons, such as lasers and microwaves, could enable the destruction of satellites from a distance.

Another trend is the increasing role of private companies in space exploration, which could lead to the development of new military technologies and strategies. For example, SpaceX has been developing reusable rockets and launching satellites into orbit, which could be used for military purposes. The increasing commercialisation of space could also lead to the development of new military technologies and strategies, as private companies seek to protect their assets in space.

The future of the westernisation of space is likely to be shaped by the increasing influence of Western nations and their cultural, economic, and political practices. One of the key trends is the increasing commercialisation of space, which is largely driven by Western companies. For example, SpaceX, Blue Origin, and Virgin Galactic are all private companies that are developing new technologies and strategies for space exploration.

Another trend is the influence of Western cultural practices on space exploration. For instance, the naming of celestial bodies often reflects Western cultural and historical references, which can be seen as a form of cultural imperialism. The increasing influence of Western nations in space exploration could lead to the establishment of new international norms and regulations, which could reflect Western cultural, economic, and political practices.

Recent Developments in the Militarization and Weaponization of Space

Recent years have witnessed significant developments in the militarisation and potential weaponisation of space, transforming it into a new arena for strategic competition:

Anti-Satellite (ASAT) Tests: Countries like Russia, China, India, and the USA have conducted ASAT tests, showcasing capabilities to disable or destroy satellites. Notably, Russia's 2021 ASAT test led to international criticism due to the creation of space debris, endangering space operations and the International Space Station.[18]

(a) Space Forces and Commands: The establishment of dedicated space forces or commands by major powers signals a shift in military strategy. The United States created the Space Force in 2019, followed by similar initiatives by other nations to secure their space assets and operations.

(b) Advanced Space Technologies: There's been rapid development in technologies that could serve dual-use purposes, including laser systems for satellite tracking and potential blinding, and ground-based systems for satellite interception. Hypersonic missile programs, which rely on space for navigation and targeting, are also advancing, with nations like the US, Russia, and China at the forefront.

(c) Space-Based Interceptors: Recent mentions in policy documents and executive orders, particularly from the US, suggest plans for 'Iron Dome' like defences using space-based interceptors against hypersonic and ballistic threats, indicating a move towards weaponising space for defensive purposes.

(d) Nuclear Threats in Space: Allegations and concerns have arisen regarding the development or deployment of nuclear weapons in space by some nations, raising the specter of nuclear weaponisation of outer space, although this is explicitly banned by international law.

(e) International Tensions and Diplomacy: The increasing militarisation has led to diplomatic efforts to curb an arms race

18 "Global Counterspace Capabilities Report", Secure World Foundation, April 9, 2025, https://swfound.org/ counterspace/. Accessed on April 9, 2025.

in space. The UN has seen discussions on non-binding norms and behaviours for space, but consensus on treaties like the Prevention of an Arms Race in Outer Space (PAROS) remains elusive.

(f) Private Sector Involvement: The role of private companies in space has complicated the landscape, with entities like SpaceX providing commercial satellite services that have military applications, blurring the lines between civilian and military use.

These developments highlight an evolving landscape where space is not only a domain for scientific exploration but also a potential battleground, necessitating urgent dialogue, transparency, and possibly new international agreements to manage the risks of conflict and ensure the sustainable use of space.

Militarisation of space and nuclear weapons

States have avoided weaponising space until recently, despite the fact that space has been militarised since the 1950s, when the USSR and the US utilised satellites for spying purposes.[19] Conversely, states are progressively employing space-based military capabilities in contemporary conventional combat for logistical support, reconnaissance, and command and control of military operations. The significance of space-based assets in modern combat and their relevance to military dominance underscore their potential influence on national and international security matters. This has prompted certain participants to note that the issue is not if space will be weaponised, but rather when it will occur.[20]

Prospective Trajectories: An arms race in space might potentially exacerbate the already hostile ties between the major space powers. The potential negative consequences of this development include the aggravation of the global security crisis and, most importantly, the escalation of the threat to the prosperity that humans have achieved through the peaceful utilisation of space.[21]

19 Martand Jha, "This is How the Space Race Changed the Great Power Rivalry Forever", *The National Interest*, July 27, 2017, https://nationalinterest.org/feature/how-the-space-race-changed-the-great-power-rivalry-forever-21690. Accessed on April 3, 2025.

20 "The Future of Space-Based Warfare in Brief", The Hague Centre For Strategic Studies, Future Issue No. 06, 2009, https://hcss.nl/wp-content/uploads/2022/01/01.03_.2009_-_Future_Issue_-_Space-Based_Warfare_.pdf. Accessed on March 24, 2025.

21 "Militarisation of space and nuclear weapons", Institute of International Relations Prague, October 21, 2024, https://www.iir.cz/en/militarisation-of-space-and-nuclear-

The potential for a disastrous escalation of tensions exists, characterised by a cycle of arms races and mutual deterrence, alongside the corresponding action-reaction dynamics in US and NATO ties with Russia. The recommencement of arms control discussions about strategic stability and the implementation of steps to diminish the likelihood of conventional and nuclear conflict might certainly aid in alleviating this issue. The primary prerequisite is the cessation of the Russian-Ukrainian conflict and the political resolve to tackle the enduring security concerns in Europe. This development could positively influence the resolutions of other problem areas.[22]

Strategies to Deter Weaponisation:

The Outer Space Treaty of 1967 imposes limitations on the deployment of weapons of mass destruction (WMDs) in space, although it does not encompass all categories of space weaponry. Discussions for more comprehensive agreements are still in progress.

Transparency and Confidence Building Measures: Establishing a culture of open communication among spacefaring nations regarding their space programmes can reduce mistrust.

Collaboration on space exploration and research can play a crucial role in promoting unity and teamwork among nations, offering a beacon of hope in the face of potential conflicts.

The current state of affairs

Numerous countries, such as the United States, China, and Russia, actively develop technologies with potential military applications in space. Notably, the international community is currently engaged in a lively discussion on effectively addressing the issue of preventing an arms race in outer space, a reassuring sign of collective concern and action.

Way Ahead

Exploring the vast expanse of space, the weaponisation of space is contingent upon the decisions made by the various nations with space capabilities. Opting for collaboration and peaceful space utilisation, which could involve using space for scientific research, communication, and

weapons. Accessed on February 5, 2025.

22 Ibid 1.

exploration, can preserve its status as a domain for peaceful advancement rather than conflict.

The militarisation and westernisation of space are two trends that are shaping the future of space activities. The militarisation of space reflects the growing importance of space in international relations, as countries seek to expand their military presence in space. The westernisation of space reflects the increasing influence of Western nations and companies in space exploration and development. The interplay between these two trends is complex and multifaceted, with implications for international relations, space security, and the long-term sustainability of space activities. As space activities continue to evolve, it is likely that the militarisation and westernisation of space will remain important trends, shaping the future of space exploration and development.

The reflection warns of the dangers of space militarisation and calls for renewed arms control talks between rival nations.

Regulatory Controls: Nations have to take part in international accords to prevent an arms race and offer a fair method to militarise space technology. Enhanced international cooperation and communication can help to produce laws and regulations stressing for the peaceful use of space.

Promoted should be research and development investments in dual-use technology that satisfy military and civilian purposes. By improving openness in military advancements affecting space, this approach not only promotes creativity but also lowers the possibility of confrontation.

Governments should also support the establishment of monitoring systems equipped to follow developments in space technology. Such models would guarantee states follow accepted conventions and accords on the appropriate use of space, therefore encouraging responsibility.

Essential public participation and lobbying for laws enabling the peaceful use of outer space is policy-oriented. By educating people on the consequences of space militarisation, one can foster peace and inspire governments to implement more favourable policies about space technology and uses.[23]

Space technology militarism raises serious questions for world security and international affairs. The results for peace and collaboration in outer space are complicated by the junction of military achievements with technical development.

23 Ibid UNOOOSA.

States collectively working and strict implementation of the regulations on space activity will be crucial in reducing the risks of a growing arms race. An equal approach giving the peaceful use of space first priority guarantees a brighter future for all people.

Conclusion

The militarisation and westernisation of space represent significant developments in the modern era, driven by technological advancements and geopolitical interests. The militarisation of space involves the deployment of military technology and weaponry in outer space, while westernisation refers to the adoption of Western cultural, economic, and political practices by other nations. The interplay between militarisation and westernisation in space is complex and multifaceted, reflecting the changing geopolitical landscape and the increasing influence of Western nations in space exploration.

When the Space Race was in full effect, it was in its very nascent stage. Development and expansion of the Indian space programme is due to aid and assistance from both the US and the USSR. Indian space scientists and engineers were trained in both these countries. This led the Indian Space Research Organisation (ISRO) to become one of the best space research institutions in the world.[24] The India needs to invest in R&D to maintain the leading globally in this realm.

24 Ibid (The National Interest).

Chapter 10

Space Technology Led Warfare: A Threat to Human and Environmental Existence on Earth

-Ajay Revansidha Tambulkar and K. Ratnabali

Introduction

The Universe in which we all exist today with our competing and conflicting interests, began with an explosion of space itself, popularly known as the 'Big Bang'[1] and is constantly expanding. Life has evolved to consciousness and further with improvement in scientific knowledge, the horizon of human outreach expanded beyond the planet earth. This is evident from the launch of first satellite from earth Sputnik[2], entry and

1 Tony Rothman, A Little Book about the Big Bang, The Belknap Press of Harvard University Press Cambridge, 2022; Andrew May; Anand Narayanan, Where do we come from? What are we? Where are we going?, iWonder, Rediscovering School Science, Issue I, Azim Premji University, 2018, available at https://cdn.azimpremjiuniversity.edu.in/media/publications/downloads/i-wonder-Issue-1-Aug-2018.pdf; When it all Began: Big Bang. In: The Evolving Universe and the Origin of Life. Springer, New York, NY, 2009; What is the Big Bang Theory? The Big Bang Theory explains how the universe began 13.7 billion years ago, available at https://www.space.com/25126-big-bang-theory.html; Bickersteth, P. (2022).

2 Fabio Tronchetti, Harbin Institute of Technology Harbin, Fundamentals of Space Law and Policy, Springer Briefs in Space Development, DOI 10.1007/978-1-4614-7870-6 ISSN 2191-818X (electronic) ISBN 978-1-4614-7870-6 (eBook) Springer New York Heidelberg Dordrecht London, 2013; Bin Cheng, Studies in International Space Law, Oxford Scholarship Online, Oxford University Press, 1997; Fabio Tronchetti , The Exploitation of Natural Resources of the Moon and Other Celestial Bodies, A Proposal for a Legal Regime, Studies in space law, Vol. 4, Martinus Nijhoff Publishers and VSP, 2009.

presence of envoys of humankind in orbit, deployment of space station to the recent recapture of reusable launch vehicle by Spacex[3]. These consistent developments in space technology have been strategically utilised by States to shape security and military interests, enabling them to use space as zone of force multiplier and power projection. The tussle between US and erstwhile USSR is a history of complex dynamics between technological inventions and political ambitions.

Today, claims and conflicts of human society are no longer limited to this planet and the air space above it. With escalation of armed conflicts to the fourth frontier of warfare, outer space is being viewed as an ultimate high ground from where earth below could be controlled.[4] In the light of these developments in space technology and potential use of such technology in military operations and war, this chapter delves into nuances of space warfare and its environmental impacts as it has direct correlation with the survival of human species.

Space Technology: Genesis to present status of 'dual use'

The earliest satellites and 'space-based technology'[5] were designed and deployed for scientific experiments to discover the facts about vast expanse of universe. Later, space technology led satellites were focussed on civilian applications such as Earth Observation Satellites, Communications and Navigation Satellites, Astronomical satellites, Satellites for weather monitoring or forecasting, etc. The benefits of television, radio communication, navigation and positioning, internet and interplanetary scientific expeditions was ushered by such civilian space missions and these innovations contributed in enhancing the standard of life on planet earth. Interestingly, satellites guided humanity in multiple ways, from discovery of ozone hole over Antarctica to monitoring of forest fires and natural disasters as an early caution sign. Satellites have also helped to capture

---

3 Ellen Phiddian, Cosmos science journalist, Tower recaptures SpaceX rocket booster, Cosmos Magazine, October 14, 2024, available at https://cosmosmagazine.com/space/exploration/spacex-super-heavy-recapture/.

4 John Pike, The military uses of Outer Space; A New Era in Outer Space, Our Common Agenda Policy Brief 7: For All Humanity – The Future of Outer Space Governance, May 2023; Shipman, H.L. (1989). The Military Uses of Outer Space. In: Humans in Space. Springer, Boston, MA. https://doi.org/10.1007/978-1-4899-6104-4_14

5 What are space-based technologies? p. 3, The Accenture Space for Growth report, Why every company has a stake in the new space economy, available at https://www.accenture.com/content/dam/accenture/final/industry/aerospace-and-defense/document/Accenture-Space-for-Growth-PDF.pdf.

photographs of manmade disasters like, nuclear power plant disaster at Chernobyl. Every aspect of human life, from communication to air traffic management is augmented by intervention of Space technology.

On the other hand, along with these civilian pursuits, evidently[6] outer space and space technology has been used for military purposes even before the first human spaceflight. The R&D of first Inter-Continental Ballistic Rocket, R-7 Semyorka[7] by Soviet Union was started in 1954 and it was launched into outer space in August, 1957, two months prior to the first artificial satellite launch. This ultra-long-range multistage rocket was later added to the arsenal of the Soviet Army making it one of the space superpowers. This underlines the space race with earliest instances of testing of weapons in outer space as a precursor of militarisation of space.

Eventually, in cold war era, satellites were explicitly used to monitor activities of adverse State and gather intelligence imageries and information to assert 'technological superiority'[8], thereby setting the trend of using space technology as a support to military purposes. Since the journey of earth-bound satellites that began from Sputnik 1[9], the space tech-regime has grown exponentially[10], from small experimental satellites to deployment of giant space station, development of reusable launch vehicles, anti-satellite tracking and striking system, technology ensuring the possibility of human presence in outer space and most recently, counter-space weapons, etc. The

6 Bowen, B., War in Space: Strategy, Space-power, Geopolitics 1st Edition. Edinberg: Edinburgh University Press, 2020.

7 Presidential Library Collection, The first soviet intercontinental ballistic rocket R-7 launched, Pervov M. A. Intercontinental ballistic missiles of the USSR and Russia. Moscow, 1998; Umansky S. P. Launch vehicles. Spaceports. Moscow, 2001.

8 Kruppa, J., Sanders, K. and Martinez, M., 2021. Achieving Space Superiority in an Era of Great Power Competition. The Journal of the Joint Forces Staff College.

9 Supra n. 2.

10 Brian C. Odom, The Rise of the Commercial Space Industry Early Space Age to the Present, Palgrave Studies in the History of Science and Technology, 2024; OECD Handbook on Measuring the Space Economy, 2nd Edition, OECD Publishing, Paris, 2022, https://doi.org/10.1787/8bfef437-en.; Space Economy Initiative, UNOOSA, Insights Report 2021; John Schmidt and Paul Thomas, The Accenture Space for Growth report, Why every company has a stake in the new space economy- What are space-based technologies? Pg. 3, available at https://www.accenture.com/content/dam/accenture/final/industry/aerospace-and-defense/document/Accenture-Space-for-Growth-PDF.pdf; Thomas Cortez, Brendan Omana, and Dr. Philip Ritcheson, The Future of the Space Economy Potential Implications for the Intelligence Community, Deloitte Report, 2024.

weaponisation and militarisation of space became inevitable for States with their terrestrial conflicts extending into airspace and outerspace.

Today, earth's orbits and outer space region have become a core area of surveillance for security and military interests across the globe. Since the past three decades, almost all top space faring nations have developed space technology-based military capabilities. In fact, every satellite is potentially helpful for providing critical information to military establishments, for example, even Earth Observation or Navigation Satellites meant for civilian purpose can guide military operations by providing precise images or information indicating positions, installations or military objects of enemy party. This brings us to the 'dual-use'[11] potential of space technology and this increases the legal complexity of regulating or limiting the non-peaceful (offensive military) use of space technology. The dual-use means potential of space technology and assets to be used for both civilian and military purposes.[12] Conceptually, defining or categorising dual use is in strict sense difficult because of rising multi-pronged usage of technology. Philosophically, the intent of user of means (technological tools) determines the potential nature and end outcome.

Space technology, by its very nature, is global and in many aspects it goes beyond strict politically conceived territorial divisions of States; satellites are a material consequence and producer of the 'geopolitical shrinking'[13] of Earth. The existing space technological capabilities (potential dual-use, both civilian and military) employed in armed conflicts are broadly of five categories[14]: co-orbital capabilities, wherein objects are placed into orbit and then manoeuvred to approach their target spacecraft, to interfere in ways that can be destructive; direct ascent capabilities, includes ground, air, and sea launched missiles that destroy their target spacecraft through kinetic impact; directed energy capabilities consist of systems that use focused energy, such as laser or microwave beams to destroy or interfere with space systems; electronic warfare capabilities uses radiofrequency

11 Forge, J. A Note on the Definition of 'Dual Use'. *Sci Eng Ethics* 16, 111–118 (2010), available at https://doi.org/10.1007/s11948-009-9159-9;

12 European Commission, Final report: Data and information collection for EU dual-use export control policy review, November, 2015.

13 *Ibid*

14 Victoria Samson, "Space and Counterspace Technologies: Assessing the Current Threat Environment," Observer Research Foundation Issue Brief No. 745, October 2024,; Bleddyn E. Bowen, War in Space Strategy, Spacepower, Geopolitics, Edinburgh University Press, Edtn. 2020.

interference with satellite communications; and cyber capabilities uses network and software techniques to interfere with or destroy computer systems relevant to space capabilities.

The space technology enabled capabilities of national military forces and certain non-state actors have resulted into the frequent military use of space, along with support for nuclear weapons infrastructure, radio-frequency jamming, use of lasers, manoeuvrable unmanned space objects, and more capable direct-ascent anti-satellite weapons are among the new capabilities for disrupting and destroying satellites. Therefore, it is an undeniable fact that space technology has gone beyond mere civilian utility and peaceful use. Perhaps, dual use of space technology makes it more complex for determining the legitimacy of use of such technological weapons and their international control or disarmament, this makes scale and impact of ongoing wars more challenging for the world order. The instances of use of space technology in military operations or warfare and relating humanitarian challenges are discussed in subsequent part of chapter with the insights about changes in nature and scale of warfare.

The Transition in Warfare with Generations: One world with Multiple War Fronts

The present era of international relations is complex and driven by multipolar[15] power dynamics wherein the 'intervention of technology in warfare'[16] and 'change in geopolitical equations'[17] are making warfare more lethal.

Clausewitz explained that "war is an act of violence to compel our opponent to fulfil our will"[18]. War, then, is defined as a discourse of physical violence to achieve a political goal. Thomas Hobbes aptly emphasised that war, in its most basic form, is inextricably linked to gaining control over resources.

15 Frank Whelon Wayman, University of Michigan-Dearborn, Bipolarity and War: The Role of Capability Concentration and Alliance Patterns among Major Powers, Journal of Peace and Research, Vol. 21, 1984.

16 Bowen, B., War in Space: Strategy, Space-power, Geopolitics 1st Edition. Edinberg: Edinburgh University Press, 2020.

17 Tigran Yegavian, Conflicts Fueling Geopolitical Dynamics in 2024, EVN Report, available at https://evnreport.com/opinion/conflicts-fueling-geopolitical-dynamics-in-2024/;

18 Jordan Lindell, Clausewitz: War, Peace and Politics, E-International Relations, ISSN 2053-8626, available at https://www.e-ir.info/2009/11/26/clausewitz-war-peace-and-politics/.

In fact, the common root cause of warfare in all instances is conflict for resources. The type of resources may change, like, territories, oil, maritime trade routes, global trade or space-based resources. At present only handful of pioneering States possess space weapons and anti-satellite assets, whereby they play a primary role in race for space resources and in shaping the military-political situation in the world. This further leads to space technology-based power imbalance providing edge to the few against rest of the world.

A noteworthy feature of present world order is multipolarity, wherein more than two great powers, like, United States, China, Russia, India, etc. play dominant roles in the international system and exert impact on the nature and causes of international conflicts. More the power polarization, more complex the causes, means and methods of warfare are. Consequently, arms race on earth is extended to outer space, wherein space is perceived as the higher surveillance station. This was done primarily by States with the necessary change in their nature and functioning.

The way States have evolved from primitive to modern States (like, Welfare State, Digital State, Deep State, etc.), in a similar manner, the nature and form of warfare has undergone a transition from old war to new war or modern war to post-modern war[19]; from guerilla war[20] to cyber-war[21]; from direct battlefield combat using amateur weapons to present day, space-technology enabled 'precision-warfare'[22] wherein sophisticated space weapons like, nuclear warheads and Anti-satellite weapons are deployed. The multipolar world order has opened multiple war fronts with advancement in the domains of satellite communication, navigation, rocket launching capabilities, non-conventional weapons, weapons of mass destructions, satellite surveillance system and inter-continental strike capability. Today, the armed conflicts among States and non-State actors are witnessed on five fronts, land, maritime zone, airspace, cyberspace and now outer-space as well. No matter where the war is fought, the silent

19 Ozgur Tufekci, What is Distinctively New About So-Called 'New Wars'? UIIID-IJEAS, 2018.

20 Walter Laqueur, Guerrilla Warfare: A Historical & Critical Study (New Brunswick, N.J.: Transaction Publishers, 1998); Baljit Singh and Ko-wang Mei, Theory and Practice of Modern Guerrilla Warfare (New York: Asia Publishing House, 1971).

21 Nils Melzer, Cyberwarfare and International Law, Ideas for Peace and Security, UNIDR Resources, 2011.

22 Michael N. Schmitt, Precision attack and international humanitarian law, International Review of the Red Cross, Volume 87, Number 859, September 2005.

victim in war with advanced weapons raining from airspace or outerspace is environment.

Historical analysis of warfare will give us a wide spectrum of 'seven generations'[23] of warfare, each of them is distinguish with specific characteristics, from the human-to-human direct combat in wars in the first generation to the ability to shut down the enemy system from far away with the aid of automatic machines and unmanned precision guided weapons in the seventh-generation warfare. The present-day warfare places heavy reliance on 'information'[24] as a decisive factor, information superiority[25] determines the patterns and scale of armed conflicts as well as the outcomes of power-tussles. The 'exploration and use of outer space shall be carried for peaceful purpose' is the fundamental norm laid down in Outer Space Treaty, yet, certain scholars argue that, outer space has been militarized since the beginning of the 'space age' and with technological inventions, precision and lethality is taken to the next stage in military operations, eyeing space as the central axis of modern warfare.

The frequent changes in the means and methods of warfare are witnessed since past century, mainly due to industrial revolution,[26] scientific inventions in military domain and rise of nuclear powers. In World War II, heavy use of aerial technology[27] and precision weapons[28] played pivotal role in changing the outcome of war. Aircrafts designed and deployed for military purposes saw rapid and broad development during the war to meet the demands of aerial combat and converted airspace into a deadly

23 Robert J. Bunker, Generations, Waves, and Epochs Modes of Warfare, National Security Studies, California State University, San Bernardino, 1995.

24 Major General Bipin Bakshi, VSM, Information Warfare: Redefining National Security, Centre for Joint Warfare Studies (CENJOWS), SYNODOS Paper Vol - XII NO-23 / OCT 2018.

25 Information Warfare: Redefining National Security, SYNODOS Paper Vol - XII NO-23 / OCT 2018; Deganit Paikowsky, Political Science Department, Tel Aviv University, Space Technology, Patterns of Warfare and Force Build-Up: Between a Power and a Small State, Working Paper Series- Economics of National Security; Shaw J. The Influence of Space Power upon History (1944-1998), Air and Space Power Chronicles, available at www.airspace.maxwell.af.mil?airchronicles/cc/shaw.html.

26 Joseph Schumpeter, Capitalism, socialism and democracy, Allen & Unwin, 1943.

27 Vivek Kapur, Gp. Capt. Vivek Kapur, Research Fellow, Institute for Defence Studies & Analyses (IDSA), New Delhi, Precision Weapons in Aerial Warfare, IDSA Issue Brief, May, 2012; J. A. Stockfisch, A Case Study of World War II Air Power, The RAND Publication Series, 1991.

28 Ibid.

warzone, notable examples of aerial advanced weapons used in WW II are, the V-1[29], also known as the buzz bomb, was an automatic aircraft that would be known as a cruise missile today. The first aerial weapon that could go beyond stratosphere and enter outer space region is V-2. It was the world's first long-range guided ballistic missile with liquid-propellant rocket engine developed by Germany. This marked the beginning of space age of warfare even before launch of first satellite.

Later benchmark decade of 1960s in space history is the dawn of space launch, which was followed by Cold war. This phase was marked by the use of satellite data and technology for military purposes, primarily by the US and the USSR, where both tried to assert their mastery over regions of space. The US and the USSR realized that space-faring rockets could easily be fitted with nukes. Both powers then sought to prove their superiority by sending their weaponized innovations into space, and the Space ace was born. This bipolar space has become multipolar with the joining of China, the European Space Agency (ESA), India, Israel, Japan and the United Arab Emirates. New space programs are developed in countries such as Egypt, Indonesia, Iran, Malaysia, Pakistan, and Saudi Arabia. There are more than 70 States with their space agencies and ongoing space missions and 16 have launching capability. Today, space is more accessible compared to 1970s.

In 1990s, while pointing out the intricate nexus between space technology and war, Dolman[30] has opined that with the use of space technology in Persian Gulf, space warfare has evolved from its embryonic stage to infancy stage. This highlights the shift in the generation of warfare from terrestrial to outerspace. After two decades another scholar Bowen[31], based on the increased space-based aerial striking capability of States observed that "space power's time has arrived"[32] and space technology is now directly supporting the military operations.

---

29 Major Kirk M. Kloeppel, The Military Utility of German Rocketry During World War II, Air Command and Staff College, March 1997.

30 Dolman, E., Geostrategy in the space age: An astropolitical analysis. Journal of Strategic Studies, 22(2-3), pp. 83-106, 1999.

31 Bowen, B., War in Space: Strategy, Space-power, Geopolitics 1st Edition. Edinberg: Edinburgh University Press, 2020.

32 Spacepower and Space Warfare, Colonel M.V. Smith, USAF, Director of the Air Force Space and Cyber Center, Air University, JFQ / issue 60, 1st quarter 2011, available at https://ndupress.ndu.edu/Portals/68/Documents/jfq/jfq-60/jfq-60_42-45_Smith.pdf?ver=Q1CWXxuOwHaA7CU4daIaLQ%3D%3D

Since the launch of first satellite, it was well understood by US and Soviet leaders that Earths orbits are strategically important, orbits were perhaps viewed as ultimate high ground or high observation point or high firing point from. The inevitable race to master these orbits was the outcome of such tech-enabled tussle to gain necessary military advantage with space as the next frontier of warfare. At present, scholars viewed space warfare as the continuation of terrestrial (earth bound) politics by other means; in other words, what takes place in Earth orbit will essentially reflect the politics of the international system on Earth and will have long-lasting impact on earth's orbit.

The jurisprudence of war, ethics, politics and responsibility of States is indicated in the tone of Realism, 'all politics is a struggle for power and survival.'[33] This struggle for power in different spheres of global politics and survival of nations amid intense economic and technological tussle becomes the key issue related to existential crisis. Wars are mostly fought either to safeguard security or expand the security of the states; for example, Russia-Ukriane or Israel-Palestine conflicts, if looked from both the sides, conflicting parties are fighting either to defend their country (like Ukraine, Israel) or indirectly by eliminating the threat the other country poses to its security or interests.

Rise of Space Technology-based Weapons: Impact on nature and Scale of Warfare

The World Economic Forum emphasised that, "Like the internet in its early days, the space industry is standing at an inflection point."[34] On one hand, the world is witnessing Industrial Revolution 5.0 while on the other, in the name of advancement and modernisation of security and military capabilities, major powers are contesting to strengthen their arsenals with Weapons of Mass Destruction (WMDs). Paradoxically, technology enabled weapons incurring billions of rupees are held by States in pursuit of peace.

The armed conflict in Ukraine has underscored the vital role of Satellite Communication (SATCOM), Positioning, Navigation, and Timing (PNT) as well as Intelligence, Surveillance, and Reconnaissance (IST) services which were utilised to command and control the modern battlefield. The

33 Ksawery Lisinski, Explaining War: A Comparison of Realism and Constructivism, E-International Relations, available at https://www.e-ir.info/2012/05/03/explaining-war-a-comparison-of-realism-and-constructivism/

34 World Economic Forum, Space: The $1.8 Trillion Opportunity for Global Economic Growth, Insight Report, 2024.

competition in space has already taken the form of fierce contest to assert military power with the control over information to leverage decision advantage in war zone. The act of jamming, spoofing, or hacking satellite networks supporting the armed forces have been a disruptive feature of the war since its outset. The satellite communication, navigation and rockets having capability to strike over a long range has changed the geopolitical equations and heightened the 'security dilemmas'[35].

There are two broader ways of using space technology or weapons in conflict scenarios. Firstly, direct use of space weapons like Inter-Continental Ballistic Missiles (ICBM), Anti-Satellite System (ASAT) in armed conflicts. Secondly, attacking space infrastructure on or off earth, equipment, or satellites to make space applications (like, GPS, Beidou, Galileo and GLONASS) dysfunctional, thereby affecting civilian life. The traffic controls on land, in airspace and on high seas is managed with such navigation satellites, moreover, internet-based services like global banking, financing, power grids, tele-medicine, etc. are dependent on space technology. The same satellites are potential military objectives and tools in military missions or in warfare situations. The attacks on such satellites would lead to uncountable damage and disruption of global economy and international relations. In the current space weaponization and militarization era, broad category of threats to space systems include - electronic warfare, cyber-attacks, directed energy attacks and orbital-based and ground-based anti-satellite weapons.

Use of space weapons either kinetic or non-kinetic means, using space to space or ground-based earth to space weapon systems, will have catastrophic effects on civilian life on earth, this may lead to serious humanitarian crisis. In present day, space tech enabled warfare, tracing the targets and combatants of adverse State even at night, in bad weather or through smoke or blowing sand is practically possible due to advanced satellite surveillance systems. With this, war is becoming more precision guided, and thus enables distinction between military and civilian objects/ targets, however, the enhanced range and scope of destruction that today's weapon system can cause heightens the potential of causing unnecessary suffering and large-scale collateral damage. The use of aerial and space technology also challenges or at times violates the fundamental principles and rules of International Humanitarian Law and Human Rights Law.

35 World Armatnents and Disarmatnent, Stockholm International Peace Research Institute Yearbook, 1992.

The Gulf War proved the value of satellites in modern conflicts. During this war, allied forces utilised space capabilities to control the high zone of space for surveillance and achieve a decisive advantage. Satellites were deployed to provide critical information on enemy troop formations and movements, early warning of enemy missile attacks, and precise navigation in the featureless desert terrain. The advantages of satellites allowed the coalition forces to quickly bring the war to a conclusion, saving many lives.

Militarisation and Weaponisation of Outer-Space

Since the dawn of space age, Outer Space Treaty has set the foundational norm of 'peaceful use', that has been advocated by United Nations as well. However, many scholars agree to the fact that, space has been militarized since the initiation of the space age[36] as an instrument of military power.

Space militarisation is any activity in space, which is executed by a man-made object incorporated de jure or de facto in the military organization of a State.[37] Militarisation and weaponisation of outer space is a dangerous method to gain military superiority because if one State undertakes such activity then adversary State may feel compelled to pursue similar path to secure itself. For instance, the former DRDO Chief, Dr VK Saraswat, claimed on several occasions that India is developing the necessary space technologies to demonstrate the capability to destroy an enemy satellite.[38] The Russian president Putin in 2019, during a meeting with the Ministry of Defense, justified the intensified development of Russia's orbital military and dual-use systems as a defence in contrast to the United State's efforts to militarize outer space.[39] Therefore, it is established that testing of space weapon by one spacefaring State or space weaponisation attempts results in offensive-defensive ripple effects. The UN General Assembly's Special Session on Disarmament mandated that negotiations should take place in what is now the Conference on Disarmament (CD), "in order to prevent

36 Todd Harrison, Defining Space Warfare and Space Weapons, International Perspective on Space Weapons, A Report of the CSIS Aerospace Security Project, May, 2020.

37 Rajeswari Pillai Rajagopalan, ASAT weapons: A real threat to the future of Space, Space Tracker, ORF, available at https://www.orfonline.org/expert-speak/asat-weapons.

38 Ibid.

39 Schreiber, N. H. (2022). Man, State, and War in Space: Neorealism and Russia's Counterbalancing Strategy Against the United States in Outer Space Security Politics. *Astropolitics*, *20*(2–3), 151–174. https://doi.org/10.1080/14777622.2022.2143043; Ajsel Gerejhanova, Zvezdnye vojny, *Rossijskaja gazeta*, December, 2019.

an arms race in outer space" that are "held in accordance with the spirit of the Outer Space Treaty."

Outer Space as a war-zone:

The fundamental treaties and customary norms of Space Law have envisaged space as a 'common heritage of (hu)mankind' where activities shall be undertaken for 'peaceful purposes in the interest and for the benefit of all'. However, as discussed earlier in this chapter, space technology was employed to advance the military capabilities and gain superiority in conflict situations. The first such instance was, Operation Desert Storm[40] conducted by United States and allied forces against Iraq's invasion of Kuwait. This international armed conflict had first reported use of space technology for precise air strikes, communication, surveillance and navigations. It is reported[41] that, for the first time, the US used MIM-104C Patriot missile system in combat to intercept Scud missiles launched by Iraq. It was also the first time that the Air Force used stealth and space systems support capabilities against a modern, integrated air defense.

Outer Space as a testing field of advanced weapons:

The nuclear weapon tests on earth as an instrument to assert power supremacy were started by the United States in July, 1945 and its Cold War rival the Soviet Union in August, 1949. Initially, these tests were conducted underground or underwater but later it was extended to airspace and outerspace. Reportedly,[42] over 2,000 nuclear explosions for testing were conducted worldwide between 1945 and 1996, 25% of these high explosives tests, that is around 500 bombs, were exploded in the atmosphere. Among these tests, 200 were by the United States, around 200 tests by the Soviet Union and rest tests were by Britain, France and China.[43] These tests led to widespread environmental contamination.

---

40 Operation Desert Storm was primarily a sustained 43-day air campaign by the United States and its allies against Iraq between January 17, 1991, and February 28, 1991. It was perhaps the most successful war fought by the United States in the 20th century.

41 Shannon Collins, Desert Storm: A Look Back, U. S. Department of Defense, available at https://www.defense.gov/News/Feature-Stories/story/Article/1728715/desert-storm-a-look-back/

42 United Nations, the Preparatory Commission for the Comprehensive Nuclear-Test-Ban Treaty Organization (CTBTO), International Day against Nuclear Tests 29 August, available at https://www.un.org/en/observances/end-nuclear-tests-day/history.; History of Nuclear Explosive Testing, Nuclear Matters Handbook, 2020,

43 Ibid.

Certain notable case studies of nuclear tests in airspace and outer space are - aerial testing of Soviet Union's nuclear bomb - Ivan also known as Tsar Bomba in 1961[44]; which led to seismic shocks across earth and strong shock affecting entire earth. In response to this, US came up with its Starship Prime[45], a first high-altitude nuclear test in space under project Dominic 1962. This test led to negative effects on natural conditions in earth's orbits, further causing damage to nine functional satellites, radio communication, electric power-grids in the region. Another notable nuclear test conducted by Soviet Union is Project K[46], it was a series of five high-altitude nuclear explosions conducted in 1961-62. Although, precise number of nuclear weapons tests in outer space are debated, it is reported in certain findings that between 1958 and 1962 both the US and the Soviet Union conducted eight nuclear tests in space[47], these tests led to long term impact on the environment of earth and natural conditions in outer space.

Scientists explain that, testing of nuclear weapons close to earth's surface in atmosphere leads to fireball, shock wave, mushroom cloud formation and radioactive fallout that may kill living beings in the region and grossly result in destruction of the environment of the earth. Whereas, effects of nuke tests in outer space results in big flash, electromagnetic pulse, belt of high radiation around earth in orbits where explosion takes place. Consequently, such high intensity radiation in space distorts the nature (environment) of outer space[48], importantly, increase in pollutant like aluminium oxide that destroys Ozone layer, increase in insolation of earth causing rise in earth's temperature and accelerating climate change. Further, nuke tests render orbits (Specifically Low Earth Orbit) non-conducive for functioning of satellites, charged particles and prolonged radiation belt results in damage to satellites, electronic and solar components of satellites, creating havoc in orbits.

44 Tsar Bomba: The Largest Atomic Test in World History, The National WW II Museum, available at https://www.nationalww2museum.org/war/articles/tsar-bomba-largest-atomic-test-world-history.

45 Ajey Lele, Remembering Starfish Prime, The Space Review Essays and Commentary about the Final Frontier, available at https://www.thespacereview.com/article/4822/1.

46 Ibid.

47 Ibid.

48 Conall Hirsch, Nukes in Space: Exploring the Ecological and Security Implications, Central European University, available at https://ir.ceu.edu/ohpa/research_blog/articles/nukesinspace.

The burgeoning nuclear weapons among space power States and intersection of space technology with nuclear warheads poses huge threat to existence of environment on earth. The serious warning was given to humanity by the Russell-Einstein Manifesto[49]; it highlighted that war between nuclear-armed states would be destructive beyond human experience, that such a war could be the cause of 'the risk of universal death'[50]. In response to nuclear tests in space conducted by cold war rivals, United Nations passed a Resolution A45 (III), 1963, banning nuclear tests in atmosphere in outer space and underwater. The recent news reports speculating Russian deployment of nukes (nuclear warheads) in outer space indicates serious humanitarian concerns.

Space faring nations developed certain kind of weapons that can be either launched from orbits to earth or placed in orbits for potential military attack, one such weapon is, kinetic bombardment technique[51] tested by United States air force in the form of ground-based weapon resembling a kinetic bombardment, it was known as the electromagnetic railgun. Some other examples of development and testing of space weapons are hydrogen fluoride laser for space-to-space combat[52] and X-37B[53].

Another important kind of weapon tests conducted in outer space to militarise space is called as advanced counter-space capability[54] that is, Anti-Satellite test (ASAT). Out of the 29,000 trackable debris currently in orbit1, it is estimated that approximately 4,300 have been generated by destructive ASAT tests.[55] Counter-space capability is a desired degree

49 Jeffrey Boutwell, Addressing the Nuclear Weapons Threat: The Russell-Einstein Manifesto Fifty Years On, Pugwash Occasion Papers, Volume 4, Number 1, December 2005.

50 Steven E. Miller, Until the Sun Grows Cold: Persisting Nuclear Dangers in a Complacent World, 55th Pugwash Conference on Science and World Affairs, 2005.

51 Jared Keller, "The Pentagon's New Super Weapon Is Basically A Weaponized Meteor Strike". Task & Purpose, 2018, available at https://taskandpurpose.com/kinetic-bombardment-kep-weaponry/.

52 Garden, H. and Military, F. How Space Wars Will Work; How Stuff Works? 2019, available at https://science.howstuffworks.com/space-war2.htm.

53 Kiona Smith-Strickland. "What's the X-37 Doing Up There? Air & Space Magazine. Para 2, available at https://www.airspascemag.com/space/spaceplane-x-37-180957777/

54 J.B. Sheldon, Threats to Security in Space from Counter-Space Technologies, ASEAN Regional Space Security Workshop, Hoi An, Vietnam, 2012;

55 United Nations General Assembly, Destructive Anti-satellite Weapons, Open-ended working group on reducing space threats through norms, rules and principles of responsible behaviours, AC. 294/2023.

of space superiority by the destruction or neutralisation of enemy forces. In 1963, first American ASAT systems using the Nike-Zeus anti-ballistic missile and the other the IRMB Thor, were developed and it remained operational for about 10 years.[56] Later on, Soviet Union developed Killer satellite and further America developed Prototype Miniature Air-Launched System. Chinese direct-ascent anti-satellite system named, SC-19 ASAT missile and India's Mission Shakti were developed in recent past. Testing and use of such ASAT systems causes substantial amount of space debris. It changes the natural conditions of space and poses severe threat to other satellites and spacecraft in space, increasing the risk of collisions and damage to life and environment on earth.

Use of space technology in warfare: Environmental impact assessment of technology led warfare

The history of warfare provides an extensive literature on relationship between war and technology, but in many writings focus has tended to be on the significance of technology in helping nations or militaries win wars.[57] In very few cases, writers have attempted to locate war within a broader technological, economic, social, cultural and importantly environmental framework. The destruction of environment due to hostilities has been part of recent discussions under International Humanitarian Law through the works of International Law Commission, International Committee of Red Cross, United Nations Committee for Disarmament and certain other research organisations.

As per certain scholarly findings, an important correlation between war hotspots of world and biodiversity hotspots is highlighted, for instance, around 90% of the major armed conflicts during the period of 1950 to 2000 occurred within the countries having biodiversity hotspot.[58] Among these armed conflicts more than 80% wars took place directly within biodiversity

56 United Nations Institute for Disarmament Research, Geneva, Satellite warfare A challenge for the international community, Report by the French Institute for International Relations (IFRI), UNIDIR/87/4, 1987.

57 Warren Chin, Technology, war and the state: past, present and future, Re-visioning war and the state in the twenty-first century, International Affairs, July 2019; Martin van Creveld, Technology and war from 2000 BC to the Present, New York Free Press, 1989.

58 International Law and Policy Institute (ILPI), Protection of the Natural Environment in Armed Conflict An empirical study, Oslo, Norway, 2014; T. Hanson, Warfare in Biodiversity Hotspots, Conservation Biology, 2009, pp. 578–87.

hotspot regions[59]. This underlines the direct destructive impact of warfare on environment and war - a causative factor for 'ecocide'[60]. Ecocide denotes "various measures of devastation and destruction which have in common that they aim at damaging and destroying the ecology of geographic areas to the detriment of human life, animal life and plant life".[61]

The first four phases of industrial revolution experienced by the world so far has two sides, one, the beneficial aspect that it added to the standard of human life on planet earth, and the other flip side being, the stark reality that human society is turning into profit centred market society, with policies, at certain times, detrimental to societal values and environmental ecosystem. The militarisation and weaponisation of space, development and deployment of space technology on defensive or offensive fronts in warfare have shown us the flip side of technological advancement with its negative impact, like, use of guided ballistic-missiles to target adverse nation and its people may cause superfluous injuries; use of nuclear warheads guided by space technology may result in loss of lives, wanton destruction of property and natural ecosystem; anti-satellite systems or counter-space weapons may cause unprecedented impact on lives and environment on earth.

The space technology has taken warfare to its next level. The impact of space technology on warfare shall be analysed in comparison to the parallelly ongoing Industrial Revolution 5.0[62] (IR 5.0). The IR 5.0 attempts to make technology more human-centric while use of advanced space technology in military operations and warfare is making war more machine-centric. War is becoming more lethal with unimaginable extent of destruction caused by proliferation of space (based) weapons or counter-space weapons[63].

59 Ibid.

60 Richard A Falk, Princeton University, Environmental Warfare and Ecocide- Facts, Appraisal, and Proposals, Bulletin of Peace Proposals, Vol. 4, No. 1, 1973.

61 Sarlieve Maud, Ecocide: Past, Present, and Future Challenges, Springer Nature Switzerland AG, 2021,

62 Susu Nousala, Gary Metcalf and David Ing, Industry 4.0 to Industry 5.0, Explorations in the Transition from a Techno-economic to a Socio-technical Future (Edtd.), Springer Nature Singapore Pte Ltd., 2024; Sudipta Ghosh, Decoding the Fifth Industrial Revolution, available at https://www.pwc.in/decoding-the-fifth-industrial-revolution.html;

63 Dr. Rajeswari Pillai Rajagopalan, Electronic and Cyber Warfare in Outer Space, Space Dossier 3, UNIDR, May 2019.

The ubiquitous coverage of satellites offers State and non-state actors a unique, fact-based perspective that can help us to overcome greatest challenges posed by power struggles, security tensions and could contribute in avoiding future armed conflicts. Information gathered from spacecrafts can be used for truly peaceful purposes as well as for the benefit and in the interest of all, like, use of information to track presence and movement of terrorists or belligerents, track the deployment of arms by rogue elements, improve border security, monitor the critical international borders causing infiltration and potential conflicts, etc.

The term 'peaceful purposes' enshrined in Outer Space Treaty is not clearly defined in any authoritative document, whereas in State practices, it is perceived in generic sense as a military, commercial, and scientific activity in space. Eventually with advancement in technology like, invention of ballistic or nuclear weapons, it was discussed by members of international community that the placement of weapons or the targeting of objects in space be excluded. But recent developments suggest that this norm against the weaponisation of space is now threatened. Certain cases or instances of use of space technology for military operations or to effectuate warfare are discussed below.

Space technology in Gulf War of 1991

The invasion of oil rich Kuwait by Iraq in 1990 led to intense war, wherein US allied with 42 States and under Operation Desert Storm, war was fought against Iraq's illegal invasion. Scholars consider this as the first space war wherein space technology was directly used by US and allies to gain advantage in war. In the first Gulf War, the destruction of infrastructure and environmental consequences were on huge scale, hundreds of oil well fires burnt uncontrollably in Kuwait and it affected air quality on a global scale. In this war, 600 oil wells were destroyed, causing the daily release of up to 500,000 metric tons of pollutants.[64] This armed conflict had severe effects on the air quality of the region. Iraq's destruction of oil bases led to serious damage to the coastal and desert ecology of southern Iraq, Kuwait, and Saudi Arabia-from the fires and spills, from military fortifications and land mines, from attacks on oil and petrochemical installations.

This Gulf war marked a paradigm shift in the conduct of war and a revolution in military affairs (RMA) caused by technological advances,

64 The Environmental Impacts of the Gulf War 1991: Interim Report, International Institute for Applied Systems Analysis, Austria, 2004.

use of computers, communication networks and satellites made it more techno-driven war giving edge to space power nation.[65]

Space technology in Russia-Ukraine War

This second Rapid Damage and Needs Assessment (RDNA2)[66] jointly developed by the World Bank Group, the Government of Ukraine, the European Commission, and the United Nations, presents an assessment of one year of war impacts.

The Russia-Ukraine war is having catastrophic impact on all environmental components including air, water, soil, and biota in agricultural fields, forests, rivers and alike aquatic ecosystem. The destruction of civilian infrastructure, like, residential and commercial buildings, hazardous industrial units and energy installations e.g. power plants, oil refineries, is resulting into emission of pollutants of serious nature, e.g. asbestos, PM2.5, Carbon dioxide and Green House Gases.

As per estimates, due to armed-conflict in Ukraine's Donetska, Kharkivska, and Luhanska region, forests cover of 1,83,181 hectares has been damaged due to fire caused by explosive weapons and an estimated 20 percent of the forest is now inaccessible due to impact of war on forest environment.[67] Natural ecosystem of forests and forestry sector has suffered gross destruction amounting to over USD 1.5 billion and forest resource losses are around USD 523 million.

The Intergovernmental Panel on Climate Change (IPCC)[68] coefficients and metrics highlights that the burning of over 440,000 hectares of natural landscapes resulted in emission of Carbon dioxide equivalent and triggered

65 Alvin Toffler and Heidi Toffler, War and anti-war: survival at the dawn of the 21st century (London: Little, Brown, 1993.

66 World Bank; Government of Ukraine; European Union; United Nations. *Second Ukraine Rapid Damage and Needs Assessment (RDNA2): February 2022 - February 2023 (English).* Washington, D.C. : World Bank Group http://documents.worldbank.org/curated/en/099184503212328877

67 Fire damage in the forestry sector (183,181 ha) is based on Fire Bulletin data for all Oblasts, except for ykolaivska, for which State Forest Resource Agency's data has been used.

68 World Bank; Government of Ukraine; European Union; United Nations. *Second Ukraine Rapid Damage and Needs Assessment (RDNA2) : February 2022 - February 2023 (English).* Washington, D.C. : World Bank Group http://documents.worldbank.org/curated/en/099184503212328877

a net increase of 120 million tonnes of greenhouse gases[69]; in economic terms, the estimated damage quantity goes up to USD 3 billion.[70] The air in war zone between Russia and Ukraine is highly polluted due to frequent fire incidents in forests, grasslands, oil depots and other ecosystems; the estimated loss is of USD 14 billion. In order to restore the environment after war, for instance, to restore or recover forests, over USD 1 billion is needed and the time required would be a decade period till 2033. The capacity building activities for strengthening environmental governance will require an estimated USD 420 million.

The most long-lasting environmental impact of war is 'natural resource depletion'[71]. War activities with advanced weapons of mass destruction and aerial-space weapons causes frequent and high intensity usage of fuel and energy sources. For instance, as per the impact analysis reported by United Nations Environment Program (UNEP)[72], Global petroleum consumption for military purposes is 6 percent of the gross world consumption, in other words, it accounts to one-half of the total consumption of all developing countries. The United States's 85 percent of energy consumption is for military purposes. It is pertinent to note that the manufacturing of weapons and military capabilities before war also contributes to environmental impact, for instance, in the manufacturing of arms, satellite, missiles, counter-space weapons and space nukes, etc. minerals and metals like, iron, copper, aluminium etc. are used in heavy quantities, which leads to depletion of resources.

Space technology-based warfare also leads to generation of hazardous waste; well-known issue of space debris is one such impact. Development, testing and use of chemical, nuclear, cyber-electronic material, as a part space weapons, results into large scale waste generation and severe impact on environment.

Space technology in Isarel-Palestine War

The use of Arrow 2 missile system by Israel to intercept Iranian made ballistic missile, suspected to be launched from Yemen against Israel's city,

69 Ibid.

70 Ibid.

71 Asit K Biswas, Scientific Assessment of Long-Term Environmental Consequences of War, The Environmental Consequences of War: Legal, Economic, and Scientific Perspectives, Cambridge University Press, Cambridge, UK, 2001.

72 United Nations Environment Program, Internal Documents on Peace and Security (1991).

highlighted that a segment of the armed-conflict has extended to outer space. As per the Human Rights Watch analysis, the Israeli forces are using satellite enabled surveillance technologies, artificial intelligence (AI) and other digital tools to determine the military targets or objectives in Gaza. The intersection of cyber-electronic-space technology is providing edge to continue fight with precision.

The United Nation, European Union and World Bank together conducted assessment of state of the environment in the Gaza Strip since the outbreak of armed conflict. Gaza Strip is one of the most densely populated area with severe strain on natural ecosystem for routine water, land and other resources. The disrupted water ecosystem in the region has been described as 'ecological catastrophe and a main climate change vulnerability'[73]. Since the outbreak of war till ceasefire, per day more than 300 aerial bombings with space enabled positioning, reconnaissance, surveillance has resulted into total targets of 22000 sites in Gaza.[74] The heavy grade 25000 tons of explosives were used in this conflict which scholars claim to be equivalent to use of two nuclear bombs.[75] These facts and figures conspicuously indicate the threshold of environmental impact this war is having on environment.

Limits on space technology led warfare: Intersection of International Space Law and Humanitarian Law

The United Nations General Assembly, through its Resolution 75/36, emphasised the need for all States to work together to reduce threats to space systems through the further development and implementation of norms, rules and principles of responsible behaviours with the aim of maintaining a peaceful, safe, stable, secure and sustainable outer space environment. In another recent instance, the United Nations General Assembly passed a resolution that urged governments to refrain from conducting harmful direct-ascent (DA) anti-satellite (ASAT) experiments in outer space. The said resolution received support of 155 nations, while nine nations, including China and Russia, voted in opposition. The UN Resolutions, although do not create binding obligations for member states yet they serve certain purposes. The Resolution emphasises the global need to address the issue of space weaponisation, militarisation and potential

73 United Nations Environment Programme (2024). Environmental impact of the conflict in Gaza: Preliminary assessment of environmental impacts. Nairobi, available at wedocs.unep.org/20.500.11822/45739.

74 *Ibid.*

75 *Ibid.*

threats from space warfare. It also clarifies the trend of state practices on certain key issues and creates ground for further legal developments, like negation of agreements.

As ICRC[76] clarifies that the military use of outer space or warfare activities in outer space do not remain unregulated in a legal vacuum, perhaps such activities affecting environmental factors are addressed together by the Charter of the United Nations, Space Law treaties and International Humanitarian Laws.

Responsibility and liability of States in the context of this topic can be discussed under two heads; one, liability for use of force in space, use of weapons in space and space warfare; second, liability for causing environmental hazards due to space technology-led warfare.

Liability for use of Force in Space

The United Nations Charter governs the lawfulness of the resort to threat or use of force by one state against another and the UN Charter is applicable[77] to outer space activities. Article 2(4) of the Charter provides: *"All Members shall refrain in their international relations from the threat or use of force against the territorial integrity or political independence of any state, or in any other manner inconsistent with the Purposes of the United Nations."*

International Court of Justice has underlined that prohibition on use of force enshrined in Article 2 is the 'cornerstone'[78] of the Charter and also a 'customary rule'[79], therefore, it creates liability on States for their unlawful use of force. The International Law Commission has stressed this provision as 'a conspicuous example of a peremptory norm'[80]. In other words, it is *jus cogens*[81], meaning, established universal rule of International Law applicable in *rem*. Therefore, every state is obliged to follow this norm while undertaking military activities or using force in outer space domain. Article

76 Gilles Doucet and Stuart Eves: Protecting Essential Civilian Services on Earth from Disruption by Military Space Operations

77 Art. III of Outer Space Treaty, 1967.

78 Armed Activities on the Territory of the Congo (Dem. Rep. Congo v. Uganda), Merits, Judgment, I.C.J. Rep. 168, 2005

79 Military and Paramilitary Activities in and against Nicaragua (Nicaragua V. U.S.), I.C.J. Rep. 392, 1984.

80 Draft Conclusions on Subsequent Agreements and Subsequent Practice in Relation to the Interpretation of Treaties, conclusion 7(3), annexed to U.N. Doc. A/RES/73/202.

81 Art. 53, Vienna Convention on the Law of Treaties, 1969.

2 (4) of the Charters limits the unlawful use of force by States in outer space impacting life and environment on earth. In cases having threshold lower than use of force but are taken as harmful interference by State impacting environment of space and consequentially that of earth, States can resort to Article IX of the OST and undertake consultation process or retorsion to resolve the issue.

Unlawful threat or use of force by State gives rise to international State responsibility. In case any State commits unlawful acts in orbits or on earth, using space capabilities affecting environment in conflict situations, e.g. use of ICBM or ASAT damaging natural ecosystem on earth. In such scenario, perpetrator State shall, cease the unlawful act,[82] make full reparations for unlawful act[83] and creates the right of the victim State to take non-forcible countermeasures[84]. International community of States is made responsible not to render aid or assistance in furthering such unlawful activities. Chapter VII of the UN Charter further provides a mechanism of collective defence by the Security Council in case of unlawful action by any State which causes far reaching impact.

Liability for causing environmental hazards by use of weapons in space and space warfare:

Liability of States for causing environmental damage, due to military or war activities in general and space technology-led military or war activities in particular, is established under multilateral conventions in the realm of Public International Law, International Space Law, International Humanitarian Law, International Criminal Law and Human Rights Law.

International Space Law:

International Space Law, through fundamental treaty framework developed by the United Nation's initiative through UNCOPUOS and later UNOOSA, provides five treaties[85] as the legal framework governing outer space activities. These instruments prohibits weaponisation, militarisation and contamination of space affecting life and environment on earth. State parties to the treaty are prohibited from orbiting any weaponry including

82 Responsibility of States for Internationally Wrongful Acts, Art. 30

83 Ibid., Art. 31.

84 Ibid., Art. 22.

85 Space Law Treaties and Principles (Unoosa.org, 2018), available at http://www.unoosa.org/oosa/en/ourwork/spacelaw/treaties.html

nuclear weapons around the Earth, from installing such weapons on celestial bodies and from stationing any weapons in space.[86] The moon and other celestial bodies are to be used exclusively for peaceful purposes. The establishment of military bases, installations and fortifications, the testing of any type of weapons and the conduct of military manoeuvres on celestial bodies is forbidden.[87]

Space law treaties, in particular the Outer Space Treaty, which recognizes the common interest of all mankind in the progress of the exploration and use of outer space for peaceful purposes. Its Article IV prohibits the placement in orbit of objects carrying nuclear weapons or other weapons of mass destruction, the installation of such weapons on celestial bodies and the stationing of such weapons in outer space in any other manner. It also prohibits testing of any type of weapons and the conduct of military manoeuvres. However, the testing of ASAT by four space powers, generated space debris, has raised concerns about violation of Article IV.

Article IX of OST imposes obligation on States to conduct activities in outer space with due regard to interests of all state parties, avoid harmful contamination, adverse changes in the environment of earth and not to do harmful interference. In case of acts against the said provision, States can undertake consultation to overcome unlawful activities. Use of ICBM, precision missiles, laser weapons for jamming, use of cyber weapons for spoofing etc. may lead to harmful interference in space that may further affect lives and environment on earth; for instance, in 2011, Iran brought down a US RQ-170 Unmanned Aerial Vehicle by jamming its satellite communication links and spoofing the GPS signals it received, in another instance Iran used laser weapon against US satellite to disrupt it.[88] Russia, in its ongoing armed conflict with Ukraine, was reported to have used jamming systems to jam GPS signals in Ukraine in 2014[89].

International Criminal Law:

There are recent developments regarding analysis of environmental destruction taking place in wars and urgent need to fix legal liability for

86 United Nations Treaties and Principles on Outer Space, 4, (Article IV of Outer Space Treaty).

87 Ibid.

88 T. Harrison, K. Johnson and T.G. Roberts, Space Threat Assessment 2018, Center for International and Strategic Studies, available at https://csis-prod.s3.amazonaws.com/s3fs-public/publication/180823Harrison_Space Threat Assessment_FULL_WEB.pdf.

89 Ibid.

the wanton damage caused to environment by use of advanced technology enabled weapons. Recognising 'ecocide'[90] as a war crime is advocated by scholars. The UN General Assembly further urged Member States to label crimes that affect the environment as serious crime[91] and endorsed principles on the protection of the environment in relation to armed conflicts that had been set out by the International Law Commission.[92] Draft policy to fix liability for environmental crimes is under consideration.

International Criminal Law through Rome Statute[93], Art. 8 (2) (b) (iv) provides that, an attack with widespread, long-term and severe damage to the natural environment which would be clearly excessive in relation to the concrete and direct overall military advantage, will amount to war crime. Further, Art. 8 (2) (b) (xx) provides that, employing weapons, projectiles and material and methods of warfare which are of a nature to cause superfluous injury shall be treated as war crime.

International Humanitarian Law:

International humanitarian law (IHL), provides fundamental rules of warfare, it protects stakeholders, human made and natural assets, it also prohibits use of certain type of weapons in all kinds of warfare. Basically, IHL attempts to reduce the effects of war and balance principle of humanity vis-à-vis military necessity. The framework of IHL placing limits on methods and means of waging war, are Genevan Conventions, Hague Conventions of 1907, the 1977 Additional Protocols to the Geneva Conventions and a series of agreements on specific weapons, like, Chemical Weapons, Biological Weapons and Cyber Weapons etc.

International Humanitarian Law (IHL) sets limit on military activities of States in the armed conflict, including those that are carried out in outer space, or the effects of which extend to outer space.[94] IHL provides

90 Supra n. 60, 61; Giovanna Maria Frisso, Ecocide: The Environment as Victim at The International Criminal Court, ICD Brief, February 2023; Peter Doran, Criminalising 'Ecocide' at the International Criminal Court, Environment Justice Network Ireland, April 2021.

91 UN General Assembly Resolution 76/185, 16 December 2021

92 UN General Assembly resolution 77/104, 7 December 2022.

93 Rome Statute of the International Criminal Court

94 International law includes IHL. See also International Court of Justice, Legality of the Threat or Use of Nuclear Weapons, Advisory Opinion, 8 July 1996, para. 86.The applicability of IHL in outer space is confirmed by Article III of the Treaty on Principles Governing the Activities of States in the Exploration and Use of Outer Space, including

customary principles and treaty norms wherein protection of stakeholders and protection of environment in armed-conflict scenario is contained. The use of space technology, satellites or anti-satellites, ballistic missiles and other counter-space techniques involving kinetic, cyber and electronic attacks, if goes beyond the set limits relating to means and methods of warfare under Hague Rules and Geneva Codes, will attract regulatory norms provided in Geneva Codes and Hague Conventions. The use of weapons of mass destruction launched with the help of missiles using satellite enabled surveillance and navigation system may result into violation of fundamental norms of Humanitarian Law such as, Principle of distinction, Principle of precaution[95], Principle prohibiting indiscriminate attack[96] and Principle of proportionality[97].

The IHL regime further prohibits actions affecting environment in armed conflict by specific customary rules which are applicable to outer space, for instance -

- The use of means and methods of warfare which are of a nature that can cause superfluous injury or unnecessary suffering and the use of which may be indiscriminate, is prohibited.[98]
- No space object nor any of its constituent parts may be attacked, unless and for such time as they would be military objectives.[99]
- Prohibition on attacks, destruction, removal or rendering useless objects that are indispensable to the survival of the civilian population[100], wherein environment and natural habitats supporting livelihood of civilians in also protected. This rule extends to military activities on earth and in outer space.
- While assessing the proportionality of an attack, all foreseeable

---

the Moon and Other Celestial Bodies (Outer Space Treaty), which requires states to "carry on activities in the exploration and use of outer space ... in accordance with international law". International law includes IHL.

95 Article 57 of Additional Protocol I, 1977.

96 Article 51.4 of Additional Protocol I, 1977.

97 Articles 51.5 (b) and 57.2 (a) (iii) of Additional Protocol I, 1977.

98 Rules 70 and 71, ICRC Customary IHL Study; 2 ICJ, Nuclear Weapons case, Advisory Opinion.

99 Rule 10, 11 and 12, ICRC Customary IHL Study; Article 52(2), Additional Protocol I.

100 Article 54(2) of Additional Protocol I, 1977.

direct and indirect incidental damage to civilian objects (environmental components like agricultural land, grazing fields, forests etc. are considered as civilian infrastructure or objects) in outer space or on earth must be considered.[101]

- The environmental modification techniques as a part of warfare methods are prohibited, such as - changing or manipulation of natural processes like overcrowding orbits and creating potential threats, composition or structure of the earth's environment or of outer space having widespread, long-lasting or severe effects, as the means of war time destruction, damage or injury is prohibited.[102]

Conclusion

The development of dual-use space technology is transforming the world in an unprecedented manner and every sector of global economy is intercepted by space technology. Security, military capabilities and techniques of warfare are also largely affected by space innovations and modern warfare is becoming more precise and lethal due to space technology. All space faring nations are heavily investing in upscaling of their national military-space capabilities and to ultimately gain space supremacy. Geopolitics, geoeconomics, global security dilemmas, ongoing wars and ecocide are intricately inter-connected phenomenon which requires timely attention to build sustainable earth with its peaceful and safe orbits and outer space.

The environmental impact assessment of war is significant from ethical, social, economic, political, technological and legal point of view. As the end outcome of every war is direct or indirect destruction of natural and manmade assets, therefore, international institutions like, the United Nations Environment Program, UN Security Council, World Bank, UNIDR and ICRC should resolutely come up with nuanced framework to conspicuously establish that the destruction of environment in war is crime against humanity. The liability of States and non-state actors for destruction of environment due to military and war activities should be fixed in clear terms. For this, Protocol to Genva Convention, Hague Conventions and Rome Statue may be amended to re-craft and add certain provisions; further, absolute liability of States should be created for causing damage to

101 ICRC, International Humanitarian Law and the Challenges of Contemporary Armed Conflicts, ICRC, Geneva, 2015.

102 Articles I and II, Convention on the Prohibition of Military or Any Other Hostile Use of Environmental Modification Techniques, 1976.

environment by use of space-based technology in warfare. The responsible use of space technology should become part of responsible State practices in the interest and for the benefit of all lives on earth, including humanity.

Chapter 11

Evolving Air Power in Modern Conflicts: A Legal Perspective

-Kishore Kumar Khera

Evolving Airpower

Power empowers. In the kinetic domain, empowering tools have gradually transformed from the brute physical strength of the soldiers to cavalry, artillery and mechanised forces for surface battles. In the maritime domain, vessels of different shapes and sizes with firepower operating on surface and sub-surface defined the power matrix. With the advent of aircraft in the early 20th century, air power has now become a key tool for power expression for battles on the surface and in the maritime arena. Reach, speed, quantum and precision are four defining features of air power that practically define the battlespace environment. These air power attributes have steadily grown and enhanced the power projection.

Airpower has evolved dramatically over the past century, transforming from a fledgling military experiment into a dominant force in modern warfare. World War I (1914–1918) saw the birth of airpower with aircraft used as reconnaissance and spotting artillery. Fighters[1] Emerged to gain air superiority and bombing raids were primitive. The air combat and strike tactics developed slowly. By World War II (1939–1945), technological improvement resulted in faster, more reliable monoplanes[2] and organisationally air forces came into being independent from the army and

1 Aircraft such as the Sopwith Camel and Fokker Dr. I, were employed in combat operations.

2 The Supermarine Spitfire played a significant role in WWII.

navy[3]. Paratroopers and air transport started to gain relevance. Fighters, bombers, and transport aircraft started playing decisive operational roles. Large-scale strategic bombing campaigns[4], Carrier-based aviation[5] And Airborne operations[6] Defined the way battle progressed. Jet propulsion[7] For aircraft transformed the air power. For the next five decades, supersonic fighters[8] Dominated air combat with air-to-air missiles that replaced gun-based dogfights. Strategic bombers[9] Carried nuclear weapons for deterrence and the development of intercontinental ballistic missiles (ICBMs) changed the strategic balance. Aerial refuelling extended operational ranges and introducing precision-guided munitions (PGMs) redefined the strike paradigm. The stealth technology[10], long-range PGMs and air superiority fighters dominated conflicts towards the end of the 20th century but thereafter, Unmanned Aerial Vehicles (UAVs), emerged for reconnaissance and strike missions. The battle space transparency is enhanced with network-centric warfare integrated with real-time intelligence from satellites and aircraft. Now is a period of UAVs & 5th Gen Fighters like the F-22, F-35, Su 57 and J20 II. The UAVs have revolutionised surveillance and targeted strikes democratising the air power owing to low cost, low risk and commercial availability. Combat air power projection which was restricted to a few powerful militaries, is now available to a multitude of states and non-state actors. Hypersonic weapons and artificial intelligence (AI) are transforming airpower albeit slowly because of technical challenges. Cyber warfare and electronic warfare[11] Have become critical elements. The future of airpower will have under development 6th generation fighters and enhanced role of AI, directed energy weapons,

3 The Royal Air Force, as an independent entity, came into being in 1918.

4 The firebombing of Dresden and Tokyo are suitable examples in this arena.

5 For example, the Battle of Midway.

6 Normandy landing, Operation Market Garden and Operation Varsity in WWII brought airborne operations into focus.

7 German Me 262 redefined the way aero-engines were designed with its first jet flight on July 18, 1942.

8 MiG-21 and F-4 Phantom dominated the combat spaces for over five decades.

9 B-52 Stratofortress and Tu-4 capable of carrying nuclear weapons and undertaking long-range missions were critical in retaining balance during the Cold War era.

10 The operationalisation of F117 and its usage forced the redefinition of inherent capability and technological base for surface-based guided weapon systems.

11 Operations like GPS jamming and spoofing can be undertaken with little hardware and cost. Such spoofing operations in Myanmar in April 2025 affected the aircraft carrying relief material after an earthquake.

swarming drones and space-based assets permitting operational freedom to autonomous aircraft and loyal wingmen.[12].

Airpower and Transforming Warfare

Airpower has gone from rudimentary biplanes to sophisticated, networked, and autonomous systems that dominate modern warfare. The evolution of airpower over the last 100 years has profoundly transformed warfare. It has reshaped military strategy, tactics, and the global balance of power.

Before airpower, warfare was largely ground-based and static, with trenches and large-scale land battles. Air reconnaissance during WWI allowed armies to track enemy movements, reducing the effectiveness of static defences. By WWII, airpower enabled blitzkrieg tactics, combining tanks, infantry, and aircraft for rapid breakthroughs. Air forces introduced strategic bombing, directly targeting enemy industries, infrastructure, and cities.[13]. Air superiority became a critical objective—whoever controlled the skies often won on the ground and the seas. Aircraft carriers in the Pacific Theater made naval warfare air-centric. Airpower became a pillar of nuclear deterrence, with strategic bombers (B-52, Tu-95) and later ICBMs shifting warfare from conventional battles to potential mutual assured destruction (MAD). Jet aircraft and supersonic interceptors defined Cold War aerial combat (F-4 Phantom vs. MiG-21). The Cold War saw the rise of high-altitude aerial reconnaissance.[14] To track enemy movements. The Gulf War (1991) demonstrated the power of precision-guided munitions (PGMs) and stealth technology (F-117 Nighthawk). Instead of mass destruction, modern airpower allows surgical strikes against key military targets with minimal collateral damage.[15]. The rise of UAVs, like the Bayraktar, Predator and Reaper, has changed warfare by allowing remote-controlled and autonomous attacks.

The End of Traditional Frontlines

Airpower has erased traditional battle lines. Enemies can be engaged from thousands of miles away using UAVs, bombers, or missiles. Cyber

12 XQ-58 Valkyrie is an apt example in this domain.

13 Attacks on London, Dresden, Hiroshima, and Tokyo in WWII.

14 MiG-25, U-2 and SR-71 Blackbird redefined strategic reconnaissance with high altitude and high speed often out of reach of surface-based weapon systems and most interceptors.

15 Indian strike on terror network in Pakistan and Pakistan Occupied Kashmir on May 7, 2025, encapsulates this attribute.

warfare and electronic warfare (e.g., GPS jamming, and hacking enemy air defences) are now part of aerial combat. Hypersonic missiles reduce reaction time, making defences harder to maintain. The use of a hypersonic missile by Houthis to hit an Israeli airfield in April 2025 is possibly the first use of such a weapon by a non-state actor. AI-driven aircraft (e.g., the "loyal wingman" concept) fly alongside manned fighters. Swarming drones could overwhelm defences without risking pilots. Space-based warfare (e.g., satellite disruption, orbital weapons) will expand airpower's reach beyond the atmosphere.

Airpower has turned warfare into a fast, precise, and technologically driven domain. It has shifted conflicts from mass land battles to high-tech, remote-controlled, and even space-based engagements. Future wars may be won without a single soldier setting foot on the battlefield—a stark contrast to the trenches of WWI.

IHL and Airpower

International Humanitarian Law (IHL) has evolved significantly in response to the use of airpower in warfare. Initially, IHL was designed to regulate land and naval warfare, but the introduction of aircraft in combat forced legal frameworks to adapt. Over the past century, new treaties, conventions, and customary laws have been developed to address airpower-related concerns, particularly civilian protection, targeting, and aerial bombardment. International Humanitarian Law (IHL) needs to evolve continuously to address the challenges posed by modern airpower, including autonomous drones, AI-driven targeting, hypersonic weapons, and space-based warfare. While existing laws provide a foundation, they require updates, clarifications, and stronger enforcement mechanisms.

Expansion of Airpower Verticals and IHL

Over the past 115 years or so, airpower has undergone a profound transformation, shaping modern warfare in unprecedented ways. From its early use in reconnaissance to its current role in precision strikes, surveillance, and multi-domain operations, airpower has significantly evolved across four critical dimensions: speed, reach, quantum, precision and battlespace transparency. The evolution of these capabilities has had a lasting impact on the conduct of warfare, as well as on compliance with International Humanitarian Law (IHL), which seeks to regulate armed conflict and protect civilians from the effects of war.

Speed

Over the years, the speed of airpower has increased dramatically, fundamentally transforming the nature of warfare and raising new questions about compliance with International Humanitarian Law (IHL). At the dawn of aviation in the early 20th century, aircraft such as the Wright brothers' Flyer flew at speeds of around 50 kilometres per hour. During World War I, aircraft were primarily used for reconnaissance and achieved speeds of roughly 190 km/h. The interwar period and World War II brought significant technological advancements, with aircraft like the P-51 Mustang reaching speeds of up to 700 km/h. The post-war era introduced jet engines, allowing speeds to surpass 965 km/h, as seen in the F-86 Sabre. By the 1960s and 1970s, aircraft like the SR-71 Blackbird and MiG-25 (Tri sonics) pushed the boundaries further, flying at over 3,400 km/h. While modern combat aircraft such as the F-22 Raptor typically cruise at speeds around Mach 2 (2400km/h), recent developments in hypersonic weapons and aircraft aim to exceed Mach 5 (6,174 km/h), ushering in a new era of high-speed military capability.

This surge in speed has had profound impacts on the nature of warfare. High-speed aircraft enable faster operational tempo, allowing militaries to conduct strikes, reconnaissance, and deployments more rapidly than ever before. Speed contributes to tactical surprise and enhances the effectiveness of precision strikes, enabling deep penetration into enemy territory with minimal warning. The ability to project power across long distances in short periods has reshaped military doctrine, favouring swift, precise actions over prolonged engagements. In modern warfare, this has led to an emphasis on stealth, offensive capability, and fast disengagement, rather than traditional massed formations.

However, the increasing speed of airpower poses significant challenges to compliance with International Humanitarian Law. One of the primary issues is the compression of decision-making time. High-speed engagements leave little room for careful assessment of targets, which increases the risk of violating the principles of distinction and proportionality—key tenets of IHL that require distinguishing between combatants and civilians and avoiding excessive force. Higher speeds impact air operations in three distinct ways – one by reducing time to identify the target system which can lead to error secondly, strike error increase leading to a greater probability of unwarranted damage and lastly by enhancement of Circular Error of Probability (CEP) owing to higher speed, the necessary weight of attack increases and resultant greater damage than that is necessary for achieving military objectives. The complexity of modern battlefields, particularly in urban environments, further exacerbates these risks. Rapid operations in such settings make it difficult to ensure that all actions conform to legal and ethical standards.

Moreover, the technological sophistication that accompanies high-speed airpower often results in remote or standoff engagement. While this reduces risk to military personnel, it can create a psychological and informational distance from the battlefield, potentially diminishing situational awareness and the human judgment necessary for lawful targeting. It also complicates accountability and oversight, especially when autonomous or AI-assisted systems are involved in the decision loop.

Nevertheless, advancements in speed have also brought certain opportunities for better compliance with IHL. High-speed surveillance and reconnaissance platforms enhance the collection of intelligence, which can support more accurate and informed targeting decisions. The integration of digital systems and data networks in modern aircraft further allows for rapid information processing and dissemination, which, if managed responsibly, can support lawful and ethical decision-making in combat.

Range

The reach of airpower has undergone significant evolution. In the early 20th century, aircraft had very limited operational range, often restricted to a few dozen miles. The Wright brothers' inaugural flights in 1903, for instance, lasted under a minute and covered less than a mile. During World War I, the range of combat aircraft modestly expanded, allowing for short-range reconnaissance and limited bombing missions. By World War II, advances in engine technology and aircraft design enabled long-range strategic bombing campaigns, with aircraft such as the B-17 Flying Fortress and the B-29 Superfortress capable of reaching targets hundreds of miles away.

The post-World War II era witnessed a dramatic extension in airpower's reach with the advent of jet propulsion and aerial refuelling. Strategic bombers like the B-52 Stratofortress and reconnaissance platforms such as the U-2 and SR-71 could conduct intercontinental missions. In the contemporary era, airpower reach has been further extended by multirole fighter jets, long-range drones, and hypersonic weapons systems. Air-to-air refuelling capabilities allow for virtually unlimited range, and unmanned systems can be piloted from across the globe. These advancements enable states to project power across vast geographical distances with unprecedented speed and precision.

The increasing reach of airpower has profoundly affected warfare. It has enabled states to engage adversaries far beyond their borders, reducing the need for forward-deployed ground forces and allowing for a more agile and flexible force posture. Long-range strike capabilities facilitate preemptive and retaliatory operations against strategic targets, while global surveillance platforms provide continuous intelligence, surveillance, and reconnaissance (ISR) coverage. The ability to conduct operations from standoff distances also enhances survivability by minimising exposure to hostile air defences. Consequently, airpower's extended reach has contributed to the globalisation of conflict and the transformation of strategic doctrines.

However, this expansion in operational reach also raises critical concerns regarding adherence to International Humanitarian Law. IHL principles such as distinction, proportionality, and precaution are more difficult to observe when operations are conducted over long distances and from remote locations. The physical and psychological detachment of drone operators, for instance, can reduce the immediacy and contextual awareness necessary for lawful targeting. Furthermore, reliance on remote sensing and intelligence data may result in errors or misidentification of targets, increasing the risk of harm to civilians and civilian objects.

At the same time, the extended reach of airpower can support compliance with IHL when employed with adequate safeguards. Persistent surveillance and precision-guided munitions can enhance targeting accuracy and reduce collateral damage. Long-duration ISR missions can provide comprehensive situational awareness, allowing for better-informed decision-making. Nevertheless, the increasing reliance on remotely operated and autonomous systems necessitates robust legal frameworks, oversight mechanisms, and rules of engagement to ensure accountability and compliance with international norms.

Quantum

Since its advent in the early 20th century, airpower has undergone a remarkable transformation in both scale and scope. The quantum of airpower—referring to the volume, diversity, and sustained availability of aerial capabilities for military use—has expanded exponentially over the past century. From a handful of rudimentary aircraft used primarily for reconnaissance in World War I, the world's militaries now operate vast and complex fleets, including fixed-wing fighters, bombers, helicopters, drones, transport aircraft, and surveillance platforms. This growth is not only quantitative but also qualitative, as modern air forces are capable of sustained, integrated, and highly coordinated operations across multiple domains.

The increase in the quantum of airpower has significantly altered the character and conduct of warfare. Greater numbers and types of aircraft have enhanced force projection, enabling states to maintain a persistent presence in distant theatres of operation. Modern air forces can execute continuous air campaigns, maintain air superiority, provide close air support to ground forces, and conduct logistical operations on a global scale. Furthermore, the proliferation of unmanned aerial vehicles (UAVs) has contributed to the sustained presence of airpower in conflict zones without incurring direct risk to human pilots, allowing for prolonged operations in otherwise inaccessible or high-risk environments.

This expanded quantum has also led to a form of asymmetric dominance, where technologically advanced states can impose overwhelming airpower against adversaries with limited or no aerial capabilities. As a result, air campaigns are often decisive in shaping the outcomes of conflicts, sometimes even in the absence of large-scale ground operations. However, this dominance can also create strategic overreliance on airpower, potentially leading to civilian harm or unintended escalation when used without complementary political or humanitarian strategies.

The implications of this increase in airpower for compliance with International Humanitarian Law (IHL) are complex and multifaceted. On one hand, the sheer scale of air operations raises concerns about the proportionality and distinction principles under IHL. As the number of aerial sorties increases, so does the potential for incidental harm to civilians, particularly in densely populated or urban areas. High-tempo air campaigns can strain the legal review process, increasing the risk of unlawful targeting due to operational pressures or inadequate intelligence.

On the other hand, the increased quantum of air assets can also facilitate better adherence to IHL if accompanied by robust rules of engagement, precision-guided munitions, and advanced surveillance capabilities. For instance, large fleets of drones and reconnaissance aircraft can enhance situational awareness and allow for more deliberate targeting processes, potentially reducing civilian casualties. The diversity within the expanded quantum—such as the availability of non-lethal air platforms for evacuation, supply drops, or communication relays—can support humanitarian operations and the protection of civilians in conflict zones.

Battle Environment

Since its advent in the early 20th century, airpower has evolved not only in terms of speed, reach, and quantum but also in its ability to transform battlespace transparency. Battlespace transparency refers to the ability to observe, monitor, and understand the operational environment in real-time or near-real time. In the early stages of air warfare, aircraft were primarily used for visual reconnaissance, providing limited and often delayed intelligence. During World War I and II, aerial photography became a key tool for mapping enemy positions and movements, offering a new dimension of situational awareness compared to ground-based intelligence.

The Cold War era marked a significant advancement in battlespace transparency with the introduction of high-altitude reconnaissance aircraft such as the U-2 and SR-71 Blackbird, capable of capturing strategic intelligence deep within enemy territory. This era also saw the rise of space-based assets, including satellites, which further expanded the scope and persistence of aerial surveillance. In the contemporary period, airpower has integrated real-time data gathering, processing, and dissemination through sophisticated airborne platforms such as JSTARS (Joint Surveillance Target Attack Radar System), AWACS (Airborne Warning and Control System), and unmanned aerial vehicles (UAVs) equipped with high-resolution sensors. These systems collectively offer a persistent, multilayered view of the battlespace, allowing military commanders to make informed decisions with unprecedented speed and accuracy.

The impact of increased battlespace transparency on warfare has been profound. Enhanced surveillance capabilities have significantly improved command and control, target identification, and threat assessment. Real-time intelligence feeds from UAVs and reconnaissance aircraft enable dynamic targeting, allowing for rapid response to emerging threats and changes in the operational environment. This transparency contributes to more efficient and coordinated joint operations across air, land, and sea domains. Furthermore, it reduces the fog of war, enabling a clearer understanding of enemy intentions, movements, and capabilities.

However, the expansion of battlespace transparency also presents new challenges and implications for compliance with International Humanitarian Law (IHL). On one hand, improved situational awareness can enhance adherence to IHL principles by enabling more accurate distinction between combatants and civilians, and more precise targeting that minimises collateral damage. High-resolution imagery and real-time surveillance can support proportionality assessments and allow for post-strike evaluations, which are crucial for accountability and legal review.

On the other hand, the overwhelming flow of information may lead to data saturation, where critical details are overlooked or misinterpreted under the pressure of rapid decision-making. Moreover, increased transparency may create unrealistic expectations for perfect intelligence, potentially leading to overreliance on aerial surveillance at the expense of human intelligence and on-the-ground context. In some cases, the ability to observe the battlefield in detail may also raise ethical concerns about the psychological detachment of operators from the human consequences of military actions.

AI Integration with Airpower

The integration of artificial intelligence (AI) with airpower has become one of the most transformative elements of modern military operations. AI enhances airpower in multiple ways, including autonomous operations, mission planning, data analysis, and target identification. AI-driven systems, such as UAVs, are capable of executing missions with minimal human intervention, including reconnaissance, surveillance, and precision strikes.

AI technologies allow for faster, more accurate decision-making by processing vast amounts of real-time data. For example, AI algorithms can identify high-value targets, recommend optimal attack plans, and adjust to changing conditions in the battlespace. Additionally, AI-driven systems can operate in environments where human intervention is limited or impossible, such as during high-risk surveillance or in contested airspaces.

While AI integration increases the speed and precision of airpower, it also introduces new challenges for compliance with International Humanitarian Law (IHL). One of the primary concerns is the lack of human oversight in AI-driven systems, which may lead to errors or unintended harm to civilians. The potential for AI systems to malfunction or be hacked poses significant risks to operational integrity. Moreover, the complexity of autonomous systems makes it difficult to determine accountability in the event of violations of IHL.

Cyber and Space Integration with Airpower

The integration of cyber and space capabilities with airpower has further expanded the operational scope of modern military forces. Cyber capabilities support air operations by enabling secure communications, real-time data sharing, and electronic warfare, such as jamming enemy radar systems or disabling communications. Space-based assets, such as satellites, provide critical intelligence, surveillance, and reconnaissance capabilities, along with global positioning and communication systems that ensure seamless coordination of air operations.

The synergy between airpower, cyber, and space has redefined modern warfare, enabling forces to operate across multiple domains simultaneously. The integration allows for rapid, coordinated responses to threats, improving strategic decision-making and providing a more comprehensive view of the battlespace. However, the reliance on these interconnected domains introduces vulnerabilities, particularly regarding the security of cyber and space infrastructure. A cyberattack on air operations or a disruption of satellite communication could severely affect the effectiveness of airpower, raising questions about accountability and proportionality in the context of IHL.

IHL Principles & Their Application to Airpower

Airpower can both conform to and challenge the basic tenets of International Humanitarian Law (IHL), depending on how it is used. IHL is built around key principles of Distinction (Differentiating between combatants and civilians) and Proportionality (Military action must not cause excessive harm to civilians relative to its military advantage). To ensure that airpower application aligns with International Humanitarian Law (IHL), military leaders must be well-versed in several critical areas. Their training and decision-making must balance operational effectiveness with legal and ethical considerations.

Military leaders must internalise the four key principles of IHL and apply them in real-world air operations:

- **Distinction.** Ensure airstrikes differentiate between combatants and civilians.

- **Proportionality.** Avoid attacks where civilian harm outweighs military advantage.
- **Military Necessity.** Only target legitimate military objectives.
- **Humanity.** Prevent unnecessary suffering (e.g., banning incendiary or indiscriminate weapons).In urban warfare, leaders must ensure precision-guided munitions (PGMs) are used to avoid civilian casualties instead of area bombing.

Understanding Legal & Ethical Responsibilities in Air Warfare

What constitutes a war crime in aerial warfare? Who holds accountability for unlawful airstrikes? Executive leaders, Commanders, Intelligence officers, Planners, Pilots and System Operators have a role to play in the outcome of a mission. Who will be accountable? Legal frameworks governing air warfare include the Geneva Conventions, UN resolutions and national military laws. Commanders must ensure all operators follow strict engagement protocols to prevent unlawful killings outside active battle zones.

Some measures to retain legitimacy that may be adopted are covered here. Use of AI and real-time surveillance to confirm military targets before strikes, development of "no-strike lists" for protected sites (hospitals, schools, refugee camps, religious sites), enhancement of Battle Damage Assessments (BDA) to track and verify post-strike outcomes. AI-assisted target recognition systems can minimise false identifications in crowded urban areas and implementing robust Rules of Engagement (ROE) can limit collateral damage. Clear ROEs that enforce IHL compliance, such as verification of intelligence before strikes, pre-strike legal review of all air missions and specification of abort criteria when civilian harm is likely to be too high. The use of only specific weapons with minimal MAE (Mean Area of Effectiveness) in civilian-dense areas can minimise the probability of unwarranted civilian casualties.

Strengthening Accountability & Post-Strike Assessments

Transparent investigations into wrongful airstrikes and holding commanders accountable for disproportionate attacks though desirable have rarely been implemented. After an airstrike in Afghanistan (2019) that killed civilians, NATO reviewed its intelligence failures and improved target vetting but no one was penalised for the unwarranted deaths.

Training & Simulations for Ethical Decision-Making

Wargames and case studies on past air campaigns play a pivotal role in grooming future leaders in ethical decision-making. This effort can be augmented by virtual reality (VR) simulations for pilots and commanders to practice real-time decision-making under IHL constraints. Interdisciplinary education—mixing military training with legal, ethical, and technological studies, is a step in the right direction to ensure airpower is used in consonance with IHL.

Recent conflicts have witnessed several instances where the use of airpower has led to alleged violations of International Humanitarian Law (IHL). Notable examples include: Israeli Airstrikes in Lebanon and Gaza. Israel used an AI system called "Lavender" to automate target selection for airstrikes in Gaza. AI allegedly marked thousands of targets, with minimal human verification. High civilian casualties raised concerns about proportionality and distinction violations under IHL. Israeli airstrikes resulted in the deaths of civilians. In 2023 and 2024, Israeli airstrikes in Gaza have been reported to violate International Humanitarian Law (IHL) in several key areas like indiscriminate and disproportionate attacks resulting in high civilian casualties. Between October 7, 2023, and February 19, 2024, the Israeli Air Force conducted over 29,000 attacks in Gaza. The rate of Palestinian fatalities during this period was reportedly higher than in any recent global conflicts, raising concerns about indiscriminate and disproportionate use of force. From October 12, 2023, to June 30, 2024, multiple attacks on hospitals in Gaza were documented even though medical personnel and facilities are protected under IHL, provided they are not used for hostile acts. An airstrike on April 1, 2024, killed seven aid workers from the World Central Kitchen in Gaza. This attack drew condemnation from the United Nations Security Council, which urged immediate action to investigate and prevent such violations of IHL. The pattern of these attacks raises serious concerns about compliance with international law. In 2024, over 124 journalists were killed in 18 countries, with more than 70% of these deaths attributed to Israeli actions in Gaza. This includes 85 journalists, among them 82 Palestinians, who lost their lives due to Israeli military operations. In Myanmar too, military indiscriminate airstrikes targeting civilians and civilian infrastructure, including villages, schools, and medical facilities are reported by the Karen Human Rights Group listing 227 such attacks, resulting in at least 417 civilian casualties. These actions have been described as war crimes and potential crimes against humanity under international law. Such incidents highlight significant concerns regarding the protection of journalists in conflict zones. Investigations by organizations like Amnesty International have called for these incidents to be examined as potential war crimes, emphasising the need for accountability and adherence to IHL.

Broader Implications and International Responses

The international community has expressed alarm over the increasing disregard for IHL in various conflicts. The International Committee of the Red Cross has highlighted a deficit in political leadership for mediating peace agreements, leading to prolonged conflicts and escalating humanitarian needs. This situation underscores the critical importance of adhering to IHL principles, especially concerning the use of airpower in warfare. These instances highlight the ongoing challenges in ensuring compliance with IHL during air operations. They underscore the necessity for rigorous adherence to the principles of distinction, proportionality, and precaution to protect civilian lives and property.

Is IHL Evolving Fast Enough?

The evolution of International Humanitarian Law (IHL) has not always kept pace with the rapid advancements in air power in conflicts. While IHL has evolved to address the challenges posed by aerial warfare, it often lags behind technological and tactical developments. The Hague Conventions of 1899 and 1907 attempted to regulate aerial bombardment, but air power was in its infancy. WWI saw increased use of air power, including bombings of cities, but there were few legal frameworks to regulate these actions. By WWII, strategic bombing campaigns raised serious humanitarian concerns, but IHL lacked specific rules on proportionality and civilian protection in air warfare. Post-WWII, the 1949 Geneva Conventions established broad protections for civilians but did not specifically address aerial warfare. The principle of distinction (between combatants and civilians) and proportionality (avoiding excessive civilian harm) became more clearly articulated, though their application to air power remained vague. Cold War era witnessed the 1977 Additional Protocols to the Geneva Conventions explicitly prohibited indiscriminate attacks, including those by air power. The principles of precaution in attack (avoiding civilian harm as much as possible) were introduced, but enforcement remained a challenge. Modern air warfare has shifted towards long-range strikes, unmanned aerial vehicle strikes and guided weapons, raising new legal debates on accountability and targeting rules. Conflicts in Iraq, Syria, and Ukraine have shown the difficulty of applying IHL when air power is used in densely populated areas. The rise of AI-assisted targeting and autonomous drones presents new legal and ethical questions that IHL has yet to fully address.

Has IHL Kept Pace? Partially—While IHL has evolved to regulate air power, it often reacts after new technologies and tactics emerge. Enforcement remains weak, as seen in cases where airstrikes result in high civilian casualties but legal accountability is limited. The future of IHL will likely require new treaties or stronger enforcement mechanisms to address AI-driven warfare, cyber-attacks on air systems, and autonomous weapons. The evolution of International Humanitarian Law (IHL) for modern airpower-dominated conflicts should be driven by a combination of states, international organizations, civil society, and legal experts to ensure its relevance, legitimacy, and enforceability. Governments control military operations and sign international treaties. Without state commitment, any evolution of IHL will be ineffective. Development of national military doctrines that integrate new IHL standards and encouraging compliance through military training and internal accountability mechanisms are the keys.

The UN has the global reach and legitimacy to push for legal reforms. The International Committee of the Red Cross (ICRC) should continue leading research on air warfare and IHL. The UN Security Council and General Assembly can create new legal frameworks and pressure states to adopt them. Agencies like the UN Human Rights Council (UNHRC) and the UN Office for Disarmament Affairs (UNODA) can push for better oversight of airstrikes. Courts interpret IHL and hold violators accountable. Legal experts refine laws based on real-world conflicts. The International Criminal Court (ICC) and International Court of Justice (ICJ) should adjudicate cases of unlawful air warfare. Legal scholars and institutions should propose new legal norms for autonomous weapons and drone strikes. NGOs drive awareness, advocate for victims, and push states to uphold IHL. Groups like Human Rights Watch (HRW), Amnesty International, and Airwars document airstrike impacts and lobby for legal changes. They can pressure governments through public campaigns and litigation. AI researchers shape the future of air warfare. Their involvement ensures realistic, enforceable laws by encouraging ethical AI in targeting decisions and transparency in algorithms. Researchers need to work with policymakers to balance military necessity and humanitarian concerns. A hybrid approach is needed with all stakeholders and led by the ICRC & UN as neutral mediators.

A Turkish-made Kargu-2 drone allegedly hunted down and killed a Libyan fighter in 2020 without human intervention making it possibly the first autonomous lethal AI attack in history. The U.S. "Project Maven" used in Afghanistan, Syria, and Iraq is an AI-powered surveillance system for detecting insurgent activity and guiding drone strikes. It analyses drone footage to detect enemy movements and weapons. It uses machine learning to improve strike accuracy over time however, it has the potential for AI bias leading to misidentification of combatants.

As air power increasingly relies on Artificial Intelligence (AI), autonomous weapons, and drone warfare, International Humanitarian Law (IHL) faces new challenges. Key concerns include ensuring human oversight, preventing unlawful killings, and holding actors accountable when AI-driven airstrikes violate Modern air warfare involves AI-assisted targeting that processes vast data to identify threats. However, levels of automation vary in Human-in-the-Loop, a human operator makes the final decision after AI suggests targets. But Human-out-of-the-Loop is a fully autonomous system that makes decisions without human input (not yet widely deployed). IHL requires human judgment in targeting decisions to ensure proportionality and distinction. But how much human involvement is enough? AI relies on training data, which may reflect biases, leading to wrongful attacks or False Positives as AI might misidentify civilians as combatants (e.g., mistaking a farmer with a shovel for a fighter with a rifle). AI models still lack contextual understanding and they struggle with human intent. IHL must clarify liability when AI-driven strikes result in unlawful deaths. Is it the programmer, the operator, or the commanding officer who is responsible? Military advantage must outweigh civilian harm. AI as yet lacks the moral judgment to weigh human suffering and cannot implement the rule of proportionality.

A short-term solution is to expand IHL guidelines that require human sign-off on all AI-targeted or autonomous strikes. In the long run, banning fully autonomous lethal systems (like landmine bans) and the creation of AI auditing mechanisms for real-time oversight of air operations would be ideal.

AI-powered air warfare outpaces legal evolution, creating an urgent need for updated IHL frameworks. Governments, international courts, and civil society must act before autonomous weapons make IHL obsolete in air warfare is already shaping modern conflicts, but international law struggles to keep pace. The AI-assisted drones (e.g., MQ-9 Reaper) plan for "signature strikes," where AI analyses behaviour patterns to determine targets. In 2021, a US drone mistakenly killed an Afghan aid worker and 10 civilians due to flawed AI pattern recognition. AI's reliance on metadata (phone calls, movement patterns) can lead to false positives and unlawful killings. AI-driven strikes must meet transparency and accountability standards to ensure human oversight.

Emerging Treaties and Legal Proposals

The United Nations Group of Governmental Experts (GGE) is debating limits on Lethal Autonomous Weapon Systems (LAWS). Some states (Russia and, the U.S.) oppose a full ban, arguing AI weapons enhance precision and reduce casualties. A legally binding agreement to ensure "meaningful human control" over AI weapons. The International Committee of the Red Cross (ICRC) warns that AI weapons risk violating core IHL principles and proposed mandatory human oversight. AI decisions must be transparent and reviewable. Military AI should have a legal chain of command and States must disclose AI targeting methods to ensure compliance with IHL. The European Union is pushing for strict regulations on AI in warfare through the AI Act (2024). It classifies AI-driven lethal systems as "high risk" and requires ethical audits before deployment.

New Challenges for IHL

Defining Legal Boundaries for Autonomous & AI-Powered Air Warfare

AI and autonomous drones (e.g., "loyal wingman" projects) could select and engage targets without human oversight. It is necessary to establish clear legal accountability—who is responsible if an AI-driven drone commits a war crime? The programmer? The commander? A mandatory "human-in-the-loop" principle for AI-controlled air strikes will ensure human decision-making in lethal force. The development of new treaties to regulate AI weapons, similar to nuclear and chemical weapon bans will create the necessary legal framework.

Stricter Regulations on UAV Warfare & Targeted Killings

UAVs allow low-risk, remote-controlled warfare, leading to potential misuse in undeclared conflicts and assassinations. Defining legal limits on UAV strikes, especially in non-war zones (e.g., Pakistan, Yemen) is an operational necessity. The introduction of transparency and accountability for drone operations like reporting civilian casualties and strengthening restrictions on "double-tap" strikes (hitting the same area twice, harming rescuers) are necessary changes.

Regulating Hypersonic & Space-Based Air Weapons

Hypersonic missiles and space-based military assets reduce reaction time, making traditional IHL principles (e.g., proportionality, distinction) harder to apply. Updating of IHL to cover hypersonic weapon use, ensuring they comply with proportionality and distinction rules. And expansion of existing treaties (e.g., Outer Space Treaty) to ban the use of space-based weapons for strikes needs due deliberation.

Strengthening Enforcement & Accountability Mechanisms

Almost all airpower-related war crimes go unpunished due to state interests and lack of enforcement. It is essential to establish an independent international body to investigate airstrike-related war crimes and impose sanctions or penalties for nations and entities using airpower indiscriminately. Ideally, real-time monitoring of airstrikes via satellite and AI-based verification is essential but is unlikely in the current environment.

Adapting the Concept of Civilian Protection

Modern airpower has blurred the line between military and civilian infrastructure (e.g., cyber warfare, dual-use targets). Redefining "civilian objects" to account for cyberinfrastructure, data centres, and AI systems that support airpower and strengthening protections for urban warfare scenarios, where airpower is increasingly used in populated areas.

As airpower becomes faster, more precise, and increasingly autonomous, IHL must evolve to ensure ethical, legal, and humanitarian considerations keep pace with technological advancements. The key focus areas should be AI accountability, drone warfare transparency, hypersonic weapon regulation, enforcement mechanisms, and stronger civilian protections.

Gestalt

The evolution of airpower over the past 115 years has revolutionised warfare, introducing new capabilities and challenges. The increasing speed, reach, quantum, and transparency of airpower have enhanced military effectiveness and strategic flexibility, while also complicating compliance with International Humanitarian Law. The integration of AI, cyber, and space technologies has further transformed airpower, enabling more precise and autonomous operations but also raising concerns about accountability and potential violations of IHL principles. As airpower continues to evolve, the key challenge will be balancing technological advancements with the ethical and legal imperatives that govern the conduct of armed conflict.

Section III

Protection of Persons and Cultural Heritage

Chapter 12

The Protection of Journalists in Conflict Zone

-Kanika Sharma

Introduction

Globally, the number of conflicts whether political, criminal, or military in nature – has doubled in the past five years, and this is reflected in increasing number of killings and kidnapping of journalists in conflict zones. The world has witnessed unprecedented surge in the killing of journalists during Russia-Ukraine war and Isreal-Gaza war. Numerous journalists were injured, harassed or kidnapped in war zones; or killed when targeted by one side or another or caught in the crossfire of violence. The ongoing conflicts are a clear illustration of vulnerability of journalists reporting from the conflict zone. The dangers posed to journalists and media staff working in unrest situations and conflict zones is well established with the killings of a number of journalists and media workers in 2024.[1] The year is considered as the deadliest year for the journalists by the Committee to Protect Journalists (CPJ).[2]

1 Special Report, Committee to Protect Journalists, www.cpj.org.

2 The Committee to Protect Journalists (CPJ) was founded in 1981 by a group of US correspondents who realized they could not ignore the plight of colleagues whose reporting put them in peril on a daily basis. The idea that journalists around the world should come together to defend the rights of colleagues working in repressive and dangerous environments led to CPJ's first advocacy campaign in 1982. Today, CPJ's networks are made up of journalists, researchers, and advocates, working together to support journalists and press freedom around the world. https://cpj.org/about/history/.

The International Federation of Journalists (IFJ) has alleged that a large number of journalists and other media personnel have been abducted, killed or deliberately targeted because of their professional work by the state and non-state forces. In February 2025, the International Federation of Journalists (IFJ) published its 34th annual report on journalists and media staff killings globally. Some of the highlights of the report are as follows.[3]

- 2024 was among the five deadliest years since the International Federation of Journalists (IFJ) began its Killed List in 1990, with recorded killings of 122 journalists worldwide. There is an alarming 30% increase in imprisoned journalists and media workers, with figures rising from 393 in 2023 to 516 last year.
- The Gaza strip accounted for almost half of journalists killed worldwide, with 64 casualties in 2024. In the Asia Pacific region, 22 journalists were killed last year – an 83% increase from the year before.
- In Latin America and the Caribbean, there was a fall in the number of killings, with nine journalists murdered compared to 11 in 2023. In the Middle East and the Arab World, there were 77 killings recorded by the Federation.
- 14 women journalists were killed in 2024, while reporting in Palestine, Syria, Ukraine, Iraq, Somalia, Sudan and the Philippines.
- In 2024, there was a 30% increase in imprisoned journalists. The number of journalists and media workers imprisoned rose from 393 in 2023 to 516 in 2024, highlighting the worsening state of press freedom worldwide.

The IFJ in its earlier report has brought out that extremist groups also consider foreign reporters as bargaining chips and have resorted to kidnapping them to gain political concessions or to make money through ransoms. The cases in point were the gruesome beheading of Western and Japanese journalists in Pakistan, Syria and Iraq by Islamists, allegedly in retaliation against foreign policies of countries in these regions.

Journalists reporting in conflict areas play a vital role in bringing to the attention of the international community the horrors and realities of the conflict. They risk their life to ensuring access to reliable information

3 https://www.ifj.org/fileadmin/user_upload/IFJ_Killed_List_report_2024.pdf.

to influencing opinion of the people and parties to conflict. The killings and attacks against these people are the clear threat that poses to the flow of information worldwide. The laws of armed conflict or International Humanitarian Law (IHL), comprise comprehensive rules regarding the protection of journalists as civilians and war correspondents and POWs. Although they are protected under IHL, human rights law and various other instruments, the increasing number of killings and violence against this group raise serious questions about the adequacy and enforcement of the international legal frameworks available for their protection.

Protection of Journalists: Initial Action

Historically, the protection of Journalists' coverage of conflict garnered international attention at the end of the nineteenth century. Several attempts have been made of all to "protect" journalists on dangerous assignments abroad. Instructions for the Government of Armies of the United States in the Field, 24 April, 1863 (The 1863 Lieber Code) was the first attempt to codify the laws of war that provides for special protection to journalists.[4] The Lieber Code strongly influenced the further codification of the laws of war and the adoption of similar regulations by other states. They formed the origin of the project of an international convention on the laws of war presented to the Brussels Conference in 1874 and stimulated the adoption of the Hague Convention II 1899 and IV of 1907 Respecting the Laws and Customs of War on Land. The 1899 Hague Convention in Article 13 provides for the treatment of captured journalists.[5] It was later restated in Article 13 of the 1907 Hague Convention.[6] Further, the Convention Relative to the Treatment of Prisoners of War, 27 July 1929 (The 1929

4 Instructions for the Government of Armies of the United States in the Field, 24 April, 1863, Article 50 Moreover, citizens who accompany an army for whatever purpose, such as sutlers, editors, or reporters of journals, or contractors, if captured, may be made prisoners of war, and be detained as such.

5 The Hague Conference 1899, Article 13 Treatment of Captured Journalists, sutlers etc.: Individuals who follow an army without directly belonging to it, such as newspaper correspondents and reporters, sutlers, contractors, who fall into the enemy's hands, and whom the latter think fit to detain, have a right to be treated as prisoners of war, provided they can produce a certificate from the military authorities of the army they were accompanying.

6 The Hague Conference 1899, Article 13 Individuals who follow an army without directly belonging to it, such as newspaper correspondents and reporters, sutlers and contractors, who fall into the enemy's hands and whom the latter thinks expedient to detain, are entitled to be treated as prisoners of war, provided they are in possession of a certificate from the military authorities of the army which they were accompanying.

Geneva Convention) incorporated the provision relating to the journalists in Article 81.[7] The proposal for international protection of journalists and the media came from the League of Nations' Conference of Press Experts, held in Geneva in 1927 and convened after a League Assembly Resolution recommending the cooperation of the press in the organisation of peace. The resulting draft resolutions hinted at the conflict in goals between the representatives of the media and the states, and were ultimately all rejected by the states. The states that responded to these resolutions were less than favourable to journalist demands, stressing that journalists should not be singled out for special protection and that the sovereign right of the state could not be compromised for foreign journalists. They were especially reluctant to give a proposed panel of journalists review power over decisions by states to expel journalists from their territory. Notably, the recommendation that came closest to adoption by the Conference suggested that journalists be issued some form of identity card. However, once again debates about whether states or professional organisations should be responsible for issuing these cards stalled the resolution, and nothing ever came of the proposal.

The United Nations has been little more receptive to the idea of journalist protections than its predecessor. The body first addressed journalists' rights in 1947, when the Commission on Human Rights in its first Session established a Sub Commission on Freedom of Information and of the Press.[8] The subcommittee and the conference it convened are notable for their deference to states. Statements made at the conference reveal the concern of states that the media might be used as a tool to undermine the sovereignty of a state or legitimacy of its government. But neither the conference nor the subcommittee directly addressed the questions of wartime protection or the status of journalists under IHL. The international community first addressed the issue of physical protection of journalists when the International Federation of Editors-in Chief, along with the International Commission of Jurists in Geneva and representatives from the ICRC, prepared a draft convention for the safety of journalists. This draft convention, known as the Montecantini Draft, proposed the creation of an

7 Convention Relative to the Treatment of Prisoners of War, 27 July 1929, Article 81 Persons who follow the armed forces without directly belonging thereto, such as correspondents, newspaper reporters, sutlers, or contractors, who fall into the hands of the enemy, and whom the latter think fit to detain, shall be entitled to be treated as prisoners of war, provided they are in possession of an authorization from the military authorities of the armed forces which they were following.

8 E/CN.4/Sub.1/33, 27 June 1947.

International Committee for the Protection of Journalists on Dangerous Missions, which was to be an independent group of five to seven individuals from prominent press organisations, chosen by the UN Secretary-General. This committee would be responsible for issuing all journalists identity (ID) cards and keeping track of all journalists on dangerous missions. While on dangerous missions, journalists were expected to wear a recognisable emblem designed by the committee. The Montecantini Draft also imposed obligations on states. States would be prevented from arresting or detaining any journalist for anything undertaken within his or her journalistic capacity and required to release any journalist arrested as soon as possible and return him to his home country. Ultimately, however, the Montecantini Draft was never referred to any UN body for consideration. The UN first addressed the issue of journalist protection in 1970 with the creation of the International Professional Committee for the Safety of Journalists. This Safety Committee operated much as the Montecantini Draft had imagined, issuing ID cards and keeping records of journalists on dangerous missions. However, unlike the Montecantini Draft, the Committee imposed obligations upon journalists, requiring them to provide a declaration of honour to use the card only on professional assignments, to not participate in hostilities, and to neither bear arms nor wear a uniform.

The UN General Assembly (UNGA) has addressed the safety of journalists by recognising that certain type of protection can be granted to the journalists under Geneva Conventions and by also showing the need of additional humanitarian instruments to ensure the better protection to the journalists engaged in dangerous missions and particularly in areas where an armed conflict has taken place.[9] The UNGA again took up the issue in 1973 and passed a resolution proposing a 'Draft Convention to Ensure the Protection of Journalists Engaged in Areas of Armed Conflict'.[10] After consulting various professional groups, the UN Draft was completed and submitted to the UNGA member states for comment. The Montecantini Draft and the UN Draft are markedly different in their approach, revealing the separate goals of their drafters - professional organisations and states, respectively. Both drafts propose creating a special status designation for journalists, but while the Montecantini Draft proposes that this designation would be granted by a journalist's employer or by the Committee, the UN Draft would determine a journalist's status "by virtue of his country's law practice," thus reserving broad power to the state to deny such status.

9 UN General Assembly Resolution 2673(XXV), 9 December 1970.

10 UN General Assembly Resolution 2673(XXVIII), 2 November 1973.

Moreover, the UN Draft proposes that the issuance of identification cards be contingent on a journalist conducting himself "in a manner consistent with the highest standards of journalistic integrity and . . . not to engage in any political or military activities," compliance with which would be decided by national authorities. Also distinct is the quality of protection. The Montecantini Draft would prevent, under any circumstances, the arrest, detainment, and imprisonment of a journalist, as well as a judgment against him by "any authorities whatsoever for bona fide activities undertaken solely in connexion [sic] with carrying out his professional mission." The UN Draft, in contrast, merely requires that states extend to foreign journalists the same protection given their own journalists and "do all that is necessary" to protect journalists from danger. The drafts differ regarding enforcement as well: the Montecantini Draft included penalties upon states for violating the Convention, while the UN Draft lacks any enforcement provision at all.

Unfortunately, neither draft came to fruition and instead, the question of protection of journalists was taken up during the drafting of the Additional Protocol I (AP I) to the Geneva Conventions, resulting in the incorporation of Article 79 on Measures of Protection for Journalists. The authors of the protocol debated establishing a special status for journalists, but ultimately decided against it, arguing that "any increase in the number of persons with a special status necessarily accompanied by an increase of protective signs, tends to weaken the protective value of each protected status already accepted." Article 79 of the AP I was the extent of international attention given to the protection of journalists until the most recent effort in the late 1980s when Waleed Sadi, a member of the Sub-Commission on Prevention of Discrimination and Protection of Minorities, introduced a draft resolution entitled "Protection of Journalists" to the Committee on Human Rights. The result of this was a call for further research into how such protection might be extended. The resolution never made it out of committee. This history of state concern over the role of journalists suggests that any convention increasing the rights of journalists at the expense of state sovereignty, especially during wartime when state concern for sovereignty is heightened, has little chance of gearing state support. Thus, a convention increasing state protection of journalists must preserve state sovereignty, especially in regards to (1) the ability to expel individuals, and (2) preserving the state's own conception of freedom of expression within the bounds dictated by the International Covenant on Civil and Political Rights.

Protection Under International Humanitarian Law

Defining Journalist and War Correspondents

General protective principles and the protection of journalists are part of the *jus in bello* or IHL, which comprises a set of rules 'designed to regulate the treatment of the individual – civilian or military, wounded or active' in armed conflicts. IHL applies the principle of distinction and hence protects combatants and civilians differently. IHL recognises persons attached to the armed forces as a special group of protected persons. It governs protection of journalists who operate in armed conflict as (i) independent journalists who work independently as freelancer or as a part of media organisation and (ii) war correspondents (including embedded journalists) who are accredited to the armed forces and who are attached to the military units during armed conflict. Under the current legal protections, both have two different statuses, depending on their relationship with the armed forces and a 'civilian journalist' may not be confused with the 'war correspondent' the latter are journalists who accompany the armed forces of a state without being member thereof.[11] War correspondents are treated as a special category of non-combatants known as individuals "accompanying the armed forces."[12] War correspondents are specifically mentioned in Geneva Convention III and are protected by Prisoner of War (POW) status as persons accompanying the military and if captured or detained during hostilities they are afforded fundamental rights including humane treatment, protection from acts of violence, including torture, medical and scientific experimentation, insults and public curiosity, access to medical care, minimum standards regarding conditions of captivity, the right to have contact with their families, the right to relief from organisations like ICRC, and the right to fundamental judicial guarantees, if they are subject to trial.[13] On the other side, Independent journalists are considered as civilian and are entitled to be treated as 'protected person' under Article 4

11 *Customary International Humanitarian Law*, Volume II, Chapter 10, Rule 34.

12 Geneva Convention (III) Relative to the Prisoners of War, 1949, Article 4A provides Prisoners of war, in the sense of the present Convention, are persons belonging to one of the following categories, who have fallen into the power of enemy… (4) Persons who accompany the armed forces without actually being members thereof, such as civilian members of military aircraft crews, war correspondents…, provided that they have received authorization from the armed forces which they accompany, who shall provide them for that purpose with an identity card similar to the annexed model.

13 *Ibid*, Article 13, 15-17, 29-33.

of the IV Geneva Convention.[14] Independent journalists remain civilians are 'solely' affording the protection of Article 75 of AP I, which establishes the minimum guarantees of humane and non-discriminatory treatment of all persons in the power of a Party to a conflict. Both are protected against attacks and detention.

Embedded Journalists: Embedded journalism[15] took birth during the 1990-91 Gulf War. It was the first war in which war correspondents could instantaneously broadcast their stories to the world. However, due to operational secrecy, censorship limited the reporting effectiveness of war correspondents.[16] During the Kosovo Conflict (1998–1999), the US/NATO military leaders recognised that combat journalists could be used as 'force multipliers' on the battlefield, developing public opinion and enhancing military morale. At the outset of the Iraq War, the US Department of Defence (DoD) encouraged the military to deploy reporters to embed with the troops. It is estimated that over 300 journalists participated in the DoD initiated training before joining as embedded journalists. They were taught combat skills, for example, providing immediate medical attention to wounded US soldiers until medical personnel arrived, operating on military helicopters, detecting land mines, surviving a chemical weapons attack, and conducting land navigation. In addition to responding to press

14 Convention (IV) Relative to the Protection of Civilian Persons in Times of War, 1949, Article 4Persons protected by the Convention are those who, at a given moment and in any manner whatsoever, find themselves, in case of a conflict or occupation, in the hands of a Party to the conflict or Occupying Power of which they are not nationals.

15 Distinct types of war correspondents are those that are 'embedded' with the military, a term that has gained popularity since the beginning of the First Gulf War. Embedded reporting is defined as living, eating, moving in combat with the military units that the journalist is attached to.

16 Today's embedded journalist is a product of the military press relations created from a common history of conflict and cooperation. The Vietnam experience led the US military to maintain greater control of press access in times of military engagement due to mistrust of the media by many senior military leaders. The First Gulf War (1990–1991) required a higher level of military-press cooperation to address the need for media integration into the combat mission. It was America's first war where war correspondents could instantaneously broadcast their stories to the world. The military had good intentions to increase media access, but operational secrecy still threatened media relations due to the mission. In response, the military created an elaborate system of accreditation, press pools, and military-media escorts to be used until the conflict ceased. While this system increased the war correspondent's coverage of the war, censorship issues limited their reporting effectiveness. Out of the 1600 reporters approved to cover the war, only 186 accompanied combat units into action. Moore Douglas W., Twenty-First Century Embedded Journalists: Lawful Targets? *The Army Lawyer*, July 2009, pp. 1-32.

inquiries and providing briefings to members of the press on US military operations, the military practice has also been to embed journalists with units during military operations. Embedded journalists are assigned to a unit, and they eat, sleep, and move with the unit.[17]

Protection Against Attacks

The main and most important provision of IHL explicitly referring to the protection of journalists in international armed conflicts ('IACs') is Article 79 of AP I[18], which was included as a specific provision relating to journalists in the body of IHL. It provides that journalist engaged in dangerous professional missions in areas of armed conflict, whether independent journalists or war correspondents accompanying the armed forces, are to be considered as civilians within the meaning of Article 50(1) AP I[19]. In other words, a journalist, who is undoubtedly a civilian, does not lose this status by entering an area of armed conflict on a professional mission, even if he is accompanying the armed forces or if he takes advantage of their logistic support. Thus, attacks on journalists are strictly prohibited

17 The United States, Department of Defence Law of War Manual (June 2015, updated July 2023), para 4.24, pp. 173-175.

18 Protocol Additional to the Geneva Convention of 12 August 1949, and relating to the Protection of Victims of International Armed Conflicts (Additional Protocol I), 8 June 1977. Article 79 Measures of Protection of Journalists:

1. Journalists engaged in dangerous professional missions in areas of armed conflict shall be considered as civilians within the meaning of Article 50, paragraph 1.

2. They shall be protected as such under the Conventions and this Protocol, provided that they take no action adversely affecting their status as civilians, and without prejudice to the right of war correspondents accredited to the armed forces to the status provided for in Article 4 (A) (4) of the Third Convention.

3. They may obtain an identity card similar to the model in Annex II of this Protocol. This card, which shall be issued by the government of the State of which the Journalist is a national or in whose territory he resides or in which the news medium employing him is located, shall attest to his status as a journalist.

19 *Ibid*, Article 50 Definition of civilians and civilian population

1. A civilian is any person who does not belong to one of the categories of persons referred to in Article 4 A (1), (2), (3) and (6) of the Third Convention and in Article 43 of this Protocol. In case of doubt whether a person is a civilian, that person shall be considered to be a civilian.

2. The civilian population comprises all persons who are civilians.

3. The presence within the civilian population of individuals who do not come within the definition of civilians does not deprive the population of its civilian character.

under IHL. Journalists are afforded the whole set of protections relative to civilians, including under Articles 51 and 57 AP I and Geneva Convention IV. This is, however, only the case unless and for as long as they do not take any action adversely affecting their status as civilians, as outlined in Article 79(2) AP I. As soon as they take direct part in hostilities, they lose their protection under this Article. Journalists have a duty to not engage in any actions adverse to their status of civilians and may be held accountable for acts of perfidy pursuant to Article 37(1)(c) AP I and for spying pursuant to Article 46 AP I. Although AP II relative to non-international armed conflicts ('NIACs') does not contain specific provisions on the protection of journalists, their protection as civilians also extends to such conflicts. Journalists are protected pursuant to Article 13 of AP II as well as by the minimum guarantees of Common Article 3 Geneva Conventions.

According to the ICRC Customary Law Study, state practice has established the protection of and respect for journalists engaged in professional missions in armed conflicts as a norm of customary international law. This is applicable to both IACs and NIACs, providing an equivalent protection to journalists in both types of conflicts. This has been manifested in Rule 34 of the Study.[20] The fact that both APs have not been universally ratified is thus irrelevant to the protection of journalists under this Rule. This can be evident from the fact that this rule is set forth in numerous military manuals and also supported by official statements and reported practice.[21] This practice includes that of States not party to AP I. Moreover, the illegality of attacking journalists is manifested by Article 85(3)(e) AP I, under which an attack on civilians can be considered a war crime.[22]

Protection Against Arrest and Detention

Another threat to the protection of journalists is their arrest and detention during armed conflict by the belligerent state. Journalists if arrested and

20 *Customary International Humanitarian Law,* Volume II, Chapter 10, Rule 34, Civilian journalists engaged in professional missions in area of armed conflict must be respected and protected as long as they are not taking a direct part in hostilities.

21 *Ibid.*

22 Additional Protocol-I, Article 85(3) In addition to the grave breaches defined in Article 11, the following acts shall be regarded as grave breaches of this Protocol, when committed wilfully, in violation of the relevant provisions of this Protocol, and causing death or serious injury to body or health:...(e) making a person the object of attack in the knowledge that he is ' hors de combat '... (5) Without prejudice to the application of the Conventions and of this Protocol, grave breaches of these instruments shall be regarded as war crimes.

detained by the authorities of belligerent state enjoyed protection under Article 75 of AP- I that *inter alia* provides for the prohibition of violence to life, health or physical or mental wellbeing, outrages upon personal dignity, the taking of hostages, collective punishments, threats and fair and humane detention and trial.

Article 79(2) of AP I[23] also refers to specific protections in case of detention pursuant to Article 4(A)(4) Geneva Convention III as POWs. The protection as POW relates inter alia to persons accompanying the armed forces without actually being members thereof, including war correspondents. Thus, in case of falling into the hand of the adversary, war correspondents benefit from all protections relative to POWs. Article 4(A)(4) Geneva Convention III, however, does not relate to nationals of a Party to the conflict nor to nationals of co-belligerent or neutral States maintaining diplomatic relations with the belligerent State. However, both the Articles only apply to IACs. In the case of NIACs, journalists are at least protected by the minimum guarantees enshrined in Common Article 3 that provides for the humane and non-discriminatory treatment of persons taking part in hostilities which would include journalists. These are similar to and amplified by AP II but still more restricted than those afforded under Article 75 AP I. The protections under AP II are listed in Article 5 which protects both persons who have been deprived of their liberty because of the reasons related to the armed conflict and persons who have been deprived for other reasons.[24] Nevertheless, violations of journalists' rights in detention, such as fair trial and humane treatment are considered grave breaches of IHL and lead to prosecution.[25] Article 79(3)

23 Additional Protocol-I, Article 79(2). They shall be protected as such under the Conventions and this Protocol, provided that they take no action adversely affecting their status as civilians, and without prejudice to the right of war correspondents accredited to the armed forces to the status provided for in Article 4 A (4) of the Third Convention.

24 Protocol Additional to the Geneva Convention and Relative to the Protection of Victims of Non-International Armed Conflict, 8 June 1977, Article 5 Persons whose liberty has been restricted: 1. In addition to the provisions of Article 4, the following provisions shall be respected as a minimum with regard to persons deprived of their liberty for reasons related to the armed conflict, whether they are interned or detained:..........(3) Persons who are not covered by paragraph 1 but whose liberty has been restricted in any way whatsoever for reasons related to the armed conflict shall be treated humanely...

25 *Ibid*, Article 6 Panel Prosecutions.

AP I[26] is considered an additional protective measure in relation to arrests as it provides for the carrying of identification cards. Such cards, however, neither confer a special status as 'journalist' nor are they indispensable, but simply attest to the fact that journalists are authorised to accompany the armed forces. In case of war correspondents, identity cards are mandatory under Geneva Convention III and must be carried at all times.

Radio and television facilities are considered as "civilian objects" under IHL, and Article 48 of AP I requires armed forces to distinguish between civilian objects and military objectives and to direct operations only against the latter. It says that attack must be limited to military objectives and in case of doubt, it is presumed that an object normally used as civilian object is civilian.[27] It follows that civilian objects, along with the civilian population, enjoy general protection under IHL. The question which emerges is whether journalists and media infrastructure could be considered legitimate targets because they disseminate propaganda, which may indirectly support the war effort. For instance, in Rwanda during Civil War in 1993-1994, the local media, particularly the extremist radio station Radio-Television Libre des Milles Collines (RTLM), nicknamed "Radio Genocide" or "Hutu Power Radio," played a significant role in inciting the Rwandan genocide that took place from April to July 1994.[28] In such instances, media and journalists become

26 Additional Protocol-I, Article 79(3) They may obtain an identity card similar to the model in Annex II of this Protocol. This card, which shall be issued by the government of the State of which the journalist is a national or in whose territory he resides or in which the news medium employing him is located, shall attest to his status as a journalist.

27 *Ibid*, Article 52 General Protection of Civilian Objects:

1. Civilian objects shall not be the object of attack or of reprisals. Civilian objects are all objects which are not military objectives as defined in paragraph 2.

2. Attacks shall be limited strictly to military objectives. In so far as objects are concerned, military objectives are limited to those objects which by their nature, location, purpose or use make an effective contribution to military action and whose total or partial destruction, capture or neutralization, in the circumstances ruling at the time, offers a definite military advantage.

3. In case of doubt whether an object which is normally dedicated to civilian purposes, such as a place of worship, a house or other dwelling or a school, is being used to make an effective contribution to military action, it shall be presumed not to be so used.

28 The International Criminal Tribunal for Rwanda convicted three Media Leaders for incitement to genocide, conspiracy, and crimes against humanity, extermination and persecution. Ferdinand Nahimana, and Hassan Ngeze were sentenced to life imprisonment and Jean Bosco Barayagwiza was sentenced to 35 years imprisonment. This case addressed the role of the media in the context of international criminal

legitimate military objective; however, the principle of proportionality and the obligation to give due warning, so as to avoid, or at least limit, loss of human life, injury to civilians and damage to civilian objects, need to be observed.[29] In ongoing war, Israeli aircraft have struck the headquarters of Iran's state broadcaster in Tehran; however, Iran's foreign ministry has alleged that air attack amounts to a "war crime." The Israeli military later stated that the "communication centre" was being used by the Iranian military "under the guise of civilian activity."[30]

The International Committee of the Red Cross (ICRC) offers protection for journalists in situations of armed conflict. ICRC helps media professionals working in armed conflict situations by promoting international humanitarian law, with the aim of preventing violations of the law and enhancing protection; by providing training to journalists in first aid and IHL, providing background to their reporting and information regarding the ways in which the law protects them and by helping journalists on dangerous assignments who are in need of humanitarian assistance. In addition, it focuses on safeguarding the physical safety of those in detention. It's hotline enables journalists, their families or employers to report cases of journalists who have been arrested, captured, detained, reported missing, wounded or killed. The four-year action plan of ICRC for the implementation of international humanitarian law contains an objective 3 on enhanced protection of journalists and the role of the media with regard to international humanitarian law. The 32nd International Conference of the Red Cross and Red Crescent received a progress report on the steps taken by States, national societies and ICRC to ensure the protection of journalists, and media equipment and installations. These included integrating the protection of journalists into the international

---

justice. Available at: https://unictr.irmct.org/en/news/three-media-leaders-convicted-genocide.

29 Peter Prive, *Freedom of Expression, and the Protection of Journalists in Conflict Situations*, August 17, 2024, available at: https://waccglobal.org/freedom-of-expression-and-the-protection-of-journalists-in-conflict-situations/.

30 David Gritten, Israel bombs Iran state TV during live broadcast, BBC News, 16 June 2025, available at: https://www.bbc.com/news/articles/c3w46pw2xn0o. The attack was preceded by an Israeli evacuation order for the densely-populated Tehran district where the state broadcaster lies. In that statement, the Israeli military said it planned to target "military infrastructure" in the area "in the coming hours." Israel Attacks Iran's State Television, Live on the Air, The New York Times, 16/17 June 2025, available at: https://www.nytimes.com/2025/06/16/world/middleeast/israel-iran-state-tv-attack.html.

humanitarian law training provided to different militaries, and providing training for journalists in conflict zones.

UN Resolutions Related to the Protection of Journalists

Subject of safety and protection of journalists during armed conflict and other dangerous situations has been developed in the form of soft law also. The United Nations and its organs have time and again urged the states to do their best to prevent violence against journalists and also to become the parties to the international instruments containing provisions relating to the prohibition of torture and other cruel, inhumane and degrading treatment or punishment.

A. UN Security Council Resolutions:

Condemning the attacks on journalists, the UN Security Council (UNSC) has adopted the resolutions 1265 (1999); 1296 (2000); 1502 (2003). However, the UN Security Council Resolution 1738 (para 1) specifically addresses the protection of journalists. It condemns all attacks against journalists, media professionals and associated personnel in armed conflicts, and calls on all parties to end such practices. It recalls that journalists are protected as civilians under humanitarian law, unless they take action adversely affecting their status as civilians, and recalls that media equipment and installations are civilian objects protected from attack, unless they are military objectives (paras 2–3). The resolution also condemns media incitement of violence against civilians (such as genocide, crimes against humanity and serious violations of humanitarian law) and calls for the perpetrators to be brought to justice (para 4). It then calls on all parties to conflicts to comply with their obligations towards civilians (including journalists) and to prevent violations of humanitarian law, including through prosecutions (paras 5–7). However, the resolution is innovative in that it specifically states that the deliberate targeting of civilians 'may constitute a threat to international peace security' to which the Council may respond (para 9). It is also significant in urging all parties to a conflict to 'respect the professional independence and rights of journalists' and media personnel (para 8), and urges states to become parties to Protocols I and II (para 10).[31]

Again in 2015, expressing the deep concern at the growing threat to the safety of journalists, media professionals, and associated personnel posed by terrorist groups and strongly condemning incidents of killings,

31 UNSC Resolution S/RES/1738, 23 December, 2006

kidnapping and hostage taking committed by terrorist groups UNSC, adopted another Resolution.[32] The Resolution urges Member States to take appropriate steps to ensure accountability for crimes committed against journalists, media professionals and associated personnel in situations of armed conflict and through the conduct of impartial, independent and effective investigations within their jurisdiction and to bring perpetrators of such crimes to justice.[33]

B. UN General Assembly Resolutions:

Expressing the concern at the threat to the safety of journalists posed by non-State actors, including terrorist groups and criminal organisations the UNGA in the year 2013 adopted the Resolution on 'Safety of Journalists and Issue of Impunity' and condemned unequivocally all attacks and violence against journalists and media workers, such as torture, extrajudicial killings, enforced disappearances and arbitrary detention, as well as intimidation and harassment in both conflict and non-conflict situations.[34]

Most recently, in 2023 UN General Assembly adopted the resolution on the Safety of Journalists and Issue of Impunity wherein Staes were called upon to develop and implement effective and transparent legal frameworks and measures for the protection of journalists and media workers and for combating impunity, taking a gender-responsive approach, including, where appropriate, through the creation and strengthening of special investigative units or independent commissions, the appointment of a specialised prosecutor and the adoption of specific protocols and methods of investigation and prosecution; to immediate and unconditional release of journalists and media workers who have been arbitrarily arrested, arbitrarily detained or taken hostage or who have become victims of enforced disappearances the immediate and unconditional release of journalists and media workers who have been arbitrarily arrested, arbitrarily detained or taken hostage or who have become victims of enforced disappearances.[35]

---

32 UNSC Resolution 2222 (2015) Adopted by the Security Council at its 7450th meeting, on 27 May 2015.

33 Id. Para 6.

34 UNGA Resolution A/RES/68/163 18 December 2013. Since then, Various Resolutions were adopted by UNGA: A/RES/69/185 dated 18 December 2014; A/RES/70/162 17 December 2015; A/RES/72/175 dated 19 December 2017; A/RES/74/157 dated 18 December 2019; A/RES/76/173 dated 16 December 2021.

35 UNGA Resolution A/RES/78/215 dated 22 December 2023.

C. Human Rights Council Resolutions

Since its establishment in 2006, the Human Rights Council has regularly addressed the issue of safety of journalists in the context of the right to freedom of expression and opinion. Resolution 21/12 was the first Council resolution to have a specific focus on safety of journalists. In that resolution, the Council expressed, inter alia, its concern and called upon parties to armed conflict to respect their obligations under international human rights law and international humanitarian law, including their obligations under the Geneva Conventions and, where applicable, the Additional Protocols, the provisions of which extend protection to journalists in situations of armed conflict, and to allow, within the framework of applicable rules and procedures, media access and coverage, as appropriate, in situations of international and non-international armed conflict. It also provides for ensuring accountability through the conduct of impartial, speedy and effective investigations into such acts falling within their jurisdiction, and to bring to justice those responsible and to ensure that victims have access to appropriate remedies.[36] Following previous resolutions[37], Human Rights Council expressed the serious concern at attacks and violence against journalists and media workers in situations of armed conflict, including the specific risks faced by women journalists.[38]

D. UN Educational Scientific Cooperation Organisation Initiatives

The UN Educational Scientific Cooperation Organisation (UNESCO) is committed to provide holistic support to safety of journalists covering physical, psychological and digital safety, promoting access to lifesaving, humanitarian information for local populations affected by crises and conflicts and supporting journalists that have been forced into exile. It has taken numerous actions in providing safety to journalist in the form of adopting resolutions, Declarations and Executive Council decisions. It adopted Resolution 29 on the 'Condemnation of violence against journalists. The resolution invited the Director-General 'to condemn assassination and any physical violence against journalists as a crime against society, since

36 Human Rights Council Resolution A/HRC/RES/21/12 dated 9 October 2012.

37 General Assembly and Human Rights Council resolutions on the safety of journalists, in particular Assembly resolution 76/173 of 16 December 2021 and Council resolution 45/18 of 6 October 2020, as well as Council resolution 50/15 of 8 July 2022, on freedom of opinion and expression, and Security Council resolutions 1738 (2006) of 23 December 2006 and 2222 (2015) of 27 May 2015, on the protection of civilians in armed conflict.

38 A/HRC/RES/51/9 dated 6 October 2022.

this curtails freedom of expression and, as a consequence, the other rights and freedoms', and to urge the authorities to prevent, investigate, punish and remedy such crimes.[39] Member States, in 2015, were encouraged again by UNESCO to promote journalists, producers of social media and media worker's safety. In order to achieve this, UNESCO encouraged the Member States to take advantage of the opportunities, practices and knowledge which is available through the 'United Nations Plan of Action on the Safety of journalists' and the problem of impunity.[40]

Furthermore, UNESCO has issued number of Declarations regarding safety of journalists and impunity *viz.* the Belgrade Declaration on Media in Conflict Areas and in Countries in Transition, established in 2004[41] and the Medellin Declaration on Securing the safety of journalists and combating impunity, 2007. UNESCOs' aim in establishing such declarations was to discover ways and methods for providing and enhancing support for the media operating in conflict zones and thus, to be able to design a suitable framework of action in order to achieve that.

Recently, UNESCO has reported a 42 per cent increase in attacks on journalists reporting on environmental issues between 2019 and 2024, highlighting the evolving nature of risks confronting the media. UNESCO recorded 68 killings of journalists in countries experiencing armed conflict, a slight low as compare to 72 killings in 2023, forty-four (44) journalists and media workers were killed in line with or in relation to their work in countries experiencing conflict, compared to 28 in 2022 and 20 in 2021. This amounts to 59% of all journalists killed that year, recording more than half of killings in a single year for the first time since 2017, and reversing the trend which had seen a decrease in the percentage of killings occurring in countries experiencing armed conflict. There was a notable spike in journalists killed in countries not experiencing armed conflict in 2022 (60), the highest ever recorded by UNESCO, with Mexico accounting for

39 UNESCO Resolution 29 of 1997 on Condemnation of Violation against Journalists.

40 UNESCO 196th Executive Board Decision on Safety of Journalists and the Issue of Impunity 196/EX/31/20 April 2015, para16.

41 Belgrade Declaration on 'Media in Conflict Areas and in Countries in Transition, 2004 sought to create a much more focused strategy than that of the existing humanitarian assistance plan in order to provide a much more sustainable and continuing media assistance framework founded on freedom of expression and progress of civil society. It emphasizes putting an end to the practice of impunity for attacks on journalists., (para 3).

almost a third of those killings (19).[42] Noticing the increase in killings, UNESCO Executive Board in May 2025, adopted the decision wherein it deplored the rise in journalist killings as well as the continued high frequency of threats, attacks, reprisals, and online and offline violence against journalists, including cases of disappearances, imprisonment, arbitrary detention and other harmful acts.[43]

Regional Initiatives

A. The Organisation for Security and Cooperation in Europe (OSCE): The OSCE is an organisation consisting of 57 States from Europe, Central Asia and North America. The OSCE oversees a number of issues including security, economic development and human rights protection. Its principal mandate is to make sure that the Member States maintain and promote freedom of the media – a core membership requirement. The OSCE published a report on the safety of journalists in 2011. It reported that the safety and protection of journalists has become a major problem for members of the OSCE due to the fact that there has been a significant rise in violence towards journalists. Further, the report by the OSCE sets out clear and sufficient practices for dealing with the issue of safety of journalists. The report also produced evidence of several blockades on the freedom of media. Such blockades included the forbidding of foreign journalists from accessing State territory, and the problem of the physical safety of journalists. In November 2018, the Ministerial Council OSCE adopted Decision 3/18 on the Safety of Journalists. In this landmark document, the participating States committed themselves to improve the safety of journalists on different inter-related aspects, including physical, legal, economic and online threats and attacks, with a special focus on the distinct risks faced by women journalists.[44]The recent 2023 Report in addition to reporting the risks faced by the journalists including women journalists focussed on the challenges and safety issues of the journalists in exile.[45]

42 Director-General's Report on the Safety of Journalists and the Danger of Impunity (CI-24/COUNCIL.34/7), 2024.

43 UNESCO 221 Executive Board Decision on Safety of Journalists and the Issue of Impunity 221/EX/Decisions 2-17 April 2025, 5.1.F Para 6.

44 Organization for Security and Co-operation in Europe Office of the Representative on Freedom of the Media Special Report on The Sixth Roundtable of The Safety of Journalists Project Police Prevention and Fight, Against Impunity, August 2023

45 Special Report on the Third Roundtable on The Safety of Journalists Project, Organization for Security and Co-operation in Europe, Office of the Representative

B. Council of Europe: Several resolutions as well as recommendations on the problem of the safety of journalists and the combating of impunity have been adopted by the Parliamentary Assembly of the Council of Europe. The Council emphasised greatly, in Resolution 1428 (2005) the need for Member and Observer States to make sure that journalists can safely practice their profession within their territories. The Council of Europe, in 2012, approved a 'Strategic Framework on Human Rights and Democracy' which aims to strengthen the efficiency of the human rights strategy of the EU both outside and within. The creation of the status of EU special delegates for human rights, by the 'European External Action Service', was mandated to endorse essential human rights which include freedom of media in States outside the EU in order to make sure that journalists are being protected from both violence and intimidation. More importantly, the Council has approved the right for journalists to not reveal their information, except in certain conditions. This may well permit the protection of journalists from becoming a target by preventing them from appearing as witnesses. Guidelines were adopted by the Committee of Ministers of the Council of Europe in 2007, on Protecting Freedom of Express and Information in Times of Crisis. They highlighted the issue of impunity in conflict zones. They expressed the need to have a broader range of protection for journalists outside their physical safety. Moreover, the protection should also incorporate journalist's freedom of movement, as well as protection of their bases. Sates are encouraged to protect the privacy of sources in situations of conflict, as stated by the Committee of Minister of Council of Europe. The significance of the value of protecting journalists' information was expressed in *Prosecutor v Tlaic*[46], by the International Criminal Tribunal for the form Yugoslavia. The Tribunal held that "compelling war correspondents to testify before the International Tribunal on a routine basis may have a significant impact upon their ability to obtain information and thus their ability to inform the public on issues of general concern. The Appeals Chamber will not unnecessarily hamper the work of professions that perform a public interest."

The significance of the standard for the protection of the sources of journalists' reports was expressed in *Goodwin v. UK*[47] by the European Court. It stated that "protection of journalistic sources is one of the basic conditions for press freedom, as is reflected in the laws and the professional

on Freedom of the Media, 7 March 2023.

46 *Prosecutor v. Brdjanin & Talic*. Case No. IT-99-36-AR73.

47 *Christine Goodwin V. The United Kingdom*, 28957/95 [2002] ECHR 588 (11 July 2002)

codes of conduct in a number of Contracting States and is affirmed in several international instruments on journalistic freedom." The Court stated that where a superseding requirement towards the public interest was absent, a demand to reveal their sources would therefore be in violation of the freedom of expression expressed in the ECHRs Article 10. The Council was urged to help Member States to train their law-enforcement, judges and police in order to protect journalists from violent threats, as recommended by the Parliamentary Assembly of the Council of Europe.

C. **The Organisation of African Union:** The African Commission on Human and Peoples' Rights (the African Commission), meeting at its 49th Ordinary Session adopted the resolution on Safety of Journalists and Media Practitioners in Africa urging all parties involved in situations of armed conflicts to respect the independence and freedom of journalists and media practitioners to exercise their profession and guarantee their safety and security in accordance with international humanitarian law.[48] Further, the Declaration of Principles of Freedom of Expression and Access to Information in Africa (the Declaration) was adopted by the African Commission at its 65th Ordinary Session which was held from 21 October to 10 November 2019 in Banjul, The Gambia. The Declaration establishes or affirms the principles for anchoring the rights to freedom of expression and access to information in conformance with Article 9 of the African Charter which guarantees individuals the right to receive information as well as the right to express and disseminate information. The Peace and Security Council (PSC) of the African Union (AU) held its 1230th meeting (Open Session) on 2 September 2024, on Protection of Journalists and Access to Information in Situation of Armed Conflicts in Africa expressed the concern of attacks on journalists and threats to journalists and humanitarian workers in conflict situations and condemned all violations and abuses committed.

The United States Department of Defence, Law of War Manual (June 2015, updated July 2023), recognises that journalists play a vital role in free societies and the rule of law and in providing information about armed conflict. The are civilians and are protected as such under the law of war. Journalists do not form a distinct class of persons under the law of war, but instead receive protection through the general protections afforded civilians. Thus, in general, the rights, duties, and liabilities applicable to civilians also apply to journalists. Although generally journalists are

48 ACHPR/Res.185(XLIX)11, 49th Ordinary Session, Held in Banjul, The Gambia, From 28 April - 12 May 2011

civilians, journalists are not precluded from being considered combatants, whether privileged or unprivileged, if they otherwise acquire such status. For example, members of the armed forces sometimes serve as journalists or in some other public affairs capacity, and these persons have the same status as other privileged combatants. Non-State armed groups sometimes use their members for propaganda or other media activities, and such personnel are not precluded from being considered unprivileged belligerents. In addition, although engaging in journalism would not be a basis to consider a person an unprivileged belligerent, an unprivileged belligerent would not be precluded from being considered as such because he or she works as a journalist.[49]

Conclusion

The nature of modern warfare has vastly changed the role of journalists in conflict and, therefore, the reliability of the protections afforded to them. Undoubtedly, there have been undeniable advancements over recent years to strengthen the safety of journalists and address prevailing impunity for violations of their rights. There now exist numerous prevention, protection, monitoring and complaint mechanisms at the international and regional levels, often with multiple purposes and functions, which are utilised by States, the United Nations system, international and regional organisations, and media and civil society actors, Non-Governmental Organisations like IFJ, Reporters without Borders etc. in order to enhance the safety of journalists. Despite the attention given to the safety of journalists at the international and regional levels, attacks on journalists are increasing, raising legitimate questions about the impact of these mechanisms at all levels. After analysing the rules relative to the protection of journalists, the question remains whether they are in fact respected and implemented in reality. To some answer is in supplementary, humanitarian rules are indeed observed, as evidenced by the sometimes-extraordinary accounts given to us on television or in the papers. Nevertheless, violations are not infrequent. One possible solution might be for journalists themselves to contribute towards creating the conditions likely to compel authorities to respect the rules of international humanitarian law, for fear of intolerable pressure by world opinion. The IFJ once again has called for the adoption of a UN Convention to protect journalists, an initiative that has never been more urgent.

49 The United States, Department of Defence Law of War Manual (June 2015, updated July 2023), para 4.24, pp. 173-175.

Chapter 13

Protecting the Protectors: Navigating Recent Challenges to Medical Personnel in the Context of International Humanitarian Law

-Anna Bashir and Ms. Mehvish Mehraj

Introduction

Within the stage of armed conflict, where humanity's limits are regularly pushed to the extreme, medical staff hold a specially safeguarded position in international humanitarian law (IHL). Committed to relieving human suffering without discrimination, they are the guardians of neutrality and impartiality in the midst of violence. And yet, with all their legally protected status, the past decade has witnessed a disquieting rise in attacks specifically aimed at medical professionals and medical facilities. From the destruction of hospital facilities in Syria and Gaza to the harassment and detention of health professionals in Myanmar and Ukraine, the systematic disregard of medical impartiality has become a hallmark of crisis in modern conflict areas. This dilution of respect for humanitarian principles calls for immediate academic attention to both the effectiveness and enforcement of legal guarantees under IHL.[1]

Medical staff broadly construed to comprise physicians, nurses, paramedics, hospital personnel and medical transport teams are specifically protected under the 1949 Geneva Conventions and their Additional Protocols.

1 Julia Neuberger, "The Educated Patient: New Challenges for the Medical Profession", *Journal of Internal Medicine*, vol. 247, no. 1 (2000), pp. 6–10 at p. 6.

These documents codify principles of distinction, proportionality and necessity, which together exclude the targeting of medical units and require respect for their humanitarian role. That said, the character of armed conflict itself has been radically altered since the middle part of the 20th century. Contemporary warfare is now marked by prolonged civil wars, asymmetrical conflicts with non-state armed actors and hybrid warfare blurring the distinction between combatants and civilians. This has made it difficult to apply and enforce IHL norms, leaving medical workers exposed to politically inspired attacks, reprisal executions and the deliberate targeting of medical facilities as military objectives.[2]

The intentional or indiscriminate targeting of hospitals is a war crime under international law. However, impunity for such crimes persists. The ICC's limited jurisdiction, states' hesitance to prosecute under universal jurisdiction, and the politicisation of international accountability mechanisms have all combined to thwart efforts to hold perpetrators accountable. Meanwhile, humanitarian aid militarisation and the use of counterterrorism laws to limit medical support in areas of conflict also diminish the protective legal regime under IHL. These realities pose tough but essential questions: Are the current legal frameworks sufficient to protect medical staff in armed conflicts today? What normative and structural weaknesses weaken their protection? And how can accountability be practically imposed in a growing, splintered international order. This chapter attempts to steer these questions through a critical analysis of the legal, political and operational obstacles to the safeguarding of medical personnel in the realm of international humanitarian law. Grounded in a doctrinal and case-based approach, the chapter starts by charting the development of protections given to medical personnel under IHL, including the Geneva Conventions, customary international law and jurisprudential evolution. It then situates these protections in the reality of contemporary warfare, examining recent trends of abuses and the legal grey areas manipulated by combatants.

Historical Background and Development of Norms

The protection of medical staff during armed conflict developed over a long historical path influenced by humanitarian necessity and the cruel realities of warfare. Early codifications like the 1864 Geneva Convention and the 1863 Lieber Code established the basic principles for the humane care of

2 Vanina Mihaylova and Adolf Alakidi, "Professional Challenges for Healthcare Professionals", *Burgan Journal of Public Health*, vol. 15, no. 2 (2023), pp. 27–34 at p. 27.

the wounded and the neutrality of medical service.[3] These early attempts were subsequently built upon and improved by successive treaties, such as the Hague Conventions of 1899 and 1907, which established primitive guidelines for the conduct of hostilities and the treatment of medical missions. Yet, the large-scale atrocities of the World Wars spurred a more widespread effort, resulting in the 1949 Geneva Conventions. These tools represented a seminal normative transition by enacting a global duty to safeguard medical personnel, installations and transports and by characterising infractions as serious breaches open to international sanction. The post-war era also saw the establishment of international institutions, like the International Committee of the Red Cross (ICRC), which took a leading role in the promotion and implementation of these norms.[4]

The acceptance of the 1977 Additional Protocols also answered to the challenges of contemporary warfare, in this case, by dealing with non-international armed conflict and asymmetric warfare situations. All these, however, have been at a slower pace than the evolution of the character of warfare, notably with increasing activity by non-state actors and in urban battlefields where civilian and military targets are often confused with each other. Accordingly, the historical evolution of IHL simultaneously signals increasing international agreement regarding the inviolability of medical personnel and the ongoing difficulty of bridging legal ideals and operative realities.[5]

Early Humanitarian Thought and Pre-Geneva Initiatives

The notion that the injured and caregivers must be exempted from the brutality of war is not a recent creation. Evidence of such a norm is discovered in early codes and religious teachings that taught compassion and clemency even in times of armed conflict. But it was not until the 19th century that a rational legal system for the protection of medical staff arose, spurred on by the humanitarian ideals of people such as Henry Dunant,

3 Adam Roberts, "Foundational Myths in the Laws of War: The 1863 Lieber Code, and the 1864 'Geneva Convention'", *Melbourne Journal of International Law*, vol. 20, no. 1 (2019), pp. 158–196 at p. 158.

4 Samantha Frances Bradley, "Protection of Detainees from Sexual Violence under International Humanitarian Law", *Journal of Conflict and Security Law*, vol. 25, no. 3 (2020), pp. 381–422 at p. 381.

5 Igor P. Blishchenko, "Adoption of the 1977 Additional Protocols", *International Review of the Red Cross* (1961–1997), vol. 37, no. 320 (1997), pp. 511–514 at p. 511.

whose time at the Battle of Solferino in 1859 resulted in the establishment of the International Committee of the Red Cross (ICRC) in 1863.[6]

The first official legal codification of safeguards for medical staff was with the Geneva Convention of 1864, which mandated belligerent parties to attend to wounded combatants and protect medical teams. Though crude and narrow in scope, largely dealing with the wounded and military medical staff in the field, the Convention set the stage for contemporary humanitarian law by promulgating the Red Cross symbol, a symbol of protection and neutrality. At the same time, the Lieber Code of 1863, issued during the American Civil War, established initial rules of warfare and recognised medical personnel's special status, an effort one of the earliest to set rules for conduct in war from a state-based point of view.[7]

The Hague Conventions and Early Twentieth-Century Developments

The Hague Conventions of 1899 and 1907 enlarged legal protection during War. Although their basic concern was with the laws of warfare and weapons and tactics of combat, they also included principles of humanitarian treatment and offered some protection to medical formations and hospital ships. In particular, these conventions drew upon the Geneva tradition by developing concern for sparing installations and personnel involved in caring for the wounded and sick.[8]

Yet the First World War revealed the serious shortcomings of such legal protection as did exist. The extensive employment of chemicals, the bombardment of medical facilities and the heavy toll among civilians demonstrated the shortcomings of current legal standards. These failures led to a reconsideration of humanitarian law during the interwar years, though such fundamental reform awaited the post-Second World War period.[9]

---

6 Maartje Abbenhuis, *War, Peace and International Order?: The Legacies of the Hague Conferences of 1899 and 1907*, vol. 23 (Taylor & Francis, 2017), p. 12.

7 Hans van Loon, "The Hague Conference: Its Origins, Organization and Achievements", *Svensk Juristtidning* (SvJT), 1993, pp. 293–307 at p. 293.

8 Erazak Manapovich Tileubergenov, Sergei Igorevich Pelevin, Anatoliy Anatolievich Vasiliev and Eduard Igorevich Danilyanc, "Political and Legal Defining the Regulations of War in the Hague Convention of 1907", *Journal of Advanced Research in Law and Economics*, vol. 7, no. 3 (17) (2016), pp. 672–677 at p. 672.

9 Leo Van Bergen, "'Would It Not Be Better to Just Stop?' Dutch Medical Aid in World War I and the Medical Anti-War Movement in the Interwar Years", *First World War Studies*, vol. 2, no. 2 (2011), pp. 165–194 at p. 165.

The Geneva Conventions of 1949: A Transformative Framework

The Second World War atrocities, such as hospital attacks, the execution of medical professionals, and the categorical denial of care to civilians, served as the impetus for the most fundamental revamp of humanitarian law in recent history. The upshot was the promulgation of the Four Geneva Conventions of 1949 that collectively redefined the extent and content of legal protections within armed conflict. The First Geneva Convention directly dealt with the "Amelioration of the Condition of the Wounded and Sick in Armed Forces in the Field," and enshrined the duty to respect and protect medical transport, units and personnel. Article 19 made it clear that medical units "may in no circumstances be attacked," while Article 24 gave special protection to personnel assigned solely for medical work. Significantly, the Conventions also endorsed the principle of impartiality, mandating that care be provided without discrimination based on nationality, race, religion or political opinion.[10]

The Geneva Convention relative to the Protection of Civilian Persons in Time of War added protections to civilians, such as those delivering medical care, expanding recognition that the effects of war were no longer strictly confined to combatants. International law first acknowledged in a formal way that civilian medical volunteers needed legal protection as actors in the humanitarian response.[11]

The 1977 Additional Protocols: Responding to New Forms of Warfare

During the post-World War II decades, the international landscape of conflict evolved significantly. The process of decolonisation, the emergence of non-international armed conflicts (NIACs) and the growing role of non-state armed groups made assumptions in the Geneva Conventions insufficient. With a view to filling these lacunae, the Additional Protocols I and II, adopted in 1977, brought important developments. Additional Protocol I widened protections in international armed conflicts (IACs) and reasserted the protected nature of medical units, mandating that they must not be utilised to cover up military operations. Article 12 of Protocol I reaffirmed that "medical units shall be respected and protected at all times

10 Boyd Van Dijk, *Preparing for War: The Making of the 1949 Geneva Conventions* (Oxford University Press, 2022), p. 212.

11 Ebunoluwa Bamigboye and Victor O. Ayeni, "Laying the Foundations for Jus Post Bellum: The Conservationist Principle in the Law of Occupation as a Foundation for a Fourth Additional Protocol to the Geneva Conventions", *International Journal of Comparative Law and Legal Ethics Practice* (IJOCLLEP), vol. 4 (2022), p. 61.

and shall not be the object of attack." It also added legal precision to the prohibition against reprisals against medical staff and defined under what circumstances protection could be lost, essentially, if employed to cause acts injurious to the enemy beyond their humanitarian role.[12]

Additional Protocol II was revolutionary in dealing with non-international armed conflicts, previously mentioned under Common Article 3 of the Geneva Conventions only. While narrower than Protocol I, it achieved important legal acknowledgement that in internal conflicts like civil wars and insurgencies, medical personnel and facilities must also be respected and protected. Article 9 of Protocol II provides that "medical and religious personnel shall be respected and protected and shall be granted all available help for the performance of their duties." In spite of these developments, there remained problems. The small number of ratifications, in particular of Protocol II and the non-belief of many non-state entities in obligations arising under international treaties, watered down the effective application of these reforms. The 1977 Additional Protocols were, however, an important step towards bringing IHL into conformity with the realities of new conflicts.[13]

Jurisprudential and Institutional Developments

The latter half of the 20th and early 21st centuries also saw notable improvements in humanitarian jurisprudence and enforcement. The creation of ad hoc tribunals, including the International Criminal Tribunal for the former Yugoslavia (ICTY) and the International Criminal Tribunal for Rwanda (ICTR), created case law affirming the proposition that attacks on medical staff and facilities would amount to war crimes. The establishment of the International Criminal Court (ICC) formalised this acknowledgement. In accordance with Article 8 of the Rome Statute, "intentionally directing attacks against hospitals and places where the sick and wounded are collected, provided that they are not military objectives," is deemed a war crime.[14]

12 Knut Dörmann, "Applicability of International Humanitarian Law to Computer Network Attacks" (International Committee of the Red Cross, 2015), available at: https://www.icrc.org/sites/default/files/external/doc/en/assets/files/other/applicabilityofihltocna.pdf, accessed on 26 March 2025.

13 Claude Pilloud, Yves Sandoz, Christophe Swinarski and Bruno Zimmermann (eds.), *Commentary on the Additional Protocols: of 8 June 1977 to the Geneva Conventions of 12 August 1949* (Martinus Nijhoff Publishers, 1987), p. 128.

14 Article 8, Rome Statute of the International Criminal Court, 17 July 1998, 2187 UNTS 90 (entered into force 1 July 2002).

Concurrently, the International Committee of the Red Cross (ICRC) was an integral force in the codification of customary IHL, which continues to bind states irrespective of ratification of the treaty. The ICRC's 2005 research on customary international law confirmed that the fundamental principles relating to the protection of medical personnel are accepted as customary norms, thus enhancing their universality and applicability even in conflicts including non-signatories or irregular forces.[15]

Legal Framework: Protection of Medical Personnel

The safeguarding of medical staff during armed conflict is solidly established in the body of international humanitarian law, mainly codified in the 1949 Geneva Conventions and their 1977 Additional Protocols.[16] The First Geneva Convention obliges medical staff, facilities and vehicles to be respected and protected in all cases, adhering to the principle of medical neutrality.[17] This safeguard is reaffirmed under Additional Protocol I, which explains prohibitions against attacking medical units and reaffirms that these protections are not dependent upon the status of the wounded or sick.[18] United Nations Security Council Resolution 2286 (2016) reaffirmed the global condemnation of such attacks, but its absence of binding enforcement powers has limited its real-world effectiveness. The difference between international and non-international armed conflict also makes the legal framework more complex, typically having less effective protections in internal conflicts where abuses are most common. As modern warfare evolves, so too must the institutional and legal frameworks that are intended to maintain the sanctity of humanitarian medical care.[19]

---

15 International Committee of the Red Cross (ICRC), *Overview of Operations 2005* (December 2004), available at https://www.icrc.org/sites/default/files/external/doc/en/assets/files/other/icrc_overview_appeal_2005.pdf (last accessed 27 May 2025).

16 Protocol Additional to the Geneva Conventions of 12 August 1949, and relating to the Protection of Victims of International Armed Conflicts (Protocol I), 8 June 1977, 1125 UNTS 3 (entered into force 7 December 1978).

17 Convention for the Amelioration of the Condition of the Wounded and Sick in Armed Forces in the Field (First Geneva Convention), 6 August 1949, 75 UNTS 31 (entered into force 21 October 1950).

18 Julianto Jover Jotam Kalalo and Chyntia Novita Kalalo, "Legal Protection Against Health Workers in Taking First Aid Medical Measures", *Musamus Law Review*, vol. 1, no. 1 (2018), pp. 40–52 at p. 40.

19 United Nations Security Council Resolution 2286 (2016), Adopted at the 7685th meeting on 3 May 2016, UN Doc. S/RES/2286 (2016).

Geneva Conventions

The foundation of international humanitarian law is the Geneva Conventions of 1949 and notably the First and Fourth Conventions, which together form the legal framework for the protection of medical staff and facilities in the midst of armed conflict. The First Geneva Convention is particular to the "Amelioration of the Condition of the Wounded and Sick in Armed Forces in the Field," and it requires that medical staff, units and transport will be respected and protected at all times. Article 19 of the First Convention says that fixed medical establishments and mobile medical units shall never, under any circumstances, be attacked but shall always be respected and protected by the parties to the conflict.[20]

Additional Protocols of 1977

The 1977 Additional Protocols to the Geneva Conventions offer more specific guidance. Additional Protocol I (API), which is applied to international armed conflicts, reiterates and extends protections under Article 12, which medical units shall not be targeted and should be placed in ways that reduce risk. It also launches the prohibition of indiscriminate attacks, which are not allowed if they do not discriminate between the legitimate military objectives and the persons or objects entitled to protection, i.e., medical personnel. The Additional Protocol II (APII), which covers non-international armed conflicts, was the major breakthrough, since most modern conflicts constitute this type. It provides protection for medical units and transport in civil wars and internal unrest, which indicates growing concern for non-state armed groups and greater violence inside state frontiers.[21]

Customary International Humanitarian Law

In addition to treaty law, customary IHL provides an important source of legal protection for medical staff, especially when treaty law is either non-committal or not applicable. The International Committee of the Red Cross (ICRC) has catalogued a plethora of customary rules that underpin the protections embedded in treaty law. Rule 25 of the Customary Rule, for

20 Theresa U. Akpoghome, "Legal Framework to Ensure Sufficient Medical Equipment, to Train Medical Staff and to Observe Sanitary Standards", *KAS African Law Study Library*, vol. 7, no. 4 (2021), pp. 544–568 at p. 544.

21 LawBhoomi, "Medical Professional and Related Laws in India", *LawBhoomi*, 12 January 2022, available at: https://lawbhoomi.com/medical-professional-and-related-laws-in-india/, accessed on 26 April 2025.

example, dictates that "medical staff assigned solely to medical tasks must be respected and protected in all situations." This rule is applicable in both international and non-international armed conflicts and is binding on all parties irrespective of ratification.[22]

Customary law also covers prohibitions on attacks on medical facilities (Rule 28) and the duty to search for and treat the wounded and sick without discriminatory distinction (Rule 110). These rules are especially significant in asymmetric warfare, where non-state actors frequently disregard treaty-based obligations, but are nevertheless subject to customary norms. The ubiquity of customary law, therefore, fills significant normative gaps and underpins the universality of protections for medical personnel.[23]

The Principle of Medical Neutrality

One of the key notions supporting the legal framework is medical neutrality, the duty of parties to a conflict to not only avoid attacking medical professionals and facilities but also to allow their autonomous functioning. This norm finds its normative traction both within treaty law and customary law. Abuses of medical impartiality, like attacks on ambulances, refusal of access to medical care or criminalisation of medical treatment for suspected insurgents, have become more common. These abuses tend to take advantage of loopholes in the law, for instance, the use of national security or counterterrorism as a justification, thus eroding the fundamental principles of IHL. The duty of respect and protection for medical staff is not dependent on the status of the sick or wounded. Disruption of this function is not only a violation of the law but is also a moral failure in the midst of human suffering.[24]

22 Robert Heinsch, "Methodological Challenges in Ascertaining Customary International Humanitarian Law: Can Customary International Law Respond to Changing Circumstances in Warfare?", in *Law-Making and Legitimacy in International Humanitarian Law* (Edward Elgar Publishing, 2021), pp. 170–194 at p. 170.

23 World Jurisprudence, "Understanding Customary International Humanitarian Law Principles", *World Jurisprudence*, 26 October 2024, available at: https://worldjurisprudence.com/customary-international-humanitarian-law/, accessed on 16 April 2025.

24 Leonard Rubenstein, "Medical Neutrality and Political Engagement", in *Challenging Medical Neutrality: Healthcare Ethics in Armed Conflict and Other Complex Settings* (Springer Nature Switzerland, Cham, 2024), pp. 189–207 at p. 189.

International and Non-International Armed Conflicts

The distinction between International and Non-International Armed Conflicts significantly affects the legal protection afforded to medical personnel under international humanitarian law. In International Armed Conflicts (IACs), involving conflicts between States, medical personnel enjoy extensive protection under the Geneva Conventions of 1949 and Additional Protocol I, which explicitly recognize their status, ensure their immunity from attack and mandate their repatriation if captured. In contrast, Non-International Armed Conflicts (NIACs), which occur within a single State involving government forces and non-State armed groups or between such groups, offer more limited and less detailed protections primarily under Common Article 3 of the Geneva Conventions and Additional Protocol II. Unlike IACs, NIACs often lack clear mechanisms for recognizing medical personnel, and domestic laws may criminalize their assistance to enemy combatants, placing them at greater risk. Nevertheless, customary international law has helped bridge this gap by affirming that medical personnel must be respected and protected in all types of armed conflicts.[25]

While Common Article 3 ensures basic protection, humane treatment and non-discriminatory treatment of the wounded, it is not as specific and enforceable as in IACs. The circumscribed application of Additional Protocol II, with fewer ratifications and only applying under tight criteria (organised armed groups, prolonged hostilities), undermines protection in insurgencies, civil wars and internal conflicts. Such a dualism has resulted in normative fragmentation and inconsistent enforcement, resulting in the susceptibility of medical staff in NIACs.[26]

United Nations Instruments and Resolutions

The United Nations Security Council has more recently actively engaged in responding to violence against healthcare in conflict. Resolution 2286 (2016), which was passed unanimously, condemned attacks on medical

25 Ben McGuckin, "The Conflict Between Armed Conflicts: Dispensing with the Distinction Between International and Non-International Armed Conflicts" (Durham Global Security Institute Working Paper No. 1, 2018), available at: https://www.dur.ac.uk/media/durham-university/research-/research-institutes/durham-global-security-institute/pdfs/McGuckin2017TheConflictBetweenArmedConflicts-FinalforDGSI1.pdf, accessed on 12 March 2025.

26 UN Secretary-General, *Report on the Protection of Civilians in Armed Conflict*, UN Doc. S/2022/381 (2022).

staff in armed conflict firmly and called on states to abide by their international law obligations.[27] The resolution constituted a significant political recognition of the increasing attacks against medical staff, but has been criticised for failing to include binding legal obligations or concrete enforcement processes. Other pertinent tools are the UN Secretary-General's Reports on the Protection of Civilians in Armed Conflict, which every year point to the targeting of healthcare services as a significant issue. Without effective mechanisms for investigation, sanction or enforcement, however, such resolutions remain nominal.[28]

Contemporary Challenges to the Protection of Medical Personnel

Today's challenges to the protection of health personnel involve the escalating targeting of healthcare workers and health facilities in conflict areas, which weakens the provision of key medical services. Such threats make it difficult to obey international humanitarian law and require stringent enforcement mechanisms to ensure medical neutrality.[29]

Increasing Complexity of Armed Conflicts

The modern battlefield differs significantly from the traditional interstate conflicts to which most of international humanitarian law (IHL) was originally tailored. These features are difficult to reconcile with the practical application of legal safeguards for medical personnel. In urban combat, for example, the blurring of civilian, military and humanitarian actors within densely populated environments tends to create challenges of distinction and identification. Medical units that are proximate to military bases or that are sporadically used by armed groups tend to be drawn into the conflict through collateral damage. Most non-state actors are not trained in or respectful of IHL, which leads to widespread abuses, such as targeting medical personnel who are seen as assisting the enemy.[30]

---

27 UN Security Council Resolution 2286 (2016), Adopted at the 7685th meeting on 3 May 2016, UN Doc. S/RES/2286 (2016).

28 P. Preston Reynolds, "A Legislative History of Federal Assistance for Health Professions Training in Primary Care Medicine and Dentistry in the United States, 1963–2008", *Academic Medicine*, vol. 83, no. 11 (2008), pp. 1004–1014 at p. 1004.

29 Alan Gregg, *Challenges to Contemporary Medicine* (Columbia University Press, 1956), p.126.

30 Mariusz Goniewicz and Krzysztof Goniewicz, "Protection of Medical Personnel in Armed Conflicts, Case Study: Afghanistan", *European Journal of Trauma and Emergency Surgery*, vol. 39 (2013), pp. 107–112 at p. 107.

Deliberate Targeting and Criminalisation of Medical Personnel

Arguably, the most disturbing trend of the last few years has been the intentional attack on medical staff, ambulances and healthcare facilities. In contrast to collateral damage, attacks of this type tend to be deliberate acts of war, intended to shatter enemy troops' morale or intimidate civilian populations. Both Syria, Yemen and South Sudan have seen repeated and well-documented attacks on healthcare providers and facilities.[31] The resort to "double-tap" attacks, where a second shot is delivered against first responders who have reached the scene, constitutes a blatant IHL and medical neutrality violation. States have practised the criminalisation of health, particularly within counterinsurgency settings. Care given to wounded fighters, even for humanitarian reasons, has resulted in the arrest, prosecution or intimidation of medical personnel, discouraging the delivery of neutral care.[32]

Erosion of the Principle of Medical Neutrality

The doctrine of medical neutrality, which was once a foundation of humanitarian practice, is increasingly undermined. Medical staff are frequently suspected, especially in polarised or ethnically divisive conflicts, where charges of bias will be met with reprisals. In politically volatile situations, local medical personnel can be coerced or intimidated into working for one side against another. The spread of surveillance technologies and biometric data capture has also undermined the perceived impartiality of medical missions, particularly when humanitarian actors have to transmit data to security actors. Perceived complicity is damaging to trust and puts both patients and practitioners at risk.[33]

Inadequate Legal Enforcement and Impunity

Although the normative system for the protection of medical staff is strong, its mechanisms for enforcement are weak and unreliable. Violations of IHL, such as attacks on healthcare, seldom lead to prosecution or substantial

31 Ronald T. Libby, *The Criminalization of Medicine: America's War on Doctors* (Bloomsbury Publishing USA, 2007), p. 223.

32 Angela Perone, "From Punitive to Proactive: An Alternative Approach for Responding to HIV Criminalization that Departs from Penalizing Marginalized Communities", *Hastings Women's Law Journal*, vol. 24 (2013), p. 363.

33 Paul Gilbert, "Medical Neutrality", in *Challenging Medical Neutrality: Healthcare Ethics in Armed Conflict and Other Complex Settings* (Springer Nature Switzerland, Cham, 2024), pp. 59–70 at p. 59.

accountability. Political interests, evidentiary difficulties and jurisdictional limitations in international courts usually hinder justice. The International Criminal Court (ICC) has only issued a few indictments against persons for targeting medical personnel in particular, and most states do not have domestic laws to prosecute the same under the principles of universal jurisdiction. Even where legal frameworks are available, the application is selective and politically charged, and perpetrators operate with impunity.[34]

Challenges Posed by Counterterrorism and Security Frameworks

New conflicts are becoming more and more interwoven with counterterrorism operations, creating legal and operational challenges for humanitarian actors. Numerous states have passed counterterrorism legislation that makes material support of listed groups criminal offences, which may include providing medical assistance.[35] Such legislations have a chilling impact on humanitarian activity, especially in areas held by non-state parties. For instance, giving medical treatment to a wounded insurgent would be interpreted as assisting terrorism in some states' law, even though such treatment is required by IHL. Military action conducted under counterterrorism imperatives could overlook or supplant humanitarian concerns, thus placing medical protection beneath security needs.

Technological Warfare and New Threat Vectors

The digitisation of war and the emergence of cyber war introduced new dangers to the security and effectiveness of medical personnel. Cyberattacks on hospital facilities already reported during peacetime pose a far greater threat during armed conflict. Compromising hospital systems, manipulating patient information or cutting off communications can have fatal effects in areas of war. The application of drones and artificial intelligence (AI) for targeting and surveillance raises serious issues regarding the misidentification of medical facilities as military targets. The recourse to algorithmic decision-making, with insufficient human involvement, could cause erosion of the principle of distinction at the core of IHL.[36]

34 V. Ern, "Moral Neutrality", *Work*, vol. 49, no. 11 (1996).

35 James Cockayne, "Challenges in United Nations Counterterrorism Coordination", in *Research Handbook on International Law and Terrorism* (Edward Elgar Publishing, 2014), pp. 666–682 at p. 666.

36 David Herrera, Jörg Meyle, Stefan Renvert and Lijian Jin, "White Paper on Prevention and Management of Periodontal Diseases for Oral Health and General Health", *FDI World Dental Federation* (2018), pp. 2020–11.

Stigmatisation and Psychological Trauma

In addition to physical attacks, healthcare workers are increasingly subjected to stigmatisation, psychological trauma and burnout, especially during long conflicts with extensive casualties and weak institutional protection. They are subject to attacks on their integrity and allegations of bias or espionage, decimating their legitimacy and moral voice among affected populations. Numerous healthcare professionals work under chronic threat, with little mental health assistance or legal action available. The psychological cost of such a deployment, seeing so many casualties, having to work under fire or being compelled to make life-or-death triage decisions, is impossible to overestimate. This erosion of morale and resistance eventually affects the humanitarian mission itself.[37]

Case Studies: A Tale of Violation of Legal Responses

This part discusses significant cases in which legal safeguards to medical professionals were violated during military confrontations, illuminating gaps between operational international laws and their enforcement. Through the case studies, difficulties in providing accountability and maintaining medical neutrality are carefully evaluated.

Ukraine: Medical Neutrality Under Siege

The Russian Federation's 2022 invasion of Ukraine has led to indiscriminate attacks on civilian infrastructure, including ambulances and hospitals. The World Health Organisation (WHO) confirmed more than 700 attacks on medical facilities, just in the conflict's first year alone. Russian troops have reported targeting health centres deliberately, especially in besieged cities like Mariupol and Kharkiv. These events not only contravene the Geneva Conventions but also seem to be part of an overall strategy to terrorise civilians and erode the strength of public services.[38]

In response, various human rights organisations have demanded war crime investigations, and proof is being gathered by international bodies, including the International Criminal Court, which has initiated a formal investigation of war crimes allegedly committed in the Ukraine conflict.

37 Shmuel P. Reis, Hedy S. Wald and Paul Weindling, "The Holocaust, Medicine and Becoming a Physician: The Crucial Role of Education", *Israel Journal of Health Policy Research*, vol. 8 (2019), pp. 1–5 at p. 1.

38 Arun Raschidy, Healthcare and Conflict in the Gaza Strip: Assessing the Impacts and Legal Implications (Master's thesis, University College Tilburg, Tilburg School of Humanities and Digital Sciences, Tilburg University, 2024), p. 64.

The case could be used as a means to strengthen legal accountability mechanisms, although much will hinge upon the cooperation of states and the capacity to arrest suspects, particularly senior military personnel or state leaders.[39]

Syria: Systematic Targeting in a Protracted Conflict

The conflict in Syria is one of the most extreme recent instances of the deliberate targeting of medical staff and hospitals. Under the government and its loyalist forces since the beginning of the civil war in 2011, doctors, patients and medical facilities have repeatedly been subjected to charges of the intentional bombing of hospitals, sieges to withhold medical access and criminalisation of healthcare delivery in opposition-held territory. More than 600 attacks on hospitals and clinics were registered between 2011 and 2020, according to Physicians for Human Rights, and a total of more than 900 medical staff lost their lives. Medical healthcare was weaponised as a means of warfare, to break down enemy morale and force civilian populations into submission.[40]

The Syrian government enacted laws that effectively criminalised the provision of medical attention to opposition fighters, terming doctors who treated them as collaborators or terrorists. Such criminalisation went against the duties under Common Article 3 of the Geneva Conventions that require humane treatment of all wounded individuals. The abundance of evidence has seen legal accountability remain low. While the UN Commission of Inquiry on Syria has provided extensive reports documenting war crimes such as attacks on hospitals, moves to refer the case to the International Criminal Court (ICC) have been prevented at the UN Security Council, primarily because of Russia and China's use of their veto powers.[41]

Yemen: A War of Attrition with Collateral Medical Devastation

In Yemen, the war between Houthi rebels and the Saudi-led coalition has yielded a humanitarian disaster, with the healthcare system being one of its

39 Robert Angevine, John K. Warden, Russell Keller and Clark Frye, *Learning Lessons from the Ukraine Conflict* (Alexandria, VA: Institute for Defense Analyses, Document NS D-10367, May 1, 2019), at p. 124.

40 Human Rights Watch, *"Targeting Life in Idlib": Syrian and Russian Strikes on Civilian Infrastructure* (15 October 2020), available at https://www.hrw.org/report/2020/10/15/targeting-life-idlib/syrian-and-russian-strikes-civilian-infrastructure (last accessed 17 March 2025).

41 Liana Melkonian, Regional Protracted Conflict in Syria (PhD diss., Lebanese American University, 2022), p. 321.

main victims. Airstrikes by coalition forces have hit hospitals, clinics and ambulance services repeatedly. Médecins Sans Frontières (MSF) reported numerous attacks on its facilities, including the 2016 bombing of an MSF-supported hospital in Hajjah, which killed 19 individuals. Most often, they occurred even though the GPS locations of the medical facilities had been provided well in advance to coalition forces.[42]

Saudi-led coalition's reliance on precision-guided munitions has created serious questions regarding whether such attacks were intentional or caused due to intelligence failings. Global outrage led the UN Panel of Experts on Yemen to conclude that most of these strikes amounted to war crimes. Yet, the absence of an institutionalised investigatory or judicial process with the ability to hold the perpetrators of such abuses accountable has weakened legal recourse. Local investigations in Saudi Arabia have typically cleared military commanders of blame, questioning their autonomy and integrity.[43]

Afghanistan: Dual Threats from Insurgents and Counterinsurgents

Afghanistan has a unique dynamic in which both insurgent forces and state-sponsored military actions have added to the risk faced by medical workers. The most notable example is the 2015 American bombing of the MSF hospital in Kunduz, which marked a turning point in the world's discussion of medical neutrality. The bombardment that killed 42, including doctors and patients, was universally condemned. Even though internal investigations were carried out by the U.S. military and the incident was termed a human error caused tragic mistake, no criminal charges were brought, and the hospital was never reconstructed.[44]

Taliban and other insurgent elements have consistently intimidated, abducted or murdered healthcare providers perceived as being on the government's or foreign side. Clinics that are located in Taliban-controlled zones of operation tend to operate under threat, with the tacit threat of

42 Nawsherwan, Sumaira Mubarik, Shafaq Naeem, Rabia Mubarak, Chuanhua Yu, Wang Yan and Mangmang Sang, "Health Dynamics in War-Torn Yemen: Insights from 32 Years of Epidemiological Data (1990–2021)", *Population Health Metrics*, vol. 23, no. 1 (2025), p. 4.

43 Sumaira Mubarik Nawsherwan, Shafaq Naeem, Rabia Mubarak, Chuanhua Yu, Wang Yan and Mangmang Sang, "Health Dynamics in War-Torn Yemen: Insights from 32 Years of Epidemiological Data (1990–2021)", *Population Health Metrics*, vol. 23, no. 1 (2025), p. 4.

44 Kersti Larsdotter, "Regional Support for Afghan Insurgents: Challenges for Counterinsurgency Theory and Doctrine", *Journal of Strategic Studies*, vol. 37, no. 1 (2014), pp. 135–162 at p. 135.

retaliation for attending to members of the opposite faction. This dual threat, international forces conducting counterinsurgency operations on one hand, insurgent elements exerting ideological control on the other, has significantly undermined the safety and neutrality of medical actors within Afghanistan.[45]

Occupied Palestinian Territory: Medical Care Amid Systemic Restriction

Within the Gaza Strip and West Bank, medical provision has been hindered by a variety of administrative and physical barriers introduced by the Israeli government. In instances of mass conflict, for example, Operation Protective Edge (2014) and Operation Cast Lead (2008-09), hospitals and ambulances were targeted in airstrikes, resulting in high numbers of civilian fatalities. Although the Israeli military claimed that these buildings were being utilised for military purposes, an exception under IHL, the principle of proportionality and precautionary measures have usually been argued as insufficiently taken into account.[46]

Palestinian healthcare providers have been impacted too by restrictions on movement, delays at border crossings and access problems in securing permits, which considerably hamper urgent care. In other instances, healthcare providers have been wounded or even killed in the line of duty while attending to protests or incursions. While UN agencies and NGOs have expressed ongoing concerns, Israel's domestic investigatory processes have been condemned for being both opaque and ineffective, resulting in pervasive impunity.[47]

Legal Responses: Limited but Emerging Avenues of Accountability

In spite of these serious violations mentioned earlier, there is still rare and uneven legal accountability. International tribunals usually do not have jurisdiction or political backing in most instances, while domestic

45 Paul Lushenko, Srinjoy Bose and Scott N. Romaniuk, "Blending Counterinsurgency to Defeat Hybrid Threats", in *Handbook of Terrorist and Insurgent Groups* (CRC Press, 2024), pp. 83–93 at p. 83.

46 Majdi M.K. Ashour, "Healthcare in the Times of Increased Adversity: Changes in Out-of-Pocket Payments, Treatment Seeking Behaviours and Public-Private Mix in the Gaza Strip", (2023), p. 86.

47 Bilal Irfan, Izzeddin Lulu, Adam Hamawy, Abdallah Abu Shammala, Susan Kullab, Mohamed Fawaz, Abd Al-Karim Sammour *et al.*, "Combating Infections Under Siege: Healthcare Challenges Amidst the Military Assault in Gaza", *World Medical & Health Policy*, vol. 17, no. 1 (2025), pp. 188–213 at p. 188.

prosecutions are frustrated by insufficient capacity, will or laws. Yet, there are new doors to justice and deterrence. Universal jurisdiction, employed by some countries like Sweden and Germany, has facilitated the prosecution of war crimes perpetrated outside their territories, including assaults on medical facilities. The UN Security Council Resolution 2286 (2016) specifically denounced attacks on healthcare during conflict, though it is not binding.[48]

The growing documentation activities of institutions like the ICRC, MSF, Amnesty International and Human Rights Watch, in addition to the application of digital evidence and satellite images, have reinforced the evidentiary foundation for prospective prosecutions. The expansion of international criminal law into command responsibility and individual criminal liability holds promise for redress, but is such an outcome the exception and not the norm?

Accountability and Enforcement Gaps

Despite strong international legal regimes safeguarding medical staff, there remain huge gaps in the prosecution of perpetrators. Lax enforcement mechanisms, restricted jurisdictional scope and political impediments tend to prevent justice from taking place, enabling abuses to be sustained with impunity and weakening humanitarian law's efficacy.

The Role of the ICC, Universal Jurisdiction and Ad Hoc Tribunals

Although a legal framework for safeguarding medical staff in armed conflict exists in good form, mechanisms of accountability, especially international criminal trials, have usually not effectively functioned in responding to violations. The International Criminal Court (ICC) under the Rome Statute has jurisdiction over war crimes, including "intentionally directing attacks against hospitals and places where the sick and wounded are collected" (Article 8(2)(b)(ix)). In reality, the ICC has rarely opened cases in particular for attacks against healthcare and the jurisdiction of the Court is frequently narrowed down by state non-ratification, political restrictions or complementarity problems.[49]

48 Jason S. Rathod, "Emerging Markets, Vanishing Accountability: How Populations in Poor Countries Can Use Aggregate Litigation to Vindicate Their Rights", Transnational Law & Contemporary Problems, vol. 24 (2014), p. 69.

49 Cedric Ryngaert, "The International Criminal Court and Universal Jurisdiction: A Fraught Relationship?", *New Criminal Law Review*, vol. 12, no. 4 (2009), pp. 498–512 at p. 498.

ICC verdicts are largely dependent on cooperation from states, which is erratic and politically inspired. For instance, even though the ICC initiated investigations in cases of assaults on hospitals, like in Darfur and Ukraine, arrest warrants have never been followed by prosecutions because there was either a deficiency of political will or capacity to arrest suspects. Moreover, the ICC is restricted to prosecuting crimes committed after 2002 and has jurisdiction only over citizens of state parties or referral cases referred by the UN Security Council, where veto politics may hinder referrals, as in the Syrian case.[50]

Ad hoc courts, like the former Yugoslavia tribunal (ICTY) and Rwanda tribunal (ICTR), have been an important force in the evolution of international criminal law, including war crimes related to healthcare. The ICTY, for example, dealt with the shelling of hospitals during Sarajevo's siege. These courts, however, were short-lived and locally focused. No new ad hoc court has been established in the past few years, evidencing a slackening of political energy for mass-scale international criminal justice institutions. International criminal law makes doctrinal provision for the seriousness of assaults against medical personnel, institutional constraints, jurisdictional deficiencies and reluctance on the part of states enormously compromise enforcement.[51]

Problems of State Compliance and Enforcement Deficits

Protection of medical staff in armed conflict is not just a matter of legal norms, but also of their implementation and enforcement at the national level. State respect for IHL, however, is generally weak, particularly in the case of prolonged or internal conflict. Even if states have ratified the Geneva Conventions and Additional Protocols, their national legal systems often lack the legislative, judicial or administrative mechanisms to prosecute effectively. In most cases, military justice mechanisms are employed to investigate and try suspected war crimes, compromising impartiality and transparency. Investigations are sometimes delayed, narrow in scope or designed to shield institutional interests instead of bringing about justice. This has the effect of conferring de facto impunity even on serious abuses.[52]

50 Caroline Fournet, "Medical Evidence at the International Criminal Court – Dosage and Contraindications", in Caroline Fournet, Pia Hüsch and Katrin Fenrich (eds.), *Biolaw and International Criminal Law* (Brill Nijhoff, 2020), pp. 364–386 at p. 364.

51 Ademola Abass, "The International Criminal Court and Universal Jurisdiction", *International Criminal Law Review*, vol. 6, no. 3 (2006), pp. 349–385 at p. 349.

52 Dustin Lewis and Naz Modirzadeh, *Taking into Account the Potential Effects of Counterterrorism Measures on Humanitarian and Medical Activities: Elements of an*

Non-state actors, who are increasingly central to the conflicts of today, are not signatories to international agreements and are frequently out of reach of enforcement mechanisms. Although IHL binds all actors in a conflict, compliance by non-state actors depends on political incentives, ideological bent and involvement by humanitarian actors, all of which are extremely variable. Adding to the problem is that there are no strong sanctions or coercive tools to be used by the international community when states do not comply.[53]

Humanitarian Law vs. Counterterrorism Measures

There is a high and escalating tension between the legal norms of international humanitarian law and counterterrorism legal and operational policies. Since the post-9/11 era, states have been increasingly adopting domestic and international counterterrorism legislation that has profound consequences for humanitarian interventions and the safety of medical professionals.[54]

Several of these legislations criminalise dealing with listed terrorist groups, such as treating their members, even when it is required under IHL. This puts humanitarian actors in a legal dilemma: rendering impartial care, as stipulated by the Geneva Conventions, can at the same time subject them to liability under domestic counterterrorism laws. These legal frameworks thus undermine the principle of medical neutrality since medical assistance is no longer regarded as humanitarian of humanitarianism but more as probable material support for terrorism.[55]

The UN Security Council Resolution 2462 (2019), which calls for states to criminalise material support to terrorism, does not have sufficient humanitarian carve-outs, adding to the legal complexity. Groups like

---

Analytical Framework for States Grounded in Respect for International Law (2021), at p. 212.

53 Muhammad Tanvir Hashem Munim, "Universal Jurisdiction and the International Criminal Court (ICC): A Pragmatic and Holistic Approach to the Consideration and Application of Universal Jurisdiction by the ICC", *Journal of Rights & Justice*, vol. 3 (2022), p. 4.

54 Dustin Lewis and Naz Modirzadeh, "Taking into Account the Potential Effects of Counterterrorism Measures on Humanitarian and Medical Activities: Elements of an Analytical Framework for States Grounded in Respect for International Law" (2021), p. 65.

55 Tristan Ferraro, "International Humanitarian Law, Principled Humanitarian Action, Counterterrorism and Sanctions: Some Perspectives on Selected Issues", *International Review of the Red Cross*, vol. 103, nos. 916–917 (2021), pp. 109–155 at p. 109.

the ICRC and Médecins Sans Frontières have consistently requested humanitarian exemption of medical services from counterterrorism measures, but change is slow and patchy. The aggregate impact of these tensions is the discouragement of medical staff from working in high-risk settings, especially in non-state actor-controlled zones.[56]

International Responses and Initiatives

International institutions and states have implemented a number of initiatives to enhance the protection of medical staff, ranging from advocacy campaigns to creating monitoring mechanisms and improved legal frameworks. Actions such as UN resolutions and efforts by the International Committee of the Red Cross seek to induce compliance with humanitarian law and enhance accountability for breaches.

United Nations Mechanisms and Resolutions

The United Nations (UN) has been at the forefront of bringing into focus the situation of medical staff in war zones and promoting global standards to better protect them. One such milestone here is UN Security Council Resolution 2286 (2016), which emphatically denounces attacks on medical facilities and staff in armed conflict.[57] The resolution calls on all sides to armed conflicts to respect their international humanitarian obligations, including the protection of medical services. It invites states to carry out serious, impartial and independent investigations into reported abuses and prosecute those who are guilty.[58]

In spite of its normatively clear language, Resolution 2286 has weak enforceability due to the non-binding nature of Security Council resolutions unless adopted under Chapter VII of the UN Charter. The resolution is not followed by the creation of any autonomous monitoring or accountability system, but instead draws upon voluntary state initiative and institutional channels that already exist. Its implementation has been followed up very rarely, and some states, especially those engaged in modern conflicts, have

56 Peter Weiss, "Terrorism, Counterterrorism and International Law", *Arab Studies Quarterly* (2002), pp. 11–24 at p. 11.

57 UN Security Council Resolution 2286 (2016), Adopted by the Security Council at its 7685th meeting, on 3 May 2016, UN Doc. S/RES/2286 (2016).

58 Suleymanov Alim Vidadievich, "United Nations Role in Resolution of International Conflicts", Bulletin of the Peoples' Friendship University of Russia. Series: International Relations, vol. 17, no. 1 (2017), pp. 86–94 at p. 86.

evidenced little political will in turning its provisions into national action.[59] The UN Secretary-General's Report on Children and Armed Conflict and fact-finding missions by the UN Human Rights Council have also registered attacks on healthcare, bringing international attention to the subject.

The Role of the International Committee of the Red Cross (ICRC)

The ICRC is still the chief protector and champion of international humanitarian law, with an expert mandate for the safeguarding of medical staff and facilities in war. With its Health Care in Danger (HCiD) program initiated in 2011, the ICRC has especially aimed at averting violence against health care professionals and ensuring safe access to health care. The HCiD initiative has undertaken field work, hosted diplomatic forums and worked with local health ministries and militaries to apply contextual strategies. These have involved setting up safe areas around hospitals, educating armed combatants in IHL and developing early-warning mechanisms for medical evacuations. Though the initiative has increased awareness and spurred practical reforms, its effectiveness is hindered by its use of dialogue and persuasion, as opposed to binding implementation.[60]

NGO Advocacy and Documentation Efforts

Civil society groups, particularly international non-governmental organisations like Médecins Sans Frontières (MSF), Physicians for Human Rights (PHR), Amnesty International and Human Rights Watch, have been instrumental in documenting violations and calling for accountability. Their missions to fact-find, witness testimonies and collection of digital evidence have helped raise the profile of attacks on medical care in conflicts like Syria, Yemen and Gaza. MSF's suspension of operations in some conflict zones following repeated attacks, e.g., northern Yemen and Kunduz, Afghanistan, was indicative of the security crisis for humanitarian actors and prompted international outcry.[61]

59 United Nations General Assembly, Special Session, *Resolutions* (United Nations, 1963), p. 134.

60 Georges Willemin, Roger Heacock and Jacques Freymond, *The International Committee of the Red Cross*, vol. 2 (BRILL, 1984), p. 231.

61 L. M. Salazar García, *Enablers and Constraints of Creation and Sharing of Knowledge Assets: A Case of NGO Policy Advocacy* (PhD diss., University of Oxford, 2005), p. 115.

Regional Initiatives and Humanitarian Networks

Regionally, there have been dissimilar levels of interaction with the problem of safeguarding medical professionals. The European Union has made a number of policy declarations and has supported projects for consolidating legal responsibility and assisting humanitarian actors within fragile environments. The African Union and the Organisation of American States have also included health care protection in wider peace and security frameworks, but have had limited operational initiatives. Transnational networks of health professionals and professional associations, including the World Medical Association (WMA) and Safeguarding Health in Conflict Coalition (SHCC), have also come to be increasingly involved in standard-setting, advocacy and promoting accountability. They have created codes of conduct, issued incident reports and lobbied for global action, including through UN and ICC submissions.[62]

Technological Innovations and Evidence-Based Approaches

New technologies have increasingly facilitated the documentation and examination of medical facility attacks. Satellites, geolocation software and remote sensing devices are now utilised to confirm allegations of airstrikes and medical infrastructure destruction. These technologies have been utilised by groups like Amnesty International's Evidence Lab and Berkeley's Human Rights Centre to construct admissible evidence for possible war crimes trials. Digital evidence, when married to chain-of-custody procedures, promises future successful prosecutions.[63] Yet difficulties still exist as regards data security, authentication and the admissibility of such evidence in formal court proceedings. Excessive reliance on distant technologies sometimes leaves out on-the-ground circumstances, and this can sometimes result in decontextualised or incomplete interpretations.[64]

Recommendations for Strengthening Protection and Accountability

To ensure the protection of medical staff, it is important to step up international legal enforcement through greater cooperation between

62 John Bryant, "Mapping Local Capacities and Support for More Effective Humanitarian Responses", *HPG Policy Brief*, no. 75 (2019), p. 10.

63 Henry Ahn, Mohit Bhandari and Emil H. Schemitsch, "An Evidence-Based Approach to the Adoption of New Technology", *Journal of Bone and Joint Surgery (JBJS)*, vol. 91, no. Supplement_3 (2009), pp. 95-98 at p. 95.

64 Christine Spratt and Paul Lajbcygier (eds.), *E-learning Technologies and Evidence-Based Assessment Approaches* (IGI Global, 2009), p. 226.

states and institutions. Expanding training in humanitarian law for military forces, enhancing documentation and reporting of abuses and facilitating independent investigations can assist in bridging accountability gaps.

Enhancing Legal Clarity and Harmonisation

One of the primary needs for enhancing the protection of medical staff in armed conflict is clarifying and harmonising relevant legal rules. International humanitarian law (IHL), international human rights law (IHRL) and national counterterrorism laws frequently coexist without adequate consolidation, resulting in inconsistency and tension. It is necessary that states and global organisations act towards the legal codification of medical neutrality as a non-derogable principle, especially in the context of broad counterterrorism regimes that now criminalise medical assistance to all groups involved in conflict.

For that purpose, interpretative guidance provided by international organisations like the ICRC and the UN Human Rights Committee ought to receive more prominence within national legal orders in order to ensure that counterterror policies don't supersede humanitarian imperatives. Model law and best practice guides could assist nations in integrating humanitarian exceptions into local law in a predictable and legally valid fashion. The Rome Statute might be amended or clarified to legally include a broader range of attacks on medical facilities and personnel, particularly in non-international conflicts.

Strengthening Monitoring and Reporting Mechanisms

The absence of systematic reporting and independent monitoring has complicated prevention and response to attacks on medical staff. International organisations like the UN Office for the Coordination of Humanitarian Affairs (OCHA), together with the World Health Organisation (WHO), should be given specific mandates to gather, verify and report data on such attacks. An autonomous international monitoring body may be created to gather and process statistics on attacks on health professionals and facilities, similar to the UN Monitoring and Reporting Mechanism (MRM) for serious violations against children.

Promoting Domestic Implementation and Capacity Building

For international standards to be of practical effect, they have to be translated into local law and day-to-day working practice. Training courses for military officers, police forces and irregular armed groups must have modules on IHL with special reference to the protection of healthcare. Their integration into military rules of engagement and national operational manuals would give respect for medical neutrality a place of institutional prominence. Capacity-building assistance should be provided to judicial, prosecutorial and investigative institutions in conflict or post-conflict countries to allow them to prosecute these kinds of crimes. International donors and legal development institutions should give the highest priority to such activities within rule-of-law programming.

Reinforcing Accountability through International and Hybrid Mechanisms

With the constraints of domestic enforcement, it is imperative to reinvigorate international and hybrid accountability mechanisms. The International Criminal Court (ICC) ought to give priority to the investigation of attacks on health facilities where jurisdiction is available and ought to frame policy papers or prosecutorial approaches particular to these crimes, similar to its earlier emphasis on sexual violence.

Hybrid tribunals and internationalised domestic courts could also offer potentially effective alternatives, especially in post-conflict situations where national institutions are weak but support from outside is politically acceptable. An attempt must also be made to engage universal jurisdiction, particularly in those jurisdictions with a strong tradition of the rule of law. Strategic litigation and the use of arrest warrants, even in absentia, can help establish a global climate of deterrence and diminish the impunity that is so widespread today.

Safeguarding Humanitarian Space and Medical Neutrality

Countries and international bodies must strive to uphold the operational autonomy of humanitarian organisations, especially in situations where counterterrorism measures threaten neutrality. UN declarations and resolutions should directly invoke humanitarian exceptions in all counterterrorism actions, and donors should make donor assistance conditional on the promotion of such exceptions in beneficiary states. Medical workers must be permitted to attend to all patients without threat of retribution or prosecution. Legal changes must enshrine this principle, whereas institutional mechanisms like safe areas, protected transport corridors and demilitarised health facilities must be fortified and upheld by both sides of the conflict.

Leveraging Technology for Prevention and Accountability

Technological advances hold out the prospect of powerful instruments for deterrence and documentation. Cell phone applications, secure reporting platforms and satellite-based verification systems can enable medical staff and humanitarian agencies to report attacks in real time, safeguard evidence and enable swift response. To reap these advantages, there is a need for international organisations to invest in interoperable and secure platforms to share data among humanitarian actors while protecting confidentiality. Capacity-building activities must incorporate training in digital documentation methods for frontline staff, and collaboration must be fostered between humanitarian actors and academic institutions to enhance data integrity and analysis.

Fostering Political Will and Global Solidarity

Legal and institutional change has to be driven by political will. Continued advocacy, public campaigns and diplomatic efforts are needed to mobilise international action. States, the international community and civil society have a duty to regularly condemn attacks on healthcare workers as breaches of international law and common human decency. Global solidarity can also be conveyed in symbolic and material forms of support to impacted medical staff, such as global acknowledgement, protection awards and post-traumatic care. The celebration of medical professionals risking their lives working in conflict areas should be formalised in world forums, reiterating their critical role in promoting humanitarian values.

Conclusion

The changing character of armed conflicts, characterised by long-lasting non-international conflict, the proliferation of asymmetric warfare and the increasingly diffuse distinction between combatants and civilians has presented unprecedented challenges to the security and impartiality of medical professionals. While the Geneva Conventions and customary international humanitarian law contain explicit protections for healthcare personnel, abuses against health workers have also grown alarmingly common and systematic. The deliberate targeting of hospitals, the criminalisation of medical aid under counterterrorism laws and the widespread impunity for such actions have not only undermined core humanitarian principles but also exacerbated human suffering in already fragile contexts.

This chapter has traced the historical development of legal norms protecting medical personnel, outlined the contemporary accountability and enforcement challenges and surveyed the international community's responses. While activities like United Nations resolutions, ICRC efforts and civil society campaigns have helped raise awareness and provide policy direction, they have lacked in restricting violations or securing effective redress. Most importantly, the chapter has presented evidence of the structural flaws of the prevailing accountability architecture, varying from jurisdictional deficiencies to political complacency, undermining which states and armed forces have been able to operate with impunity.

Chapter 14

The Protection of Cultural Property during Armed Conflict: Law and Practice

-Rashmi Salpekar

"Destroying a country's cultural heritage is the fastest way to undermine its national identity. [...] And saving a country's cultural heritage is the best path to reconstruction and revival of society."[1]

Introduction

Culture creates a sense of belongingness for all individuals. It is an identity and pride for the individual and thus for the country. The countries have been partitioned and united due to their culture. Each culture created and developed a style of architecture, literature, jewellery, etc. The succeeding generations have adopted the same. This is how each culture has developed its heritage for its generations to come. It gives a path to follow, a reason to live and a trust to go forward.

United Nations Educational, Scientific, and Cultural Organisation (UNESCO), an UN specialised agency is a leading organisation in the area of cultural property. It has defined cultural heritage as "artefacts, monuments, buildings, sites and museums that provide a variety of cultural benefits".[2] This includes cultural property that have "symbolic, historic, artistic, aesthetic, ethnological or anthropological, scientific and/ or social significance". Cultural property can be tangible and intangible. The

1 Søren la Cour Jensen, "Chair of Blue Shield Denmark, Backup Ukraine Wins Award", *The Blue Shield* (May 2025), https://theblueshield.org/backup-ukraine-wins-award/.

2 UNESCO, Cultural Heritage, UIS.UNESCO.ORG, https://uis.unesco.org/en/glossary-term/cultural-heritage.

intangible includes "practices, representations, expressions, knowledge and skills". It also covers the instruments, objects, and cultural spaces which are associated with communities, groups and individuals so much that based on these objects, one can identify individuals/groups' culture.

Due to the strong belongingness towards culture and cultural property, during armed conflicts, cultural property is sometimes deliberately targeted by enemy countries. Along with the loss of life and property, cultural property also becomes victims of the armed conflicts. It is disheartening to note that over the centuries, various works of art have been lost, cultural sites damaged or destroyed and many have undergone alterations during armed conflicts. The following incidents will prove the argument:

The leading centre of teaching of Mahayana Buddhism was Nalanda. However, at the end of the 12th Century, invader Bakhtiyar Khilji demolished The Monastery. His armed forces killed the Monks and burned the entire library which was considered as the wealth of knowledge. It is stated that this library was burning for three long months.[3] The extensive destruction of cultural property committed during World War I[4] and World War II[5] was alarming for the international community. Once upon a time, the destruction of cultural property was understood as the collateral damage, but during World War II, it was seen that destruction of cultural property was an intentional act of cultural cleansing. This fact prompted the international community to act and provide specific legal protection.

The targeting of cultural heritage is seen as a feature of many recent armed conflicts, too. The massive and intentional destruction of cultural property in Bosnia-Herzegovina, Croatia and Kosovo has been done during the 1991–1999 armed conflict Yugoslav Succession[6]. It was called as the "greatest destruction of cultural heritage in Europe since World War II". Taliban destroyed the Bamiyan Buddha statues in Afghanistan in

3 Ancient Nalanda University Ruins, NALANDA, http://nalanda.nic.in/en/tourist-place/ancient-nalanda-university-ruins.

4 World War I witnessed destruction of various cultural property, for example, destruction of cultural property in Rheims, Leuven and Arras, and many more. Protect Cultural Property in the Event of Armed Conflict, UNESCO, https://www.lacult.UNESCO.org/lacult_en/docc/DossierProtegerBienesCulturales_Ingles.pdf.

5 Anne Rothfeld, "Nazi Looted Art: The Holocaust Records Preservation Project", 34 *Prologue MAG.* 2 (Summer 2002), https://www.archives.gov/publications/prologue/2002/summer/nazi-looted-art-1.

6 Magnus Bjarnason, The War and War-Games in Bosnia and Herzegovina from 1992 to 1995 (2001).

March 2001[7] are still fresh in memory. Syria and Iraq have also faced such intentional destruction of cultural property as the terrorist group, namely Daesh, intentionally attacked cultural property to create a "caliphate".[8] The group used bulldozers and explosives to destroy the Syrian city of Palmyra in the year 2015. There were reports that Daesh has looted century old manuscripts and thousands of books from libraries and universities in Mosul, Iraq, and then sold in the international art market. Unfortunately, the group burned down Mosul's university library and destroyed the central public library. In addition, videos showed militants destroying artefacts in the Mosul Museum with hammers. In 2012, during the occupation of northern Mali, a significant amount of cultural heritage was destroyed, particularly in Timbuktu.[9] This included the destruction of mausoleums, mosques, and ancient manuscripts. Fourteen of the sixteen mausoleums inscribed on the UNESCO World Heritage List in Timbuktu were destroyed during this armed conflict. The attack was carried out by the Islamist group Ansar Dine, often in conjunction with Al-Qaeda in the Islamic Maghreb (AQIM) and the Movement for Oneness and Jihad in West Africa (MUJAO).

Recent years are also full of evidence of the destruction of cultural property during armed conflicts. As per the news reports, in 2022, Russia launched its full-scale invasion of Ukraine and with it, a direct assault on Ukrainian culture. It was informed by Ukraine's Ministry of Culture and Information Policy that more than 1,400 cultural heritage sites have been damaged or destroyed by Russian forces. UNESCO has so far verified 501 of these sites, including museums, churches, libraries and monuments.[10] There is some evidence that Russia has been targeting Ukrainian cultural elements.[11] In

7 Luke Harding, "Taliban Blow Apart 2,000 Years of Buddhist History", *The Guardian* (Mar. 3, 2001), https://www.theguardian.com/world/2001/mar/03/afghanistan.

8 Nicole Winchester, "Targeting Culture: The Destruction of Cultural Heritage in Conflict", *Lords Library* (2022), https://lordslibrary.parliament.uk/targeting-culture-the-destruction-of-cultural-heritage-in-conflict/.

9 Lazare Eloundou Assomo, "Cultural Heritage at Risk in Mali: The Destruction of Timbuktu's Mausoleums of Saints", Getty Conservation Institute, https://www.getty.edu/publications/cultural-heritage-mass-atrocities/part-2/14.

10 "Russia Has Conducted Direct Assault on Ukraine's Culture", *Times Of India* (July 11, 2025), https://timesofindia.indiatimes.com/world/europe/russia-has-conducted-direct-assault-on-ukraines-culture/articleshow/101234567.cms.

11 "Beyond the Battlefield: The Price of War and Fight for Peace—Ukraine: A Deeply Cultural War", *Times Of India* (July 8, 2025), https://timesofindia.indiatimes.com/world/europe/beyond-the-battlefield-the-price-of-war-and-fight-for-peace-ukraine-a-deeply-cultural-war/articleshow/101234567.cms.

recent armed conflict between Israel and Palestine, as per the Press release of OHCHR, it is stated that "... religious and cultural sites in Gaza investigated by the Commission constituted civilian objects at the time of attack and suffered devastating destruction for which the Commission could not identify a legitimate military need. Artefacts were destroyed, removed or looted. Further, "in the occupied West Bank, including East Jerusalem, the Commission found that Israeli authorities have appropriated, developed and profited from cultural heritage sites representing Palestinian, Jewish and other cultures, displaced Palestinian residents from those sites, and blocked or severely restricted Palestinians from accessing such sites."[12]

Role of International Organisations in Protecting Cultural Property

International organisations have dedicated aims and objectives relating to the protection of cultural property. The treaties to protect cultural property are adopted by the UN through its specialised agency -UNESCO[13]. UNESCO is instrumental at each step for the protection of cultural property.

The process of identifying potential World Heritage sites begins with a country recognising cultural properties that it considers significant, in accordance with the guidelines of the UNESCO World Heritage Centre. Once these cultural properties are identified, they are compiled into a Tentative List based on specific selection criteria. Following this, the sites are nominated for World Heritage status. Expert evaluations are then conducted by professionals from the International Council on Monuments and Sites (ICOMOS) and the World Conservation Union (IUCN), who review the nominations and provide recommendations to UNESCO's World Heritage Committee. The selection of sites is guided by a unified set of ten

12 Israeli Attacks on Educational, Religious and Cultural Sites in the Occupied Palestinian Territory Amount to War Crimes and the Crime Against Humanity of Extermination, UN Commission, June 10, 2025, https://www.ohchr.org/en/press-releases/2025/06/israeli-attacks-educational-religious-and-cultural-sites-occupied-palestinian.

13 UNESCO was established in the year 1945. Its constitution recognises that wars begin in the minds of men, it is in the minds of men that the defences of peace must Memory of the World Programme, UNESCO, https://www.UNESCO.org/en/memory-world.

The main purpose of *UNESCO* is to serve in advancing, through the educational and scientific and cultural relations of the peoples of the world. Its main objective is to achieve international peace and the common welfare of mankind, for which the *United Nations* Organisation was established and which its Charter proclaim see: UNESCO Constitution, UNESCO, https://www.UNESCO.org/en/legal-affairs/constitution?hub=66535.

criteria outlined in the Operational Guidelines for the implementation of the World Heritage Convention, ensuring a standardised approach to site evaluation and designation. [14]

UNESCO is maintaining various types of lists and registers under various conventions to identify, safeguard and protect the cultural property. The main aims of these lists are to preserve and promote the world's diverse cultural heritage for the international community of present and future. The names of the lists are as follows:

- World Heritage List under the 1972 World Heritage Convention[15]
- Lists of Intangible Cultural Heritage under the 2003 Convention for the Safeguarding of the Intangible Cultural Heritage[16]
- Register of Good Safeguarding Practices. It is a compilation of all conventions, its principles and how it is protecting cultural heritage. It helps the new states to understand the good practices regarding safeguarding living cultural heritage.
- Memory of the World Register under the 1992 Memory of the World Programme[17]
- International Register of Cultural Property under Special Protection under the 1954 Hague Convention and its Second Protocol[18]

The above lists are created to cover different types of cultural heritage, tangible, intangible, documentary, and property under armed conflict protection. In general, the process of listing the cultural property is similar with each other. The main steps are - nominations from States Parties, evaluation by the experts, and then decisions by specialised committees created under respective conventions or the Director-General of UNESCO.

14 The Criteria for Selection, UNESCO, https://whc.unesco.org/en/criteria

15 World Heritage Convention 1972, UNESCO, https://whc.UNESCO.org/en/convention.

16 Convention for the Safeguarding of the Intangible Cultural Heritage 2003, UNESCO, https://ich.UNESCO.org/en/lists.

17 The Memory of the World Programme aims to safeguard the world's documentary heritage of archives, manuscripts, rare books, audiovisual materials, and such other from collective amnesia, neglect, decay, and deliberate destruction. See: Memory of the World Programme, UNESCO, https://www.UNESCO.org/en/memory-world.

18 UNESCO Convention for the Protection of Cultural Property in the Event of Armed Conflict, https://www.UNESCO.org/en/legal-affairs/convention/protection/.

Besides UNESCO, several other international organisations are actively involved in the protection of cultural property. These include the International Centre for the Study of the Preservation and Restoration of Cultural Property (ICCROM), which focuses on conservation training and research; the International Council on Monuments and Sites (ICOMOS), dedicated to the preservation of historic monuments and sites; and the International Council of Museums (ICOM), which works to safeguard museum collections and promote the role of museums in society. Together, these bodies contribute to the global effort to preserve cultural heritage.

It is important to note that, in addition to international organisations, non-governmental organisations (NGOs) also play a significant role in protecting cultural property, especially during armed conflicts. Notably, the International Committee of the Red Cross (ICRC) and The Blue Shield are two NGOs that contribute extensively to safeguarding cultural heritage both in times of war and peace. Through the efforts of such civil society groups, NGOs actively participate in the protection and preservation of cultural property, complementing the work of international bodies. The International Committee of the Red Cross (ICRC) was established in 1863 with the primary goal of providing protection and assistance to victims of armed conflict and strife worldwide. It carries out this mission through direct action, the promotion and development of International Humanitarian Law (IHL), and encouraging respect for IHL among both states and non-state actors.[19] The Blue Shield, originally known as the International Committee of the Blue Shield, was founded in 1996 to protect endangered cultural heritage across archives, libraries, monuments, sites, and museums. This organisation was created by four NGOs: the International Council on Archives (ICA), the International Council of Museums (ICOM), the International Federation of Library Associations and Institutions (IFLA), and the International Council on Monuments and Sites (ICOMOS). The Blue Shield uses the emblem of the 1954 Hague Convention on the Protection of Cultural Property and is recognised as a distinguished professional organisation. It holds an advisory role within the Committee of Protocol 1999, which oversees the implementation of the Protocol 1999 among State Parties. In 2014, the International Committee of Blue Shield (ICBS) and the Association of National Committees of the Blue Shield (ANCBS) agreed to merge. This amalgamation was officially approved in 2016 and ratified during the 2017 General Assembly, and

19 *International Committee of the Red Cross, History of the ICRC, https://www.icrc.org/en/document/history-icrc.*

today, both ICBS and ANCBS operate collectively under the name "The Blue Shield." [20]

The growing number of actors to protect cultural property indicated "a shift from 'national patrimony' to 'common cultural property'" and this shift also indicates a shift from right perspective to duty perspective.[21]

Recognition of Culture as a Human Right

Cultural property and its protection are recognised in international human rights law and international humanitarian law. Thus, the protection mechanism is available for both peacetime and wartime. The Universal Declaration of Human Rights (UDHR) of 1948, along with the International Covenant on Civil and Political Rights (ICCPR) and the International Covenant on Economic, Social and Cultural Rights (ICESCR), both adopted in 1966, establish a rights-based framework for the protection of cultural rights. Article 27 of the UDHR and the ICCPR specifically guarantee the right to culture. This article emphasises key elements such as the right of every individual to participate in cultural life and to access cultural goods. Additionally, it highlights the importance of safeguarding the cultural rights of various ethnic, religious, and linguistic minorities, ensuring that their cultural identities are respected and protected.

ICESCR has special significance as its name includes 'culture' explicitly. Right to profess culture is the soul of each provision; meaning thereby, the implementation and enjoyment of rights provided in ICESCR is not possible without the right to profess culture. It recognises that as per the UDHR, "the ideal of free human beings enjoying freedom from fear and want can only be achieved if conditions are created whereby everyone may enjoy his economic, social and cultural rights, ...".[22] The ICESCR ensures the protection of economic, social and cultural rights, including the right to self-determination of all peoples, covering the right to determine political status and to freely pursue economic, social and cultural development.[23]

20 The Blue Shield, http://theblueshield.org.

21 P. Ishwar Bhat, "Protection of Cultural Property under International Humanitarian Law: Some Emerging Trends", 2001 *ISIL Yearbook on International Humanitarian Law and Refugee Law*, http://www.worldlii.org/ int/journals/ISILYBIHRL/2001/4.html.

22 International Covenant on Economic, Social and Cultural Rights art. 15, ¶ 3, Dec. 16, 1966, 993 U.N.T.S. 3.

23 International Covenant on Economic, Social and Cultural Rights art. 15, ¶ 4, Dec. 16, 1966, 993 U.N.T.S. 3.

It also emphasises the right to take part in cultural life[24] and to benefit from the protection of the moral and material interests resulting from any scientific, literary or artistic production of which an individual is the author[25]. The state parties are required to take necessary steps for the conservation, development and diffusion of culture.[26] The State parties are also required to respect the freedom pertaining to the creative activity.[27] Additionally, state parties need to recognise the benefits derived from the encouragement and development of international contacts and cooperation in the cultural fields.[28]

Culture is deeply intertwined with cultural property, making it difficult to separate the two. While the right to culture is included in the International Covenant on Economic, Social and Cultural Rights (ICESCR), which has a comparatively weaker binding obligation than the International Covenant on Civil and Political Rights (ICCPR), individuals often regard culture not just as a right but as a fundamental aspect and way of life. In this sense, culture is closely connected to an individual's life, liberty, and dignity. Recognising this vital link, many countries have incorporated the protection of cultural property during armed conflicts into their domestic laws. Moreover, this protection has also been reinforced through regional and international treaties adopted by various organisations, reflecting the global commitment to safeguarding cultural heritage even in times of conflict.[29]

Cultural Property during Armed Conflicts and Response of International Humanitarian Law

Cultural property, as discussed earlier, has become a victim of armed conflicts for ages. States had customs to protect the cultural property during armed conflicts. Gradually, codification has been made by states for their domestic usages, and later on, it took shape as customary law under international law. Amongst these, Liber Code 1863 is one of the fundamental codes which was codified by Francis Liber on the directions

24 Art 15 (1) (a), ICESCR, 1966.

25 Art 15 (1) (c), *ibid.*

26 Art 15 (2), *Id.*

27 Art 15(3), *Id.*

28 Art 15 (4), *Id.*

29 Council of Europe, Association of Southeast Asian Nations (ASEAN), Arab League Educational, Cultural and Scientific Organization (ALECSO) have adopted instruments to protect cultural property, including in the situation of armed conflicts.

of Abraham Lincoln. Liber code is a set of rules to be followed by military personnel during a civil war. Article 35 of the Lieber Code (Instructions for the Government of Armies of the United States in the Field, 1863) mandates the protection of certain cultural and scientific property during armed conflict, even within besieged or bombarded areas. Specifically, it requires the safeguarding of "classical works of art, libraries, scientific collections, or precious instruments, such as astronomical telescopes, as well as hospitals". This article emphasises that such protection should be provided "against all avoidable injury".

Article 17 of the Brussels Declaration, adopted in 1874, emphasises the protection of civilian objects during wartime, specifically requiring that all necessary measures be taken to preserve buildings dedicated to art, science, or charitable purposes. The extensive destruction witnessed during World War I and World War II underscored the urgent need for the international community to establish specific legal protections for cultural property. Historically, it was common for occupying powers to alter or destroy cultural property to impose their own cultural dominance. To address this, the Hague Regulations of 1899 and 1907 included provisions for the special protection of cultural property, notably in Article 27, as well as in Article 5 of the 1907 Hague Convention (IX) concerning Bombardment by Naval Forces in Time of War. These regulations also placed a duty on local inhabitants to mark cultural property with distinctive emblems to identify and safeguard them. Similar protective measures were incorporated into the Hague Rules of Air Warfare in 1922/23, particularly in Articles 25 and 26, further reinforcing the international legal framework aimed at preserving cultural heritage during armed conflict.

Under Customary International Humanitarian Law, Chapter 12, Rules 38 to 41 specifically address the protection of cultural property during armed conflicts. These rules, grounded in consistent state practice, outline important obligations for parties involved in conflicts. Rule 38 requires that each party exercise special care to avoid damaging buildings dedicated to religion, art, science, education, charitable purposes, or historic monuments during military operations, except when such sites serve as military objectives. It further mandates that property of great cultural importance must not be targeted unless absolutely necessary for military reasons. Rule 39 explicitly prohibits the destruction or damage of cultural property that holds significant value to the heritage of any people. Rule 40 forbids the seizure, destruction, theft, pillage, misappropriation, or vandalism of important cultural property. Finally, Rule 41 prohibits the illicit export of cultural property from occupied territories and calls for the return of such property to the appropriate authorities of the occupied area, reinforcing the commitment to preserving cultural heritage even amid conflict.[30]

Coming to codified contemporary International Humanitarian Law (IHL), it consists mainly of four Geneva Conventions, 1949 and two Additional Protocols.[31] IHL is applicable during armed conflicts. It covers both international and non-international armed conflicts. Its approach towards cultural property and heritage is that destruction or damage to cultural property and heritage is damage to the cultural heritage of all mankind.

The Geneva Conventions of 1949 recognise cultural property as part of civilians' belongings, with Article 27 of the Fourth Geneva Convention specifically affirming that protected persons are entitled to respect for their person, honour, family rights, religious beliefs and practices, as well as their customs in all circumstances. This provision serves as a fundamental basis for safeguarding the cultural property during armed conflicts.

Furthermore, the Additional Protocols to the Geneva Conventions, especially Protocol I, explicitly address the protection of cultural property—referred to as cultural objects and places of worship. Article 53 of Protocol I prohibits any hostile acts directed at historic monuments, works of art, or places of worship that represent the cultural or spiritual heritage of peoples. It also forbids the use of cultural property to support military operations and any reprisals against such property. Additional Protocol II reinforces these protections, primarily through Article 16, further strengthening international legal safeguards for cultural heritage in times of conflict.

Hague Convention on the Protection of Cultural Property 1954 (CCP) and its Protocols

The most direct international agreement focused on protecting cultural property during armed conflict is the Hague Convention of 1954, formally known as the Hague Convention for the Protection of Cultural Property in the Event of Armed Conflict, adopted on May 14, 1954. The development of this convention can be traced back to earlier efforts, beginning with the Roerich Pact of 1935. Building on the protections outlined in the 1899

30 International Committee of the Red Cross, Customary International Humanitarian Law, https://ihl-databases.icrc.org/en/customary-ihl/.

31 International Committee of the Red Cross, International Humanitarian Law Treaties, https://ihl-database.icrc.org/en/ihl-treaties.

and 1907 Hague Regulations, the Roerich Pact—proposed by Professor Nicholas Roerich—was endorsed at the Seventh International Conference of American States and subsequently signed on April 15, 1935, under the guidance of the Pan-American Union's Governing Board.

After the devastation of World War II, the Netherlands submitted a proposal to UNESCO in 1948 to further strengthen the legal protection of cultural property. In response, UNESCO's General Conference established a committee of government experts in 1951 to draft a new convention. This committee presented draft versions in 1952, which were revised and circulated to governments for feedback. The final draft was adopted at a conference held at The Hague from April 21 to May 14, 1954. The Convention officially came into force in 1956, with UNESCO serving as its depository. The 1954 Hague Convention primarily focuses on the safeguarding and respectful treatment of cultural property during armed conflicts, establishing a cornerstone for international cultural heritage protection.[32] The list of identified cultural property is given in the International Register of Cultural Property under Special Protection. This cultural property is said as "very great importance".

The 1954 Hague Convention outlines several key features for the protection of cultural property during armed conflict. Article 1 provides a detailed and comprehensive definition of cultural property, encompassing both movable and immovable assets of great importance to the cultural heritage of all peoples. This includes monuments of architecture, art, or history—whether religious or secular—as well as archaeological sites, groups of buildings with historical or artistic value, works of art, manuscripts, books, and other objects of artistic, historical, or archaeological significance. The definition also covers scientific collections and important archives or reproductions of these types of property. Additionally, buildings primarily intended to preserve or exhibit movable cultural property, such as museums, large libraries, and archive depositories, are recognised as cultural property. Even refuges intended to shelter cultural assets and centres housing a large concentration of monuments are included within this scope.

The Convention establishes two levels of protection: general and special. Under general protection, state parties are obligated to safeguard their cultural heritage during armed conflict by taking necessary precautions.

32 The Hague Convention on the Protection of Cultural Property in the Event of Armed Conflicts, art. 2, May 14, 1954, 249 U.N.T.S. 240.

They are also required to protect cultural property located within occupied territories, ensuring its preservation despite the challenges of war.[33]

Under the special protection regime of the 1954 Hague Convention, cultural property is granted immunity from any acts of hostility as well as from being used for military purposes, including the use of its surrounding area. To qualify for this special protection, the cultural property must not be utilised for military activities and must be located at a sufficient distance from any military objectives. This system is designed to ensure that important cultural sites are safeguarded from damage or exploitation during armed conflict.[34]

The 1954 Hague Convention stipulates under Art 28 that Parties to the Convention must take all necessary steps to prosecute and impose sanctions on all persons who violate its provisions.

The Convention applies mainly to international armed conflict. However, the Convention extends the scope of the Convention to the non-international armed conflict wherein the state parties are required to "respect" the cultural property.[35] This provision was indeed not sufficient, but having a provision addressing non-international armed conflict was itself a progressive step in the era of the 1950s.

The Convention grants an exception in case of "imperative military necessity". However, lacks clarity on the same. Therefore, the possibilities of misuse of this clause cannot be denied. The Convention mandates that state parties adopt national legislation for the implementation of The 1954 Hague Convention. Therefore, it is silent on international criminal responsibility and extradition clauses and thus makes the 1954 Hague Convention weak in implementation and execution. To address limitations of the 1954 Hague Convention, two further Protocols were adopted in 1954 and in 1999.

The 1954 Protocol

The Protocol for the Protection of Cultural Property in the Event of Armed Conflict, adopted in 1954 and coming into force in 1956, aims to strengthen the safeguards established by the Hague Convention. Its primary objectives are to prevent the unlawful expropriation of cultural property, ensure the

33 *Ibid*, art. 5.

34 *Ibid*, art. 9.

35 *Ibid*, art. 19.

restitution of cultural objects that have been illegally exported, and prohibit the retention of cultural property as war reparations. This Protocol plays a crucial rôle in reinforcing the protection and recovery of cultural heritage during and after armed conflicts.[36]

The 1999 Protocol

The Second Protocol to the 1954 Hague Convention for the Protection of Cultural Property in the Event of Armed Conflict, adopted in 1999 and entering into force in 2004, introduced a significant advancement in cultural heritage protection. One of its key features is the establishment of "enhanced protection," a higher level of safeguarding for cultural property that is recognised as being of the "greatest importance for humanity." This protection applies to cultural sites and objects listed by UNESCO on the International List of Cultural Property under Enhanced Protection, ensuring these invaluable assets receive the utmost care and legal safeguards during armed conflicts.[37]

The concept of "enhanced protection" introduced by the 1999 Protocol to the 1954 Hague Convention adds an additional layer of safeguarding for cultural property. While the original 1954 Convention provides a system of general protection, the 1999 Protocol grants enhanced protection to cultural property that meets specific criteria: it must be adequately protected under domestic law, not used for military purposes, and not serve to shield military sites. This elevated level of protection is officially conferred when a cultural property is entered on UNESCO's International List of Cultural Property Under Enhanced Protection.

The process for granting enhanced protection status is clearly outlined in the 1999 Protocol. A committee established under the Protocol is responsible for considering requests from state parties to include cultural properties within their jurisdiction on the enhanced protection list. Additionally, the International Committee of the Blue Shield (ICBS) and other non-governmental organisations can recommend cultural properties for consideration. The committee's final decision requires a four-fifths majority vote of its members to approve the inclusion of a property under

36 International Committee of the Red Cross, *Customary International Humanitarian Law Database*, IHL DATABASES (last updated May 20, 2025), https://ihldatabases.icrc.org/eng/.

37 Art 10, Second Protocol to the *1954 Hague Convention* for the Protection of Cultural Property in the Event of Armed Conflict, 1999 (Protocol 1999)

the enhanced protection category, ensuring a rigorous and collaborative selection process.[38]

The 1999 Protocol clearly affirms the immunity of cultural property from attack during armed conflict. This immunity can only be lifted in exceptional circumstances, specifically if the cultural property is being used for military purposes. Otherwise, the protection remains firmly in place to safeguard cultural heritage even amid warfare.[39]

Further, under the precautionary measures, the Protocol 1999 have laid down duties for both conflicting parties. It is stated that everything feasible should be done to check before the attack that cultural property listed under Art 4 should not be the target of the attack. If it is, then cancel or suspend the attack. The state parties should refrain from targeting any cultural property which may be harmed incidentally and for any purpose other than a military advantage. The means and methods chosen for the attack should be to minimise the incidental damage to the protected cultural property. [40] The duty laid down for the other conflicting party is to shift movable cultural property to a safe place during armed conflict, not to keep any military objective near the cultural property.[41]

Regarding protection in occupied territory, a state party in occupation of the territory is prohibited from carrying out excavation, alteration and destroying any cultural property which will conceal or destroy the cultural property.[42] It has imposed an obligation on the State Party to adopt legislative, administrative or disciplinary measures to suppress the illicit export, removal of or transfer the ownership of cultural property from occupied territory.[43]

Loss of enhanced protection status is possible only if cultural property has become the military objective, or it is used for a military purpose.[44]

---

38 Refer Art 11 with articles 10, 26, and 27, Second Protocol to *The 1954 Hague Convention* for the Protection of Cultural Property in the Event of Armed Conflict, 1999 (Protocol 1999)

39 Art 5, Second Protocol to *The 1954 Hague Convention* for the Protection of Cultural Property in the Event of Armed Conflict, 1999 (Protocol 1999)

40 Art 7, *Ibid*

41 Art 8, *Ibid*

42 Art 9, *Id*

43 Art 21, *Id*

44 Art 13, *Id*

It may be noted that clear evidence is required for taking out the status of enhanced protection. Moreover, status of special protection under 1954 Hague Convention remains intact even after loss of enhanced protection status.

The Protocol 1999 also provides enforcement supportive provisions. It has established individual criminal responsibility for five serious violations. The state parties are required to recognise violations of Protocol 1999 as criminal offences under domestic legislation and to give appropriate punishment for offences. In its Art 15, a list of violations is given as follows:

a. making cultural property under enhanced protection the object of attack;

b. using cultural property under enhanced protection or its immediate surroundings in support of military action;

c. extensive destruction or appropriation of cultural property protected under the Convention and this Protocol;

d. making cultural property protected under the Convention and this Protocol the object of attack;

e. theft, pillage or misappropriation of, or acts of vandalism directed against cultural property protected under the Convention.

Out of the above five types of violations, the first three, that is, from 15 (a) to (c), have universal jurisdiction. It applies to both international and non-international armed conflict.

As mentioned earlier, a state party is required to adopt appropriate measures to prevent any form of cultural property destruction; in addition to that, a committee of the state party is established under Protocol 1999. The committee is composed of 12 state party[45] members, required to meet once in year in ordinary sessions. The committee can meet more than once in a year, called an extraordinary session. The composition of 12 members represents diverse cultures and different regions across the

45 In determining membership of the Committee, Parties shall seek to ensure an equitable representation of the different regions and cultures of the world. See: Second Protocol to the Hague Convention for the Protection of Cultural Property in the Event of Armed Conflict, art. 10, 15, 24, Mar. 26, 1999, in *Second Protocol to the Hague Convention of 1954 for the Protection of Cultural Property in the Event of Armed Conflict*, deposited by UNESCO, entered into force Mar. 9, 2004.

world.[46] The main functions of the committee are: Granting, suspending or cancelling protection given to the listed cultural property; monitoring the implementation of the Protocol and promoting the identification of cultural property, receiving and considering requests regarding international assistance, determining the use of the fund and monitoring its operation, and developing guidelines for the implementation of the Protocol 1999.[47] In determining membership of the Committee, Parties shall seek to ensure an equitable representation of the different regions and cultures of the world.

Upon analysis, it becomes clear that the 1999 Protocol offers a stronger and more comprehensive framework for protecting cultural property during armed conflicts compared to the original 1954 Hague Convention. However, its effectiveness is limited by the fact that relatively few states have ratified the Protocol. The introduction of the enhanced protection category has created an implicit hierarchy between cultural properties granted special protection under the 1954 Convention and those granted enhanced protection under the 1999 Protocol. Enhanced protection is reserved for sites deemed of the greatest importance to humanity. Yet, if a state possessing such culturally significant property is not a party to the 1999 Protocol, its heritage cannot receive enhanced protection. These gaps and limitations undermine the Protocol's overall goal of robustly safeguarding cultural heritage worldwide during conflict.

Security Council Resolutions for the Protection of Cultural Property

The United Nations have given the key function of maintaining peace and security in the world to the Security Council. The resolutions adopted by the Security Council create binding obligation. Thus, resolution of security council consisting of protection of cultural heritage during armed conflicts have great significance. Mainly two resolutions can be referred in this context- 2199 (2015) and 2347 (2017).

In 2015, the United Nations Security Council adopted Resolution 2199, emphasising the responsibility of UN member states to prevent terrorist groups operating in Iraq and Syria from profiting through the trade of oil, antiquities, hostages, and from receiving donations. The resolution unanimously condemned any form of trade with groups such as the Islamic State of Iraq and the Levant (ISIL, also known as Daesh), the Al-

46 *Ibid*, art. 24.

47 *Ibid*, art. 25.

Nusrah Front, and other organisations linked to Al-Qaida. It strongly denounced the deliberate destruction of cultural property in Iraq and Syria, particularly by ISIL and the Al-Nusrah Front. The resolution called on all member states to cooperate with international bodies such as Interpol and UNESCO to take effective measures to stop the illicit trade in cultural, scientific, and religious artifacts that had been illegally removed from these countries during the armed conflicts.[48]

In the year 2017, Security Council adopted a resolution 2347 (2017) in response to the attacks on cultural property by non-state actors. With this, Security Council considered protection of cultural property as one of the key elements to maintain peace and security in the world. In this Resolution, the Security Council condemns the unlawful destruction of cultural heritage, by terrorist groups. It urges member states of UN to develop broad law enforcement and judicial cooperation in preventing and countering trafficking in in cultural property. [49] This Resolution is of great importance, as it is not in relation to any state in particular, but it is in general for all, thus applicable for all states and non-state entities. This Resolution was adopted unanimously. UNESCO Director General, called this Resolution 2347 as historic and stated that weapons are not enough to defeat violent extremism. Building peace requires culture also; it requires education, prevention and the transmission of heritage.[50]

Instruments adopted by Regional Organisations for the Protection of Cultural Property during Armed Conflicts

Council of Europe have adopted Convention on Offences relating to Cultural Property (Nicosia Convention, 2017), and European Convention on the Protection of the Archaeological Heritage (Revised) (Valletta Convention, 1992). Both these conventions provided legal provisions to protect cultural property during armed conflicts. The African Union (AU) has seen the impact of destruction of cultural property due to various armed conflicts in Africa. It has adopted AU Model Law on the Protection of Cultural Property and Heritage (2018) which is useful as a guide for

48 "Unanimously Adopting Resolution 2199 (2015), Security Council Condemns Trade with Al-Qaida Associated Groups, Threatens Further Targeted Sanctions," UN Press Release, U.N. Press Release SC/11775, ¶ 1–2 (Feb. 12, 2015), https://press.un.org/en/2015/sc11775.doc.htm.

49 S.C. Res. 2347, ¶¶ 1–2, U.N. Doc. S/RES/2347 (Mar. 24, 2017), https://main.un.org/securitycouncil/en/s/res/2347.

50 UNESCO, UN Security Council Adopts Historic Resolution for the Protection of Heritage, https://whc.unesco.org/en/news/1648.

state members to enact and adopt national legislations to protect cultural property even during armed conflicts. North Atlantic Treaty Organisation (NATO) has adopted Military Manuals and Training to military personnel for the implementation of 1954 Hague Convention. It has a unit namely Civil- Military Cooperation (CIMIC). It works with civilian authorities and experts in heritage to identify cultural property and to protect the same. Interpol, even though a global organisation, however, its regional bureaus and specialised units take initiative to combat illicit trafficking of cultural property which generally escalates during armed conflicts.

Regional organisations are able to contribute only when political will is positive. Most of the armed conflicts occurred with regional states, thus in such situation regional organisations find powerless to fulfil its commitment. Reginal organisation's instruments at times find overlapping with the international instruments, which may develop issues, of non-coordination.

Response of International Courts towards Protection of Cultural Property

An analysis of cases adjudicated by various international courts, both *ad hoc* and permanent, shows that sanctions have been imposed for the destruction of cultural property or the alteration of cultural structures by occupying forces in occupied territories. The protection of cultural heritage has long been a priority for the international community, as reflected in key legal instruments and tribunals. Notable examples include the Charter of the International Military Tribunals (IMT) at Nuremberg[51], the International Criminal Tribunal for the Former Yugoslavia (ICTY)[52], and the Extraordinary Chambers in the Courts of Cambodia[53]. These bodies have jurisdiction over crimes specifically related to cultural heritage and cultural property, underscoring the global commitment to preserving cultural assets even in the aftermath of conflict.

51 Charter of the International Military Tribunal art. 6(b), Aug. 8, 1945, 82 U.N.T.S. 279.

52 Statute of the International Tribunal for the Former Yugoslavia art. 3(d), May 25, 1993, S/25704, annex.

53 Law on the Establishment of the Extraordinary Chambers, with Inclusion of Amendments as Promulgated on 27 October 2004 (NS/RKM/1004/006) Art. 7: Law on the Establishment of the Extraordinary Chambers in the Courts of Cambodia for the Prosecution of Crimes Committed during the Period of Democratic Kampuchea, NS/RKM/1004/006, art. 7 (Cambodia 2004).

The Nuremberg Tribunal held Nazi leaders accountable for crimes against cultural heritage. On October 18, 1945, the chief prosecutors of the IMT brought charges against 24 leading German officials. A case worth mentioning is that of Alfred Rosenberg. He was a key Nazi figure. He was found guilty of organising and directing a unit for looting cultural property. This operation involved the systematic seizure of art, books, and other cultural items from occupied territories and Jewish individuals. He was tried as a major Nazi war criminal before the IMT, Nuremberg in 1945. Further, Rosenberg was found guilty on all the counts of conspiracy, crimes against peace, war crimes, and crimes against humanity, and thus sentenced to death. He was hanged on October 16, 1946.

The International Criminal Tribunal for the former Yugoslavia (ICTY) has played a pivotal role in shaping legal precedent by establishing criminal liability for the intentional destruction of cultural property. During the wars in the 1990s across the former Yugoslavia, hundreds of religious and cultural sites were deliberately destroyed as part of a systematic effort to erase the identity and heritage of targeted groups. From its earliest cases, the ICTY affirmed that the destruction of cultural heritage constitutes a crime under customary international law. Furthermore, the Tribunal recognised that such widespread and deliberate attacks on cultural heritage can amount to crimes against humanity, emphasising that "all of humanity is indeed injured by the destruction of a unique religious culture and its concomitant cultural objects." This jurisprudence has significantly reinforced the international legal framework protecting cultural property during armed conflicts.

In 2001, the Tribunal issued an indictment against four accused for crimes committed during the 1991 siege of the Croatian coastal town of Dubrovnik. While the indictment and subsequent trials included charges of murder and inhumane treatment of civilians, the intentional damage caused to this UNESCO World Heritage site played the main role in both the presentation of evidence and in public perception of these trials. This was the first time that crimes against cultural heritage took central stage in an international criminal trial.

International Criminal Court

The Rome Statute of the International Criminal Court (ICC) recognised crimes against persons and crimes against property. Both these categories are included in the description of the crimes recognised under the ICC as international crimes. The crimes recognised by the ICC are: genocide[54], crimes against humanity[55], war crimes[56], and the crime of aggression[57]. In the Preamble of the Rome Statute, it is clearly stated that "all peoples are united by common bonds, their cultures pieced together in a shared heritage." This sets the foundational principle that cultural heritage is not merely the property of a single nation or group, but belongs to all of humanity. Damage to it is, therefore, damage to the heritage of all. The inclusion of the destruction of cultural property as a crime under the recognised international crimes is given below:

War Crimes: Crimes committed as part of a plan or policy, or as part of a large-scale commission of such crimes[58] in international or non-international war, are punishable as war crimes under the Rome Statute. Art 8 (2) (b) (ix) meant for international armed conflict and Art 8 (2) (e) (iv) meant for armed conflicts not of an international character provides: "Intentionally directing attacks against buildings dedicated to religion, education, art, science or charitable purposes, historic monuments, ... provided they are not military objectives" will be considered as war crime.

Recognising the importance of investigating and prosecuting crimes against or affecting cultural heritage and to highlight the seriousness of these crimes, the Office first brought charges relating to cultural property in the Al Mahdi case in the Situation of Mali in September 2015. In September 2016, Mr Ahmad al-Faqi al Mahdi was convicted of the war crime of intentionally directing attacks against buildings dedicated to religion and historic monuments. This case, focusing solely on crimes against cultural heritage, was symbolic and sent a clear message that the intentional targeting of cultural heritage is a serious crime and should be duly punished.

Crimes Against Humanity: The 15 forms of crimes against humanity are listed in the Rome Statute. Crimes against humanity encompass the acts when committed as part of a widespread or systematic attack directed against any civilian population, with knowledge of the attack[59]. It also provides that persecution against any identifiable group or collectively on

54 Rome Statute of the International Criminal Court, art. 6, July 17, 1998, 2187 U.N.T.S. 90.

55 *Ibid*, art. 7.

56 *Ibid*, art. 8.

57 *Ibid*, art. 8bis.

58 *Ibid*, art. 8.

59 *Ibid*, art. 7.

political, racial, national, ethnic, cultural, religious, gender or other grounds that are universally recognised as impermissible under international law, in connection with any act referred to in this paragraph or any crime within the jurisdiction of the Court[60] will be considered crimes against humanity. Since unlawful destruction of cultural property constitutes a war crime in both international and non-international armed conflict under Art 8 of the Rome Statute, it can also constitute a crime against humanity under Art 7(1)(h).[61]

International Court of Justice

The International Court of Justice (ICJ) has rarely dealt with the issue of destruction of cultural property during armed conflicts. However, before coming on case directly applicable to the issue of protection of cultural property during armed conflicts, few references of cultural property by the jurists are worth mentioning over here.

Judge Weeramantry in the *Legality of Nuclear Weapons* case favoured a view that all property listed or scheduled by high contracting parties form considerable segment of cultural heritage.[62]

Recently, on December 7, 2021, the ICJ decided *Armenia v. Azerbaijan* relating to the same issue. This case is of more relevance as the ICJ applied the Convention on the Elimination of All Forms of Racial Discrimination (CERD) 1965 for the crime of destruction of cultural property during armed conflict. In this order, the ICJ indicated provisional measures to protect the cultural heritage of minorities and their right to equal participation in cultural activities. In the court's analysis, it was considered that the alleged violations of rights by Azerbaijan are plausible regarding the "discrimination against persons of Armenian national or ethnic origin ... through vandalism and desecration affecting Armenian cultural heritage."[63] In addition, the ICJ found that a link between the plausible violation of these rights and the provisional measures requested exists in relation "to prevent, prohibit and punish vandalism, destruction or alteration of

60 *Ibid*, art. 7 (1) (h), *Id.*

61 Roger O'Keefe, "Protection of Cultural Property under International Criminal Law", *Melbourne Journal of International Law*, Vol. 11, 2010, p. 44.

62 Legality of the Threat or Use of Nuclear Weapons: Advisory Opinion, I.C.J. Rep. 226, 467 (1996).

63 Application of the International Convention on the Elimination of All Forms of Racial Discrimination (Armenia v. Azerbaijan), *Provisional Measures*, ¶ 61, I.C.J. Case No. 180 (Dec. 7, 2021) (order).

Armenian historic, cultural and religious heritage and to protect the right to access and enjoy that heritage. These measures, in the Court's view, are directed at safeguarding plausible rights invoked by Armenia under the CERD.[64] Two judges of the ICJ gave a dissenting opinion, in which they both questioned the application of CERD for the issue of the destruction of cultural heritage. One of the judges in his dissenting opinion stated that "[c]considerations of race and racial discrimination cannot and do not apply to monuments, groups of buildings, sites and artefacts"[65]. Racial discrimination cannot be done with monuments.

Conclusion and the Way Ahead

The world has made significant progress in many areas, with globalisation and liberalisation blurring traditional boundaries. Yet, the deep emotional attachment and sense of belonging to culture remain unmatched. Many armed conflicts stem from a profound disrespect for cultural property, with culturicide—deliberate destruction of culture—often used as a weapon to erase particular races, creeds, or religions.

While an international legal framework to protect cultural property exists, as discussed earlier, this protection is not absolute. The allowance for "military necessity" often weakens strict adherence to safeguarding cultural heritage during armed conflicts. Additionally, modern warfare increasingly involves advanced technologies such as AI-powered weapons or lethal autonomous weapons systems (LAWS), posing new challenges in identifying and protecting cultural property from being targeted.

The existing international legal regime, including the 1954 Hague Convention and its Protocols, follows the PPP model: Protection, Prevention, and Precaution. However, none of these instruments mandate compensation for deliberate destruction of cultural property. The Rome Statute of the ICC is an exception, with provisions for reparations to victims. A landmark case in this regard is the conviction of Ahmad Al Mahdi, who was sentenced to nine years in prison and ordered to pay €2.7 million in reparations for the destruction of cultural heritage in Timbuktu between June and July 2012—a UNESCO World Heritage site. Although Al Mahdi was indigent, the ICC's Trust Fund for Victims has taken on the responsibility of raising funds to compensate the victims. Additionally, Al

64 *Ibid*, paras. 67, 68.

65 *Ibid*, Dissenting Opinion Judge Yusuf, para. 13.

Mahdi was ordered to pay a symbolic one euro to UNESCO and Mali for the damage caused.

This case also highlighted the positive role of UNESCO, which mobilised efforts for the restoration of the damaged mausoleums with support from the European Union and Switzerland. The rehabilitation efforts included the reconstruction of the mosques of Djingareyber, Sankore, and Sidi Yahia, along with safeguarding ancient manuscripts—many of which had been burned or stolen. UNESCO's success was made possible through close collaboration with Malian authorities, local communities, the Timbuktu masons' guild, and the United Nations Multidimensional Integrated Stabilisation Mission in Mali (MINUSMA). This example underscores the importance of restoration alongside protection, prevention, and precaution, suggesting that restoration should be made a mandatory component of cultural property protection frameworks.

Looking ahead, as humanity ventures into outer space for exploration and settlement, celestial bodies like the moon, sun, and other planets hold cultural significance for various communities. However, the current UNESCO lists focus primarily on man-made, state-recognised cultural property. There is a growing need to broaden the definition of cultural heritage to include outer space and celestial bodies, recognising them as part of the shared cultural heritage of all humanity.

In summary, while significant strides have been made in protecting cultural property, challenges remain, especially in the context of evolving warfare technologies and expanding cultural frontiers. Strengthening legal frameworks to include mandatory restoration, expanding the scope of cultural heritage, and fostering international cooperation will be essential steps forward in preserving humanity's diverse cultural legacy for future generations.

Chapter 15

Territorial Jurisdiction of International Criminal Court over Nationals of Non-Party States: Principles and Practice

-Vinai Kumar Singh

Introduction

Since the Rome Conference, the US opposition to jurisdiction of ICC over non-state party committed crimes in the territory of State Parties set forth it controversial and which still struggle with the difficulty of asserting jurisdiction. The first phase, which can be identified with the "delegated theory", has been characterized capable to provide the sound legal foundation for ICC jurisdiction. Such a theory, despite receiving enormous support from international community, in last two decades, has shown many deficiencies. The shortcomings of the "delegated theory" have therefore paved the way for the advent of second phase, characterized by "Conferral Theory", which is found consistent with the juridical character of the ICC's power and the power of international courts and tribunals more general. The recent approach of Pre-Trial Chamber in 2024 in the Situation in State of Palestine case fostered the idea of "functionalism" a progressive revision of the "conferral theory" with a view to simplifying and streamlining it.

The chapter will firstly briefly outline the legal basis, scope and content of the territorial criminal jurisdiction under the Rome Statute. It will then discuss the scope and content of the International Criminal Court's (the ICC) jurisdiction over the nationals of non–party States accused of committing crimes on the territories of States Parties. Nevertheless, the concept of 'territorial jurisdiction' has received renewed emphasis and reassessment since the importance of strengthening the ability of the ICC has been articulated with much greater emphasis to exercise jurisdiction over nationals of non-party States committing crimes in the territories of State Parties. While the territorial jurisdiction principle itself is universally acknowledged as a fundamental principle of international law, its precise scope and limitations and that of its corollary aspects have become the subject of considerable discussion and certain issues, such as relevance of "delegated theory" construing that state possess a right to delegate their criminal jurisdiction to an international tribunal or other states, subjects of lively controversy. The basis of jurisdiction of the Court becomes crucial when its jurisdiction is challenged by a party to a dispute, and the court or tribunal has to determine the proper contours of their own jurisdiction. The legal basis, content and scope of Article 12 of the Rome Statute, already investigated in some depth by eminent scholars still require further examination.[1] There were few instances when the ICC, in recent times, has claimed competence to prosecute nationals of non-party states without their consents such as Myanmar/Bangladesh, Afghanistan, Situation in the State of Palestine, and Russia.

History of Article 12 of the Rome Statute and Modes of Territorial Jurisdiction

The competence of the ICC to determine jurisdiction is governed by Article 12 of the Rome Statute. A unique title "Pre-condition to the exercise of jurisdiction" to Article 12 different from a general title of "bases of jurisdiction" was the result of debates to enlarge the scope of the jurisdiction of the ICC in respect of serious crimes (such as crime of genocide) as those crimes are deemed to be concern of the international community. The Rome Conference deliberated to adopt one between several alternatives viz., 'inherent jurisdiction' versus 'treaty crimes', and 'universal

1 M. Morris, "High Crimes and Misconceptions: The ICC and Non-Party States," *Law & Contemporary Problems*, vol. 64, no. 1 (2001), pp. 13-66; Michael P. Scharf, "The ICC's Jurisdiction over the Nationals of Non-Party States: A Critique of the U.S. Position," *Law & Contemporary Problems*, vol. 64, no. 1 (2001), pp. 67-116; Hans-Peter Kaul, "Precondition to the Exercise of Jurisdiction" in Antonio Casses, Paola Gaeta and John R. W. D. Jones, *The Rome Statute of the International Criminal Court: A Commentary* (Oxford University Press, 2002), pp. 583-616; Dapo Akande, "The Jurisdiction of the International Criminal Court over Nationals of Non-Parties: Legal Basis and Limits," *Journal of International Criminal Justice*, vol. 1, no. 3 (December 2003), pp. 618-650.

jurisdiction' versus 'automatic jurisdiction'.[2] It is worth mentioning that Article 12 employs language whereby States have to by their conduct agree to the jurisdiction of the Court. Three bases of jurisdiction are generally contemplated under the Rome Statute: first, crimes committed on the territory of the State Party; secondly by their nationals regardless of place of crime, and thirdly non-party state accepting the jurisdiction of the ICC on an *ad hoc* basis. Article 12 aims prosecution of individuals for crimes committed on the State Parties territory or by their nationals or by non-party state on adhoc basis. In brief, Article 12 of the Rome Statute unquestionably represents legal norms and has various dimensions which merit further consideration.

Principle of Consent and Monetary Gold doctrine

The issue may involve a question whether the ICC exercises its jurisdiction on the basis of only on the permitted objective, or take into account the teleological limitations of jurisdiction. The Rome Statute foresees the three situations of permitted objectives in which the ICC may lawfully claim competence to have jurisdiction over nationals of non-parties. "First, the ICC may prosecute nationals of non-parties in situations referred to the ICC Prosecutor by the UN Security Council (UNSC). Secondly, nationals of a non-party are subject to the ICC jurisdiction when they have committed a crime on the territory of a state that is a party to the ICC Statute or has otherwise accepted the jurisdiction of the Court with respect to that crime. Thirdly, jurisdiction may be exercised over the nationals of a non-party where the non-party has consented to the exercise of jurisdiction with respect to a particular crime." In the first two scenarios, the consent of the state of nationality is not an essential requirement to the exercise of jurisdiction.

On the other hand, the teleological limitation of jurisdiction of the ICC exists as argued by few that "it is against the treaty norm to apply treaty provisions over non-party states without their consent for the commission

2 William A. Schabas, *An Introduction to the International Criminal Court* (Cambridge University Press, 2004); Manoj Kumar Sinha, "International Criminal Court: A Backgrounder," *World Focus*, no. 266 (August 20010, pp. 1-6; Anupam Jha, *International Criminal Court: Theory and Practice* (Satyam International, 2020); Srinivas Burra, "India and the International Criminal Court" in Seokwoo Lee (ed.), *Encyclopedia of Public International Law in Asia*, vol. 3, (Brill|Nijhoff, 2021), pp. 402-403; U C Jha, "ICC and Indian Military Justice System", in Vahida Nainar and Saumya Uma (ed.), *Pursuing Elusive Justice: Mass Crimes in India and Relevance of STA* (OUP, 2013), pp. 315-333.

of crime committed in the territory of State Party".[3] It is argued that violation of treaty norms relates to state party as a basis of international responsibility. This is a doctrine which appears in international law since the adoption of Vienna Convention on the Law of Treaties 1963. This teleological approach has found doctrinal basis in the decision of the International Court of Justice (ICJ) in *the Monetary Gold case*[4]. ICJ, in this case, has ultimately declined to decide the case due to lack of jurisdiction, as Albania, a necessary party to the dispute, had not consented to the ICJ's jurisdiction and Albania was not before the court. Albania was a third party who was not involved in this proceeding. The proposition of the case is popularly known as *Monetary Gold doctrine* that recognizes the '*principle of consent*' and requires the consent of the State in international adjudication. The ICJ observed that "it could not adjudicate on Italy's claim because doing so would necessarily involve determining Albania's rights to the gold, and Albania had not consented to the ICJ's jurisdiction".[5] There is an important practical condition to apply *Monetary Gold doctrine* that "if the rights and responsibilities of the third state is a necessary prerequisite for the determination of the case before the court".[6] The central issue in this case was third party legal interest such that Albania's interests formed the subject of the case and Albania was not a party to the proceeding. This '*principle of consent*' was followed by ICJ in 1995 in *the East Timor Case*[7] where ICJ ruled that it lacks jurisdiction on the matter because Indonesia, a necessary party to the dispute, had not consented to the Court's jurisdiction. The case is related to the principle of self-determination for the people of East Timor. The central issue was Australia's entering the Timor Gap Treaty with Indonesia regarding the maritime area of East Timor. Portugal alleged that they were rightful administering power in East Timor and Indonesia had no authority to negotiate with Australia regarding the maritime area.

The *Monetary Gold doctrine* outlined by ICJ have been refined and altered in several other cases (*Certain Phosphate Lands in Nauru (Nauru v. Australia), Preliminary Objections (1992); Military and Paramilitary Activities in and Against Nicaragua (1984); Land, Island and Maritime*

3 M. Morris, "High Crimes and Misconceptions: The ICC and Non-Party States," *Law & Contemporary Problems*, vol. 64, no. 1 (2001), pp. 13-66.

4 *Monetary Gold case (Italy v. France, United Kingdom and United States)*, ICJ Reports (1954), p. 19.

5 *Ibid.*

6 *Ibid.*

7 *Case Concerning East Timor (Portugal v. Australia)*, ICJ Reports (1995) 91.

Frontier case (1990)[8] where it found that the legal interests of a third party unrelated to the dispute, did not constitute the same subject matter of the ruling to be issued between contesting parties. Consequently, ICJ held that the absence of a third state does not prevent it from continuing to determine the dispute between contesting parties. Akande takes the view that the ICC is exercising jurisdiction over individuals, it will not need to rule as a prerequisite on the responsibility of that non-party state.[9] This view found foothold and is further expanded in the application submitted by the Prosecutor to the Pre-Trial Chamber-I (PTC) under Article 19 (3) of the Rome Statute on 22 January 2020, claiming for the territorial jurisdiction of the ICC in Palestine.[10] In this regard, the Prosecutor takes the view that it is wrong to apply *the Monetary Gold principle* before the ICC for a number of reasons, namely, the ICC is not meant to settle disputes between states, but rather investigates the criminal responsibility of individuals.[11] The Prosecutor's holds a view that the negotiation of Article 12 of the Rome Statute, after full deliberation, has explicitly rejected the application of the *Monetary Gold doctrine* on the ground it prevents the court from investigating serious crimes and arise question of judicial efficiency.[12]

The "principle of consent" has its general scope in the area of treaty obligations, but it needs consideration is whether such a proposition can be treated as an absolute one and can it, in all circumstances, apply effectively even including a specific objective of instrument to deter and punish those who might escape justice? This "principle of consent" presents a formidable challenge to international criminal justice, therefore, the responsibility cannot be avoided by jurists to develop appropriate legal propositions to support the emerging norms. Also this situation reminds us to ICJ engagements with *non-liquet* in *the Lotus and Nuclear Weapons*

8 *Certain Phosphate Lands in Nauru (Nauru v. Australia), Preliminary Objections*, ICJ Reports (1992) 241, 261-262. See also *Military and Paramilitary Activities in and Against Nicaragua, (Nicaragua v. United States), Jurisdiction and Admissibility*, ICJ Reports 1984, 392, 431; *Land, Island and Maritime Frontier case, (El Salvador/ Honduras), Application for Intervention by Nicaragua*, ICJ Reports (1990), 92, 122.

9 Akande, *note 1*; Akande, "The Monetary Gold Doctrine and the ICC: Can the ICC determine the Territorial Boundaries of Israel and Palestine?", *EJIL Talk! blog*, June 16, 2020, available at: https://www.ejiltalk.org/the-monetary-gold-doctrine-and-the-icc-can-the-icc-determine-the-territorial-boundaries-of-israel-and-palestine/.

10 *Situation in the State of Palestine*, No. The ICC-01/18, 22 January 2020, Pre-Trial Chamber-I, available at: Ihttps://legal-tools.org/doc/clur6w/pdf/.

11 *Situation in the State of Palestine, ibid.*

12 *Situation in the State of Palestine, ibid.*

Advisory opinions, "whether any international legal rule exists that would prohibit it".[13] Rao puts it "the international community often engaged in further clarification, codification and progressive development of the law even when the principles involved in such an exercise are already regarded as well-established in international law"[14]. In other words, it is pertinent to explore whether states do engage in customary practice delegating the criminal jurisdiction to any international tribunals and whether that delegation can be for a crime committed in the territory of a state party by nationals of a non-party State and that too without their consent. Therefore, it is important to explore the different dimensions of territorial jurisdiction stipulated in Article 12 of the Rome Statute to prosecute accused of serious crimes to deter the impunity.

Evolution in the Interpretation Since Rome Statute

It has been contended, during negotiation of the Rome Statute, that in some respects provisions of Article 12 of the Rome Statute are inconsistent with some of the established norms recognized in 'territorial jurisdiction' which may *prima facie* suggest that nationals of non-party state without consent of non-party state cannot be matter of the jurisdiction of the Court. It is argued that the State is entitled to shield its national interest where necessary or prevent jeopardizing the interest of the nation by simply withholding ratification of any such international instruments. This point was asserted by the United States at the time of negotiations of Article 12 of the Rome Statute. Scheffer puts it: "United States emphasized that the Rome Statute exposes nonparties in ways that parties are not exposed. United States advanced a view that while certain conduct is prohibited under customary international law and .... establishment of, and a state's participation in, an international criminal court are not derived from custom but, rather,

13 Yogesh Kumar Tyagi, "Judicial Statesmanship Without Political Courage : The ICJ Advisory Opinion on Nuclear Weapons," *Indian Journal of International Law*, vol. 37 (1997), pp. 185-200; Bharat Desai, Non Liquet And The ICJ Advisory Opinion on the Legality of the Threat or Use Of Nuclear Weapons : Some Reflections," *Indian Journal of International Law*, vol. 37 (1997), pp. 201-218; V. S. Mani, "The Nuclear Weapons and the World Court," *Indian Journal of International Law*, vol. 37 (1997), pp. 167-184; B. S. Chimni, "The International Law of Jurisdiction: A TWAIL Perspective," *Leiden Journal of International Law*, vol. 35 , no. 1 (March 2022), pp. 29 – 54.

14 P. Sreenivasa Rao, "Advisory Opinion of the International Court of Justice on Legality of the Threat or Use of Nuclear Weapons: An Assessment From Indian Perspective," *Indian Journal of International Law*, vol. 37 (1997), 219-249

from the requirements of treaty law".[15] Akande considers that "this position requires careful examination as emerging practice of "delegated theory" which implying transfer of jurisdiction to international tribunals, has gained recognition in recent times".[16]

Serious controversy arose about the scope of *territorial jurisdiction over nationals of non-party States without its consent* recognized in Article 12 of the Rome Statute during the time of its negotiations. The United States opposed inclusion of such provision conferring jurisdiction to the ICC over nationals of non-party state.[17] Two significant competing views are noted in the recent time. Morris adopts the view that the exercise of the ICC jurisdiction over nationals of non-parties without the consent of that non-party would amount violation of international law.[18] This view found a legal basis on a well-established principle of Article 34 of the Vienna Convention on the Law of Treaties (VCLT) 1963 providing that a treaty may not impose obligations on non-parties without the consent of those parties. This view was supported by Ruth Wedgwood.[19] Akande and Sadat, on the other hand, consider Article 12 as a source of contemporary international law.[20] They argued that "It would be justified under international law to claim competence of the ICC to exercise jurisdiction over nationals of states that are not parties to the Rome Statute without the consent of those states."[21] However, Akande and Sadat relied upon two different theories to claim the above position.[22]

15 David Scheffer, "The United States and the International Criminal Court," *American Journal of International Law*, vol. 93 (1999), pp. 12-22.

16 Akande, "The Jurisdiction of the International Criminal Court over Nationals of Non-Parties: Legal Basis and Limits," *note 1*.

17 Scheffer, *note 15*.

18 Morris, *note 1*.

19 Ruth Wedgwood, "The Irresolution of Rome," *Law & Contemporary Problems*, vol. 64, no. 1 (2001), pp. 193-214.

20 Akande, "The Jurisdiction of the International Criminal Court over Nationals of Non-Parties: Legal Basis and Limits," *note 1* and Leila Nadya Sadat, "The Conferred Jurisdiction of the International Criminal Court," *Notre Dame Law Review*, vol. 99, no. 2 (2023), pp. 549-609.

21 Akande, "The Jurisdiction of the International Criminal Court over Nationals of Non-Parties: Legal Basis and Limits," *note 1* and Sadat, *note 20*.

22 Sadat, *note 20*.

Legal Status of Delegated Theory and Conferral Theory in International Criminal Law

This section aims to provide contemporary interpretations of basis on the jurisdiction of the Court. This not only includes interpretations supported by the ICC, but also highlights diverging views. The interpretation of jurisdiction of ICC today is influenced by the practice of States, international institutions and courts who have recognized this obligation. In the last two decades since establishment of ICC in 2002, there is a deeper understanding that ICC needs different capacities of jurisdiction to prosecute accused of serious crime. This brings us to the question as to which one among "Delegated theory" or "Conferral Theory" is appropriate to justify a court's jurisdiction extending over nationals of non-party State committed crime in the territory of the State Party.

Delegated Theory: A Basis for Jurisdiction

The "delegated theory" in the ICC system has been introduced as a natural progression from its jurisprudential progeny, which actually meant to prosecute serious crimes committed in the territory of the State Party or by its nationals. The "delegated doctrine" authorizes a State "to delegate criminal jurisdiction to an international tribunal over a crime committed by nationals of a non-party state and does not require consent of the state or nationality of the accused person for that purpose". Scharf claimed there is practice of transfer of accused for prosecution of nationals of non-parties without their consent under international criminal law such as anti-terrorism treaties.[23] It has been argued that the anti-terrorism treaties set forth an international obligation of 'extradite or prosecute' which recognize a right of state with custody of an accused of such crimes under these treaties to prosecute, therefore it may amount a delegation of jurisdiction by the national of states jurisdiction to the state of custody. In brief, the purpose of these treaties is to facilitate the prosecution of accused. Moreover, the consent of a State or nationality of the accused (whether it a party or a non-party) is irrelevant for prosecution by a state of custody.

An intriguing exchange between Morris and Akande on practice of "delegated theory" has provided initial thought on its scope and limitation.[24] The "delegation theory" which constitutes the legal foundation

23 Scharf, *note 1*.

24 Morris, *note 1*; Akande, "The Jurisdiction of the International Criminal Court over Nationals of Non-Parties: Legal Basis and Limits," *note 1*.

of the conduct actually followed by States is the *principle of territorial jurisdiction*. The *principle of territorial jurisdiction* has thus proved to be a seminal source for basis of jurisdiction which states have derived a wide range of powers aimed at securing effective prosecution of accused of crimes committed within its territory and by its nationals.[25] Serious crime committed in other State territory by any nationals continues to fall within the parameters of the concept of territorial jurisdiction and that delegation of national jurisdiction to another State or international tribunal is a legitimate exercise of the rights of State in preventing the impunity from prosecution. If States were not given power to delegate/ confer jurisdiction upon international tribunal, it would be deemed to be prejudicial to the interests of the international community as a whole. Similar analogy may equally apply over a situation if a crime committed by nationals of a non-party State. In brief, the territorial jurisdiction principle has been invoked as an overriding principle which can be relied upon to invalidate any attempt to weaken its prosecutorial power over the crimes committed in its territory as incompatible with it and to support the emerging trends viz., delegated theory.

The "delegated theory" in the present context has been criticized by Morris, *inter alia*, on two grounds. First "it is argued that this power of delegating criminal jurisdiction to international tribunals by States without the consent of the state or nationality of the accused is fundamentally ambivalent. Secondly, it is argued, that this delegation of criminal jurisdiction exercise by states is not common in international criminal law".[26] Morris was of the view that no delegation from States exists to serve the purpose of jurisdiction, but on the contrary it amounts unlawful.

Akande points out that "these arguments fail to take account of precedent of practice of "delegation of criminal jurisdiction" evolved from Nuremberg Tribunal to Ad hoc tribunals and to Special Courts for Sierra Leone (SCSL)".[27] Akande considers the above arguments of Morris termed as "High Crimes and Misconception" fails to properly give account for the many treaties in which states delegate their national criminal jurisdiction

25 Kai Ambos, ""Solid Jurisdictional Basis"? The ICC's Fragile Jurisdiction for Crimes Allegedly Committed in Palestine, *EJIL Talk! blog*, March 2, 2021, available at: https://www.ejiltalk.org/solid-jurisdictional-basis-the-iccs-fragile-jurisdiction-for-crimes-allegedly-committed-in-palestine/.

26 Morris, *note 1*.

27 Akande, "The Jurisdiction of the International Criminal Court over Nationals of Non-Parties: Legal Basis and Limits," *note 1*.

to other states/international tribunals.[28] He is of opinion that the earlier view that prosecution of nationals of non-party state without their consent over crimes committed in territory, has now yielded to the view that, having regard to the delegated theory, a state unquestionably has lawful power to delegate such jurisdiction to international tribunals. Discussion, however, centers around the situation or conditions when nationals of a non-party State may not be subject to jurisdiction of the ICC.

The controversy regarding that states may not delegate their criminal jurisdiction without the consent of the state of nationality, it will be seen is substantially resolved by a more precise analysis of its operation, Akande argued.[29] There are many instances where the exercise of criminal jurisdiction by international tribunals over the nationals of non-party state. Akande has examined a large number of treaties and sought to derive from them evidence of state practice in support of 'delegated theory' transferring jurisdiction to international tribunals by States and relying on this evidence argues that the state practice reflected in such treaties suggesting competence of the ICC to exercise jurisdiction over nationals of states that are not parties to the Rome Statute and that without the consent of those states.[30]

Akande examines the history of establishment of international criminal tribunals and its constituent instruments.[31] A survey of constituent instruments of international criminal tribunals indicates that a delegation from States exists permitting them to exercise territorial or universal jurisdiction. The Agreement for the Prosecution and Punishment of Major War Criminals of the European Axis and Establishing the Charter of the International Military Tribunal (IMT) adopted on 8 August 1945 provided a legal basis to prosecute Nazi leaders (non-party) for atrocities committed against the Jewish people of Europe. This trial, known as the Trial of the Major War Criminal, was "a collective exercise of delegation of criminal jurisdiction to a treaty-based international court and sets a precedent

28 Akande, "The Jurisdiction of the International Criminal Court over Nationals of Non-Parties: Legal Basis and Limits," *note 1*.

29 Akande, "The Jurisdiction of the International Criminal Court over Nationals of Non-Parties: Legal Basis and Limits," *note 1*.

30 Akande, "The Jurisdiction of the International Criminal Court over Nationals of Non-Parties: Legal Basis and Limits," *note 1*.

31 Akande, "The Jurisdiction of the International Criminal Court over Nationals of Non-Parties: Legal Basis and Limits," *note 1*.

for the ICC".[32] Therefore, the Nuremberg Tribunal is an example of the delegation by states of criminal jurisdiction to an international tribunal. Same trend could be noticed in the establishment of International Criminal Tribunals for the Former Yugoslavia (ICTY) and International Criminal Tribunal for Rwanda (ICTR). ICTY and ICTR assume jurisdiction from resolutions of the United Nations Security Council (UNSC) which was delegated to it by UN member states collectively. This trend of delegation by a state of its criminal jurisdiction to a treaty-based international court can be seen also in the Special Court for Sierra Leone (SCSL). SCSL derived its authority from a treaty entered between the UN and Sierra Leone to prosecute accused committed serious international crimes in Sierra Leone. Importantly, SCSL had indicted one non-national Charls Taylor, the Head of State of the neighbouring state of Liberia in respect of his participation in the armed conflict in Sierra Leone. In all these, no attempt was made to obtain the consent of the state of nationality.

In brief, due to the seriousness of the crimes, the consent of non-party State committing crime in the territory of the State Party cannot operate as a bar to international prosecution. Supporters to this reasoning view the consent of non-party State a priori is in general a tactic used for ensuring limitation and asking for departure from it.

Limitations and Controversy

There are, however, some important limitations imposed upon 'delegated theory' by international law itself which is noted by Akande. Following situations limited the competence of the ICC to exercise jurisdiction over nationals of non-parties: (a) The Court cannot do more than the states themselves could have done (*nemo dat quod non habet*). According to this, Palestine cannot delegate criminal jurisdiction to the Court over alleged ICC crimes committed on its territory by Israeli citizens, as it does not have jurisdiction over those crimes itself under the Oslo Accords; (b) Another limitation can be emerged from the international regime of immunity that provide immunity to head-of-state (*immunity ratione personae and Arrest Warrant case*[33]). Thus, customary international law deprives jurisdiction of the ICC over heads of state unless the Court has received an explicit waiver of immunity from their country of origin. In other words, the court, in

32 Akande, "The Jurisdiction of the International Criminal Court over Nationals of Non-Parties: Legal Basis and Limits," *note 1*.

33 Arrest Warrant of 11 April 2000 Case (Democratic Republic of the Congo v. Belgium), 2002.

this situation, necessarily runs the risks of undermining the international regime of immunity. By virtue of Article 98(1), the jurisdiction of ICC may be limited to apply over non-party State as state can only delegate to the Court which it possess; (c) Interpretation of Article 98(2) extends to cover agreements with non-parties known as Status of Forces Agreements (SOFA) which would in a nutshell amounts that non-party decide not to prosecute; (d) Another type limitation can be seen from complementarity principle which requires the Court to relinquish its jurisdiction if a state is investigating or prosecuting the accused in question; (e) Another form of limitation can be drawn from Article 15 which provides that the Prosecutor cannot open an investigation without the permission of a Pre-Trial Chamber. In all these situations, the negotiators of the Rome Statute put restrictions over the Court's adjudicative and enforcement jurisdiction beyond what they were required to do under international law; and (f) State Party, in some cases, is under an international obligation to extradite its own nationals present in its territory to the non-party as per doctrine "either prosecute or extradite".

Situation in the State of Palestine and Conferral Theory

(i) Broad Consultations on the Jurisdiction of ICC over Crimes Committed by Nationals of Non-consensual Non-party State

ICC, *Situation in the State of Palestine: ICC Pre-Trial Chamber I rejects the State of Israel's challenges to jurisdiction and issues warrants of arrest for Benjamin Netanyahu and Yoav Gallant case (2024)*, have now recognized that Article 19 applies not only over non-party State but also without consent of national State.[34] Israel, on 23 September 2024, made two requests before the Pre-Trial Chamber (PTC) to take account of Article 18 and 19 of the Rome Statute in dismissing the applications for arrest warrants for Benjamin Netanyahu and Yoau Gallant on the ground of Court lacks jurisdiction over crimes committed in Palestine by Israeli nationals.

In the first request, Israel challenged the consideration of the applications for warrants of arrest for Mr Benjamin Netanyahu and Mr Yoav Gallant, submitted by the Prosecution on 20 May 2024 and contended that the Court lacks jurisdiction over the Situation in the State of Palestine in

34 Pre-Trial Chamber Decision on Israel's challenge to the jurisdiction of the Court pursuant to article 19(2) of the Rome Statute, ICC-01/18-374, 21 November 2024, available at: https://www.icc-cpi.int/court-record/icc-01/18-374.

general, and over Israeli nationals.[35] In the second request, Israel requested that "the PTC-I should direct the Prosecution to provide a new notification of the initiation of an investigation to its authorities under Article 18(1) of the Statute". [36] Israel further requested the PTC-I to not continue any proceedings before the Court in the relevant situation against it.

While rejecting the first request from Israel, the PTC-I, on 21 November 2024, affirms its earlier determination made on 5 February 2021 and held that the acceptance by Israel of the Court's jurisdiction is not required, as the Court can exercise its jurisdiction on the basis of territorial jurisdiction of Palestine.[37] PTC-I, in its 5 February 2021 determination, actually exercised its criminal jurisdiction in the Situation in the State of Palestine and that the territorial scope of this jurisdiction extends to Gaza and the West Bank, including East Jerusalem.[38] To put the issue in correct perspective, it is worth to mention that Prosecutor Fatou Bensouda's request on 22 January 2020 for a ruling on the Court's territorial jurisdiction in Palestine to put the investigation on 'the soundest legal foundation' drew criticism on the ground of double standards and unnecessary procedural.[39] It was considered a "State of Exception" as the Court was actually having the necessary jurisdiction.[40] In response to Prosecutor Fatou Bensouda's request to confirm that the ICC have jurisdiction over the "Situation in the State of Palestine, PTC triggered broad amicus participation."[41] PTC-I, ultimately, concluded that ICC has jurisdiction over crimes committed by

35 *Ibid.*

36 Pre-Trial Chamber Decision on Israel's request for an order to the Prosecution to give an Article 18(1) notice ICC-01/18-375, 21 November 2024, available at: https://www.icc-cpi.int/court-record/icc-01/18-375.

37 Pre-Trial Chamber Decision on Israel's challenge to the jurisdiction of the Court pursuant to article 19(2) of the Rome Statute, *note 34*.

38 *Situation in the State of Palestine*, No. ICC-01/18, 5 February 2021, PTC- I, para 22, available at: https://www.icc-cpi.int/sites/default/files/CourtRecords/CR2021_01165.PDF.

39 Souheir Edelbi, "State of Exception': Judicial Discretion and the Amicus Curiae Mechanism in the ICC's Palestine Proceedings," *Opinio Juris blog*, 2 September 2024.

40 *Ibid.*

41 *Situation in the State of Palestine*, No. ICC-01/18, 5 February 2021, PTC- I, para 12, available at: https://www.icc-cpi.int/sites/default/files/CourtRecords/CR2021_01165.PDF (the Court's jurisdiction in the present Situation have been fulfilled: Professor John Quigley; Professor William Schabas; Professor Richard Falk; On other hand, Professor Malcom N. Shaw: Court's jurisdiction in the present Situation have not been fulfilled).

nationals of States Parties and by the nationals of non-States Parties on the territory of a State Party. "With regard to the argument that 'Palestine's ability to delegate its jurisdiction to the Court is limited because it does not have criminal jurisdiction with respect to Israelis, the Prosecutor does not consider these limitations in the Oslo Accords to be obstacles to the Court's exercise of jurisdiction."[42]

With regard to second request, the PTC-I found Israel's challenge is premature on the ground that States are not entitled to challenge the Court's jurisdiction under Article 19(2) prior to the issuance of a warrant of arrest.[43]

(ii) Establishment of Panel of Experts by Office of the Prosecutor of ICC in 2024

At this stage of case (2024), extensive consultations with international law experts and States on two occasions took place to deliberate lawfulness of jurisdiction of ICC over a crime committed by nationals of non-party States. These elaborate consultations on such fundamental questions in a time bound manner has thus gone far beyond the drafting process of the Rome Statute. First consultation exercise was carried out at the initiative of the Office of the Prosecutor of ICC, at the time of submitting application on 20 May 2024. Karim Khan, the ICC Chief Prosecutor, sought advice of a panel of renowned legal experts comprising non-official ICC lawyers of having institutional, historical and practical knowledge, to test the evidence review and legal analysis in relation to these arrest warrant applications.[44] The Panel included two academic advisers Professor Marko Milanovic, Professor Sandesh Sivakumaran. They, unanimously, affirmed

42 *Situation in the State of Palestine*, No. ICC-01/18, 5 February 2021, PTC- I, para 25, available at: https://www.icc-cpi.int/sites/default/files/CourtRecords/CR2021_01165.PDF.

43 Pre-Trial Chamber Decision on Israel's request for an order to the Prosecution to give an Article 18(1) notice ICC-01/18-375, 21 November 2024, available at: https://www.icc-cpi.int/court-record/icc-01/18-375.

44 The Panel is composed of experts of immense standing in international humanitarian law and international criminal law, including Sir Adrian Fulford PC, former Lord Justice of Appeal and former International Criminal Court Judge; Baroness Helena Kennedy KC, President of the International Bar Association's Human Rights Institute; Elizabeth Wilmshurst CMG KC, former Deputy Legal Adviser at the UK Foreign and Commonwealth Office; Danny Friedman KC; and two of my Special Advisers – Amal Clooney and His Excellency Judge Theodor Meron CMG. Available at: https://www.icc-cpi.int/about/otp/special-advisers-to-the-prosecutor/panel-of-experts-in-international-law/report-of-the-panel-of-experts-in-international-law

the assessment and findings of the Prosecutor[45] and held a view that "the ICC has jurisdiction in relation to crimes committed on the territory of Palestine, including Gaza, since 13 June 2014, under Article 12(2)(a) of the ICC Statute" [46]. "They also agreed that the Court is having jurisdiction over crimes committed by Palestinian nationals inside or outside Palestinian territory under Article 12(2)(b) of the Statute".[47] The report of Panel Experts concluded that "the ICC therefore has jurisdiction over Israeli, Palestinian or other nationals who committed crimes in Gaza or the West Bank. It also has jurisdiction over Palestinian nationals who committed crimes on the territory of Israel, even though Israel is not an ICC State Party".[48]

(iii) Amicus Participation Exercise Carried out by PTC: Is "Delegated Theory" Still Controversial?

Immediately after Prosecutor, on 20 May 2024, seeking arrest warrants against two Israeli officials along with three senior members of Hamas, the United Kingdom (UK) on 10 June 2024[49] sought permission from PTC-I to submit amicus curiae observation and was granted permission to do so on 27 June 2024[50]. The UK argues to take account of the Oslo Accords which make it clear that Palestine itself does not have criminal jurisdiction over Israeli nationals. It asked first to "resolve the issue of jurisdiction of ICC before determining the application for arrest warrants". Here, it is important to highlight that Israel has earlier in 2019 and Germany in

45 Panel of Experts in International Law convened by the Prosecutor of the International Criminal Court, 20 May 2024, available at: https://www.icc-cpi.int/sites/default/files/2024-05/240520-panel-report-eng.pdf

46 Statement of ICC Prosecutor Karim A.A. Khan KC: Applications for arrest warrants in the situation in the State of Palestine, available at: https://www.icc-cpi.int/news/statement-icc-prosecutor-karim-aa-khan-kc-applications-arrest-warrants-situation-state

47 *Note 45.*

48 *Note 45.*

49 Pre-Trial Chamber-I, Request by the United Kingdom for Leave to Submit Written Observations Pursuant to Rule 103, Situation in Palestine, ICC-01/18, 10 June 2024, available at: https://www.icc-cpi.int/sites/default/files/RelatedRecords/0902ebd180892e1f.pdf.

50 Pre-Trial Chamber-I Public redacted version of 'Order deciding on the United Kingdom's request to provide observations pursuant to Rule 103(1) of the Rules of Procedure and Evidence, and setting deadlines for any other requests for leave to file amicus curiae observations', Situation in Palestine, ICC-01/18, 27 June 2024, available at: https://www.icc-cpi.int/sites/default/files/CourtRecords/0902ebd1808bb469.pdf.

2020 proposed this position claiming that the court lacks jurisdiction with regard to the Situation in Palestine.[51]

Following the UK's, 19 other states (total 70 requests) applied and were granted permission on 22 July 2024 to submit amicus observations.[52] The UK did not proceed with this request and their request was considered withdrawn after expiry of the last date to submit their brief. Likewise, other states raised issues in their briefing included "whether Palestine qualifies as a state entitled to stand before the ICC; whether the Oslo Accords restricts Palestine's authority to exercise criminal jurisdiction over Israeli nationals and thereby prevents the ICC from continuing such jurisdiction; and whether Israel failed to pursue its own criminal investigations under the ICC's complementarity regime, which prioritizes genuine domestic investigations over international proceedings".[53] In brief, it was argued that Oslo Accords will be in effect of denying the Court's jurisdiction with respect to Israeli nationals allegedly responsible for crimes committed on the territory of Palestine. These arguments makes the assumption that the ICC would get what powers possessed by state parties domestically, popularly described as "*nemo dat quod non habet*". This position questions the usefulness of 'delegation theory' or 'theory of conferral' on the ground that Palestine may not confer such criminal jurisdiction to the Court which it does not possess it in principle.[54] PTC-I finds that *the nemo dat quod non habet* provision, will not create a problem of jurisdiction, but it refers to cooperation within the meaning of Articles 97 and 98 of the Rome Statute.[55]

---

51 Press Release, Ministry of Foreign Affairs, The International Criminal Court's Lack of Jurisdiction over the So-Called "Situation in Palestine" (Dec. 20, 2019) (Israel); Observations by the Federal Republic of Germany as Amicus Curiae, Situation in the State of Palestine, ICC01/18-103 (March 16, 2020).

52 The US, Germany, Hungary, Czech Republic, Argentina and the Democratic Republic of the Congo have submitted their observations challenging the Court's jurisdiction based on the Oslo Accords; PTC-I Decision on requests for leave to file observations pursuant to rule 103 of the Rules of Procedure and Evidence, ICC-01/18, 22 July 2024, available at: https://www.icc-cpi.int/sites/default/files/CourtRecords/0902ebd1809006d1.pdf.

53 Available at: https://s3.documentcloud.org/documents/6589835/Israel-AG-Brief-on-ICC-Jurisdiction-in-Palestine.pdf.

54 Available at: https://s3.documentcloud.org/documents/6589835/Israel-AG-Brief-on-ICC-Jurisdiction-in-Palestine.pdf.

55 Pre-Trial Chamber Decision on Israel's challenge to the jurisdiction of the Court pursuant to article 19(2) of the Rome Statute, ICC-01/18-374, 21 November 2024, available at: https://www.icc-cpi.int/court-record/icc-01/18-374.

In 2023, when the Courts' engagement with the *Situation in Palestine case* was at an early stage of procedural claims to assess the limitation of the Oslo Accords in relation to ICC Jurisdiction, Sadat proposed "Conferral Theory" and rejected "delegated theory" as a basis of exercising the court's jurisdiction.[56] While rejecting the "delegated theory", she submitted that "the ICC has the powers conferred upon it by States Parties to the Rome Statute, as well as those inherent to its function as an international court".[57] She tries to derive the basis of "Conferral Theory" what might be a textual understanding, by referring to provisions of the Rome Statute. She further noted that

> This competence is not derived from or transferred by each individual state's national jurisdiction but is, rather, a function of their collective action at the international level, representing, in other words, a form of "collective conferral.[58]

John Quigley, in his *amicus curiae submission*, takes a view that "jurisdiction of ICC under Article 12 of the Rome Statute is not premised on the conferral from a State Party".[59] Likewise, Adil Ahmad Haque, in his *amicus curiae submission*, points out that

> "No State Party can accept the Court's jurisdiction while selectively exempting certain persons, conduct, or territory. ..... Under the ICC Statute, States Parties do not delegate, transfer, or otherwise give their jurisdiction to the Court. Instead, States Parties accept the jurisdiction of the Court (Article 12(1)) which is governed by the provisions of its Statute (Article 1). The Court's exercise of its own jurisdiction is constrained by requirements of State acceptance (Article 12(2)-(3)), State referral (Articles 13 & 14), and complementarity (Article 17). These statutory constraints on the Court's exercise of its own jurisdiction ensure that an independent permanent international court can coexist and cooperate with sovereign States, but they should not be mischaracterized as delegations of national jurisdiction".[60]

56 Sadat, *note 22*.

57 *Ibid.*

58 Sadat, *note 22* at p. 557-558.

59 PTC-I, Situation in the State of Palestine, Written Observations Pursuant to Rule 103 (John Quigley), ICC-01/18, para 13, 29 July 2024.

60 PTC-I, Amicus curiae observations of Professor Adil Ahmad Haque submitted pursuant to the 'Decision on requests for leave to file observations pursuant to rule 103

These positions seem to refer to international institutional theory of "functionalism". According to this view, states have created the Court to perform certain functions and fulfill certain purposes within the international community. This theory justifies the authority of the ICC to exercise jurisdiction over crimes committed in the territory of the State Party by nationals of non-consensual non-party State. Few describe "ICC embodies community function".[61]

The PTC-I seems to endorse the strongly held views of John Quigley and Adil Ahmad Haque and others asserting that ICC jurisdiction flows from the Rome Statute. In so holding, the PTC-I emphatically and clearly rejected the views and submissions made on the basis of Oslo Accords depriving the courts' jurisdiction.

A survey mapping the submission of countries in the case reveals the position that there has been broad uniformity among States on whether the court may exercise jurisdiction over crimes committed by Israeli nationals in Gaza. Around 13 States Parties along with the League of Arab States (consists of 22 States) and Organization of Islamic Cooperation (30 states) joined in favour of jurisdiction. Only four States Parties argued that the court lacks exercise jurisdiction over Israeli nationals who commits international crimes in Gaza.[62]

Conclusion

In the field of international criminal law, the text of the Rome Treaty constituting the ICC, in contrast to the previous ad hoc tribunals, adopts comprehensive jurisdictional provisions. The competence of ICC, nevertheless, has evolved significantly over the last twenty years, most recently in the context of Situation in the State of Palestine. The ICC's position on jurisdiction cannot be divorced from its historical and normative context. In view of the invocation of a series of public participation by PTC, its recent decisions enjoy increasing legitimacy among commentators and States. These exercises have been seen as creating a platform in which States, scholars and practitioners could focus on the

---

of the Rules of Procedure and Evidence' of 22 July 2024 (ICC-01/18-249), ICC-01/18, paras 2&3, 6 August 2024.

61 Letizia Lo Giacco, "The ICC between Delegation Theory and Community Functions: Perils and Opportunities," *Opinio Juris blog*, 30 September 2024.

62 Adil Ahmad Haque, ""With Utmost Urgency": Arrest Warrants and Amicus Observations at the International Criminal Court," *Just Security*, 9 September 2024, available at: https://www.justsecurity.org/99916/icc-utmost-urgency-arrest-warrants/.

soundest basis of jurisdiction of ICC over non-state parties committing crime in the territory of the State Party. A number of States expressed their understanding that Article 12 of the Rome Statute is intended to govern crimes committed in territory of the State Party. PTC fostered the idea of "functionalism" stems from the relationship between Articles 1 and 12(1) of the Rome Statutes. The findings of the PTC are important because they explicitly rejected the arguments of limitation of delegation theory as raised by Israel and US. As anticipated, the PTC applied Article 12 of the Rome Statute, looking at the issue from the perspective of public international law, especially from international institutional law. In conclusion, *the Situation in the State of Palestine case* represents an interesting new step in the evolution of the jurisprudence of the ICC in relation to the law governing the jurisdiction over non-state parties committing crime in the territory of the State Party. The public participation along with the theoretical approach to jurisdictional basis of ICC is complementing each other and reinforcing legitimacy, accountability and transparency in its jurisdictional assertion over non-state parties. Another observation can be made here that the involvement of the international community adopted by PTC is to demonstrate that assertion of its jurisdiction satisfies the condition of reasonableness to exercise jurisdiction.

This chapter relates how some of the well-established principles and concepts of jurisdiction in international law, as well as some new developments in this field, has contributed to the understanding of international criminal law. However, there is still no consensus on jurisprudential aspects as to which theory may correctly provide foundation to jurisdiction of ICC to exercise over non-party state committing crime in the territory of the State Party. What complicates further is the US continued policy of opposition to ICC. What we see as highly problematic and potentially very damaging is the changing stand of States on case-to-case basis and political discourse about jurisdiction of ICC.

Bibliography

-Meenakshi Harith

Books and Monographs

Akande Dapo, et al., editors. *Human Rights and International Humanitarian Law: Conflict or Convergence?* Oxford University Press, 2021.

Altwicker, Tilmann. *The Role of International Humanitarian Law in the Protection of the Environment during Armed Conflict*. Springer, 2024.

Arai, Kyo. "Equal Application of International Humanitarian Law in Wars of Aggression: Impacts of the Russo–Ukrainian War." *Global Impact of the Ukraine Conflict: Perspectives from International Law*, edited by Shuichi Furuya, Hitomi Takemura, and Kuniko Ozaki, Springer, 2023, pp. 253–271. https://link.springer.com/chapter/10.1007/978-981-99-4374-6_12.

Arvidsson, Matilda, and Britta Sjöstedt. "Ordering Human-Other Relationships: International Humanitarian Law and Ecologies of Armed Conflicts in the Anthropocene." *The Routledge Handbook of International Law and Anthropocentrism*, Routledge, 2023, pp. 122–141. https://doi.org/10.4324/9781003201120-8.

Bothe, Michael. *New Challenges in International Humanitarian Law*. Springer, 2023.

Casey-Maslen, Stuart. *International Humanitarian Law: Rules, Controversies, and Solutions to Problems Arising in Warfare*. Edward Elgar Publishing, 2021.

Casey-Maslen, Stuart. *The War Report: Armed Conflict in 2021*. Oxford University Press, 2022.

Daly, Gavin. "Sieges and the Laws of War in Europe's Long Eighteenth Century." *Civility, Barbarism, and the Evolution of International Humanitarian Law: Who Do the Laws of War Protect?*, edited by Matt Killingsworth and Tim McCormack, Cambridge University Press, 2024, pp. 13–33.

Deeks, Ashley S. *The Law of Armed Conflict and the Use of Force: The Interplay of International Norms in Contemporary Conflicts.* Cambridge University Press, 2022.

Devetak, Richard. "Cultivating Humanitarianism: Moral Sentiment and International Humanitarian Law in the Civilising Process." *Civility, Barbarism, and the Evolution of International Humanitarian Law: Who Do the Laws of War Protect?*, edited by Matt Killingsworth and Tim McCormack, Cambridge University Press, 2024, pp. 61–84.

Furuya, Shuichi, Hitomi Takemura, and Kuniko Ozaki, editors. *Global Impact of the Ukraine Conflict: Perspectives from International Law.* Springer, 2023. https://doi.org/10.1007/978-981-99-4374-6.

Gill, Terry D., and Dieter Fleck, editors. *The Handbook of International Humanitarian Law.* 4th ed., Oxford University Press, 2021.

Gill, Terry D., and Robin Geiss, editors. *Yearbook of International Humanitarian Law: Volume 24 (2021).* T.M.C. Asser Press, 2022.

Gross, Michael L., and Don Carrick, editors. *Military Medical Ethics in Contemporary Armed Conflict: Mobilization and Care.* Oxford University Press, 2020.

Hampson, Françoise. *The Use of Force and International Humanitarian Law.* Routledge, 2024.

Houlihan, James W. *Adomnán's Lex Innocentium and the Laws of War.* Four Courts Press, 2020.

ICRC. *How Is the Term "Armed Conflict" Defined in International Humanitarian Law?* ICRC, Apr. 2024. https://library.icrc.org/library/docs/DOC/icrc-4767-002.pdf.

Killingsworth, Matt. "The State, Civility, and International Humanitarian Law." *Civility, Barbarism, and the Evolution of International Humanitarian Law: Who Do the Laws of War Protect?*, edited by Matt Killingsworth and Tim McCormack, Cambridge University Press, 2024, pp. 111–134.

Lubell, Noam, et al. *Guidelines on Investigating Violations of International Humanitarian Law: Law, Policy, and Good Practice*. University of Essex & Geneva Academy, 2020.

Lubell, Noam. *Extraterritorial Use of Force Against Non-State Actors*. Oxford University Press, 2021.

Marauhn, Thilo. "Compassion and International Humanitarian Law." *Der Schutz des Individuums durch das Recht: Festschrift für Rainer Hofmann zum 70. Geburtstag*, Springer, 2023, pp. 371–379.

McCormack, Tim, Siobhain Galea, and Daniel Westbury. "Limits to the Scope of Humanity as a Constraint on the Conduct of War." *Civility, Barbarism, and the Evolution of International Humanitarian Law: Who Do the Laws of War Protect?*, edited by Matt Killingsworth and Tim McCormack, Cambridge University Press, 2024, pp. 85–110.

Milanovic, Marko. *Cyber Attacks and the Laws of War*. Oxford University Press, 2023.

Moir, Lindsay. *Reappraising the Law of War: Historical and Legal Perspectives*. Hart Publishing, 2022.

Mührel, Linus. *The Authority of the International Committee of the Red Cross: Determining What International Humanitarian Law Is*. Brill Nijhoff, 2024. https://doi.org/10.1163/9789004687820.

Peters, Anne. "The Direct Rights of Individuals in the International Law of Armed Conflict." *The Individualization of War: Rights, Liability, and Accountability in Contemporary Armed Conflict*, edited by Jennifer Welsh, Dapo Akande, and David Rodin, Oxford University Press, 2023, pp. 58–88. https://doi.org/10.1093/oso/9780192872203.003.0003.

Sandoz, Yves, and Marco Sassòli. *The Law of Armed Conflict: A Contemporary Critique*. Edward Elgar Publishing, 2023.

Sassòli, Marco. *International Humanitarian Law: Rules, Controversies, and Solutions to Problems Arising in Warfare*. 2nd ed., Edward Elgar Publishing, 2023.

Sassòli, Marco. *International Humanitarian Law: Rules, Controversies, and Solutions to Problems Arising in Warfare*. With assistance from Lizaveta Tarasevich, Edward Elgar, 2024.

Schmitt, Michael N., and Liis Vihul, editors. *The Tallinn Manual 3.0 on International Law Applicable to Cyber Operations*. NATO CCDCOE and Cambridge University Press, forthcoming 2025.

Svicevic, Marko, and Martha M. Bradley, editors. *Mozambique's Cabo Delgado Conflict: International Humanitarian Law and Regional Security*. Routledge, 2024. https://doi.org/10.4324/9781003317647.

Vec, Miloš. "All's Fair in Love and War or the Limits of the Limitations: Juridification of Warfare and Its Revocation by Military Necessity." *Civility, Barbarism, and the Evolution of International Humanitarian Law: Who Do the Laws of War Protect?*, edited by Matt Killingsworth and Tim McCormack, Cambridge University Press, 2024, pp. 34–60.

Welsh, Jennifer, Dapo Akande, and David Rodin, editors. *The Individualization of War: Rights, Liability, and Accountability in Contemporary Armed Conflict*. Oxford University Press, 2023. https://doi.org/10.1093/oso/9780192872203.001.0001.

Journal Articles

"International Humanitarian Law: Necessity, Distinction and the 'Standard of Civilisation.'" *Journal of International Humanitarian Legal Studies*, vol. 14, no. 2, 2023, pp. 250–273. https://doi.org/10.1163/18781527-bja10062.

Abraksia, Nicholas. "The Killing of Ayman al-Zawahiri: On Its Legality and Why the U.N. Should Clarify the 'Unable or Unwilling' Doctrine." *Case Western Reserve Journal of International Law*, vol. 56, no. 1–2, 2024, pp. 545–568.

Abuloye, Ayoola. "The Legal Protection of Children as Victims of Armed Conflict." *ISIL Yearbook of International Humanitarian and Refugee Law*, 2023, pp. 91–103.

Ackermann, Tobias, and Sebastian Wuschka. "International Humanitarian Law and International Investment Law: Mapping a Developing Relationship." *Yearbook of International Humanitarian Law*, vol. 25, 2022, pp. 41–69. https://doi.org/10.1007/978-94-6265-619-2_2.

Akande, Dapo, and Emanuela-Chiara Gillard. "Conflict Classification and the Law Applicable to Detention and the Use of Force." *International Review of the Red Cross*, vol. 103, no. 916–917, 2021, pp. 1535–1554.

Al Qaralleh, Amir Salameh. "Jordan and Syrian Humanitarian Refugees' Dilemma: International Law Perspective." *Heliyon*, vol. 8, no. 5, 2022. https://scholar.google.com/scholar?output=instlink&q=info:knb4j51YfRkJ:scholar.google.com/&hl=en&as_sdt=0,5&as_ylo=2022&as_yhi=2023&scillfp=11947722078840687003&oi=lle.

Alexander, Amanda. "Filling the Gaps: The Expansion of International Humanitarian Law and the Juridification of the Free-Fighter." *Journal of International Humanitarian Legal Studies*, vol. 14, no. 2, 2023, pp. 274–303. https://doi.org/10.1163/18781527-bja10075.

Bagheri, Saeed. "Turkey's Extraterritorial Use of Force against Armed Non-State Actors." *Israel Law Review*, vol. 56, no. 2, 2023, pp. 143–170.

Baig, Khurram, et al. "Comparative Study of International Human Rights Law and International Humanitarian Law: Case Study of Their Commonalities." *Pakistan Research Journal of Social Sciences*, vol. 2, no. 3, 2023. https://prjss.com/index.php/prjss/article/download/74/65.

Benarji, Chakka. "Justice to the Victims of Armed Conflict in Darfur in Sudan and the Role of Regional Human Rights Mechanisms." *ISIL Yearbook of International Humanitarian and Refugee Law*, 2020–21, pp. 152–171.

Ben-Naftali, Orna. "The Fog of Law: IHL and the Urban Battlefield." *Harvard International Law Journal*, vol. 63, no. 1, 2022, pp. 145–178.

Boothby, William H. "Autonomous Weapon Systems and Customary International Humanitarian Law." *Journal of Conflict and Security Law*, vol. 26, no. 1, 2021, pp. 55–76.

Bothe, Michael. "Revisiting the Martens Clause: The 'Conscience of Humanity' and the Law of Armed Conflict." *Journal of International Humanitarian Legal Studies*, vol. 12, no. 1, 2021, pp. 8–23.

Breau, Susan. "Climate Change and International Humanitarian Law: New Challenges for Protection in Armed Conflict." *International Review of the Red Cross*, vol. 103, no. 918, 2021, pp. 876–894.

Breitegger, Alexander. "Increasing Visibility of Persons with Disabilities in Armed Conflict: Implications for Interpreting and Applying IHL." *International Review of the Red Cross*, vol. 105, no. 922, 2023, pp. 99–134.

Cakmak, Cenap, and Gokhan Guneysu. "Exploring Foundational Convergence between the Islamic Law of Armed Conflict and Modern International Humanitarian Law: Evidence from al-Shayne's Siyar al-Kabirr." *International Review of the Red Cross*, vol. 102, no. 915, 2020, pp. 1153–1178.

Chakka, Benarji, and Bitar, Mohammad. "Combating Human Trafficking: A Study of Anti-Human Trafficking Law and Policies in Cambodia, Myanmar, and Thailand." *ISIL Yearbook of International Humanitarian and Refugee Law*, 2023, pp. 18–58.

Chaudhury, Sanghamitra, and U.C. Jha. "Challenges to the Third Geneva Convention in Contemporary Armed Conflicts." *ISIL Yearbook of International Humanitarian and Refugee Law*, 2020–21, pp. 83–110.

Crenn, S., and C. Mohr. "The Protection of Persons with Disabilities in Armed Conflict: An Empty Shelf in an IHL-Specialized Library?" *International Review of the Red Cross*, vol. 105, no. 922, 2023, pp. 55–59.

Crowe, Jonathan. "Ethics and International Humanitarian Law: A Philosophical Appraisal." *Leiden Journal of International Law*, vol. 33, no. 1, 2020, pp. 59–78.

Durham, Helen. "Sexual Violence in Armed Conflict: A Contemporary Challenge to the Application of IHL." *International Review of the Red Cross*, vol. 104, no. 919, 2022, pp. 341–359.

Fabiano, Joao. "Should Weaponised Moral Enhancement Replace Lethal Aggression in War?" *Israel Law Review*, vol. 56, no. 2, 2023, pp. 201–224.

Ferraro, Tristan. "International Humanitarian Law, Principled Humanitarian Action, Counterterrorism, and Sanctions: Some Perspectives on Selected Issues." *International Review of the Red Cross*, vol. 103, no. 916–917, 2021, pp. 109–156.

Frias, Sanchez Alejandro. "Bringing Terrorists to Justice in the Context of Armed Conflict: Interaction between International Humanitarian Law and the UN Conventions against Terrorism." *Israel Law Review*, vol. 53, no. 1, 2020, pp. 71–100.

Funke, Carolin. "No Context Is Too Challenging: Promoting, Doing and Achieving Inclusion in the Humanitarian Response in South Sudan."

International Review of the Red Cross, vol. 105, no. 922, 2023, pp. 375–395.

Gaggioli, Gloria. "Legal Protection of the Natural Environment from the Effects of War." *International Review of the Red Cross*, vol. 104, no. 919, 2022, pp. 215–235.

Garcia, Ana Dols. "Armed Groups, IHL and the Invisible World: How Spiritual Beliefs Shape Warfare." *International Review of the Red Cross*, vol. 102, no. 915, 2020, pp. 1179–1200.

Gasser, Hans-Peter. "Neutrality and IHL in the Context of the Russia–Ukraine Conflict." *Swiss Review of International Law*, vol. 80, no. 2, 2023, pp. 201–218.

Gill, T. D. "Rethinking the Scope of Application of International Humanitarian Law and Its Place in the International Legal System." *The Military Law and the Law of War Review*, vol. 60, no. 1, 2022, pp. 58–70. https://doi.org/10.4337/mllwr.2022.01.04.

Greenman, Kathryn. "Of War and International Investment Law." *International and Comparative Law Quarterly*, vol. 73, no. 3, 2024, pp. 579–608.

Gutman, Roy. "The View from Syria: In War on Terror, Humanitarian Law Takes." *Case Western Reserve Journal of International Law*, vol. 52, no. 1 & 2, 2020, pp. 9–26.

Hassan, Samia Awad Mohamed, and Somia Abdelrhman Mohamed Ali. "Limitations on Warfare Methods: A Brief Examination Under International Humanitarian Law." *Journal of Advances in Humanities Research*, vol. 2, no. 4, 2023, pp. 1–19. https://www.jadhur.com/index.php/journal/article/download/189/46.

Henderson, Christian. "US and UK Military Strikes in Yemen and the *Jus ad Bellum*." *International and Comparative Law Quarterly*, vol. 73, no. 3, 2024, pp. 767–792.

Herzberg, Anne. "Lex Generalis Derogat Legi Speciali: IHL in Human Rights Regulation of Courts Operating in Situations of Armed Conflict." *Israel Law Review*, vol. 54, no. 1, 2021, pp. 84–119.

Hrnjaz, Milos, and Mina Radoncic. "Geneva, We Have a Problem: Internationalisation of Armed Conflicts through Indirect Intervention Remains a Dead Letter." *Israel Law Review*, vol. 57, no. 1, 2024, pp. 102–134.

Jha, U.C. "Lawfare - To Win Without Fighting." *ISIL Yearbook of International Humanitarian and Refugee Law*, 2023, pp. 1–17.

Kumar, Amit. "Is Article 21 of the Rome Statute Aiming for Legality or Hierarchy?: A Dilemma." *ISIL Yearbook of International Humanitarian and Refugee Law*, 2020–21, pp. 56–82.

Laurent, Ambre. "The Influence of International Humanitarian Law in Peacemaking: An Analysis of the Role of IHL During the Negotiations Between the FARC-EP and the Government of Juan Manuel Santos in Colombia." 2023. https://www.diva-portal.org/smash/get/diva2:1778507/FULLTEXT01.pdf.

Leary, Emma O. "Politics and Principles: The Impact of Counterterrorism Measures and Sanctions on Principled Humanitarian Action." *International Review of the Red Cross*, vol. 103, no. 916–917, 2021, pp. 459–478.

Lord, Janet E. "Accounting for Disability in International Humanitarian Law." *International Review of the Red Cross*, vol. 105, no. 922, 2023, pp. 60–98.

Lukin, Annabelle, and Alexandra García Marrugo. "The International Laws of War: Linguistic Analysis from the Perspectives of Register, Corpus and Grammatical Patterning." *Journal of International Humanitarian Legal Studies*, vol. 14, no. 2, 2023, pp. 223–249. https://doi.org/10.1163/18781527-bja10065.

Macak, Kubo, and Ellen Policinski. "In Pursuit of a Treaty's Soul: A Study of the Object and Purpose of the Fourth Geneva Convention." *International and Comparative Law Quarterly*, vol. 73, no. 2, 2024, pp. 385–416.

Madhukumar, Aswathy. "Re-Defining Civilian Security Within the Concept and Acts of Direct Participation in Hostilities." *ISIL Yearbook of International Humanitarian and Refugee Law*, 2020–21, pp. 111–151.

Malik, Rupal, and Benarji Chakka. "Autonomous Weapon System: Exploring the Autonomy and Accountability under International Humanitarian Law." *Indian Journal of International Law*, vol. 63, no. 3–4, 2023, pp. 307–333.

Maltez, Mar. "'Impossible': Some Challenges of Implementing International Law in the Area of Humanitarian Affairs for Persons with Disabilities."

International Review of the Red Cross, vol. 105, no. 922, 2023, pp. 217–229.

Matyas, David. “Humanitarian Access Through Agency Law in Non-International Armed Conflicts.” *International and Comparative Law Quarterly*, vol. 69, no. 2, 2020, pp. 451–476.

Maurer, Daniel D. “Meta-Law of Armed Conflict Principles.” *Texas Tech Law Review*, vol. 56, 2023, pp. 113–140. http://texastechlawreview.org/wp-content/uploads/TTLR-Vol.-56-Book-1.Maurer.PUBLISHED10.pdf.

Mégret, Frédéric. “Another Look at the Gendered Constitution of the Laws of War: Semantic Fields, Hegemonic Masculinities and the Reproduction of Heteronormativity.” *Journal of International Humanitarian Legal Studies*, vol. 14, no. 2, 2023, pp. 304–348. https://doi.org/10.1163/18781527-bja10077.

Melin, Carl Victor. “IHL and Drone-Enabled Surrender.” 2023. https://www.diva-portal.org/smash/get/diva2:1790202/FULLTEXT01.pdf.

Milanovic, Marko, and Sandesh Sivakumaran. “Assessing the Authority of the ICRC Customary IHL Study: How Does IHL Develop?” *International Review of the Red Cross*, vol. 104, no. 920–921, 2022, pp. 1856–1897. https://centaur.reading.ac.uk/108017/1/Milanovic%20Sivakumaran.pdf.

Modirzadeh, Naz K., and Dustin A. Lewis. “Humanitarian Values in a Counterterrorism Era.” *International Review of the Red Cross*, vol. 103, no. 916–917, 2021, pp. 403–414.

Moir, Lindsay. “Accountability for Violations of IHL by Non-State Armed Groups.” *Yearbook of International Humanitarian Law*, vol. 23, 2021, pp. 191–212.

Mueller, Jennifer A. “Rebel Groups’ Adoption of Human Rights and International Humanitarian Law Norms: An Analysis of Discourse and Behavior in Kosovo.” *Human Rights Review*, vol. 24, no. 4, 2023, pp. 511–544. https://www.academia.edu/download/107338246/Mueller_Rebel_Groups_Adoption_2023.pdf.

Mueller-Kalandarishvili, Natia. “Transforming a Prima Facie NIAC into an IAC: Finding the Answer in IHL.” *Israel Law Review*, vol. 53, no. 3, 2020, pp. 334–354.

Nasu, Hitoshi. "Emerging Military Technologies and the Evolving Interpretation of IHL." *Asia-Pacific Journal of International Humanitarian Law*, vol. 2, 2021, pp. 17–39.

Oduniyi, Omotayo Oreluwa, and Sarah Oluwaseyi Olayinka. "Examining the Use of Digital Technologies in Rendering International Humanitarian Assistance." *ISIL Year Book of International Humanitarian and Refugee Law*, vol. 22, 2022, pp. 31–52.

Onishi, Kosuke. "The Relationship Between International Humanitarian Law and Asset Freeze Obligations Under United Nations Sanctions." *International Review of the Red Cross*, vol. 103, no. 916–917, 2021, pp. 363–384.

Osuntogun, Abiodun Jacob. "Trade in Human Trafficking and Involvement of Multinational Companies: Rethinking the Criminal Jurisdiction of the African Court of Justice and Human Rights." *ISIL Yearbook of International Humanitarian and Refugee Law*, 2020–21, pp. 24–55.

Pejic, Jelena. "Detention in Armed Conflict: Toward a Uniform Legal Framework?" *International Review of the Red Cross*, vol. 103, no. 916–917, 2021, pp. 1267–1283.

Poecke, Thomas Van, et al. "Terrorist Offences and International Humanitarian Law: The Armed Conflict Exclusion Clause." *International Review of the Red Cross*, vol. 103, no. 916–917, 2021, pp. 295–324.

Priddy, Alice. "Who Is the Civilian Population? Ensuring IHL Is Implemented for the Protection of the Entirety of the Civilian Population—including Persons with Disabilities." *International Review of the Red Cross*, vol. 105, no. 922, 2023, pp. 242–251.

Prokhorenko, Mykhailo M., et al. "Interaction of IHRL and IHL in the Field of Human Rights Promotion: International Standards and National Dimension." *Informatologia*, vol. 55, no. 1–2, 2022, pp. 42–52. https://hrcak.srce.hr/file/391554.

Put, de Van Steven. "In Search of Humanity: The Moral and Legal Discrepancy in the Redress of Violations in International Humanitarian Law." *Israel Law Review*, vol. 56, no. 2, 2023, pp. 171–200.

Raboud, Ismaël, et al. "Reflections on the Development of the Movement and International Humanitarian Law Through the Lens of the ICRC

Library's Heritage Collection." *International Review of the Red Cross*, vol. 100, no. 907–909, 2018, pp. 143–163.

Rai, Prahlad. "Legal Status of Humanitarian NGOs." *ISIL Yearbook of International Humanitarian and Refugee Law*, vol. 20–21, 2020–2021, pp. 1–23.

Rai, Prahlad. "Legal Status of Humanitarian NGOs." *ISIL Yearbook of International Humanitarian and Refugee Law*, 2020–21, pp. 1–24.

Rajan, Sanoj. "The New Frontier of War: International Counterterrorism Regime and Criminalising Humanitarian Action in India." *ISIL Yearbook of International Humanitarian and Refugee Law*, 2023, pp. 59–90.

Redaelli, Chiara, and Carlos Arévalo. "Targeting Drug Lords: Challenges to IHL Between Lege Lata and Lege Ferenda." *International Review of the Red Cross*, vol. 105, no. 923, 2023, pp. 652–673. https://international-review.icrc.org/sites/default/files/reviews-pdf/2023-06/targeting-drug-lords-challenges-to-ihl-923.pdf.

Salman, Hamza AK, et al. "Prisoners of War: Classification and Legal Protection Under International Humanitarian Law." *UUM Journal of Legal Studies*, vol. 14, no. 2, 2023, pp. 677–708. https://repo.uum.edu.my/id/eprint/29691/1/UUMJLS%2014%2002%202023%20677-708.pdf.

Salpekar, Rashmi, and Vikram Aaditya Sharma. "Terrorism and International Customary Law: A Probable Solution." *ISIL Yearbook of International Humanitarian and Refugee Law*, 2020–21, pp. 311–345.

Sassòli, Marco. "How to Develop International Humanitarian Law Taking Armed Groups into Account?" *The Military Law and the Law of War Review*, vol. 60, no. 1, 2022, pp. 71–88. https://doi.org/10.4337/mllwr.2022.01.05.

Saul, Ben. "From Conflict to Complementarity: Reconciling International Counterterrorism Law and International Humanitarian Law." *International Review of the Red Cross*, vol. 103, no. 916–917, 2021, pp. 157–202.

Schmitt, Michael N. "The Impact of Autonomous Weapons on the Development of IHL." *International Law Studies*, vol. 97, 2021, pp. 712–738.

Simmons, Claire. "The Scope of Military Jurisdiction for Violations of International Humanitarian Law." *Israel Law Review*, vol. 54, no. 1, 2021, pp. 3–23.

Sivakumaran, Sandesh. "The Influence of IHL on the Rules of Engagement: Legal and Practical Perspectives." *International & Comparative Law Quarterly*, vol. 71, no. 2, 2022, pp. 345–369.

Stucki, Saskia. "Animal Warfare Law and the Need for an Animal Law of Peace: A Comparative Reconstruction." *American Journal of Comparative Law*, vol. 71, no. 1, 2023, pp. 189–233. https://doi.org/10.1093/ajcl/avad018.

Szpak, Agnieszka. "Evolution of the International Humanitarian Law Provisions on Sieges." *Yearbook of International Humanitarian Law*, vol. 22, 2019, pp. 3–28.

Taak, Sangeeta, et al. "Sikhism and the International Humanitarian Law." *ISIL Yearbook of International Humanitarian and Refugee Law*, vol. 18–19, 2018–2019, pp. 1–21.

Trabucco, Lena, and Kevin Jon Heller. "Beyond the Ban: Comparing the Ability of Autonomous Weapon Systems and Human Soldiers to Comply With IHL." *Fletcher Forum of World Affairs*, vol. 46, 2022, p. 15. https://www.fletcherforum.org/s/Trabucco.pdf.

Trivedi, Mansi, et al. "Violation of International Humanitarian Law vis-à-vis Dispute Between Ukraine and Russia." *Remittances Review*, vol. 8, no. 4, 2023. https://remittancesreview.com/menu-script/index.php/remittances/article/download/1016/532.

Tzanakopoulos, Antonios. "Use of Force in UN Peacekeeping: Challenges Under IHL." *Oxford Journal of International Law*, vol. 41, no. 3, 2023, pp. 527–548.

Upadhyay, Santosh K. "Natural Environment During Armed Conflicts and International Humanitarian Law: A Legal Analysis of Protective Ambits." *ISIL Yearbook of International Humanitarian and Refugee Law*, 2023, pp. 104–126.

Van Dijk, Boyd. "What Is IHL History Now?" *International Review of the Red Cross*, vol. 104, no. 920–921, 2022, pp. 1621–1637. https://international-review.icrc.org/sites/default/files/reviews-pdf/2022-11/what-is-ihl-history-now-920.pdf.

Vecchia, Sara La. "The Protection of Women and Girls with Disabilities in Armed Conflict: Adopting a Gender-, Age-, and Disability-Inclusive Approach to Select IHL Provisions." *International Review of the Red Cross*, vol. 105, no. 922, 2023, pp. 161–191.

Wakefield, Alex. "'Freedom from Hatred': The Role of Khanti in Complementing the Work of International Humanitarian Law (IHL)." *Buddhism and International Humanitarian Law*, Routledge, 2023, pp. 289–306. https://library.oapen.org/bitstream/handle/20.500.12657/75921/1/9781003803300.pdf#page=308.

Watkin, Kenneth. "Proportionality and Precautions in Attack: Modern Challenges for IHL." *Military Law Review*, vol. 229, no. 3, 2022, pp. 233–262.

Weizmann, Nathalie. "Respecting International Humanitarian Law and Safeguarding Humanitarian Action in Counterterrorism Measures: United Nations Security Council Resolutions 2462 and Point the Way." *International Review of the Red Cross*, vol. 103, no. 916–917, 2021, pp. 325–362.

Young, Kirsten. "Exclusive Humanitarianism: Policy Recommendations for Genuine Inclusion of Persons with Disabilities in Humanitarian Action." *International Review of the Red Cross*, vol. 105, no. 922, 2023, pp. 396–415.

Important Documents, Reports, And Institutional Publications From The ICRC, UN, NGOS, And Other Key Organizations:

"Deliberation No. 11 on Prevention of Arbitrary Deprivation of Liberty in the Context of Public Health Emergencies." *ISIL Year Book of International Humanitarian and Refugee Law*, 2020–21, pp. 350–355.

"Draft Articles on Prevention and Punishment of Crimes Against Humanity." *ISIL Year Book of International Humanitarian and Refugee Law*, 2020–21, pp. 375–387.

"General Assembly Resolution on the Arms Trade Treaty 2023." *ISIL Yearbook of International Humanitarian and Refugee Law*, 2023, pp. 272–275.

"Humanitarian Evacuations in Violence and Armed Conflict: Internal Note, Internal Displacement Section, Division of International Protection, UNHCR." *International Journal of Refugee Law*, vol. 30, no. 2, 2018, pp. 355–372.

"ICRC and International Red Cross and Red Crescent Movement: Some Recent Documents on International Humanitarian Law and Persons with Disabilities." *International Review of the Red Cross*, vol. 105, no. 922, 2023, pp. 566–567. doi:10.1017/S1816383122001102.

"International Humanitarian Law and Cyber Operations During Armed Conflicts - ICRC Position Paper." *ISIL Year Book of International Humanitarian and Refugee Law*, 2020–21, pp. 356–364.

"Joint Guidance Note on the Impacts of the COVID-19 Pandemic on the Human Rights of Migrants." *ISIL Year Book of International Humanitarian and Refugee Law*, 2020–21, pp. 346–349.

"Key Legal Considerations on Access to Territory for Persons in Need of International Protection in the Context of the COVID-19 Response." *ISIL Year Book of International Humanitarian and Refugee Law*, 2020–21, pp. 365–368.

"Law, Humanitarian. 'ICRC Report on Detention by Non-State Armed Groups: Obligations under International Humanitarian Law and Examples of How to Implement Them.'" *International Review of the Red Cross*, vol. 105, no. 923, 2023, pp. 1165–1166.

"MLA Diplomatic Conference 2023." *ISIL Yearbook of International Humanitarian and Refugee Law*, 2023, pp. 170–264.

"Note on the Protection of Migrants in the Face of the COVID-19 Pandemic." *ISIL Year Book of International Humanitarian and Refugee Law*, 2020–21, pp. 369–374.

"Political Declaration on Strengthening the Protection of Civilians from the Humanitarian Consequences Arising from the Use of Explosive Weapons in Populated Area 2022." *ISIL Year Book of International Humanitarian and Refugee Law*, vol. 22, 2022, pp. 256–258.

"Public Law 117-351, 117th Congress an Act." *ISIL Yearbook of International Humanitarian and Refugee Law*, 2023, pp. 168–169.

"To Respect and Ensure Respect for IHL: Interview with Representatives of the French Ministry for the Armed Forces and Ministry of Europe and Foreign Affairs." *International Review of the Red Cross*, vol. 103, no. 918, 2021, pp. 843–858.

---. *IHL and the Protection of the Environment during Armed Conflict: Expert Meeting Report*. ICRC, 2024.

---. *Strengthening Compliance with International Humanitarian Law: Report of the ICRC Expert Meeting.* ICRC, 2022. https://www.icrc.org/en/document/strengthening-compliance-ihl

---. *Study on the Human Rights Impact of Autonomous Weapons Systems.* UNHRC, 2021.

Amnesty International. *International Humanitarian Law and Accountability in the Context of Syria Conflict.* Amnesty International, 2021. https://www.amnesty.org/en/documents/mde24/4560/2021/en/

European Union Agency for Fundamental Rights. *Guidance on the Application of IHL in EU Operations.* EU FRA, 2023.

Geneva Academy of International Humanitarian Law and Human Rights. *Customary International Humanitarian Law Database.* Geneva Academy, 2020. https://www.geneva-academy.ch/customary-ihl-database

Geneva Call. *IHL Compliance in Non-International Armed Conflicts: A Field Report.* Geneva Call, 2022.

Human Rights Watch. *Armed Conflict and the Protection of Civilians: A Human Rights Perspective.* HRW, 2021. https://www.hrw.org/report/2021/armed-conflict-protection-civilians

International Committee of the Red Cross (ICRC). *International Humanitarian Law and Cyber Operations During Armed Conflicts.* ICRC, 2021. https://www.icrc.org/en/document/international-humanitarian-law-and-cyber-operations-armed-conflicts

International Criminal Court (ICC). *Annual Report 2024: Updates on Investigations and Prosecutions of War Crimes.* ICC, 2024.

The International Network on Explosive Weapons (INEW). *The Human Cost of Explosive Weapons in Populated Areas.* INEW, 2022.

United Nations Human Rights Council. *Report on the Situation of Human Rights in Ukraine in the Context of the Armed Conflict.* United Nations, 2023.

United Nations Office for the Coordination of Humanitarian Affairs (OCHA). *Protection of Civilians in Armed Conflict: Global Trends 2023.* United Nations, 2023.

United Nations Office on Drugs and Crime (UNODC). *Addressing the Role of Non-State Armed Groups in Violations of International Humanitarian Law.* UNODC, 2023.

United Nations Security Council. *Report on the Protection of Civilians in Armed Conflict.* UN Security Council Document S/2022/465, 2022.

Index

U

V

W

Y

www.ingramcontent.com/pod-product-compliance
Lightning Source LLC
LaVergne TN
LVHW100347181026
850499LV00037B/378
* 9 7 8 9 3 4 8 7 3 8 4 3 1 *